A SNAKE ON THE HEART

A SNAKE ON THE HEART

History, Mystery, and Truth

The Entangled Journeys of a Biographer and His Nazi Subject

PATRICK SHANE WOLFE

IGUANA

Copyright © 2023 Patrick Shane Wolfe
Published by Iguana Books
720 Bathurst Street, Suite 303
Toronto, ON M5S 2R4

All rights reserved. No part of this publication may be reproduced, stored in a retrieval system or transmitted, in any form or by any means, electronic, mechanical, recording or otherwise (except brief passages for purposes of review) without the prior permission of the author.

Publisher: Cheryl Hawley
Editor: Paula Chiarcos
Front cover design: Ruth Dwight, designplayground.ca
Front cover photo: John in his Schutzgruppe uniform with his son Harald, early 1943, The Hague. Petersen family photo.

ISBN 978-1-77180-619-0 (hardcover)
ISBN 978-1-77180-618-3 (paperback)
ISBN 978-1-77180-617-6 (epub)

This is an original print edition of *A Snake on the Heart*.

Permission for use of certain passages has been granted by the following:
1. Horn, Michiel. *A Liberation Album: Canadians in the Netherlands, 1944–45*. Edited by David Kaufman. Toronto, Montreal, New York: McGraw-Hill Ryerson, Ltd., 1980. PERMISSION RECEIVED FROM McGRAW HILL, January 13, 2022.
2. Moore, Bob. *Victims and Survivors: The Nazi Persecution of the Jews in the Netherlands, 1940–1945*. London: Arnold, 1997. PERMISSION RECEIVED FROM AUTHOR BOB MOORE, March 3, 2022.
3. Stein, André. *Quiet Heroes: The True Stories of the Rescue of Jews by Christians in Nazi-Occupied Holland*. Toronto: Lester & Orpen Dennys, Ltd., 1988. PERMISSION RECEIVED FROM NEW YORK UNIVERSITY PRESS, March 14, 2022.
4. van der Zee, Henri A. *The Hunger Winter: Occupied Holland 1944–5*. London: Jill Norman and Hobhouse, 1982. PERMISSION RECEIVED FROM UNIVERSITY OF NEBRASKA PRESS, March 16, 2022.
5. in 't Veld, N. K. C. A. *De SS en Nederland: documenten uit SS-archieven, 1933–1945*. 2 vols. The Hague: Martinus Nijhoff, 1976. PERMISSION RECEIVED FROM THE NETHERLANDS INSTITUTE OF WAR DOCUMENTATION, April 4, 2022.
6. Mason, Henry L. *The Purge of Dutch Quislings: Emergency Justice in the Netherlands*. The Hague: Martinus Nijhoff, 1952. LICENSE RECEIVED FROM SPRINGER NATURE, April 12, 2022.

7. Hirschfeld, Gerhard. *Nazi Rule and Dutch Collaboration: The Netherlands under German Occupation, 1940–1945*. Translated by Louise Willmot. Oxford, New York, Hamburg: Berg Publishers Ltd., 1988. PERMISSION RECEIVED FROM AUTHOR GERHARD HIRSCHFELD, May 25, 2022.

8. *Holland at War Against Hitler: Anglo-Dutch Relations, 1940–1945*. Edited by M. R. D. Foot. London: Frank Cass, 1990. TAYLOR AND FRANCIS (BOOKS) LTD., UK, ADVISED THAT THEY "CANNOT DETERMINE WHERE THE COPYRIGHT IS HELD," January 19, 2022.

DEDICATION

First, to the innocent victims of the Nazi occupation of the Netherlands, particularly the Jews murdered in the Holocaust, the hostages and so-called death candidates sacrificed under the Nazi retribution policy, and the countless others who suffered during those harrowing years.

Second, to the victims of a later period, whose stories occurred off history's great stage, and to their healing and reconciliation.

Third, to the pursuit of truth and, through that process, to understanding and acceptance, especially in cases where trauma from the war has survived into the current century.

THEMES

John Petersen contributed to horrors during the war and mitigated others. He had a similarly mixed record in Canada after the war. Both victim and victimizer, he allowed himself to be largely trapped in a pattern of behaviour that prevented him from accepting the truth about himself and learning from it. His story and the stories of his birth family and of the family he later fathered illustrate the complicated and, at times, damaging threads that bind us.

Pastor Martin Niemöller, an early supporter of the Nazis who became one of their fiercest critics, wrote in 1934, while reflecting on his experience aboard German submarines during the First World War, that "we [junior officers] did see that situations involving spiritual bankruptcy did arise, situations in which it was utterly impossible to preserve a clear conscience. And the question whether we are to perish in despair or defiance, or survive all trials with a live conscience, depends wholly and solely on whether we believe in the forgiveness of sins."[1]

We are all challenged to find the truth and to forgive. These are necessities if we are to safeguard against carrying the poisons of the past with us as we and our loved ones proceed into the future.

---

[1] Martin Niemöller, *From U-boat to Pulpit* (Chicago and New York: Willett, Clark & Company, 1937), 46–47.

Facts don't necessarily reveal who we are, but our contradictions almost always do; it's the warring self—the self that's capable of both caring for others and intense self-interest—that makes a story.

—Hilton Als, *The New Yorker*

Because self-knowledge is the most difficult of the arts of living, because understanding ourselves is a prerequisite for understanding anybody else, and because we can hardly fathom the reality of another without first plumbing our own depths, art is what makes us not only human but humane.

—Maria Popova, Brainpickings

One always learns one's mystery at the price of one's innocence.

—Robertson Davies, *Fifth Business*

CONTENTS

PROLOGUE xi
PART ONE: Prewar: The Years Prior to the Nazi Occupation of the Netherlands 1
PART TWO: War and Occupation 121
PART THREE: Postwar: Internment, Release, and Readjustment 299
PART FOUR: Canada: The Final Chapters 383
EPILOGUE 425
AUTHOR'S NOTE 439
APPENDICES 441
ACKNOWLEDGEMENTS 455
SELECTED BIBLIOGRAPHY 458
INDEX 465

PROLOGUE

AN UNSETTLING PORTRAIT OF THE BIOGRAPHER AS A YOUNG MAN

On January 11, 1988, I was up all night at my office preparing the eulogy I would deliver the next day at the memorial service for my good friend, Jan Jürgen Petersen, who I knew as John, who had died a few days earlier. Despite the considerable effort I put into the eulogy, I now regard a photo I took of John's family at the reception as the most useful thing I did that day. The photo includes the second of John's four wives, Susan, to whom he was married from October 1942 to the mid-1970s; his son, Hans, from his first marriage; his children with Susan: Harald, Constance, and Onno; Ann and Phil, who started out with the family as foster children but were adopted when they aged out of care; and John Roodenburg, a boarder from 1961 or 1962 to 1965 who became like family.

Figure 1. January 12, 1988. Petersen family following John's memorial service. Left to right: John Roodenburg, Hans, Harald, Susan, Onno, Phil, Constance, and Ann, who changed her name to Kitt in the early 1990s. Author's photo.

Harald is also the baby on John's shoulders in the photo from early 1943 on the cover of this book. In 2002, Harald told me that when he was growing up, he thought he belonged to a highly functional family only to realize later that the truth was just the opposite. I mentally highlighted this remark; my perspective on my own family had followed a similar arc, although in less dramatic circumstances.

The Petersens—John and Susan and their children Hans, Harald, and Constance—emigrated from Hilversum in the Netherlands to Canada in July 1952. Their destination: Alberni on Vancouver Island.[2] They stayed initially with their sponsors, the Roelants family, who had arrived from Hilversum approximately two years earlier. It was thought that the two families were related, that Marie Roelants was John's cousin. But, as Harald learned later, this turned out not to be the case.

After several months, the Petersens moved to 114 Victoria Quay, a house built on poles next to the Somass River. The rent was thirty dollars a month. Their cookstove was fuelled with bark collected from the log booms, which Hans, who turned sixteen in December 1952, accessed from a dock at the back of their house. The Overwaitea supermarket allowed John and Susan to run a tab that John repaid later. The family also received anonymous food baskets that came, Harald believes, from one or more of the local churches. He remembers being teased by his new schoolmates during the winter of 1952–53, when he turned eleven, because he wore short pants; the family had no money for new clothes.

They also had no furniture. Driven by necessity and aided by their respective skills, John and Susan rectified this in simple and practical ways. Large crates used to ship oranges from the southern United States were fixed up and hung on the walls as cupboards. Instead of doors, Susan sewed curtains that covered their fronts. Round cheese crates became the tops of stools. John also took wood from the burn

---

[2] The cities of Port Alberni and Alberni were amalgamated as Port Alberni on October 28, 1967.

pile at the sawmill to make other furniture. Some projects, including a dining room table, were completed a little later, when he had a broken arm.

"I know, because at times, I was his other arm," Harald recalled.

During their first Canadian autumn, John found work with a roofing company, but this employment didn't last long. On one of his first days on the job, there was an accident; he broke his left arm, the same one that had sustained two breaks in a 1946 explosion when he had been defusing bombs while interned as a German collaborator after the Second World War. As with the earlier breaks, the new one required nine months to heal. By the winter or spring of 1953, the family was in dire straits. Hans quit Grade 8 at Alberni District High School and went to work at the MacMillan Bloedel plywood plant to support the family. He regarded this as liberation rather than hardship, for he was struggling at school; his ability to read and write English was limited, which is why he'd been placed in Grade 8.

The Petersens lived in Alberni for six years. For much of this time, John worked at the plywood plant with Hans. Onno was born in August 1955. The following July, John and Susan accepted an emergency placement foster child. This was Ann, who turned thirteen the next month. During the summer of 1958, they had their first boarder, Donald Grayston, a student from the University of British Columbia in Vancouver who found John "charming" and Susan "gruff." Foster children and boarders would become one of the family's defining characteristics.

When the family (except Hans who was now married) moved to Victoria at the southeastern tip of Vancouver Island in September 1958, John went to work for the Holland Life Insurance Company, which had previously employed him in the Netherlands. In mid-November, he and Susan took in their second foster child, Philip, who would turn five the next month and who was to be a companion for Onno, whose closest sibling was more than ten years his senior.

Over the next decade, the family home was sometimes called the "Petersen madhouse" as it was packed to the rafters with young people and kids. In addition to Harald, Constance, Onno, Ann, Phil, and their friends, there were at least another twelve foster kids and boarders who stayed at different times and for varying durations. Phil recalled that the household was more like an army unit than a family because, of necessity, there was a certain amount of regimentation and everyone had chores. The family was unusual in several other ways. On one hand, the kids were raised, according to Constance, "in a very black-or-white, good-or-bad environment." On the other, the family was unusually open and accommodating. One friend from the neighbourhood was almost like family, Harald and Constance agreed, because he was always there, often sleeping over on the couch, taking respite from life with his father who was "an extreme alcoholic."

Many of the foster children came through the Capital Families Association, led by Bernice Levitz Packford, who received Victoria's Honorary Citizen Award in 1971. She thought the world of John and Susan. She told me she couldn't speak highly enough about them as foster parents. "They were loving, kind, understanding, and they even took teenagers!" Even though Susan did most of the fostering work, Bernice primarily dealt with John. One day in the mid-1980s, I happened to mention to her that John and Susan had been divorced for a decade. I will never forget her thunderstruck and shattered reaction. As a Jew and prominent social activist, she would have been even more devastated had she known what I eventually learned about John's wartime past.

In addition to the foster children, Bernice was important in John's life in another way. She encouraged him to leave the insurance business and become a social worker. According to Susan, Bernice thought it would be a better use of his talents. He heeded her advice. In the autumn of 1963, during an era when specialized training and related credentials were not required, he joined the Family and Children's Service, which became part of the British Columbia government in 1973. John worked as a social worker for sixteen and a half years until he retired at the end of March 1980, the same month he turned sixty-five.

After I met my future wife, Colleen, in early July 1973, she introduced me to her parents and to John, who she considered to be a good friend. He had become her social worker at a critical juncture in her life. They had met three years before, about a month prior to her sixteenth birthday. The catalyst for their meeting was her release from reform school during the winter of 1970. She credited him with saving her life. One wrong move on her part—by which she meant a resumption of her out-of-control ways—and she could easily have been lost forever, she told me. But John *saw* Colleen and *heard* her, which was a novel experience for someone who had felt mostly unseen and unheard. John enabled a constructive, two-way connection with Colleen, something virtually all other adults had been unable to achieve. She credited him with rare insight. He not only helped her find a degree of stability at that pivotal time, he also helped her improve her relationship with her parents. He provided grounding and safety, and she held him in high regard.

John became equally important to me. As he got to know me and learned of my interest in history and writing, he offered to tell me his story, so I might write about it. This was a privilege he bestowed on no one else. By "his story," he largely meant the first half of his life. I revelled in the opportunity and in John's attention.

In 1976, over nineteen evenings from early May until early December, I listened to what he told me about his life in British North Borneo, Java, and the Netherlands, and while doing so, I made 118 pages of detailed notes. This information was augmented by several follow-up sessions, principally in 1984 and 1985.

I knew John for the last fourteen and a half years of his life. Over that period, he aged from fifty-eight to almost seventy-three, while I ranged from twenty-one to thirty-six. John was of the same generation as my emotionally distant father, a doctor who had put on a psychic straitjacket to cope with the rigours of a nine-year stint at British boarding school and who was subject to manic and depressive episodes. I came to regard John as a good friend and, in due course, as my spiritual mentor rather than as a father figure, but it's possible my judgment is clouded on this latter point. While there were a few things he told me that I held in abeyance because they engendered doubt, my predominant response and reality was to see him through rose-coloured glasses. When Colleen and I had our first child, Jamie, in 1977, John became his godfather.

Figure 2. Christmas 1982. The author standing next to John (seated) with the author's eldest children in the foreground. Pierre Wolfe photo, now in the possession of the author.

Along with my parents, Colleen and John have been the most influential people in my life. They both rocked my reality in different ways. Each of them represented a notable step away from my parents' world and into my own life. A case of opposites attracting, Colleen and I were well-matched. We both had personal development issues and we helped each other begin to address them. Our time as a couple, meaning our first three and a half years together and our subsequent twenty-four-year marriage, was tempestuous, difficult, and richly rewarding. Twenty years later, we remain good friends.

Colleen was born in Ireland and brought to Canada by her birth mother at nine months of age. The purpose of the trip was to relinquish Colleen for adoption. Her adoptive parents were kind and well-meaning, but out of their depth. Colleen's abandonment issues and emotional needs were not acknowledged or addressed. As a result, she acted out, which became a central reality of their homelife. But Colleen is also a person of sparkle and vivacity, a sun around whom others can orbit. Her effect on my life during our first months together was such that I nicknamed her Sunshine. I did this having little or no appreciation of her shadow side and what John termed her "combustible" temperament. These things would repeatedly rock our relationship.

Like her parents, I was out of my depth, largely because I didn't know myself. But it was through my relationships with Colleen and John that this slowly began to change. It was with Colleen in the latter 1970s and my daughter a decade later that I had notable encounters with the grief I carried concerning my emotional separation from my parents, especially my dad. There was also a third occasion when I met my locked-down emotional self. It was engineered and supervised by John and it, too, took place in the latter 1970s. Colleen and I were having trouble and we'd gone to see him at his home. He placed two dining room chairs facing each other in the living room and had us sit on them so our knees were touching. This didn't faze Colleen, but I broke down. I was surprised by the torrent of emotion that had broken free. My life was being cracked open by these events.

I was gaining glimmerings of subconscious issues and feelings that I needed to surface and integrate if I were to know myself better.

On some of the evenings when John first told me his story, we switched tracks to discuss reincarnation, the New Testament (which I reread at the time), and what he called "the philosophy." These were stimulating occasions. He generally had wise answers for questions I asked, and in this way, he became my spiritual mentor. This fact and the knowing and authority he presumed were two of four sides that held the core of our relationship. The third side was my lack of self-knowledge. The fourth was a shared heritage. Like me, John missed a father figure in his life and had a contentious relationship with his mother. This, I suspect, made us particularly receptive and sympathetic to each other, which, in combination with my lack of self-knowledge, rendered me especially vulnerable to his perspective and claims.

Although I'd done well at university, obtained an MA in history, and briefly taught part time at a couple of community colleges, I had little real experience of life. More importantly, I was blind to the fact that parts of my psyche had been submerged. Despite my academic credentials and facile confidence, the person I was when I listened intently to John's story and made my careful notes on what he said was essentially an amorphous and thirsty sponge. Unsettling as this portrait of the biographer as a young man is, I should add one more detail—John's initial impression of me: pompous.

I learned this later from Colleen. It is doubtless additionally revealing of me and John that I never felt this judgment from him. I felt only welcomed by him.

THE SS-ONDERSCHAARLEIDER WHO BECAME A CANADIAN SOCIAL WORKER

There are two preeminent facts about John. There is a correspondence between these facts, but they have different natures. One is an external, surface reality, the other is internal and hidden. The former pertains to John's career path. He was a social worker who had previously been a member of the SS, specifically the *Sicherheitsdienst* (SD), the SS's security and intelligence service.[3] The latter concerns his most defining behaviour, that he was a manipulator and liar, often a charming one; this was the case both during the war and for much of the rest of his life.

During the war, John's life had five major components. First and most important, the SD. Second, the insurance industry (to which he made a mysterious return on a part-time basis starting in August 1941). Third, the *Schutzgruppe*, a semi-military organization established in the spring of 1941 to relieve the Wehrmacht of rudimentary tasks, such as guarding bridges and other infrastructure and conducting inspections at checkpoints. Consisting of German citizens ineligible for active service due to age or disability, its members wore old German army uniforms like the one John is wearing in the cover photo for this book. He joined at the start of 1943. Fourth, the Dutch resistance to which he was connected by two friends. And fifth, his marriage to Susan.

"By playing a reckless game, namely playing the German authorities against each other," he wrote after the war, "I managed to remain free till 1944."[4] In response to Allied troops advancing into Belgium, the Germans declared a state of emergency in the Netherlands on September 4 and John's Schutzgruppe unit was "assigned to quarters" on the sixth.[5]

---

[3] *Unterscharführer*, or junior squad leader (*Onderschaarleider* in Dutch), was the most junior and most common noncommissioned officer rank of the SS and was the equivalent of an *Unteroffizier* in the German Wehrmacht. The rank was equivalent to a corporal in some armies and to a sergeant in others. According to his SS card, John was promoted in April 1944 to *Scharführer* (or *Schaarleider*), the equivalent of a sergeant in the British army. He maintained that he was unaware of this promotion until it was brought to his attention after the war.

[4] John's letter of June 1951 to Hans Roelants. Although the letter is undated, three letters enclosed with it all have dates from June 1951. "As proof of my Dutch-friendly feelings, I hereby enclose three letters of people who are able to judge!" John wrote toward the end of his letter. One of the enclosed letters, from Barend van Leeuwen, is dated June 17, 1951. The other two letters, one from Jan Gerrit Siewers, the other from Johan Veltmeijer, are dated June 23, 1951. All four originals are in the possession of John's son Harald.

[5] John's collaborator statement of October 29, 1946 (DNA, CABR 109786).

An example of John's reckless game is that he lied on his SS application in mid-1940, claiming that he was a Dutch citizen. Thus, while the SD viewed him as Dutch, the Schutzgruppe knew he was German. Such manipulations took a toll on him, he said.

"Every day I would wish that something would happen, so I wouldn't have to carry on this double game I was playing," he told me.

He said, "I had an image in my mind of people holding a snake to their chest. I saw myself as that snake."

This is a dramatic image, but it's also subtle and potentially confusing. I see it as a negative image of a snake, one that oppressed John and inferred he was false and hidden, a snake in the grass. But how can the snake be hidden when people are holding it to their chest? The answer: People were putting their trust in him not knowing he was playing a double game, not knowing he was a snake on the heart.

One of his social-work colleagues viewed him as an outright liar. Moreover, John knew it was not uncommon for people to have doubts about his storytelling. Maybe it was a performance, but I remember him conveying hurt and chagrin when he told me of the response of some of his co-workers to his claims: "There's no way so many things could have happened to one person."

Having been the custodian of John's story for forty-five years and having sought to make sense of it for much of the last two decades, I have concluded that multiple factors contributed to his habitual distortions and embellishments. Some of this was charming and enthusiastic storytelling; some of it was ego-driven, grandiose, and rooted in a well-hidden sense of inferiority; some of it was the product of self-deception and excessive romanticism to the point, I suspect, of creating alternate realities, which were salves for deep hurts, disappointment, and depression—a troubled coping mechanism that suggests he was occasionally mentally and emotionally unbalanced. And some of it was outright cover-up born of fear, stigma, and shame.

He once told me that the best lie is one that adheres as much as possible to the truth, that is minimalist, changing only a key detail here or there. I suspect he often practised this approach when he told me his story. I suspect, too, that over the years, I developed a bit of a sixth sense for detecting such instances. What I'm sometimes not sure about is when an obfuscation was intentional as opposed to the product of semiconscious or even unconscious reflexive habit, of an alternate reality he'd created. What does surprise me, given his "best lie" rule, is the frequency and fashion in which he broke it, telling me stories that I mostly swallowed hook, line, and sinker but have since learned are mind-boggling in their improbability and in relation to what actually, probably, or possibly occurred. (The wide range of potential scenarios generally reflects a lack of information and consequent inability to come to stronger conclusions.)

This learning is a measure of the distance I have travelled and an indication of the old skin I have shed. This learning also invokes other meanings for the snake in relation to *my* story: foremost, the ability to poison and to heal but also as a symbolic representation of the life force or kundalini power and the expansion of perspective and consciousness. I see the snake as medicine, a reminder of the caduceus I grew up viewing in my father's medical office. Psychologist James Hillman writes in *The Soul's Code* that "the snake is perhaps the most ancient and universal carrier of the genius spirit, the figure of a protective guardian, the 'genius' itself."[6]

According to John, he was an unusual victim of history and war, as well as a man without a country until he came to Canada. Although there is much to support this interpretation, what I didn't understand for a long time was how his sense of victimization was girded by trauma and emotional problems. In an aggrieved and impassioned five-page letter to his friend Hans Roelants, which he wrote during June 1951, following the family's failed first attempt to immigrate to Canada,[7] John addressed the question of his nationality this way:

---

[6] James Hillman, *The Soul's Code: In Search of Character and Calling* (New York: Warner Books, 1996), 59.
[7] The family had been stopped from boarding the airplane because son Hans had contracted contagious ringworm, which was evident on his face.

> I sent a letter of appeal [in 1937] to H. M. the Queen of the Netherlands, in which I applied for naturalisation as Dutchman. This letter of appeal was also signed by the Burgomaster of Hilversum Lambooy and the Superintendent of Police, Mr. van Beusekom. It was refused [in 1939]. The reasons:
>
> 1st My naturalisation was of no special interest to the Netherlands!
>
> 2nd Because my life was not in danger!
>
> Just think what this meant to me! I was raised in Holland by a Dutch mother. I <u>felt</u> Dutch for 100%. But notwithstanding all my trying to get away from my German nationality <u>I was pushed</u> in to it. This was the beginning of all the difficulty and trouble, which drove me in a direction that was not mine, and that would pursue me my whole life, to be ended in imprisonment after the war....
>
> These two reasons are in fact responsible for the failure of my life.[8]

There are files on John's application for naturalization in the Dutch National Archives in The Hague.[9] When his application was rejected, the letter that conveyed the decision provided no reasons for it. The reasons John cites in his letter are his own invention.

As John's letter indicates, he and his younger brother, Constant, had a German father and a Dutch mother. John believed that he and Constant were the third successive generation of the Petersen family to have had their lives fundamentally disrupted by war. He and Constant had moved from the Dutch East Indies to the Netherlands in 1922 when they were seven and five. In 1933, their mother applied to have them naturalized as Dutch citizens. For several reasons, which will be discussed, this didn't occur. This outcome had far-reaching consequences. When the Germans invaded and occupied the Netherlands in May 1940, John and Constant felt trapped by their

---

[8] John's letter of June 1951. See footnote 4.
[9] See Bibliography—Selected Primary Documentation for J. J. Petersen.

German citizenship and the country's changed circumstances, causing them to follow an uncertain path and, in the latter half of June, to join a German organization that turned out to be the SS.

Constant was stationed at Rotterdam starting in 1941 and admitted being involved in the roundup of Jews in 1942 and 1943. Based on what I regard as overwhelming circumstantial evidence, I believe John was also involved at The Hague, although there is no definitive proof in his case.

John and Constant's younger half-siblings, Wim and Miek, had a Dutch father, J. W. Kempen, and were, therefore, Dutch citizens. Despite this, Wim also served in a German organization during the war and in early 1944 became a *Begunstigende Leden* (BL), a supporting member of the SS. All three brothers regarded the Netherlands as home, but their loyalties were conflicted during the occupation. As a result, they were all jailed as collaborators after the war: John for 18.5 months, Wim for 20.5, and Constant for 32.5. The length of a sentence is generally indicative of the degree of perceived collaboration. The multiple statements they each provided to Dutch officials while imprisoned are another important source of information.[10]

There is also evidence that John and Wim cooperated with the Dutch resistance and assisted Jews in hiding, although it is more conclusive in Wim's case than John's. There is much more decisive evidence that John exempted many Dutchmen from forced labour under the Nazis. Much of this evidence is in the Dutch National Archives, which holds the files on all those who were jailed as collaborators. John's son, Hans, gave me permission to access the files

---

[10] According to researcher Dr. Maili Blauw (attachment to her email of February 14, 2007, to the author), suspected collaborators were considered "political offenders." Their postwar statements are part of the police reports into their behaviour. The *Politieke Recherche Afdelingen* (PRA), or Political Investigation Departments, compiled information for the *Bijzondere Gerechtshoven* (Special Courts), while the *Nederlands Beheersinstituut* (NBI) supervised the property of "enemies and betrayers." These organizations were created by the Dutch government to deal with these offenders and their property.

on John, which led to those on his brothers. It's possible that John and/or one or both of his brothers are mentioned in other collaborator files, which could shed additional light on their attitudes and actions during the war. But these files are to some extent an untapped resource as they haven't, to my knowledge, been systematically examined by historians.

John's chronicle is much more than the fascinating, fact-is-stranger-than-fiction Second World War account that I initially thought. It is also a psychological mystery that took many years to untangle. I have finally succeeded in telling John's story in a manner that satisfies me. I think it's a reasonable approximation of the truth. But I must emphasize the qualified nature of some of my conclusions, for there is much about John and his story that we can never know for sure. For example, the story has a mystical dimension that is often suggestive of John's seemingly credulous beliefs but which also features two noteworthy events, one of which involved me as well as John.

Moreover, one of my conclusions deserves to be flagged at the outset. Although John claimed he was pushed into his German nationality, that it drove him in a direction that wasn't his and was the cause of all his difficulties and trouble, my view is that this was a convenient cover story, that the real reason for his profound sense of victimization, which pre-dated his awareness of his nationality, was his troubled childhood and adolescence.

REPAYING A DEBT, PURSUING THE TRUTH, AND FINDING ONESELF

A reasonable approximation of the truth—that, I think, is the best we can achieve about John's history and mental health. Although it was my pursuit of the truth that drove me on through the decades to complete this project, the truth being pursued involved more than these factors. There were two others and they had more to do with me than John. One was slow self-discovery, the other was a debt I incurred through innocence and ignorance by presuming far too much.

Looking back now, it was as though a quid pro quo had to be served, that if I was going to write about how John failed to deal with his past, I first had to deal with mine. In this way, John and I remained bound together for at least fifteen years after his death. This synergistic connection is illustrated by two distinct phases: one during the first half of the 1990s, the other between 1997 and 2003.

In early 1991, three years after John's death and just a few months after the death of Colleen's adoptive mother, Colleen started seeing a therapist. She shared with me some of what she was learning. One time she observed that I was probably as remote a father to our children as my father had been to me and my younger brothers. The truth of this immediately hit home and I started to change my behaviour, not that this had any significant effect in the short term on family dynamics that had developed over a much longer period. But a dormant part of me woke up. This experience and another important discovery prompted me to consult a couple of therapists.

Around the same time, I wrote an early and partial version of John's story—a document of around two hundred pages—which I lent to Onno. With my permission, he passed it on to Susan. I spent time with her in November 1995 and again the next month and got to know John through her eyes.

"Most of it is true," Susan said about what she'd read in the manuscript. That was reassuring. But something else she said astounded me, reordered my world, and knocked off the rose-coloured glasses through which I had viewed John. Her revelation concerned the lengthy eulogy I'd given at John's memorial service almost eight years earlier. I thought I'd done a fine job, but she disclosed that my remarks had deeply offended her and Constance and Ann—the women of the family. Indeed, Constance and Ann had sat together and supported each other by holding hands. Constance told Ann to squeeze her hand if she heard anything upsetting. Not only was Constance's hand squeezed regularly, but Ann's long nails drew blood, they both told me on separate occasions. Doubtless the following passage from the eulogy was among those that offended the Petersen women:

> To me John's most essential characteristic was his desire to nurture, to encourage what is best in people, to help them grow in themselves and their relationships and help them escape situations which were negative or destructive.
>
> Always when he worked with the stuff of God's creation, he did so with great care and love and conviction.... Simply put, John was a disciple of the gospel of love.

My failing—and it was both an elementary and a gross failing—was to have proceeded based on the private, hermetically-sealed world I had shared with John without consulting family members for their perspectives. Had I done so, it likely would have alerted me to fissures in the family and some of the women's anger at John, and I may have trod more carefully. Despite being well-intentioned, my hagiographic words were, I retrospectively had to agree, an exercise in effrontery.

This is when I incurred the debt. It became a new motivation for my work: I would rebalance the scales by using multiple perspectives to tell John's story as truthfully as I could. Moreover, based on an incident Onno related and Susan confirmed, I had my first inkling that my account of John's life would not be the heroic and poignant chronicle I had once thought. It would be darker and more complicated, including odious behaviour on his part that not only flew in the face of his affability, charm, and claims of special insight but was duplicitously enabled by them.

Starting in 1997, the seven years before and after the turn of the millennium constitute the second phase of syncopation, of the synergistic two-step between the unfolding of my life and my researching and writing of John's story. During the latter 1990s and 2000, I struggled with issues concerning my relationships with my parents and Colleen. This was a time of personal reckoning and significant change for me. I separated from Colleen in November 2000. Dad died almost exactly two years later. The years 2001 and 2002 were ones of emotional consolidation. In 2003, when I spoke at least fourteen times with John's daughter, Constance, I was, in effect, rolling up my sleeves to pursue John's story with new levels of focus and vigour.[11]

Through Constance, I learned more about John's dark side and received my first insight into his peculiar and off-kilter relationship with Susan. Constance also gave me the benefit of her perspective on the rest of her immediate family in Canada, as well as the extended Petersen clan in the Netherlands. In 2004, I corresponded with John's sister, Miek. I spent more than a dozen hours with her the following January when I travelled to Amsterdam. These were vital milestones in obtaining a more rounded view of John. I also spoke to his other children—Hans, Harald, Onno, Kitt (who changed her name from Ann in the early 1990s), and Phil—and other family members, a dozen in all. In addition, I spoke to another fourteen people who knew John. And I had the benefit of knowing Mary and Shirley, his third and fourth wives.

A few years later, I took early retirement from the British Columbia Public Service to concentrate on "the book." It had occurred to me that there are no guarantees in life, especially as to longevity, and that if I found myself on my deathbed with John's story unfinished, I would be more than a little upset with myself. So, I had work to do, and it included discovering how much more my story was bound up with John's than I then knew.

---

[11] Late in the day it occurred to me that there was also a third phase to the synergistic two-step between the unfolding of my life and the writing of John's story. It was signalled by a break I took from John's story when, in mid-2015, I quite abruptly changed course and devoted the next two years to writing a memoir and family history going back to the lives of my grandparents, which brought to light information and linkages of which I had previously been unaware. After producing a solid draft of this work, I returned to John's story and what proved to be the long home stretch to its completion.

PART ONE

Prewar

The Years Prior to the Nazi Occupation of the Netherlands

Men make their own history, but they do not make it as they please; they do not make it under self-selected circumstances, but under circumstances existing already, given and transmitted from the past.

—Karl Marx, *The Eighteenth Brumaire of Louis Bonaparte*

Sooner or later Fate must bring retribution, unless men conciliate Fate while there is still time.

—Adolf Hitler, *Mein Kampf*

Be ye therefore wise as serpents, and harmless as doves.

—Jesus, Matt. 10:16

1

JOHN'S FATHER: IMAGINED AND REAL

The first evening I sat down with John, I presumed that what I was being told was true, that his story and history were essentially the same. And, broadly speaking, they were. But within that broad truth, as I was eventually to learn, was John's troubled perspective, sometimes distorted, other times purposely distorting. We were quite the pair: I, the trusting scribe and designated custodian; he, the unreliable narrator.

That first evening, John's initial subjects were his father and his paternal grandparents, his father being the primary focus. There was also a compelling subtext: John represented the third generation of the Petersen family to have the smooth flow of its life upset and overturned by war.

"Father fled" British North Borneo in an "open canoe in 1917." These are the first words of my notes. "Father" was Hans Nis Jürgen Petersen. Accompanied by his Dutch wife, Constance, who was called Stanni, and by John, Hans's destination was the neutral Dutch colony of Java. The canoe was large. Possibly remembering a family photograph of several outriggers, John said the canoe could carry thirteen.

Figure 3. Outriggers. Harbour at Lahad Datu, British North Borneo. Petersen family photo.

John's father was German, but John claimed Hans was originally Danish. He was born on January 16, 1868, at Flensburg in what had been the Duchy of Schleswig. The Petersen family had lived in Flensburg at least since the early 1800s.[12] Despite having a population that was two-thirds German, Schleswig had been ruled by the Danish crown for four hundred years. In the mid-1800s, the duchy was a repeated flashpoint between Denmark on one side and Prussia and the German Federation on the other. When, in violation of an 1852 treaty, Denmark tried to annex Schleswig in 1863, the result was not only war with Prussia and Austria in 1864 but, ultimately, the loss of Schleswig to the new German nation, which was just then beginning to emerge under the leadership of Otto von Bismarck.

---

[12] Both sets of Hans's grandparents had been residents of Flensburg, according to its *Stadtarchiv*.

With the war lost, Hans's parents, Hans Daniel and Maria Petersen, were among the 200,000 Schleswig Danes who, as John correctly stated, were given the choice to move north into Denmark or become German. In his 1951 letter, John added, "My grandparents were great patriots, who by their anti-German action were condemned to prison." He told me the same thing, comparing Hans Daniel and Maria to members of the Dutch resistance during the Second World War. He also said they died in prison and that, consequently, his father was adopted by a German couple.

John then jumped forward in the story, remarking that his father, at the age of fourteen, made his first trip to Indonesia where he worked on tobacco and rubber plantations and learned those trades. Hans also became a mechanical engineer, finishing his studies in Indonesia. In due course, he was appointed manager of the big British-owned New Darvel Bay Tobacco Company, which produced "high-quality wrapper leaf" for cigars but also had a secondary rubber plantation.[13] Located in the vicinity of Lahad Datu on the southeast coast of British North Borneo, it is where John was born on March 7, 1915.

---

[13] David W. John and James C. Jackson, "The Tobacco Industry of North Borneo: A Distinctive Form of Plantation Agriculture," *Journal of Southeast Asian Studies* 4, no. 1, (March 1973): 96. See also, Owen Rutter, *British North Borneo: An Account of its History, Resources and Native Tribes* (London, Bombay, Sydney: Constable & Company Ltd., 1922), 250. Page 22 of a report (NAUK, CO 855 27) on Trade, Crime, Planting, and General in the "East Coast Residency" in 1911 states that the New Darvel Bay Tobacco Company has "been also gradually extending their Rubber Estate on the Lower Segama, the area of which when planted up will be 1,300 acres."

Figure 4. Hans, Stanni, and John, circa 1915. Petersen family photo.

The large workforce was mostly Chinese but included some Indigenous people, John said. Their foremen, he added, were Japanese, and they were directed by Hans and the dozen white men who reported to him. Most of the Caucasians were married and had families. Stanni's younger sister, Catharina Geertruida, a nurse who was called Cato, lived with them until the summer of 1914, when she married a government surveyor. According to one source published in 1922, British North Borneo had a population of "under 500 white people ... so that ... up-country a man is lucky if his neighbours amount to half a dozen." The state capital, Sandakan, had a "European population of ... about seventy" and was "the only town worthy of the name in North Borneo."[14]

John said Hans built a house at the harbour and a train track up the mountain to the plantations. The train transported people up and down, and goods down. He added that Hans was a good manager and a kind and intelligent man who was respected by all segments of the multi-racial community he led. The local headhunters made him an honourary chief, while the Chinese declared him an "honourary Mandarin."

There was an occasion, John claimed, when the Japanese foremen, who were armed, sparked an uprising by raping some of the Chinese women. He said the Japanese made a habit of this. Alerted to the dangerous situation, Hans took immediate action to protect the small Caucasian community. To "prevent a bloodbath" and stop the Chinese descending the mountain via the railway, Hans drove the train up and down the mountain throughout the night.

John told me that the next day Hans spoke to a huge mob of Chinese in one of the large barns where the tobacco leaves were dried. One of the Chinese heckled him. In response, Hans picked the fellow up and threw him out one of the open-air windows, after which he resumed speaking to the others. John said the workers' "simple intelligence" respected Hans's decisive action. This romanticized and racist portrayal is probably representative of generalized prejudice reflective not only of his Nazi SS training but also of widespread Caucasian attitudes of

---

[14] Owen Rutter, *British North Borneo: An Account of its History, Resources and Native Tribes* (London, Bombay, Sydney: Constable & Company Ltd., 1922), 369 (under 500), 36 (Sandakan – about seventy, only town). American Consul George M. Hanson, based at Sandakan, visited British North Borneo's only internment or "detention camp" for enemy subjects, located at Tenom, on November 25 and 26, 1915. On page 3 of a five-page report (NAUK, CO 531 9), he commented, "There is always more or less trouble about food in all tropical countries, especially where there is no ice, and where people, so to speak, 'live out of time'."

dominance, whether racial, economic, military, or some combination of all three. John depicted his father as a wise and capable leader who possessed moral courage as well as physical strength.

In 1917, during the third year of the First World War, John said Hans was forced out of his job. According to John's 1951 letter, "the English newspapers ... scandalised" the fact that a German was heading an important British company at Lahad Datu. He told me the pressure in the press took two years before Hans and the family were threatened with internment. The threat was conveyed by the English consul, a family friend. Despite the war, which for a time was a far-removed reality, John correctly observed that the paucity of Caucasians brought the English and Germans together. John also told me, in a much more dubious assertion, that Hans never renewed his passport and put his German nationality in question. He states this even more strongly in his 1951 letter: "My father had evaded military service and was not registered as a German any more." Constant also believed their father had become stateless in the Dutch East Indies.[15]

The war had first intruded between Hans and the English consul in the aftermath of John's birth. The birth, I was informed, had been a miracle because Stanni had "lost her first child due to a fake doctor." In fact, Lahad Datu's two previous doctors had been imposters "masquerading as family doctors." The miracle was of a distinctly modest variety: John was delivered by a real doctor, a German, who, John said, was later interned. When Hans asked the English consul to register John's birth, the consul, according to John, replied that, despite their friendship, he could not give the English birthright to the son of a German, especially as their countries were at war and they could find themselves "looking at each other through the sights of guns."

Two years later the consul informed Hans that he was under orders to intern the Petersen family. John noted the consul gave Hans two days to get away. It was this that prompted the family's escape in

---

[15] Constant's collaborator statement of September 14, 1945 (DNA, CABR 70629).

the large canoe. According to John, the only things of material value they were able to take with them were a few gold coins pressed into pieces of soap. Everything else they owned was confiscated.

They were at sea for three weeks, often in dire circumstances. John told me they wore big hats to prevent sunstroke, and his mother supposedly told him that they "suffered a great deal."

"Why don't we just quit?" she asked Hans several times.

"You don't give up a fight," he always replied.

According to John, they were picked up by a Dutch steamer and made their way to Java.

While the foregoing is broadly true, it also contains numerous reinterpretations or reinventions and several tall tales that are outright whoppers. John's grandparents did decline the opportunity to move north into Denmark, preferring to remain in Flensburg, their hometown, but there is no evidence they resisted the Germans or were imprisoned. They certainly didn't die in jail. John's grandmother died in 1875, his grandfather in 1900. Moreover, there is no evidence that Hans, the sixth of seven children, was adopted by a German couple.

What evidence there is indicates that the family was close and assisted one another when they could. Of Hans's five older siblings, four were brothers. Johannes, born in 1865, was the fourth brother. According to the *British North Borneo Herald*, he, his wife, and their "little daughter" lived at Tawau on the east coast in the late 1890s and early 1900s, at the same time that Hans worked and lived there with his first wife, Gertrude Tuja (née Schück) Petersen, and their small children, a daughter born in 1899 and a son born in 1900.[16] The *Herald* of January 2, 1901, reported that Gertrude died, age 23, "of accidental poisoning" on December 23. The children stayed with

---

[16] *British North Borneo Herald* issues of June 16, 1899 (refers to "Mr. H. Petersen, Mr. and Mrs. Johannes Petersen"), August 1, 1899 (Mr. Petersen, a brother of Mr. H. Petersen, and his wife, arrived in Tawau; it is probable he will remain there and start some business of his own."), February 16, 1900 ("Messrs. Petersen Bros."), December 2, 1901 ("Mr. and Mrs. Johannes Petersen and little daughter"). Clippings of the relevant articles were kindly provided to the author by historian Uwe Aranas of Cologne, Germany.

Hans for a time, but at some point were sent to Europe, possibly to be raised with the family of one of Hans's brothers or sisters. As an adult, the daughter, Trudi, lived in Germany and periodically corresponded with Stanni, according to Susan, who also indicated that Trudi's brother died as an older youth.

When Hans married Stanni on April 30, 1912, in an unusual ceremony, his second oldest brother, Theodor, born in 1857, an engineer from Flensburg, played a key role. The ceremony took place at the town hall in Hilversum. Hans had been in Europe for six months in 1911, when presumably the planning for the wedding by proxy began. Theodor was Hans's representative. He held a power of attorney signed by Hans at Lahad Datu on January 12, 1912 "to do all that is legally necessary to make Constance Wilhelmina de Ridder … my lawful wedded wife."

John's statements, first in his 1951 letter, that Hans went to the Dutch East Indies when he was rather young, and second, as he told me, that Hans's objective was to learn the tobacco and rubber plantation trades, are undoubtedly true. Given his comparative youth, it is likely that John's father made these decisions in consultation with his family. Two documents provide considerable confirmation and shed light on the chronology of Hans's early career. According to the *Herald* of February 16, 1911, "Mr. Hans Petersen, Acting General Manager of the [New Darvel Bay Tobacco Company, had left] for Home [on the eighth, aboard the vessel Borneo] after 23 years absence." Based on this length of time, it appears Hans made his initial trip back to Europe in 1888.

The second document is from the German government in the early 1890s. It reads: "Petersen, Hans Nis Juergen * 1868. Accused (in 1891) of not showing for military service and of leaving the country without the required permit. Tobacco-grower. (destination USA)."[17]

---

[17] http://www.rootdigger.de/ provides a listing of almost 90,000 names titled "Emigration from Schleswig-Holstein" during the nineteenth century, which includes the referenced entry on p. 116 of the portion of the list devoted to the letter P.

The events that prompted this latter document are the basis for John's incorrect assertion that Hans never renewed his passport and put his German nationality in question. As a regular international traveller in the Far East who made at least two return trips to Europe, Hans had to have a valid passport.

John's claim that Hans was a mechanical engineer is also dubious. It's possible that his claim arose from confusion based on Hans's brother Theodor being an engineer. On the other hand, John may not have been confused at all. He may have intentionally reassigned Theodor's credentials to Hans to boost his father's résumé. This was typical of John in at least two ways: burnishing his romanticized image of Hans and claiming schooling that had not occurred. Always sensitive to his lack of academic credentials, John told me he had studied economics and commerce at Leiden University in the late 1930s, which is not true. There are other instances where John borrowed details from other people's lives to serve his storytelling. His contention that Hans finished his engineering studies in Indonesia is bogus. I have found no evidence that the country had an engineering school before 1920.

Nevertheless, John's pride in his father was well placed. Hans's career was colourful and successful. Although it is not known when he returned to British North Borneo, he is mentioned in the *Herald*'s issue of March 1, 1895. A couple of years later he was developing the Arendsburg company's plantation at Tawau, where he remained until 1902. Referring to the tobacco estates "near the government outposts at Lahad Datu and Tawau, as well as round Sandakan Bay," historian K. G. Tregonning comments, "Here the solitary and imperious Dutchmen lived gargantuan lives, topping their huge meals with immense quantities of gin, and then laboring hard enough for a dozen ordinary men."[18] The gin presumably helped them deal with the steamy climate and other difficult conditions, including the health risks, especially malaria and beriberi, which were a regular and

---

[18] K. G. Tregonning, *A History of Modern Sabah, 1881–1963* (Kuala Lumpur: University of Malaya, 1965), 86.

successful focus of attention. In 1891, the average death rate for a tobacco estate in the country was more than 20 per cent, and several had death rates over 40 per cent. But by 1893, increased government inspections produced a range of improvements for the workforce and a reduction in the death rate to 12 per cent. By 1916, it was 1.8 per cent.[19] By the time Hans became general manager of the New Darvel Bay Tobacco Company in 1911, it was the most successful operation in British North Borneo with a workforce of more than two thousand, by far the largest in the country.

Figure 5. New Darvel Bay Tobacco Company employees at a company building on the harbour. Petersen family photo.

---

[19] Tregonning, 136 (20 per cent; 40 per cent), 137 (12 per cent), 144 (1.8 per cent).

Figure 6. Lahad Datu's harbour showing wharf and train track. Petersen family photo.

Figure 7. Tobacco field. Petersen family photo.

The picture John presented of the New Darvel Bay Tobacco Company was accurate in some respects but totally off base in others. His statement that thirteen Caucasians led the company's operation is essentially correct. North Borneo's *Official Gazette* for January 2, 1913, indicates the company employed eighteen Caucasians.[20] A couple of years later, the company's European staff had increased to twenty-one, and five of them, including Hans, were identified as German. But after the Germans were "discharged ... the European staff [was] reduced to fourteen" in 1916.[21]

On the other hand, John's assertion that Japanese foremen supervised the main workforce was fantasy. Such supervision was provided "by Chinese *tindals* or overseers acting under the direction of European divisional managers."[22] His claim that the train track ran up the mountain to the plantation is another illusion. The railway, under construction in 1908, replaced the eight-mile earth road that ran from the harbour at Lahad Datu northward to the plantations, which were "uniquely situated on the rich alluvial banks of the Segama with a river frontage on either side of over one hundred miles."[23] The nonexistent Japanese foremen coupled with the nonexistent mountain renders John's uprising story one of the taller of his tall tales.

His story about the family's escape by canoe and the preceding story about the scandal fanned in British newspapers are also untrue. Hans continued in his position with the company for seventeen months following the start of the war in early August 1914. He and his assistant manager, Mr. August Zander, an Austrian, and their wives were investigated by George M. Hanson, the American consul, who visited them from December 18 to 22, 1915. According to Hanson's "Segama" report on this visit, "the only requirement exacted of these enemy

---

[20] *Official Gazette* for January 2, 1913 (NAUK, CO 855 27). The gazette does not list nationalities, only the names and occupations of sixty-one individuals at Lahad Datu.
[21] Letter of December 6, 1916, from the British North Borneo Chartered Company head office to the Colonial Office (NAUK, CO 874 432).
[22] David W. John and James C. Jackson, 103.
[23] Rutter, 41.

subjects was the usual parole under oath not to do or say anything detrimental to the interests of the local government, and not to leave the estate without proper permission." The report also states that Hans's "bank account in Singapore ... has been tied up, and, though his money is deposited in a Dutch bank, the rule against doing business with an enemy subject has been involved and he is denied the use of his capital."[24] This fact became a storied element of the family's history. "As a result of the 1914–1918 war," Wim recalled in a postwar collaborator statement, my mother "and her family were expelled [from British North Borneo] without means of support by the English."[25]

In addition, there was the growing likelihood of internment, notwithstanding the fact that Hans was "a highly respectable member of the community."[26] This was the opinion of the British North Borneo Chartered Company, the organization that governed the country from the early 1880s until just after the Second World War.[27] It was expressed in a letter of November 10, 1915, from the Chartered Company's head office in London to the Colonial Office. Three months later, in a letter of February 17, 1916, Vice Admiral W. L. Grant, the British Commander-in-Chief for China, advised the Chartered Company: "My latest orders from the Admiralty are to remove all male enemy subjects of military age and enemy subjects of either sex reasonably suspected of spying or being engaged on enemy service." The vice admiral added: "I consider that the state of affairs in the East justifies the view that any German of active mind is a potential if not actual source of danger."[28]

Fortunately for Hans, Zander, and their families, the Chartered Company's Court of Directors had previously "authorized the

---

[24] Hanson's "SEGAMA" report (NAUK, CO 531 9).
[25] Wim's statement of October 23, 1946, 14.
[26] British North Borneo Chartered Company head office letter of November 10, 1915, to the Colonial Office (NAUK, FO 383 34).
[27] The company was established by the British government in 1881 and 1882. Led by a Court of Directors in London, it also had a Governor in British North Borneo.
[28] Letter of February 17, 1916 (NAUK, CO 531 9).

Governor of North Borneo to allow both these gentlemen to leave the country on the expiration of their contracts."[29] According to the *Herald*, the two men were relieved of their duties "about the end of December" and departed Lahad Datu with their families aboard the *Kinabalu* for Tarakan in Dutch Borneo on January 19, 1916.[30] That April, an official with the Colonial Office noted that Hanson's "'Segama' report is out of date, Zander and Petersen having got away."[31] In a "supplementary report" on "Interned Enemy Subjects," date-stamped July 24, 1916, Hanson states that Petersen, Zander, and their families "have been allowed to leave the state and are now in Java. They were permitted to take only enough money to pay the cost of passage to Java and living expenses for a few weeks."[32]

The Petersens took up residence at Malang where a second son, Constant, was born at the end of the year, on December 19. But, overall, it was a difficult time, according to John. They no longer had a retinue of servants, as had been the case at Lahad Datu. Instead, at a time and place where "white women never worked," he said that Stanni and Hans both found employment. He added that this greatly bothered his father, who "sulked" about it. Moreover, at some point Hans's health took a turn. Diagnosed with what John said was kidney disease, Hans died on April 30, 1918, the sixth anniversary of his marriage to Stanni.

I sense, however, that John was pumping up the pathos here and trading more in fantasy than fact. I suspect that Hans and Stanni were able to borrow the funds they needed, possibly from their extended families or from the local Dutch and German communities or both,

---

[29] NAUK, FO 383 34. The last sentence of the report by the American Consul, George M. Hanson, reads: "I am informed that if these gentlemen are displaced in the management of this estate no objection will be made by the local government to their leaving the country in the most convenient way possible."
[30] *British North Borneo Herald*, February 1, 1916 (NAUK, CO 855 30). See "LAHAD DATO NOTES."
[31] A handwritten Colonial Office document dated April 12, 1916 (NAUK, CO 531 9).
[32] George M. Hanson, American Consul, Supplementary Report on Interned Enemy Subjects, July 24, 1916. Provided to the author by historian Uwe Aranas.

against the time when, sometime after the war, their substantial savings in Hans's Singapore bank account would once more be available to them. Indeed, there is a photo from 1917 that does not indicate the family is in straitened circumstances. It shows John with his father and Aunt Cato, who is holding her new baby born on June 22. Behind Cato is an Indigenous amah.

Figure 8. Malang, Java, 1917. Left to right: an amah, baby Frank, John's Aunt Cato, John, and his father. Petersen family photo.

Whether John was simply warming to the tale he was spinning and adding some drama, or whether he had some special emotional investment in an impecunious view of his parents' circumstances, is unclear. But he did have strong feelings about what he mischaracterized as Britain's "confiscation" of his parents' money. To get the money back, he told me his mother launched a court case that lasted approximately twelve years and resulted in a settlement of "only … 8,000 guilders." In fact, British probate records show that a Letter of Administration (with Will limited) was granted November 28, 1919, and yielded £2,316, or approximately 28,500 guilders.[33] Add to this the fact that Stanni had married J. W. Kempen, a Dutch banker, on May 6, 1919, almost seven months before. It's hard to tell what was more devastating for John: his father's death or Kempen's arrival.

Stanni and Kempen remained in Malang until July 1922, when they and the boys, John, Constant, and Wim (who had been born on November 5, 1920), relocated to Hilversum, thirty-two kilometres southeast of Amsterdam. Stanni and Kempen also had a daughter, Miek, who was born March 20, 1926. Both John and Miek said Stanni married Kempen for security rather than love.

Kempen never adopted John and Constant.

"We never existed to him," John told me.

Kempen neither spoke to John and Constant, nor punished them, according to John. If there were something to be communicated, Kempen told his wife who told the boys. They attached to her, not him. They were not his concern. Miek described her father's attitude to John and Constant as "awful." Her opinion is based on family lore; her father died six weeks after she was born. "I never knew whether my mother and father loved one another," she told me. By contrast, she said Hans and Stanni were really in love. "They were so in love,"

---

[33] England and Wales, National Probate Calendar (index of Wills and Administrations), 1861–1941. Available at http://www.ancestry.com. In 1914, $1 US = 2.46 guilders (Wikipedia, "Dutch guilder," accessed February 10, 2021.) In 1919, 1£ = $5 US; see Margaret MacMillan, *Paris 1919: Six Months that Changed the World* (New York: Random House Trade Paperback Edition, 2003), 182–184, 480.

she remarked. She referred to "father Hans" to distinguish him from her own father.

Although John emphasized his parents' financial hardship in Malang and said the fantasized court settlement only produced eight thousand guilders, might a part of him, given the welter of emotions that arose in response to his stepfather, have safeguarded the notion that an earlier return of the family's money might have forestalled Stanni's need to remarry? A second unanswerable question is this: When did John start to invent his fantasy stories about his real father?

Figure 9. Stanni marries J. W. Kempen, May 6, 1919, with Constant (left) and John (right) in front. Petersen family photo.

2

A NEW NON-FATHER AND THE ISSUE OF BELONGING

"My father left me when he should not have," John told me. He maintained that his strong philosophic outlook and his "dream in himself" came from his father who, he believed, had been a courageous man of high ideals.

Although John remembered his father "only in certain moments," one of these times was a vivid experience that occurred the night his father died. John, who had just turned three, had been put to bed. His father came to check on him, as John said was his habit, only this time his father spoke to him. The words were unforgettable.

"I'm going away," he said. "I want you to be a brave boy and to always remember me. We will meet again."

Given John's track record as a teller of tall tales, I am highly skeptical of this story and two others he told me at the same time. I'm including them here for the record and for two other reasons. First, according to the book *Dreamspeak* by Rosemary Guiley, such experiences do happen, although I question how often they happen to three-year-old children given that few of us can remember much, if anything, from that age, let alone recall dreams or unusual encounters such as the one John described. Although John insisted he had not been dreaming, Guiley refers to such experiences as "farewell encounter dreams."[34]

The second reason that slightly blunts my skepticism is that John had several psychic and mystical experiences with his son, Hans, around the time Hans turned four at the end of 1940, and two of these experiences are corroborated. They will be discussed later.

John claimed a second equally remarkable experience the night his father died. He had a dream in which he and his mother came down some steps into a large room that he interpreted to be a restaurant. His mother then introduced him to a man.

"This is your new father," she told John. Over a year later the dream came true; he said it was how he met Kempen, his stepfather.

At the breakfast table the morning after his dream, before he learned of his father's death, John said he told the family what he had experienced the night before. His use of the term "the family" is of interest here because only his mother and sixteen-month-old Constant—and possibly his Aunt Cato and her new baby, Frank, both of whom visited Stanni and family approximately half a dozen times between mid-1917 and mid-1918—could have been present. This may indicate that John transferred feelings from a later period onto this suspect event. His mother told him he'd dreamed the encounter with his father. He said he knew he had not.

He added it was the first time the family noticed strangeness in him. While there is a significant element of self-mythologizing in this statement, John's second wife, Susan, told me that John had been "strange and different" right from the beginning of their three and a half decades together. In saying this, she was referring to his interiority, his quietude, his otherworldliness, and especially to a host of interrelated subjects and activities, including his conducting séances, his belief in reincarnation, and his psychic experiences, a few of which have a degree of verification. All of which fascinated Susan and lay at the core of her relationship with him.

---

[34] Rosemary Guiley, *Dreamspeak: How to Understand the Messages in Your Dreams* (New York: Berkley Books, 2001), 252–253.

John and I discussed the events of the night his father died on at least three occasions. In December 1980, he said he remembered little from the period between his father's death and his mother's remarriage, except that for several months his father often appeared to him at night. His father would play with him, appearing first on one side of the bed, then on the other, and would tickle him and make him howl with laughter, he claimed.

John described his experiences the night his father died, his mother's reaction to his stories the next morning, and the shrouded notion that he was to have a new father as "very confusing." He had a peaceful life until his father died, he told me grandiloquently. But after this event he said he felt deserted and very alone. He noted his mother and most people didn't believe what he said. He added that he had always been very lonely and had "a feeling of not being able to belong [and of being] the odd one out."

Where John's father held an honoured place in the family's psyche, Kempen's legacy was far different. A signal event occurred when John was four months shy of his sixth birthday. This was Wim's birth. Kempen's response to the new babe was a revelation. John was amazed by how enamoured his stepfather was with Wim and by the attention Kempen lavished on him. For the next several years, Kempen doted on Wim. John said Kempen spoiled Wim in extreme ways while he ignored John and Constant, to whom he remained as silent, remote, and unreachable as ever. John told me that at mealtimes he and Constant had to stand at the table while Kempen and their mother (along with Wim, when he was old enough) sat. According to John's son, Harald, "having to stand up at the dinner table while eating" was a punishment. In mid-1925, about the time Stanni became pregnant with Miek, Kempen started complaining of what John described as "terrific headaches" and his behaviour changed. He said Kempen became very cruel to Stanni and claimed the child she was carrying was not his. The situation deteriorated to such an extent that sometime during the latter half of 1925 or early 1926, Stanni left Kempen and divorced him. She took this step, according to Susan, because Kempen didn't want any more children.

When Kempen died at the end of April, it initially appeared to be the result of a fall down the stairs at his home. But according to John, an autopsy revealed a brain tumour that had ruptured. He and his mother believed the tumour accounted for Kempen's changed behaviour. John also said his mother harboured considerable guilt for leaving Kempen when he was sick and near the end of his life and for the fact he never met his youngest child. John maintained Stanni tried to assuage her guilt by favouring Wim and Miek.

Kempen's will reinforced this bias. Half his estate went to his two grown children from his first marriage and half went to Wim and Miek. Stanni received the interest from Wim and Miek's half and was permitted to access the capital under certain circumstances until they came of age. John and Constant didn't receive anything directly. They were provided for through their mother who repeatedly told them that Wim and Miek were their benefactors.

John implied that Wim was aware of his special position in the family hierarchy and would kick John under the table with some regularity during meals. Apparently, John put up with this for some time, but one day in 1928, when he was around thirteen and Wim was about seven, his pent-up anger got the better of him and he kicked Wim back. Likely there were shouts and cries because their mother joined in by throwing a serviette ring at John, which hit him in the stomach. The physical impact was inconsequential, but the emotional affect was cutting. Stanni's action was a sharp exclamation point to her accompanying statement—John had to remember that Wim was his provider. John's response was to run away from home, although he returned later that day.

Susan, who was close to Stanni and regarded her as a second mother, maintained John was the least loved of the kids in that family and that there was some issue between John and his mother. What that issue was, Susan never specified, although a comparison of John and Constant may provide clues. Constant would be the more balanced, conventional, and successful of the two during the 1930s. John appears to have been more gifted but less disciplined, with a need to be the centre of attention and a penchant for flitting from project to project without always finishing what he started. He was a worry to Stanni.

When John told me his story, he never spoke critically of his mother. But I intuited more than once that he was not being completely forthcoming. A quarter century later, Susan implied that John held resentment toward his mother for always playing bridge when he was a boy. Susan added that Stanni had little to do with her children while she and Kempen lived in Java, where well-to-do Caucasians nearly always had servants. Although less grandly, this situation may have also prevailed in the Netherlands for the greater part of the time that Stanni and Kempen were together; there is no doubt she continued to play bridge on a regular basis.

The family didn't celebrate Christmas when Kempen was alive. John "existed in a dream world" at that time of year, he said. He would go out in the cold and walk Hilversum's downtown and look in the shop windows and "imagine that someone was going to buy for him the most marvellous toy" he saw. Of course, we need to be wary of John's claims for they were invariably self-serving and often embellished or untrue, a manifestation of how he coped with emotional upset.

John's son, Hans, heard the same story that Kempen didn't permit the family to celebrate Christmas. But he also said his father had a "poor me" complex. John's experience of Christmas during the 1922–25 period, when he was ages seven to ten, is both a case in point and important information about his life. Less clear is how much he heard from his mother during these years about his father. Did she feel constrained by Kempen's presence to talk to John and Constant about their father? If this were the case, the constraint would have ended when the family left Kempen. Either way, John and Constant likely heard more about their father once Kempen was gone, notwithstanding the guilt their mother felt given the circumstances of Kempen's demise.

Whatever the quality and quantity of this information and whenever it might have been imparted—while the family was with Kempen or after they had left him or during both periods—I suspect, in John's case, it was an emotional motherlode, the stuff of future fantasies. Whether John first soaked up this information about his father during the years Kempen was denying them Christmas or later when his mother was feeling guilty and favouring Wim and Miek, it came at a time when he felt isolated and alone within the family. These were feelings that he carried for much of the rest of his life.

Similarly, John's ideas about his father and Lahad Datu and his parents' marriage of exactly six years became personal archetypes and psychic bellwethers. What we don't know is when he began to share with others the myths he developed about his father. To what extent were they genuine fantasies rather than manipulative tall tales? His first postwar collaborator statement and his 1951 letter, which was written with the clear intent of strengthening his chances of gaining entry to Canada, are the earliest extant documentation of some of these myths. The timing of the letter is important. At least some of its tall tales were intentional fabrications or purposeful manipulations to evoke sympathy and aid his goal of coming to Canada.[35]

As his "strong philosophic outlook" and his "dream in himself" were rooted in what he regarded as his father's example, so the six-year duration of his parents' marriage also had a special hold on him. He related it to his "strangeness" and his alleged psychic gifts. About 1960, he told Harald he had misused those gifts and that, as a result, he would not be happy, except for the last six years of his life. According to Harald, this information had come from God.

---

[35] His claim on page 3 of his June 1951 letter, that his 1930s application for Dutch naturalization was refused because "1st My naturalisation was of no special interest to the Netherlands! 2nd Because my life was not in danger!" appears to be an intentional fabrication. Almost five years earlier, in his second collaborator statement (October 29, 1946), he admitted his naturalization request "was denied for … unknown reasons." His first collaborator statement (October 8, 1945) also said his naturalization request had been "denied because there was no 'direct threat to my life.'" In addition, his letter falsely claimed that his collaborator "case went on trial." He maintained that when he was released "there has been nothing whatsoever to find fault with my behaviour." Both his first collaborator statement and his letter refer to the English newspapers' indignation about a German "leading an English venture" at Lahad Datu when the two countries were at war. His letter claimed as well that his paternal grandparents were great Danish patriots.

3

JOHN'S CHILDHOOD AND YOUTH: FACT AND FICTION

John was ten months old when he arrived in Java with his parents. Malang was his home for the next six and a half years, until July 1922 when the reconstituted family left for Holland. There were three subjects he spoke about regarding this period: sickness, animals, and the Indigenous people. The only verification for any of it are Constance's and Onno's views that John's time with the Indigenous people was critical to the development of his deep interest in the seeming power of the mind to conjure, connect, and know in special ways.

As was often the case with John, there is a heightened quality to these stories, with elements of the fabulous and the romantic that suggest an overlay of accumulated emotion and experience has been added. He suffered "all the sicknesses"—diphtheria, dysentery, and malaria—between the ages of four and six and said he had them severely enough that the doctors usually thought he would die. But when he was healthy, it appears he spent most of his time with animals and the Indigenous people, even though his immersion with the latter was against his parents' wishes, especially those of his stepfather. It seems his parents didn't follow through on their instructions, and John had considerable freedom to do as he pleased. He told me he was very involved with the Indigenous people.

He also spoke of being surrounded by animals. His menagerie consisted of a miniature pony, two ostriches, a monkey, a cockatoo, a baby elephant that he would ride, a pet deer that wore a ribbon around its neck to show that it was tame, and a pair of Great Danes, a male and a female, that belonged to his stepfather. Indeed, it was as though he was the child protagonist in one of Rudyard Kipling's jungle stories. John said the Indigenous people were afraid of the dogs and would kneel when he walked by with them. The regality of this image provides a dramatic counterpoint to the sterile absence of relationship with Kempen.

John told me that the tame deer was killed by two Chinese men. They said it was an accident, but John said he knew it was not. He also said that some of the Indigenous people poisoned one of the Great Danes. The other dog lost its will to live, refused to eat, and died of malnutrition and grief. The young elephant survived but had to be left behind when the family sailed for Europe.

Where these anecdotes stress hardship and loss, John's stories about the Indigenous people emphasize discovery. According to Aldous Huxley, "there is much preoccupation with, and a widespread talent for, psychic thinking" among such societies.[36] John told me, "Indonesian people have certain powers, which have never been explained." He claimed he saw a witch doctor make it rain stones. He spoke of them putting curses on people who would become sick, shrivel up, and die unless they were able to get far enough away across the sea before the curse took effect. White men who had left wives behind in Europe and taken Indigenous women as common-law partners then abandoned them after several years were frequent targets of these curses. John spoke as well of Indigenous people who were falsely accused of some transgression, turning themselves into virtual zombies by emptying their minds to gain the assistance of bad spirits. They would become like a second shadow to their accuser, silently following

---

[36] Aldous Huxley, *The Perennial Philosophy: An Interpretation of the Great Mystics, East and West* (New York: HarperCollins, First Perennial Classics edition, 2004), 20.

him everywhere, always staring, eyes boring relentlessly into him to unravel his nerves and dominate his life. The only escape for the accuser, John said, was to give a feast of several days' duration and confess that bad spirits had made him make the accusations.

John said that fakir candidates began their training at four or five years of age, and noted he was first in touch with fakirs when he was six. With them, he practised various aspects of mind over matter. He said they were instructed to look at a rock or tree to become that rock or tree, to regulate their heartbeat and body temperature, and that he experienced a degree of success doing these things. He observed adepts walk without injury over beds of red-hot coals. He attributed this ability to their complete faith in what they were doing.

Kempen normally did his best to avoid the Indigenous people, but when there was a robbery at his bank that baffled the authorities, he agreed, as a last resort, to consult a witch doctor. John presumably accompanied his stepfather on this visit; it was the only time the two of them did anything together, according to what John told me. He said the witch doctor beckoned Kempen to look in a mirror, and when he did, he saw the face of a man he had not, nor ever would have, suspected. A trusted employee of the bank had stolen the money. Later, when challenged, the man apparently confessed.

Make of these stories what you will. It is much easier for me to endorse the two distinct sides of John's personality that are evident from his descriptions of himself as a youth in Holland. As a student, he was much more interested in tomfoolery than textbooks. Full of mischief, he said he was the life of the party and could "make things go." According to his stories, his antics got him kicked out of class frequently and expelled more than once. He favoured stink bombs and coming to school with fresh cow manure caked onto his shoes so his would be an especially smelly presence in class. He told me he liked the attention that came with "acting the fool," a tendency that was so pronounced into adulthood that both John and Susan used this phrase to describe this aspect of his behaviour.

Figure 10. Presumed school portrait of John, year unknown. Petersen family photo.

In contrast to his boisterous classroom shenanigans, the other side of his personality was contemplative and deeply serious. He probed the meaning of life and sought answers. He claimed it was not uncommon for him to go into the countryside, build a lean-to, and spend the day considering why people thought and behaved the way they did. He said that while he received no revelations, he did learn not to take things for granted and always to seek.

He told me he made a practice of visiting different churches and that he was very religious in his own way and was always seeking answers to certain questions: How could ministers or priests of the same faith but in different countries bless the weapons of soldiers who were going off to kill each other? How could the church support war and uphold the commandment not to kill? What was higher, God's law or society's law? But the men of God he spoke to never had adequate answers. He felt it was an evasion and an abrogation of responsibility when it was suggested that he would have to be a medic rather than a combatant. Although a medic was intended to help instead of fight and kill, he nonetheless functioned in support of the malignant situation that required medics in the first place. To John, the only answer was not to cooperate at all. He said he started to realize that there were social contradictions and that laws and beliefs were sometimes used to impose order and compliance over what is right.

John said his mother was against him going to church but she permitted it because it was a good outlet for his anger and frustrations. He said she knew he would come back happier, calmer, more peaceful, and added that he got strength from the church. His mother did not, however, let him formalize a relationship with any of the churches, such as becoming an altar boy. Years later, she also discouraged church involvement on the part of John's son, Hans. Neither John nor Hans gave a reason why Stanni did this. However, Miek said that when she was about ten, Stanni encouraged her to go to Sunday school as part of a well-rounded education.

John said he had one girlfriend for most of his teens. Her name was Mika, but he called her Zus, meaning sister. They met in 1928, when he was thirteen. They went for walks and did their homework together and he said he was at her home all the time, even though he didn't get along that well with her parents, who didn't really approve, especially her dad. Despite this, the relationship lasted five to six years. At the same time, it was entirely platonic. John said this was due to him, not her, and noted he never kissed her, although she probably expected it. Things ended abruptly when he was eighteen. She had promised not to cut her hair while he was at sea. When he returned and found that she had, he immediately ended their relationship and never saw her again. He told me he often thought of her afterward, but not with regret. He maintained "life was like a love" and he sustained himself with dreams of a perfect woman. These dreams, he said, were "safe from life's harsh realities and wouldn't get shot through with holes."

Romantic idealism was a mental salve and lifelong coping mechanism. While it often combined with John's aspiration and inspiration, it also contributed to his delusion and deceit. He told me that as a youth, he wanted to be a knight in modern times; he would accomplish this, he said, "by telling the truth and trying to help people." He said this with passion and enthusiasm. And there were certainly occasions when he lived up to his high ideals and conducted himself like an honourable knight. But, owing to weakness and self-deception, he was, as an adult, sometimes prone to exploitation and dishonourable behaviour. His second and third wives, Susan and Mary, who were among those who knew him best, concluded that manipulation and mendacity were among his core characteristics, along with gentleness, charm, warmth, and affability.

While these latter qualities seemed inherent in him, warmth and gentleness were also modelled by an Englishman named Timperley, who John met in 1928. Timperley was the closest John had to a father figure during his early and mid-teens. A man of about forty, Timperley was the Scout Master of John's Sea Scout pack. In his availability and acceptance, Timperley was the antithesis of John's aloof stepfather, and John soaked up the attention. John said he adored Timperley. Given John's tendency to falsify the record, I want to point out that Timperley is also notable for being a real and undisguised person. He was well known to John's family. Both Hans and Miek spoke about him to me. Timperley also led Hans's Sea Scout pack from 1949 to 1952.

John's friend Ko (Jacobus) Elhorst, who he met toward the end of 1933, is an example of someone he disguised. When he spoke to me about Ko, he always referred to him as Joe. John's supposed artistic mentor, Wiertz, was a more pronounced case of obfuscation, for after much research it turned out he didn't exist at all, which part of me still finds hard to believe. Looking at my notes, it amuses me to find an entry in the margin, John telling me: "You don't have to fictionalize Wiertz. He's dead now." The truth, which I didn't learn for several decades, is that I never needed to fictionalize Wiertz because he had always been a complete fiction.

John claimed that he first met Wiertz in about 1930 and that, like Timperley, he was about forty. However, I suspect Wiertz was modelled, in part, off a much younger man. His name was Pieter Pouwels (1910–81), a Hilversum resident and well-known painter and illustrator, who Susan confirmed John knew. Pouwels was only five years older than John. Although I have no proof of it, I suspect Pouwels was John's artistic mentor during the 1930–35 period. I also suspect Pouwels held pro-Nazi views during this period and probably shared them with John. During the war, Pouwels did illustrations for Dutch Nazi periodicals, most notably *Storm-SS*, the weekly magazine of the SS in Holland. This association hampered his postwar career. He used an alias, S. Pennick, from 1945 to 1957 for at least some of his work as an illustrator. However, he also had exhibitions using his real name during this period. It is also known that Pouwels gave painting lessons to students in Hilversum in the 1960s.

John said Timperley and Wiertz both influenced him greatly. Timperley gave important direction to John's life, both in the near and the long term. According to John, Timperley was a seaman through and through, and he taught John knot-tying, Morse code, and how to make sails, masts, and boats. John soon found that he shared Timperley's passion for sailing and the water. He said it was because of Timperley that he decided to go to nautical school and was able to skip a year when he got there.

John said Timperley also taught him a lot about his philosophy, which centred on being warm and gentle with people, and noted Timperley provided definite guidelines that helped shape the personal code John would try to live by. John said these were very key things in his life. They planted the seeds that later blossomed during his career as a social worker, especially his work with youth. Timperley, John said more than once, taught him to think, and John noted he used Timperley as an example. He not only wanted to be self-sufficient in practical matters like his mentor, he also wanted to be a teacher, someone who would help people with their lives.

"I couldn't see myself doing anything else," John said about nautical school. But later, when he described his experiences at the school, he mentioned another factor that brought him there. Nautical school was the least expensive option for his education, and this was important to his mother. He said he went to nautical school because there were no other alternatives. This is another case of John portraying himself as victimized by circumstances. It is an important example of his relationship with his mother; his schooling was an area of contention. This case also illustrates his marked sensitivity to status, a subject he opined about regularly.

He told me he wanted to be an engineer like his father, only he would be an aeronautical rather than a mechanical engineer. In support of this objective, he said he entered a three-year university-track high school program in 1927, when he was twelve. But there was a problem. Due to his lack of Dutch citizenship, he would be required to pay the higher university tuition rates applied to foreigners. He said his mother felt it would be too expensive, and this weighed on him. "What's the use?" he recounted thinking at the time. He noted he failed his first year of high school then switched to a different school that offered a more general four-year program. On another occasion he told me that his goal in life—to be an aeronautical engineer—had been taken from him.

These claims are dubious. As we shall see shortly, John didn't discover he was German until 1930, when he turned fifteen. The story about his dashed engineering aspirations is consistent with other tales he told that were meant to cover up or offset his lack of academic credentials, professional standing, or other perceived earmarks of success. He told me he'd been an officer in the SS and claimed that he'd held ranks equivalent to second lieutenant and captain when, according to his SS card, he was the equivalent of a corporal and a sergeant. When I asked Susan about his claim that he had studied economics and commerce at Leiden University, she responded bluntly: "That was his ego speaking." He didn't attend university while she knew him. She added John was impressed by professionals, particularly doctors.

John said he would talk things over with Timperley and get ideas from him and that they examined most subjects. But John didn't mention discussing his goal of being an aeronautical engineer with his mentor, which may be an indication that this purported objective was another false claim. Although this goal may already have been a dead issue because he had already changed high schools by the time he got to know Timperley, John's collaborator statement of October 29, 1946, the second of three statements he gave Dutch officials while interned after the war, refers to him attending only "H.B.S. Hoogere Burgerschool." What is clearer is that by the mid-1930s, John had set his sights on being an artist.

It's notable that John had pronounced similarities with both Timperley and the Belgian romantic painter, Antoine Joseph Wiertz (1806–65), who was, at least in part, the model for his fictional "Wiertz." (To avoid confusion, I will always refer to the artist as Antoine Wiertz.) Timperley, according to John, was a sad sort of man who had lost his father, a successful businessman, at a relatively young age, after which he had resolved to look after his mother and younger brother. Timperley never married, feeling that he couldn't become too involved with a woman because of his responsibilities. John noted that while his mentor was very self-sufficient with practical things, he was always "emotionally searching ... searching for happiness." John maintained Timperley needed a connection and a commitment to people other than his mother, which is why he worked with kids.

"People always loved him," John said, but he added they also felt sorry for him. This, I suspect, is as much a description of John's self-image as it is of Timperley. John's son Hans said his father was "one of the saddest people."

4

HITLERMANIA AND THE LARGER WORLD

Although we don't know the precise year John started paying attention to the news of the day, it probably occurred during the latter 1920s or early 1930s. We do know that the lightning rod of the 1919 Treaty of Versailles, which ended the First World War between Germany and the Allies, served as his introduction to politics, international relations, and Adolf Hitler. Known to Germans as the Versailles *Diktat*, it deprived the country of "13 per cent of its territory, 12 per cent of its population, 48 per cent of its iron industry, 16 per cent of its coal production, 80 per cent of its naval fleet, all of its colonies, and, as far as the people were concerned, all of its dignity."[37] According to Winston Churchill, "The economic clauses of the treaty were malignant and silly to an extent that made them obviously futile. Germany was condemned to pay reparations on a

---

[37] Matthew Hockenos, *Then They Came for Me: Martin Niemöller, the Pastor Who Defied the Nazis* (New York: Basic Books, 2018), 54. According to Nicolaus von Below, Hitler's Luftwaffe Adjutant, "To the mass of the German people, the [September 1, 1939] attack on Poland was no more than the means of rectifying the Versailles diktat." Nicolaus von Below, *At Hitler's Side: The Memoirs of Hitler's Luftwaffe Adjutant 1937–1945*, translated by Geoffrey Brooks (London: Greenhill Books, and Mechanicsburg, PA: Stackpole Books, 2004), 35.

fabulous scale." In April 1921, the total was pegged at 132 billion gold marks (or $33 billion).[38] The repayment process, Churchill added, was "a recognisable factor in the economic collapse which was presently to overwhelm the world, to prevent its recovery and inflame its hatred."[39] But it is also true that Germany "regularly defaulted on its payments." It paid about $4.5 billion of the total owing between 1918 and 1932, when it stopped paying for good.[40]

John identified and sympathized with Germany. He said he saw it as an outcast among nations, which had injustices inflicted upon it following the war, and he always felt the Treaty of Versailles was unjust. He noted that he grew up with this view. As the Great Depression deepened and Germany's unemployment grew steadily from 1.3 million in 1929 to over 6 million by January 30, 1933, when Hitler came to power, John said he was angered by the Dutch people who exploited Germany's situation by buying underpriced German goods.

Hitler was John's hero. He was also, according to historian Sir Ian Kershaw, "arguably the most popular head of state in the world" between 1933 and 1940.[41] John said he felt *der Führer* had a mission to fulfill and would do something. And do something he did. Through massive concentration of power, he united Germany as never before. Through massive public works projects, like the autobahn, he put the German people back to work. Unemployment was reduced to less than five million in 1934 and eliminated by 1937. And from 1933 to 1937, national income doubled. John said he was quite taken by the development of Germany from a human point of view. He noted that he was very conscious of poor people, he always sided with the underdog, and he was impressed by how Hitler restored German pride and helped the downtrodden to rise up.

---

[38] Winston S. Churchill, *The Second World War: The Gathering Storm* (Boston: Houghton Mifflin Co., 1948), 7.
[39] Churchill, 24.
[40] MacMillan, *Paris 1919*, 480.
[41] Ian Kershaw, *Hitler, 1889–1936: Hubris* (London: Penguin, 1998), xxix.

"The German people saw Hitler as an avenging saviour," he told me. Indeed, in a 1931 radio broadcast, "Call for the Führer," Pastor Martin Niemöller asked, "Where is the leader? ... When he comes, he will come as a gift, as a gift of God."[42]

Although Niemöller became the most prominent of the Nazis' German opponents and was jailed by them on numerous occasions, including from 1937 to 1945, he was an ardent supporter during the early years. He voted for the Nazis in 1924, 1928, and 1933 and "greeted Hitler's appointment [as chancellor] with euphoria."[43] In his autobiography, *From U-boat to Pulpit*, written during the summer of 1934, he states his belief that Hitler would bring light and "National Revival" to Germany, ending the long "years of darkness" from 1919 to 1932.[44]

When Hitler took power, "a wild national jubilation broke out," according to Hans Bernd Gisevius's memoir of the Nazi years, *To The Bitter End*. "Day after day people sang and marched into ever-madder states of intoxication.... Even the doubters were sucked into the torrent of joy and hope."[45]

It is apparent that John's position on Germany changed depending on his circumstances at different times in his life. For example, circa 1933, he was pro-German and believed that Hitler "had a mission to fulfill," but when he was trying to gain entry to Canada, he maintained in his 1951 letter that he had been "pushed in to" his German nationality. Doubtless his family ties to Germany contributed to his pro-German and pro-Hitler attitude as a teenager and young man. These ties included his father's nationality, the Flensburg connection, and his older half-sister, Trudi, who occasionally wrote to Stanni from Germany.

There is also the fact that John's parents were befriended by the local German community when they moved to Malang. After Hans

---

[42] Hockenos, 68.
[43] Hockenos, 74.
[44] William L. Shirer, *The Nightmare Years, 1930–1940: A Memoir of a Life and the Times*, (Boston: Little, Brown & Co., 1948), 152.
[45] Hans Bernd Gisevius, *To The Bitter End* (Boston: Houghton Mifflin, 1947), 94, 95, 93.

died, this community purchased an impressive headstone for his grave. The large, engraved plaque affixed to the headstone includes the statement *Der Heimat fern—in schwerer Zeit. Warst Du ihr treuer Sohn* (The motherland far away—in difficult times. You were a true son). The accuracy of this sentiment is debatable, however. As we have seen, Hans not only evaded German military service, he also continued to head the operation of a large British tobacco company for almost eighteen months after the start of the First World War. Indeed, American Consul Hanson's report points out that as late as December 1915 Hans still had "unrestricted liberty in correspondence concerning business affairs."[46] Nonetheless, the kindness of Malang's German community may have rekindled affection for Germany, while the prior threat of internment and the loss of his employment and home at Lahad Datu, as well as the freezing of his bank account, may have sparked bitterness toward the British. A photo of Hans's gravesite was to play an important role in how John came to be registered with the German government.

---

[46] Hanson's "SEGAMA" report (NAUK, CO 531 9).

Figure 11. Grave of Hans Petersen, 1868–1918. Petersen family photo.

When we talked in 1976, John admitted he had a real problem with his idealization of the Germans. Aspects of it continued even after the German invasion of the Netherlands in May 1940, which he regarded as a betrayal after Hitler's repeated promises to respect Dutch sovereignty and neutrality. He also didn't believe—or didn't want to believe—that Hitler knew of the Holocaust; others, in his view, were responsible for that. If Hitler were involved, it was only because he went "berserk during the war," he told me.

In the Netherlands, the Nationaal-Socialistische Beweging (NSB), the largest Dutch fascist party, was established in December 1931 under the leadership of Anton Adriaan Mussert, an engineer and civil servant.[47] It achieved its greatest popular success in the April 1935 provincial elections when it received almost 8 per cent of the vote, "making it the fifth strongest party in the country."[48] A widely reviled fringe party for the remainder of the decade, it would play a key collaborationist role during the German occupation.

While imprisoned as a collaborator after the war, John told Dutch officials that he had never been a member of the NSB.[49] This was a lie. A Hilversum police report of May 12, 1937, prepared further to his application for naturalization, states that he was a member for about a year early on, presumably sometime between 1932 and 1935 when he was sixteen to twenty years of age.[50] He told me he was not politically active. While this claim is contradicted by his NSB membership, it is supported by the apparent fact that the membership was not renewed. It is possible he was under the influence of Pieter Pouwels when he joined.

John claimed he didn't talk politics at all but read about it. He said his friends, however, were often involved. Johan Veltmeijer (1913–67), who befriended John in the latter part of 1933, was a strong socialist who belonged to the Workers Party. As John specified this was not a Communist party, I presume he was referring to the National Socialist Dutch Workers Party (NSNAP), which had less than 10,000 members and called for the Netherlands to be absorbed

---

[47] Gerhard Hirschfeld, *Nazi Rule and Dutch Collaboration: The Netherlands under German Occupation, 1940–1945* (Oxford, New York, Hamburg: Berg Publishers Ltd., 1988), 251, 326.
[48] Hirschfeld, 252.
[49] John's statement of October 8, 1945.
[50] Hilversum Police Report of May 12, 1937—Ministry of Justice documents related to John's application for naturalization—02.09.22, inventory nos. 11681 and 11668.

into the Third Reich.[51] Veltmeijer is typical of a strain of Dutch activists who initially supported Hitler but later joined the resistance to oppose him.

John said he and his friends didn't like the Communist Party and had little to do with it. He spoke of the futility of communism and contended that it was just exploiting working men. Another time he said he saw the Nazis as fighting destructive leftists who had sowed the seeds for Hitler. He was also critical of the NSB, which he said dressed in a certain way, had their marches, and engaged in some violence with the police. He said he didn't like the threat implicit in some of the party's activities and that he abhorred violence. Indeed, he was strongly inclined to pacifism. During our sessions in 1976, John mentioned his philosophy against wars and fighting several times. In 1982, he told his daughter Constance: "I spent the whole war running because I didn't want to shoot a gun."

Even if some readers doubt John's pacifism, the independence of spirit evident in some of these remarks should be noted, for it will assert itself during the occupation, even when he is working for German organizations, notably the Schutzgruppe but also the SD.

---

[51] Henry L. Mason, *The Purge of Dutch Quislings: Emergency Justice in the Netherlands* (The Hague: Martinus Nijhoff, 1952), 16.

5

NATIONALITY AND NAUTICAL SCHOOL

"After the death of my father my mother remarried a Dutchman after asking and getting back her Dutch nationality," John wrote in his 1951 letter. "She made the mistake to suppose that her children would get her nationality automatically. To the law we remained Germans. This fact came to light, when I went to sea and asked for my passport." Although most of this is true, the statement that he discovered he was German when he applied for his Dutch passport in 1933 is incorrect. The claim that his mother believed throughout the 1920s that he and Constant were Dutch appears to be true. In 1924, when the boys were nine and seven, they were sent to The Hague to stay with an aunt and uncle from September 23 to October 23. In both cases, their *Verhuizingen Binnen de Gemeente* (change-of-address documents) indicate their nationality is Dutch. It was not until 1930, when John applied for entry to a Dutch nautical school, that the truth was revealed. He said he thought he was Dutch but he was told he was German. As a foreigner, he was ineligible for the training college, according to his collaborator statement of October 8, 1945.[52]

In July 1932, John's mother, his Uncle Jan, and two others testified before a Hilversum justice of the peace. This resulted in the

---

[52] John's collaborator statement of October 8, 1945 (DNA, CABR 109786).

issuance of "a certificate of notoriety, that Jan Jurgen Petersen was born on the seventh of March 1915 at Lahad Datu (British Borneo)."[53] The acquisition of this document may have related to John's acceptance by another nautical school, Zeevaartschool Te Schiermonnikoog, where he had started classes several months before, in March. Located on Schiermonnikoog, one of the West Frisian Islands off the northeastern coast of the Netherlands, the school was situated in the centre of the island's only village, which was also called Schiermonnikoog. John was a boarding student at the school. His *rapportboekje* (nautical school report book) is in Harald's possession. It includes John's report cards dated December 22, 1932; March 24, 1933; and June 1, 1933.

This documentary evidence—the change-of-address records, the certificate of notoriety, the report cards, along with John's postwar collaborator statements and his 1951 letter (even though claims he makes in these latter documents are not always accurate or truthful)—is important because it anchors key parts of his story: his understanding that he was Dutch, the revelation that he was German, and his attendance at nautical school. These details also provide the framework for John's colourful stories about his time on Schiermonnikoog. These yarns are mostly unverified, but a couple of them have been contradicted recently (January 2021). The challenge is to distill what truth we can from the picture they present, even if it is only to confirm John as a teller of tall tales with a penchant for romanticism and grandiosity.

Nautical school loomed large in his memory. Given his inventive imagination, it is hard to tell where the line between fact and fantasy falls in many of his reminiscences. As with his Malang period, much of what he told me had a heightened quality. The ordinary often became extraordinary through some combination of setting, people, and circumstance. The island's only policeman was one of its fattest

---

[53] The certificate number is 1039. The other two witnesses were Albertus Perk, a notary public, and Berend Jan Hoetink, a candidate notary public, both of Hilversum.

residents, but remarkably also its fastest runner. Equally memorable was the one-eyed captain of the island's lifeboat-and-rescue team. He was renowned for his courage, convictions, and ability to drink huge quantities of beer from large pails without any ill effect. As a youth he reportedly lost an eye when he and some friends shot arrows straight up into the air and watched to see what would happen.

It is likely that the mythic and at times fantastical character John attributed to Schiermonnikoog indicated the significance of his time there. The island was a stepping stone away from home and a way station to the wider world. It echoed parts of his past and, as he repeatedly suggested, it foreshadowed aspects of his future.

Zeevaartschool, Schiermonnikoog.

Figure 12. Period postcard that belonged to John Petersen. Now in the possession of his son Harald.

John's education at nautical school was different from any he had before. What he learned was often in stark contrast to what Timperley emphasized: the warm and gentle attentiveness to people. John said nautical school taught him to be tough and hard, how to get out of difficulty, and to deal with physical pain. He noted the school "was a shambles" during the first months he was there, and he made it sound as though the inmates were running the asylum, where some teachers were completely out of their depth and had virtually no control over their students.

The other teachers, by and large, were tough and effective and they were backed up by the school's strict rules and severe punishments. If a student was caught doing something wrong, he was often given this choice: miss a month of school or receive a lashing with the cat-o'-nine-tails! (This unlikely claim is probably John embellishing. He may have heard stories about similar whips used in the Far East. In the early days—circa 1890—some plantation managers operated in cruel and neglectful ways. In one case, the Chinese workforce was "swindled, cheated and half-starved," according to Tregonning. Men were "flogged in the most merciless manner and [were] refused medical treatment when suffering the wounds inflicted upon them by the flogging whip, the tail of a stinging ray.")[54] The students, John said, always chose the lashes because school was too important. The whippings took place in the school attic and were attended by the entire student body. The student receiving the punishment did so with a bare back, his arms held over his head, his wrists tied to a pole. For increased effectiveness, the cat-o'-nine-tails was wetted first. Seven to twelve blows were the norm. The most John ever saw was twenty-three, he claimed.

The seamanship teacher administered the attic whippings. A former boatswain, he had a penchant for punishing people. John said he seemed to enjoy it, going about it in an almost cavalier fashion. Not surprisingly, he was a thoroughly unpopular teacher. On the day of their practical exams, several students took their revenge by throwing him overboard and making him swim the considerable distance back to shore. An eye for an eye, but it didn't end the ill will between them; it perpetuated it. The teacher took his revenge too. The student who instigated and led the rebellion received the twenty-three-blow whipping. John said he learned that there is a certain

---

[54] Tregonning, 135.

sadistic type of man who likes punishing people. He would meet more of them when he was imprisoned as a collaborator after the war.

Other teachers, while not despised like the former boatswain, also incurred the students' wrath. In one case, the students used planks and long nails to board up the doors and windows of a teacher's house. They did such a good job that when the teacher returned home that night he couldn't get in until he got a carpenter out of bed to help him. Another teacher had his garden strategically attacked several times. On one occasion his bulbs were replaced with onions; on another his prized strawberries disappeared. This latter incident led to a turn on the punishment pole for John.

He said he hadn't participated in the garden forays, but he knew about them. Such knowledge was a weighty matter because loyalty to your mates was an unwritten rule. You "never let one of your fellow students down," he said. And the importance of this rule was heightened for the small number of students who, like John, had been put ahead a year because of their Sea Scout training. The main conspirators in the garden raids were all a year older and veterans of the school's student-teacher conflicts. John's loyalty was severely tested in the aftermath of the strawberry caper.

The plot had been hatched after the guileless teacher had made the mistake of announcing in class that he would harvest his berries the next day. That night a cadre of the older boys slipped out of the school, made their way to the teacher's garden, and silently collected the treasured crop. John happily participated in the feast that followed. While there was much merriment about the success of the incursion and the excellent quality of the booty, the architects of the evening's events were careful to preserve four or five of the largest and finest berries on a small plate. These were for the *coup de grâce* that was to be administered in class the next morning. And John noted that because he was the best clown and could give the best speech, he was chosen to present the plate of berries to the teacher.

John's penchant for playing the fool and rashly doing what few others would was often accompanied by a failure to give much, if any, consideration to the likely consequences. The upshot of his bravado, he claimed, was a dramatic whipping at the punishment pole. He said he was lashed unjustly, that he was punished for all the rest even though he had not participated in the raid. His sense of unfairness and victimization makes me think something like what he described may have, in fact, occurred, although it was undoubtedly less sensational than he contended. He was given the standard choice, a suspension or a lashing; he was also offered more lenient treatment if he identified who else was involved.

"I did it," he said, taking sole responsibility and setting the stage for the final confrontation. When the whipping took place, the seamanship teacher asked him after each lash: "Who did it?" And each time he replied: "I did it."

He said he learned to deal with pain and not to betray his friends. He added that the experience was beneficial in the long run and an asset for later on.

While life at the school was, by turns, rambunctious and unsparing, the broader community had a mostly convivial spirit. Although he didn't remember their names and mixed up some of the details, John enthusiastically recalled two community festivals: the springtime Kallemooi and the Klozum, which is held on December 5 when the rest of the country celebrates Sinterklaas or Saint Nicholas' Eve. The village's other side—its danger—was the result, John said, of a long-standing feud between the local young men and the nautical-school cadets. The presence of the nautical school meant there was a disproportionate number of young men on the island and that the local ones, who mostly resided in the town, were at a disadvantage for two reasons. First, there was the attraction of all the festivities at the school. Second, and more important, were the stylish cadet uniforms, especially the one with the shiny buttons and snowy-white cap and collar, which had a proven ability to attract the girls. These uniforms even spoke silently, for there was a code that went with them. If a cadet left the top button of his tunic undone, it meant he didn't have a girlfriend and was interested in finding one. John said he was very conscious and proud of his uniform. No doubt it gave him a sense of inclusion and belonging. The code would have appealed to his romantic nature.

Figure 13. John in his nautical school dress uniform. Petersen family photo.

Resenting their disadvantage, some of the town boys responded by attacking cadets from time to time. One student was caught alone and had his face badly torn when he'd been intentionally pulled across a barbed wire fence, John asserted. Due to incidents like this, cadets generally took to walking in pairs or groups. If a problem arose, a runner would dash back to the school and ring the bell, whereupon "the whole school emptied and a great battle ensued." Several such melees occurred during John's tenure, and he attended them all. They were exercises in collective loyalty and mayhem. While John contributed to the cadets' contingent, he had no desire to fight; and he claimed he never had to. As soon as he would approach a potential opponent, they would back off, he maintained.

This had happened before. Prior to nautical school he'd gotten into scraps where fighting seemed the likely outcome, yet a fight never ensued. The other fellows always dropped it. John contended they saw something in or around him, an aura that unnerved them. He told me it was perhaps like his father speaking to the mob of Chinese workers in the drying barn. Almost fifty years later, it was still a mystery to him, he claimed. He said he didn't understand the power and determination that manifested in those situations.

Once when he was about thirteen, he intervened when a bully, who was two years older than him, was beating up his friend. "Fight me instead," John offered. The bully, to John's surprise, let it go. John didn't feel he could have won the fight. His one clear thought, he said, was to stop the beating his friend was taking. He said he felt compelled to intervene, that he had no choice.

In his whole youth he never fought, he said, a statement he later contradicted. He felt fighting was a poor way to settle an argument. In addition to his peaceable nature, there was also his size, which may have helped scare off potential opponents. He noted he grew a lot between fourteen and eighteen and was always big and tall. And there was this: He said at nautical school he took up boxing and fought a lot for the school and was known at other schools for his boxing ability. His reputation as a boxer may have deterred adversaries outside the ring. I never asked him if there was a contradiction between his attitude against fighting and his participation in competitive boxing. Of the two, I'm more suspicious of his ostentatious fight stories in which his prospective opponents always backed off. By comparison, a vivid and clearly exaggerated boxing story he told has a denouement that is downright cartoonish.

As a boxer for the nautical school, he maintained he never lost a fight until his last one. This contest was arranged by one of his trainers to make him "more humble." John was fighting a heavyweight. This didn't worry him. He expected his quickness would tire out his larger opponent. This worked fine for the first round, but John was disconcerted to discover that his hardest blows had little effect on the other fellow. He said he couldn't do anything to him. His plan backfired. During the second round, he found he was very tired as a result of having to go so fast and be so careful. When he momentarily let down his guard, he received an uppercut that, he said, lifted him off the canvas, over the ropes, and into the crowd. He said he was very humiliated, but he also learned several lessons: not to overtax himself, to know his physical limitations, and not to underestimate others.

Athletics appealed to John's ego and sometimes tempted him from fact into fantasy. In addition to boxing, he high jumped, threw the javelin, ran races, and played soccer. He told me that he never excelled, although he got quite far in soccer. But another time—succumbing to the glamour of great accomplishments—he maintained he played for the Dutch national soccer team. This was fanciful boasting. John's son Hans never heard this claim and he's sure he would have known about such a notable achievement had it been true. Tellingly, these fantasies had comforting romantic dimensions as well. When he played soccer or boxed, he would always pick a girl or woman in the crowd for whom to compete. He said he loved it when the crowd called his name. He loved the adulation of the crowds. He noted it made up for the love he didn't get at home.

***

While at the nautical school, John said he didn't go around with girls out of respect for Zus, who, he claimed, periodically travelled from Hilversum to visit him. But he did act as an intermediary between the local girls and some of the cadets. He said he made money by writing love letters for his mates. He would also sneak out of the school to meet with girls to set up times and places for couples or groups to get together. One night when he was returning to the school from one of these missions, he encountered a problem. There was no street lighting in the village, and it was very dark. He was hurrying and being as quiet as possible. In the wooded area of the village park, he moved with extra care and kept his eyes to the ground as it was pitch black. He decided to take advantage of the seclusion to pee. He took aim at the bottom of a small tree trunk close by and started to relieve himself, whereupon the damn thing moved! It scared the wits out of him. The supposed tree trunk was the dark-blue trouser leg of the policeman who had seen him earlier and was waiting for him to return. John was escorted back to the school where he was punished for breaking curfew.

This was not John's only run-in with this policeman, which helps explain his statement that the policeman didn't really like him. Contributing to the friction between them was the policeman's daughter, who John described as being the most attractive girl on the island.

"And she knew it," John noted pointedly.

In addition to being sought after, she could also be haughty and thin-skinned. When John met her on the road outside of town one summer day, she had a yoke over her shoulders, which held two buckets of milk. He offered to carry them for her. He said her response was snooty, so, he advised her she was "not the cat's meow." Insulted, she dumped one of the buckets of milk down the front of his uniform. After she strode off and John began to recover from his surprise, he said he felt ashamed to go back to the school because of what had happened to his good uniform. He retreated to the beach instead. This was a mistake. It was a hot day and the milk residue soon started to stink, he said, and this made things even worse for him when he did return to the school. He implied that his mates regarded him as an astounding sight and a wonderful source of amusement. John and his uniform would be subjected to an even worse indignity, but this would come later, after he had left nautical school.

John's role as romantic intermediary brought him once more into contact with the policeman's daughter. It also sparked an alleged episode worthy of Schiermonnikoog's bent for the slightly fantastic. According to John's telling, he was to arrange an assignation for two of his mates and one of the local girls. Plans, however, quickly shifted. Instead of one girl, there were soon three: John's contact, the policeman's daughter, and one other. The rendezvous was to take place in the bedroom of the policeman's daughter. And John found himself inveigled to come along so that there would be an equal number of boys and girls.

The policeman and his daughter lived outside the town, close to the sand dunes. Her bedroom was on the second floor, which is where she and her friends awaited the three cadets. The cadets were to enter through the window after climbing up the clay-shingled roof that dropped conveniently, farmhouse style, almost to the ground. John watched his mates negotiate the ascent and disappear through the window. He followed, but three-quarters of the way up, he encountered a loose shingle. He tried to hold it in place with his foot, but after what seemed like a long moment suspended in time, he felt the shingle give way. It not only clattered to the ground, it also, after another ominous delay, caused his own descent, slowly at first, then with a sudden rush and an awkward, uncomfortable crash landing. As if to assure his utter demise, a connected series of shingles followed him momentarily, thundering like a landslide. The shingles would have spilled painfully upon him had he not been up in a flash and running toward the dunes. He'd caught a corner-of-the-eye glimpse of the policeman, who'd appeared suddenly at the front door, shotgun in hand.

The policeman was soon in hot pursuit. John would've been caught had it not been for the little fences in the dunes used to separate the crops grown there. The simple fact was that while the policeman was the better runner, John was the better jumper. Looking over his shoulder, John saw the policeman's obese shape momentarily airborne above one of the fences in a manner that was awkward, perilous, and highly amusing. John slowed his pace to better observe what would happen. The policeman tripped but somehow managed to retain his balance. He was not so lucky the next time. When John saw his rotund form sail belly first into the sand, the hilarity of it briefly transcended his panic and he had to stop running for a few moments. This, of course, gave the policeman the opportunity to right himself and resume the chase. In the end, John got away. His two classmates later thanked him profusely for providing the diversion they needed to make their escape.[55]

***

A broken shingle was not the only thing that caused John to crash to ground. What had been rare psychic experiences became commonplace at nautical school. He said he discovered his ESP powers during his first year there. Susan dated his discovery of his psychic abilities to this period as well, although there is no corroboration for any of his stories about nautical school. He said he found he could exercise a degree of control over these abilities, and he began to abuse them. It was a lark, a game, a way to show off, to be a celebrity. He told me knowledge of his special abilities became widespread; his classmates would ask questions beyond his knowing, and he would tap into some great reservoir of knowledge and impress them with the answers. He foretold the content of exams the day before they were given. And a teacher who played the stock market sought and, to a limited extent, used his advice, though he didn't fully trust it. John said he was sucked in by others but also acknowledged that he abused his gift.

This went on for some time. His abilities peaked after he'd been at the school for several months. Then his gift turned against him. What he divined no longer happened quite as he predicted; something crucial would be different. John didn't know what to make of this change: Why should things suddenly be other than what he

---

[55] In January 2021, John's son Harald, upon reading a draft of this book, was reminded of a set of books he had read as a boy, which John also "delighted in reading." One of these books was "about a young boy who was in lust with the daughter of the rotund policeman in the small village in Terschelling [one of the West Frisian Islands], who ended up chasing him over the rooftops. It also included an episode where he peed on the guy in the darkness."

knew, or at least thought he knew? His concentration crumbled. He could think of nothing else. He said that in no time a terrible doubt replaced the certainty he'd previously possessed. The doubt not only imprisoned him, it began to consume him.

"I almost went out of my mind," he told me.

Fortunately, the new math teacher, one of several recruits hired to replace under-performing staff and bring the school up to scratch, was able to help. John reported that this young teacher knew sort of what John was going through, but he never directly asked about it. Instead, he took John under his wing, mostly by inviting him to go for walks. John described them as long rambles during which they discussed philosophy and other subjects. These diverting and instructive interludes made all the difference. The math teacher was a great help, John said. Afterward, he wanted nothing to do with his gift. He shut it out. He said he didn't use it again for four or five years, but during another of our sessions he claimed at least one apparently involuntary psychic experience within a year or so of being helped by his math teacher. As it supposedly occurred during an unlikely voyage down the west coast of Africa, the psychic experience likely never happened either.

The new math teacher and the one-eyed captain of the island's lifeboat-and-rescue team were the two most positive influences on John during his time at the school. Despite being highly focused and demanding, they were also genuinely supportive. In John's romantic parlance, they were, in their different ways, knights dedicated to noble causes.

The one-eyed captain was the only other man on the island John honoured as highly as the new math teacher. Unlike the newbie teacher, the one-eyed captain was a veteran of the community and a legend up and down the coast. He was fearless, had a great knowledge of the local waters, and regularly risked his life for others. John said the captain was "a beautiful character." Tough and hard himself, he taught the nautical students to be tough and hard. He gave them some of the best practical and philosophic training they received. He took groups of them out on practice and actual rescues in all kinds of weather. Each of them was part of a team, he said. No matter what the conditions, they had to concentrate on their work. People were counting on them. Fear, he added pointedly, was an enemy that could sink them, if they let it rule them.

On his first trial run with the captain, John was the guinea pig who went overboard into a moderately heavy sea so the other students could practise handling the boat and using the equipment to rescue him. Once the boat, which was bobbing up and down on the swells, was some distance from John, the on-board cannon fired a line that had a seat apparatus on its end. John grabbed the line and stepped into the seat as he had been instructed, expecting thereafter to be quickly pulled to safety. His mates were to coordinate their actions, some of them rowing hard to keep the line taut, the others pulling the line and bringing John in as rapidly as possible. But there were problems. The desired coordination was elusive, and the line was rarely taut, meaning that John was pulled toward the lifeboat in fits and starts. He spent a lot of time under water being pulled through swells. Much of the rest of the time, when the line went slack, he was gasping for air. He was soon exhausted and convinced he was going to drown.

Figure 14. Preparing for (or possibly following) sea rescue practice. Petersen family photo.

Despite this experience, John said he had absolute faith in the captain who John claimed was known for riding the crest of great waves onto the decks of imperilled vessels to get people to safety. One night the captain and his crew of students were "trapped" in a violent storm and had to stay out overnight. To make matters worse, one of the lads had come down with a bad fever. With nothing to do but ride out the storm, the captain reminded them that singing among sailors is a tradition. So, amidst that terrifying black tumult, they sang.

"A sailor must not be afraid to die," the captain told them.

John claimed he faced death on multiple occasions during the Nazi occupation of the Netherlands. "I risked my life several times," he wrote in his 1951 letter. But he also found himself in situations well outside the training provided by the one-eyed captain, "situations involving spiritual bankruptcy" to quote the German pastor and former seaman, Martin Niemöller.[56]

---

[56] Martin Niemöller, *From U-boat to Pulpit* (Chicago and New York: Willett, Clark & Company, 1937), 46.

6

AT SEA: A SCUTTLED CAREER

John's plan was to earn his initial qualifications at the nautical school, go to sea for a time, then return to the school for additional training. He did go to sea during the autumn of 1933, but as with much in his life during those years, his plan miscarried.

Shortly before his ship sailed, there was a panic to obtain a passport. It's remarkable that they succeeded, for they didn't start on this essential task until late in the day. John and Constant's mother applied in August to have them naturalized as Dutch citizens. The following February, the Dutch government refunded the fees of 200 guilders per application and advised Mrs. Kempen-de Ridder that her sons could reapply when they became adults. We know this based on Ministry of Justice documents in the Dutch National Archives.[57]

With the Dutch government not responding as quickly as John required, he said he next tried the British consulate, hoping to obtain British citizenship based on his birth in British North Borneo. He relied on his certificate of notoriety, issued the year before, but to the British it was insufficient proof of the date and place of birth. They required three sworn affidavits from people who had been at Lahad Datu when he was born. Given his urgent need for a passport, he

---

[57] See Bibliography — Constant and John (DNA, MJ for 1934).

didn't have the time to undertake such a project, although he did say he obtained the affidavits in the 1939–40 period thanks to his mother's work finding people to swear the affidavits.

He described his 1933 predicament in his 1951 letter: "Refused both by the Dutch government and the English Consul, I, at my wit's end, went to the German consulate." This was a misleading conflation, for the Dutch government didn't refuse him until 1939 when it ruled against his 1937 re-application. The Germans supposedly also initially denied him a passport, "because [his] father had evaded military service and was not registered as a German anymore." Afraid his ship would leave without him, John pled with the consular official. He remembered the photograph of his father's gravestone, which his mother had given him before he left home to bicycle from Hilversum to the consulate in Amsterdam. He handed it to the official who studied it intently. The German words "The motherland far away—in difficult times. You were a true son" apparently made all the difference.

"You poor devil," the man reportedly said to John, his sympathy overcoming the need for formal documentation verifying that John's father had indeed been a German citizen.

"I got my passport after much trouble and went to sea," John wrote in his letter.

But the kindness of the German consular official meant John was now listed in the registers of the German government. Twice during the coming years, he received call-up notices from the German army. He ignored them. But that would not be the end of it. Those call-up notices were a new link in the chain of events that, he said, pushed him into his German nationality, drove him in a direction that was not his, and resulted in his postwar internment as a collaborator.

This self-serving conclusion, which omits the fact that, in 1933, he looked favourably upon the new Hitler regime, was obviously influenced by the outcome of the war and his desire to gain entry into Canada. His treatment by the Dutch government still rankled when he first spoke about it to me. He maintained the government ignored the fact that his mother, stepfather, and his mother's parents were all Dutch and that he had lived in the Netherlands or on Dutch territory all his life, except for his first ten months. There is truth in this but, to repeat, the Dutch government rejected the application he made in 1937, not the one made for him in 1933. On top of this sleight of hand we find anti-Semitism. He said his application was denied because his life was not in danger and he was "not a rich Jew escaping from Germany."

During the spring of 1933, the Nazis had begun purging non-Aryans from Germany's civil service, judiciary, and universities, which led to a mass exodus of German Jews to different countries, including the Netherlands, a popular destination due to proximity, similarity of language, close social and economic ties, and, initially, "liberal refugee laws."[58] A few months later, Dutch legislation "severely restricted the ability of foreigners (and that included refugees) to find paid employment with which to support themselves and their families."[59] Successive Dutch coalition governments regarded refugees "as an unwelcome problem" and adhered to two objectives: "firstly, that the refugees were not the responsibility of the government, but of private charitable efforts, and secondly that the Netherlands was not to be treated as a country of settlement, but only as one of transmigration."[60]

Despite John's claim that German Jews brought considerable money into the country, it was, in fact, common for them to arrive "without funds ... [and] with no further planned destination," as historian Bob Moore points out. These, of course, were precisely the factors that led the fiscally conservative Dutch government, which was struggling to deal with the economic impacts of the world

---

[58] Anthony Anderson, "Anne Frank Was Not Alone: Holland and the Holocaust," 6 ("Holland and Germany had always enjoyed close ties"; "one of the world's most liberal refugee laws"). This transcript of a lecture presented at the University of Southern California on October 24, 1995, is no longer on the internet where it was previously available for years.

[59] Bob Moore, *Victims and Survivors: The Nazi Persecution of the Jews in the Netherlands, 1940–1945* (London: Arnold, 1997), 214.

[60] Moore, 214, 30.

depression, to tighten its entry policy.[61] At the same time, there is ironic truth to John's contention that the state would not profit from giving him citizenship, for after he resubmitted his application, the rationale for finally rejecting it pertained, in large part, to his poor economic prospects.

Just as the August 1933 panic to obtain a passport proved fateful, so did John's brief time at sea. The stories he told me in 1976 about this period are replete with reinvention and make-believe. They are so much taller than his tall tales about nautical school that they provoke the question, What is he trying to hide? The answer is that his sea career was a lamentable failure and a critical line of demarcation in his life. I first grasped this when I reread a sentence concerning his return from sea that appears in his collaborator statement of October 29, 1946: "I was informed that I would never be hired as a regular deck officer and I never went boating again."

This told me, although it was not explicitly stated, that his behaviour and performance were the reasons he would never be hired again. He felt diminished by this outcome in both the immediate and the longer terms. In the immediate term, it was his mother's clearly stated disappointment that stung most. In the longer term, there was the unflattering comparison to Constant, who had always followed him, first to high school, then to nautical school, and then to sea. Constant was "a real seaman," Miek said. In stark contrast to John, he had a short but successful sea career until it was brought to an abrupt and portentous end by the outbreak of the war.

In 1976, John told me that before he met his mentor, the fictional Wiertz, he was influenced by what other people thought but, afterward, he was "true to himself." But how could he be true to himself when the catalyst for this supposed transformation was an individual who did not exist?

In 1984, he provided another time-based comparison of who he became, but this one covered a much longer period. He told me there

---

[61] Moore, 29.

was no comparison between the young man of the 1930s and the person after 1952 when he came to Canada. He said he gained a purpose, that becoming a social worker in 1963 was an answer to his searching, and Canada gave him a nationality and a home and an opportunity to serve and keep his promise to repay the Canadian people. (This repayment was for kindness Canadian soldiers showed him when, as an interned collaborator, he was assigned to work for them, possibly for as long as three months from about mid-October 1945 to mid-January 1946, as will be discussed.)

John's assessment of himself, although inflated and self-congratulatory, has some substance to it. This substance suggests that the transformative influence he ascribed to Wiertz was really his disastrous time at sea, which, rather than help him be true to himself, did just the opposite, setting him up for successive difficulties that defined who the young man of the 1930s was. Consequently, his stories about his time at sea are a minefield we need to negotiate with care.

***

John told me he went aboard his ship at Antwerp, which crossed the English Channel to Southampton to pick up a load of coal destined for Quebec City, and because the dockworkers were on strike, the ship's whole crew had to work thirty-six hours to manually load the coal. None of this is true, which indicates to me that the real story of his sea career was sufficiently unflattering that he abandoned it in favour of an untrustworthy exercise in self-indulgence.

Based on several earlier discoveries and deductions, this latter-day conclusion arose from a reconsideration of a couple of his bald-faced lies. According to two of his postwar statements, he served as an apprentice deck officer or an apprentice helmsman on a Hudig & Veder cargo steamer, which he boarded at Rotterdam, not Antwerp. The second lie concerned the Southampton dockworkers. I learned they didn't strike at any point during the summer or autumn of 1933. With my reconsideration came the realization that I have no information on the route John's cargo steamer took from Rotterdam to North America. Nor did I know if the steamer was the SS *Themisto*, as he claimed.

Unreliable as his stories of this period are, some of them are nonetheless useful in that they are suggestive of his interactions with others and how he was viewed by them. For example, he told at least three stories indicating points of friction between him and the captain, two of which had him "playing the fool," and none of which would have helped him succeed in his position.

He maintained that, at eighteen, he was the youngest member of the crew. He described several rites of passage and misadventures, including "a degrading trip" when the empty steamer encountered stormy seas as she crossed the channel. He said he was on four-hour bridge watch when the storm hit. "The ship was rolling like crazy" and he was soon very sick, he emphasized. Later, at mid-ocean, they encountered a hurricane. The waves were "as high as big houses." He told me they received many distress messages and SOSs and tried to respond to the one closest to them. John claimed its radio operator had sent repeated pleas for help: "Come quickly. Rapidly taking on water …" "Water to my ankles …" "Water to my knees …" "Will not last much longer."

John reported that the steamer's first and fourth holds were damaged and many crew suffered injury as they struggled to make repairs. There may be a modicum of truth to John's hurricane story, for 1933 had a busy hurricane season. Moreover, according to the *Monthly Weather Review*'s article, "Ocean Gales and Storms, October 1933," the *Themisto* sailed from Swansea to Montreal and encountered a gale on October 15–17.[62]

John said his crewmates were a tough breed. He admired their stoicism and spoke of the calm in sailors' eyes, suggesting these qualities were the product of being routinely dwarfed by vast stretches

---

[62] "Ocean Gales and Storms, October 1933." *Monthly Weather Review* (United States: War Department, Office of the Chief Signal Officer, 1933, digitized in 2009), 311, accessed June 9, 2021.

of sea and sky and by the knowledge that their lives were mere playthings to periodic banshee storms. He said he also realized he wasn't going to like sea life.

The most notable aspect of John's depiction of his sea career is the extreme way he described the ship's captain and other senior members of the crew. He said he became aware of "discrepancies in people" when he was on the steamer. Just as he had discovered sadism and cruelty in some men during his time at nautical school, so the steamer introduced him to other malign behaviours that were made worse, he claimed, because they were practised by individuals in positions of responsibility.

He told me the captain was a "weird ... slimy ... cross-eyed" individual who was known as Captain Aye Aye for his peculiar habit of beginning sentences with the words "Aye, aye." He was the opposite of Timperley and the one-eyed captain of Schiermonnikoog's lifeboat-and-rescue team. John said Captain Aye Aye would take all sorts of chances yet would cry when significant troubles arose.

John told me that Captain Aye Aye was distrusted and disliked by most of the crew, but he was treasured by the company for his singular dedication to cutting costs, which was presumably necessitated by the global depression. What the company didn't know, according to John, was that the captain was redirecting a portion of the savings into his and a few other pockets, notably those of the first mate, who was responsible for procurement, and the chief engineer, who maintained the fuel supply records. John asserted that chicanery was used to manipulate the system that measured the amount of oil that was bunkered.

A portion of the ship's food budget was also skimmed by purchasing reduced quantities and substandard goods. This had created unhappiness among previous crews and would in due course, according to John, be the undoing of Captain Aye Aye and his accomplices. John said he never understood the captain's behaviour, particularly the frequent needless risks he took and his lack of consideration for the crew. It was a crazy way to run a ship. If you depend on the hard work and cooperation of your crew, why jeopardize their goodwill? He said it compromised the oneness of the crew and ship.

John also claimed the captain and his cronies' malfeasance caused a mutiny. But there is confusion as to when it supposedly occurred. It may have been during their passage to North America, or it may have happened on the return voyage. My notes from 1976 give the impression that it occurred during the return trip, but eight years later, when I sought clarification, John told me it happened on the way to Quebec City. He said the poor food, including maggot-filled porridge, which—perhaps tellingly—reminded me of a scene in the 1962 film *Mutiny on the Bounty*, was a primary reason for the mutiny. Captain Aye Aye was armed and provided weapons to his officers to defend his command. John implied that at some point during this incident the captain was reduced to tears. Although the mutiny was quelled, the crew's anger and protests were not. In due course the company supposedly heard their complaints, investigated, brought charges, and saw the captain, first mate, and chief engineer tried and convicted of fraud—or so John said.

I looked for evidence of these fantastic claims, but with no success. There is nothing in the records of the Raad voor de Scheepvaart (Maritime Court of the Netherlands) to support John's story. I did learn, however, that the crew's pay was twice cut by 5 per cent during 1933. Moreover, some countries had taken to subsidizing ship owners who were struggling to survive the depression and the reductions in trade and, consequently, the decreased need for ocean transport. Perhaps John's extraordinary stories are a form of venting and revenge for the failure of his sea career.

Two more of his stories are worth examining for how they present him and his relationships with others. He said that while crossing the Atlantic, he bragged about his relationships with women. His big talk was met with skepticism and a challenge. When several members of the crew dared him to join them at a brothel when they reached Quebec City, he accepted. What is striking about his braggadocio is his audacity, for what he claimed could not have been further from the truth, according to other stories he related.

John told me it was a very fancy brothel, with doctors and a dance floor, and said he was "scared silly," but he didn't back down. It was more important to him to maintain the persona that had gotten him into trouble in the first place. He liked dancing and saw it as a way he might survive the night. He would have continued dancing until the end of the evening had not his mates intervened. They presented him with a young lady and ensured that he went with her to a private room rather than back on the dance floor. John told me that once they were in the room, he sat down on a chair and began a conversation. His companion, who was sitting on the bed, became suspicious when he gave no sign that he was going to join her. "Have you been with another woman?" she asked. John assured her that he hadn't. He told her he just wanted to talk to improve his English. He said she thought this was very queer. As John persevered with his small talk, he was mentally clocking the time they'd been in the room together. While he'd been on the dance floor, anticipating what lay ahead, he'd carefully observed his mates and how long each of them would take when they went off with a woman. When he judged that enough time had elapsed, he and the girl returned to the main room.

He apparently succeeded in fooling his mates, but they had the last laugh. John told me that, having heard horror stories from doctors, anxiety turned his triumph to chagrin. In his naïveté and fear, he thought he might have picked up a disease from having been in the brothel. When he returned to the ship, he washed his whole body with permanganate to disinfect himself. The permanganate turned his skin brown, which drew attention he didn't want. He said he was laughed at.

The second story concerns a boat race. John told it for its humour, but it suggests a degree of social isolation that contrasts markedly with the charm and bonhomie he affected as a raconteur. The race was Captain Aye Aye's idea. Lifeboats were equipped with sails and manned by teams of two. The prize for the winning team was a case of champagne. John wanted to participate, but no one would crew with him.

"Everyone thought I was crazy," he said. He cited dousing himself with permanganate and his run-ins with the captain, which included typically brazen behaviour and blindness to possible consequences.

In 1976, when he first told me about the race, he said he competed anyway—by himself—that he loaded the keelless lifeboat heavily so that the extra weight would function as a keel and help keep the craft on course in the half wind. This was an effective strategy. He said he won the race. But one important detail is in doubt. John and I spoke again about the race in 1984. My notes from that occasion refer to him having a second person with him, an apprentice sailor, who John may have recruited as a last-minute teammate. This supposed alliance with the sailor is suggestive of a dubious assertion John made that he and another member of the crew became partners in a much more momentous project soon after.

The steamer headed up the St. Lawrence River to Montreal, where it was to pick up a load of grain. There were heavy mists, but Captain Aye Aye in his zeal for thrift refused the services of a pilot ship. It was a reckless and costly decision. The steamer ran aground on a sandbar. Several tugs had to be employed to free it at a price exceeding what the pilot ship would have cost. There was also a human cost. While the tugs were labouring to pull the vessel free, John maintained one of the huge foot-thick manila ropes snapped and ripped part of the tug away, severely injuring a man who was onboard.

Misfortune seemed now to dog the steamer. There were fears that the grain they had loaded had gotten wet and could lead to an outbreak of fever while they were at sea. John told me that, around this time, he realized he loved Canada and decided this was where he wanted to live. He claimed that he and a friend, another Dutchman, jumped ship. But I'm virtually certain this event never happened, although perhaps in retrospect, it seemed to John as though it did. I say this seriously as there were probably times when he believed some of his wholesale reinventions. This belief was a matter of necessity: The delusion helped him keep things together; admitting that an episode in a sequence of tall tales was untrue could undermine them all.

Based on what he told me, multiple factors could have contributed to a decision to jump ship. There was his new love of Canada and his uncertain citizenship—the fact that he now had a German passport but was still waiting for the Dutch government to rule on his mother's applications seeking naturalization for him and Constant. There was the hurricane and his discovery that he didn't like life at sea. There were his boastful claims, his diminished credibility, and the possibility that some of his experiences caused him greater embarrassment than he was willing to admit. And there was the tug accident, Captain Aye Aye's alleged carelessness and corruption, and the fear of fever from grain that may have gotten wet.

After supposedly jumping ship, John and his companion worked for a short time on a farm in Quebec until they were caught by immigration officials and expelled from the country. According to his stories, he and his friend were hired onto another freighter and travelled from North America to Greece, where they lived and worked for about three months before going their separate ways; John headed to Egypt and worked aboard another ship that travelled the northern and western coasts of Africa; he eventually returned to the Netherlands, incurring his mother's wrath because he hadn't written to his family and because, by jumping ship, he'd jeopardized his sea career; he suggested he was doubly victimized, suffering not only the opprobrium of his mother but also the betrayal of his girlfriend, Zus, who broke her promise not to cut her hair while he was away; in response, he signed onto yet another ship that took him, via the North and Baltic Seas, to Poland and Russia; upon his return, he finally faced the consequences of his actions, which consisted of having to move out of his mother's house and being blacklisted by the Hudig & Veder shipping company, supposedly for having jumped ship in Canada.

His contention that he spent time in Greece, Africa, Poland, and Russia is, in my view, nothing more than fantasy. These alleged sojourns and his purported blacklisting are, in my judgment, an elaborate series of fabrications meant to disguise that his conflicts with the captain and other onboard authority figures led to him being informed that he would never be hired as a regular deck officer, which brought his sea career to a premature and abrupt end. He said his mother was very disappointed and shamed by what had occurred. She felt he had forfeited everything that had gone into his nautical school education. She was in fear for him, and according to John, she repeatedly told him he was in danger of becoming a good-for-nothing and insisted he start making his own way in life.

John first told me he was blacklisted for two years, but a week later, when we spoke of it again, this penalty had become five years. This inconsistency, which I didn't catch at the time, was the first clue that much of what he claimed about his time at sea was a sham and a cover-up. A second clue is the length of time required for all his alleged travels, which would probably amount to five months or longer, taking him at least into early 1934, well past November when he said he and his new friend Ko started working for a German circus in Amsterdam. A third clue is that Miek never heard of him being blacklisted. She said that upon his return from sea he failed the vision portion of a required medical examination and this ended his sea career. While I am persuaded by the first two clues, I question the failed eye exam. I suspect it was a cover story that Miek, who was seven at the time, may have been told to shield her from the real reason John's sea career ended, which likely had nothing to do with his vision or his nationality or blacklisting, and everything to do with his behaviour.

***

John described himself as "an innocent in many ways" and "something of a dandy" who stuck out like a preening peacock. While his nautical school chums had prized him for his idiosyncrasies, most of his new crewmates quickly came to view him as a doubtful seaman who didn't fit the traditional mould and, as such, needed a comeuppance. They observed how he favoured his school uniform, took "spotless" care of it, and wore it every chance he got, particularly when he rowed passengers and members of the crew back and forth between the steamer and the supply-transport barge, which was his main responsibility for the few days before the steamer departed Rotterdam for the United Kingdom. Their remedy was a reverse cleansing. Four seasoned seamen contributed to a makeshift toilet, then, yelling at John from the deck, got him to manoeuver his rowboat into position beneath them. They then dumped the toilet contents upon him. John said he never lived it down.

Just as John presented Captain Aye Aye and several of his senior officers in a libellous way, was he, in this story, also taking a censorious swipe at himself and his youthful love of uniforms? Or am I giving him too much credit for subtlety? When I entertained these questions, another possibility presented itself. I saw John as a hooded cobra and myself as his mesmerized audience, as though my gullibility encouraged his adolescent hyperbole. This notion in no way negates the empathy that bound us, but it does suggest that additional dynamics may have sometimes been in play.

To take this a step further, when I first met his sister, Miek, she essentially labelled John a predator. "He wanted to be master of it all," she said. "He'd sense people's dependence, then he'd grab them." As I recollect her making these remarks, it is possible she was pointedly directing them at me. If they were a barb, it only registered superficially. But her dark assessment of her brother is important, especially given his periodic proclivity to manipulate and exploit young women, which emerged when he was a foster parent, a topic I will discuss at length later.

My final reason for highlighting the reverse-cleansing story is the same as one of John's purposes: to contrast him, as the self-described innocent and dandy, with Constant, who John claimed was not as naïve. Constant had a better idea of what to expect and how to gain acceptance. In John's colourful and probably spurious telling, when Constant came aboard the *Themisto* a year or so later, he reported for duty in a grubby uniform, two bottles of gin on display, one under either arm.

True to his name, Constant was the steadier of the two brothers. Where he was more orthodox and conforming, John was more eccentric and erratic. This became clear with their sea careers. According to John, their contrasting attitudes and abilities were evident when they were kids in school. Describing himself, John said he was a bright student with a high IQ for whom learning came easy; he also said he had a photographic memory and a logical mind. (Constance also said John had a photographic memory.) John noted he'd help others with their work, meaning he'd share answers with them during tests. When they were caught, they all got zeros. By comparison, Constant, who didn't learn as quickly or easily, reportedly worked much harder and got as good or better marks and doubtless developed good work habits in the process.

Like John, Constant was very sensitive, but with Constant it showed more, according to John. This suggests that Constant was more emotional or didn't cope as well when he was upset, but there are at least two examples from later in life that provide a different picture. One is the way Constant supposedly joined the *Themisto*, which is of questionable value because the story is likely another of John's fictions. The second example, which occurred a decade later, during the war, is more important. In a letter of June 14, 1944, to his wife, Constant is under the impression that John is to be assigned to the eastern front. He writes: "But it won't be easy for him, I wonder if he will be hard enough for it. If he is not, he will break here and that would be such a pity for him."[63]

It won't be easy for him. I wonder about Constant's phrasing. Does it include the implication that John liked things easy? While John was great at grand ideas and starting projects, he was much less effective at following them through to completion. For this and other reasons, his mother feared for his future when he was in his teens and early twenties. Just as he loved to act the fool, it is probably equally true that he preferred the easy road. This inclination was reinforced by his ability to soak up knowledge and information with little effort.

---

[63] Constant's letter of June 14, 1944 (DNA, CABR 70629).

In 1963, he was able to become a social worker because specific education and qualifications were not required. His biggest complaint in the latter 1970s, when Colleen and I spent a lot of time with him, was that his colleagues and other officials often dismissed what he had to say because he lacked credentials.

"If you want people to listen to you, get your education," he told Colleen more than once.

He did return to school to work toward a social-work degree, but he quickly gave it up. Did this reflect a lifelong pattern? Or was it simply that returning to school later in life can be difficult? He was over sixty and a few years from retirement at the time.

Perhaps Constant was the more sensitive brother in high school but changed as he got older. Or perhaps John's characterization of Constant being more sensitive was simply wrong. There are other examples where John's depictions of different situations are dramatically off base. It is as though he sometimes saw things concerning himself through a lens that was significantly askew.

"Such a sensitive, artistic soul," John's daughter Constance said of her father. He "had to use very hard survival techniques" to make it through the war. In 1964, when she was nineteen, Constance went to the Netherlands and met members of the extended Petersen family, including her Uncle Constant. Almost forty years later, she compared her father and her uncle on several occasions when we talked. They were both "lost souls," she said. Constant "even more" than John.

Constance called Constant "a very quiet man." He was married with two sons who were a few years older than Constance. The family lived in Hilversum, but Constant worked in Amsterdam for an oil company. He didn't have a happy marriage. Constance said her uncle had a mistress in Amsterdam, where he spent more and more of his time. He wanted a divorce, but his wife said she would commit suicide if he sought one. He felt trapped.

Like John's eldest son, Constant's eldest son was named Hans. I had a long-distance telephone conversation with this Hans in 2007, when he was a month shy of his sixty-sixth birthday. He told me his father's affair lasted fifteen to twenty years but was never spoken about by his parents, who stayed together for the kids. He noted they were "the worst communicators" and they never talked about things, including Constant's war experience, which was "basically taboo." Hans said he didn't know his father was a collaborator, although he suspected it. After the war, when he was between four and six years old, he remembered going every three or four weeks with his mother and brother to visit his father in prison.

"Such a sad man," Constance remarked about Constant. She added that there was a parallel between him and her father: They both behaved in ways that damaged their families. She also said the two brothers had similar natures, but Constant was "not as extreme" as John. And they both had artistic sensibilities. Where John expressed his through painting, woodworking, poetry, and in other ways, Constant was a photographer who won many international prizes, and a painter, particularly with watercolours.

Constance's most notable conclusion, which she stated on two occasions, was that Constant was not as strong as John. She said he didn't have John's strength of convictions or his beliefs.

Miek, however, had a different view. While Constance had a deeply conflicted relationship with her father, Miek was completely estranged from John for the last fourteen years of his life, since he left Susan, with whom Miek had always been close. Although Susan once told me that Miek had never liked John, she told me another time that Miek's antipathy arose after John left their marriage. This is more in line with Constance's contention that, as a teenager, Miek idealized John, who was eleven years her senior and may have served as a father figure in some respects. Constance, who had regular long-distance telephone conversations with her aunt, also said that, as an adult after the war, Miek came to view Constant as "the strongest of her brothers." He was also her favourite. Reportedly, he visited her about monthly. I suspect by "strongest" she meant that he was the most honest and didn't deny or try to hide his difficulties. Indeed, Constance told me that Miek believed Constant was the most honest man she'd ever met.

Readers should keep in mind these different ideas on strength, as well as the issue of inner resources, for they probably have a bearing on the quite different wars that John and Constant experienced. Where Constant, given his more orthodox demeanour, appears to have been more of an SS man and, in that sense, may have been somewhat more obedient and obliging, John sought to loosen the organizational ties that bound him in any way he could. Subject to our ability to navigate his labyrinth of manipulation and lies, it appears he succeeded to a surprising degree. That Constant was more conventional, and John decidedly less so, must also be remembered as factors in their notable differences.

Constant died at the age of sixty-one, on February 28, 1978, a decade before John. John had not seen Constant or Wim since leaving the Netherlands in 1952. But he had seen Miek. She came to Canada every two years to see him and Susan and other members of their family. She continued to come after the split-up, but she made a point of avoiding John. This included refusing to attend his memorial service, even though she was in the city at the time.

***

John's innocence as a seaman in 1933 was mirrored by mine decades later, hearing his tales of that period. While I'm sure he was pleased to have someone keen to listen to him, an acolyte to his cause, I suspect he recognized and was amused by my naïveté as I hung on his words, my gullibility encouraging his hyperbole as I said before when I described him as a hooded cobra and myself as his mesmerized audience.

I remember briefly noting the cartoon-like nature of Captain Aye Aye's name, but I was too enamoured by John and the privilege of hearing his story to give it much mind. Now, after learning what I have about his sea career, my response is quite different: "Captain Aye Aye? Give me a break!"

It took me only forty-plus years to write that question and that exclamation, a fact that prompted an alternate title for this book: *Captain Aye Aye and the Power of Belief.*

7

KO ELHORST, FRIE, AND THE HOLE AT THE HEART OF THE STORY

When, on his mother's order, John left home, he moved into a Hilversum boardinghouse where Ko Elhorst resided. John quickly fell in with Ko. They were fast friends during most of the decade. Through Ko, John met Johan Veltmeijer, who also became an important friend. John was the youngest of the three. Where Veltmeijer was two years older, Ko was seven years John's senior.

John described Ko as an enthusiast who would tackle anything, "a very slick fellow" and a likeable individual with a noble air. Likely influenced by the depression, Ko's politics were communistically inclined, according to John, but this tendency was overwhelmed by his desire to become wealthy. He was admired by his siblings for looking after their mother financially. But he also had trouble with the law on at least one occasion, which is probably why John hid his real name and referred to him as Joe. Found guilty of theft by an Amsterdam court on March 31, 1936, Ko had to pay twenty-five guilders or serve fifteen days detention. He also had a penchant for fraudulent activity and profiteering, which ultimately caused John to cool their friendship in the late 1930s, although they continued to have some contact during the war.

Through most of the German occupation of Holland, Ko owned a building-contracting firm. He prospered working for the German military. John said Ko overcharged for materials, a practice that was not uncommon. According to one historian, "business profits of 100 and 200 per cent (and occasionally even 300 per cent) were not infrequent." They were achieved "by including fictitious wages and non-personnel costs and corrupting German officials."[64] John said Ko was a millionaire by the end of the war, but he was also eventually imprisoned as a collaborator. Ko anticipated this, John added. He secured half his fortune in a safe hiding place. An inquiry into his firm's financial books concluded they were forged and that 285,100 guilders "had been kept out of the accounts."[65]

John was only at the boardinghouse for a short time before he and Ko relocated to Amsterdam and probably stayed initially at Ko's mother's place. John told me they managed to find employment with the Jewish-owned German Strassburger Circus for four to six weeks during its run in Amsterdam, John's first job upon his return from sea. He maintained the circus had been scheduled to go to the United States, but instead went bankrupt about Christmastime. Although these are dubious claims, it is true this circus struggled in 1933 and throughout the decade owing to boycott, extortion, and other Nazi anti-Jewish measures.[66]

Despite not knowing anything about cafeterias, John and Ko managed to display enough *savoir faire* to lease the circus's cafeteria and coat check for the duration of the Amsterdam run. John implied that he followed Ko's lead and that cocky over-confidence was their modus operandi. He said they sold themselves as being more knowledgeable than they were when they undertook a range of odd jobs at different times throughout the decade. They may have lived at the circus, for one of their responsibilities was to prepare breakfast for the performers and other personnel starting at 6:00 a.m.

---

[64] Hirschfeld, 189n.
[65] Collaborator files on Ko Elhorst (DNA, CABR 64049). Attachment to researcher Dr. Maili Blauw's email of July 10, 2009, to the author.
[66] "Circus Strassburger," Wikipedia, accessed February 6, 2020, https://nl.m.wikipedia.org/wiki/Circus_Strassburger (Jewish-owned German circus, anti-Jewish measures).

According to John, opening night was a disaster. They didn't even know how to operate the big coffee machines. But the next day was better and they were soon comfortably in the swing of things: After the breakfast cleanup, they would prepare for the afternoon and evening shows. While the food concession was profitable, the coat check reaped a bonanza. Ko had arranged to pay the fellow who stoked the fire for the big tent's heating system twenty-five guilders a week to keep the temperature hotter than necessary. John said most patrons checked their coats, and John and Ko made a lot of money.

John told me the circus people were "a breed apart, ambitious, always training." He admired their single-minded devotion, the courage their acts and stunts required, and their willingness to sacrifice themselves for one another. He spoke of their ever-present watchfulness and concern, their fear that an accident or misstep could injure or kill. Circus people "are a world within a world," he explained. He said they had their own ethics, which included a special honesty among themselves and a willingness to cheat the outside world. With their agreement with the fire stoker, John and Ko fit right in.

The double standard and flexible ethics John attributed to the circus were recurring features of his own life, notwithstanding his stories of principle and virtue, such as the moral education—including "the fallacy of society's ethics"—he said he received from the imaginary Wiertz. This flexibility likely contributed to some expediently loose storytelling, which may help explain frustrating contradictions and inconsistencies in what he had to say about these years. Case in point: When he started to tell me about this period, he emphasized that he was completely independent after his mother kicked him out of the house. But what he said other times indicates he lived at his mother's home on a repeated basis, which may have included portions of every year of the decade.

When John said he lived with Ko's family after the circus, he made two other noteworthy statements. First, that he and Ko did pretty well everything together. Second, that Ko's youngest sister, Frie, who he met during this period, was the first woman to interest him romantically. Important as these statements are, they need to be put into broader context. While there is little doubt that John and Ko routinely worked and socialized together, John also pursued, in fits and starts, his dream of being an artist and a painter, a dimension of his life that was largely separate to the time he spent with Ko.

In 2005, Miek showed me a photograph of John and Ko in paint-splattered overalls. It's typical of much of the work they did in the 1930s: painting houses, wallpapering, building cement ponds and pathways and brick walls, and doing carpentry. They even made awnings for an architect who wanted them as the finishing touch for a building he'd just completed. While they often learned as they went, their work didn't always turn out as planned and their profit margin was frequently not as large as expected. The awnings, for example, were a little crooked, so the architect refused to pay them. Less costly was a paint job they completed one afternoon under a particularly hot sun. The first coat blistered badly, necessitating the purchase of considerably more paint to get the job right. They also had difficulty gluing wallpaper.

Construction was another matter. They both had a flair for carpentry. Their success here helped compensate for setbacks elsewhere. But the fact that they were not making much money frustrated them.

It was not an auspicious time for young men in the Netherlands to make their fortunes. The government's refusal to devalue the guilder or provide public works to stimulate the economy "led to mass unemployment and social distress."[67] The situation was even more difficult for John. He told me that, as a foreign national, he had to apply to the police each month for a work permit; the same requirement applied to Constant, according to one of his collaborator statements. To "assuage nationalist opinion," desperate governments like those of Belgium, France, and the Netherlands brought in "increasing discrimination against foreign labour."[68] John told Dutch

---

[67] Hirschfeld, 251.
[68] Moore, 39.

officials after the war: "Since [returning from sea], until the start of the war, I did all kinds of jobs."[69] In addition to the circus, various types of manual labour, and pursuing an artistic career, he also participated in a few more elaborate enterprises and worked selling life insurance.

Possibly the best evidence of John's artistic pursuits is a four-page handwritten list of his paintings that he compiled in the mid-1970s, a period when his mental health went through a rough patch. I use the phrase "best evidence" with caution because I'm not sure the list is completely reliable. Part of it might reflect a delusion about art school he may have succumbed to at some point in the late 1930s or after. Yet what impresses me about the list, with columns for Year, Picture, and Whereabouts, is its substance: John's detailed recollection of numerous paintings and their disposition, whether they were sold or to whom he gave them.

The earliest period on the list is "1931," which mentions a single painting, "Heatherfields." The next period, "Amsterdam 1933–34," was much busier. John completed a work called "Blue Rhapsody" and "20 Landscapes Amsterdam." During the third period, "1934–1935," the list says he produced "Portraits - 10," "Landscapes mostly Amsterdam streets farms—lakes," "churches in & out," and "boats." It is especially noteworthy that during this latter period he apparently was involved with an art school. He uses the words "Sold in Art School" and "Sold at Art School" to describe the whereabouts of two of his paintings. The fourth period is also noteworthy for it is identified as "Wiertz, 1937–1940."

---

[69] John's statement of October 29, 1946.

Figure 15. "Small Farm, Maas River," 1942. Earliest of John's surviving paintings. Held by Harald Petersen.

***

Given that John's Wiertz does not exist, is he, by mentioning his imagined artistic mentor on his list of paintings, planting false evidence? I think this possibility is exceedingly unlikely. If I am correct, why does John mention Wiertz? Far-fetched as it may seem, I suspect, owing to trauma he experienced during the 1930s and how he reimagined certain events from that period, that he, in some manner, subsequently came to believe that his Wiertz was a real person.

John said he was in high school when he met Wiertz. After viewing some of John's work, Wiertz offered to give him free lessons. According to John, Wiertz was "a real hard teacher" who was capable of tremendous criticism. John added: "The master teaches, the boy cleans the master's brushes." John said that Wiertz's criticism brought him close to quitting several times. But after this daunting initial period, they became good friends. If there's any truth to these assertions, it may be that John received some training from Pieter Pouwels. But this is pure speculation. Although Susan confirms that John and Pouwels knew each other during the latter 1930s, there's no evidence that they did in 1931 or between 1933 and 1935.

John also claimed that when he went to nautical school and sea, Wiertz dropped in at his mother's periodically to learn if there was any news of his protégé. My intuition tells me there is something to this, but the mentor in question was not Wiertz; while it might have been Pouwels, I suspect it was Timperley. Moreover, there are additional areas of complication. Both John's mother and Constant's in-laws owned paintings by an artist named Wiertz, and Constant's in-laws considered this man a friend. This artist may have been Henri Louis (Joub) Wiertz (1893–1966), who was born in Amsterdam and worked as a technician and engineer on the design and construction of railways and harbours in China, Japan, and Australia before returning to the Netherlands in 1938 and taking up recreational painting later in life. Given the date of his return to the Netherlands, Joub Wiertz could not have been the imposing figure John said mentored him earlier that decade.[70]

Whenever John created the imaginary figure of Wiertz, it is certainly possible he chose that handle because of the connections his mother and Constant's in-laws had with the painter of that name. But if this is a factor, I believe it is only an incidental one. Much more important is the apparent influence of Antoine Joseph Wiertz, the nineteenth-century Belgian romantic painter who has a museum in Brussels dedicated to his work. John not only said his Wiertz was a well-known painter with a national reputation, he also strongly suggested his imaginary mentor was a descendent of the famous Wiertz. John described his Wiertz as an extraordinary figure—at least six feet six inches tall with bony, huge hands—and a real artist who was very dedicated and "didn't give a damn" about social standing or

---

[70] Letter of February 18, 2004, and email of March 24, 2004, from Dr. Kriszti Vákár, Department of Modern and Contemporary Art, Netherlands Institute for Art History, The Hague, to the author.

money. "He was disliked because he was too blunt." His sensitivity and his convictions were as impressive as his great size.

For me, Wiertz is the most intriguing and frustrating part of John's story. The process of sorting him out and concluding that he was a phantom of John's imagination—other than John's claims, there's not a scintilla of evidence that his Wiertz existed—required considerable time, yet part of me still wants to believe he was real. John brought him that vividly to life. Wiertz is perhaps the richest example not only of John's capacity to create alternate realities but also of my being absorbed into the romanticized world of his storytelling. Put another way, John's supposed relationship with Wiertz was like parts of my relationship with John, particularly how his story, including its falseness, bled into me. It's why coming to terms with that story has been a partial purgative for me.

John was conflicted in two fundamental ways during the mid-1930s. The first was between his dream of being an artist and his attraction to Frie. Wiertz was enmeshed in both the dream and the relationship with Frie. The second conflict was with the different sides of his personality. On one hand, he was the fun-loving individual, the "live wire" who could "make things go"; on the other, he was the solitary, contemplative young man in search of himself and his niche in the world. The former side was expressed primarily with Ko, the latter, it appears, drew psychic support, comfort, and companionship from the towering example of Antoine Wiertz, the artist, whose success John wanted to emulate.

Whether it was in the hope of making more money or because opportunities for work were scarce, John and Ko engaged in several elaborate projects that required creativity and initiative. More than once good ideas were undone by the effort required to sustain the enterprise. John believed he could develop a pill to neutralize the smell of alcohol after drinking. He said it worked. He and Ko put the mixture of peppermint, eucalyptus, and different spices into capsules and the capsules into plastic bags: four capsules per bag. Starting outside Hilversum, they sold their product to restaurants and bars.

The owners always wanted proof the capsules worked. So, either John or Ko would have a drink, take a capsule, then have the owner smell their breath. John said that even with the two of them taking turns, it didn't take too many stops before they got very drunk and couldn't get on their bicycles. They kept falling over the other side, causing them to laugh uproariously. They soon learned they could only demonstrate the product to potential customers for a short time each day. Resupplying existing customers was much easier on them. John noted that while they did a good business, they gave it up after four months. He said preparing and packaging the product took all night, selling it took all day, and the frequent consumption of liquor was both taxing and boring.

Figure 16. John (right) and Ko mugging for the camera. Petersen family photo.

In sharp contrast to this amusing but unverified enterprise, Antoine Wiertz, according to Brita Velghe, was a protagonist in the Belgian romantic movement, "a champion of monumental painting," and an "extraordinary personality." Born into an impoverished family in Dinant, Belgium, he "would take a vow of poverty throughout his life. He entered into the universe of Art in the same way others do in religion." The year he turned fourteen, he entered the Antwerp Art Academy. The next year he was awarded an annual stipend by King William I of the Netherlands. In 1828, at the age of twenty-two, the young artist participated in the *Grand Concours* in Rome. He came second, behind Jean-Antoine Verschaeren of Antwerp.[71] Antoine Wiertz proclaimed at the time, "the judges' capricious rulings are sometimes ludicrous."[72]

Velghe notes that in 1832, after again submitting work to the Grand Concours, Antoine Wiertz was awarded the Prix de Rome. In 1835, on a canvas measuring 3.95m by 7.03m, he began "his magnum opus ... 'Greeks and Troyans fighting over Patrocles' body,'" based on Homer's *Iliad*. He created an even larger version (5.20m by 8.52m) of *Patrocles*, dated 1844. His "Hell's Revolt Against Heaven," also known as "The Fall of the Rebel Angels," is 11.53m by 7.93m on "an arched canvas."

A recent assessment of Antoine Wiertz says his "pictorial sense strayed towards the excessive, or even the grandiloquent" starting about 1840 and that he was contemptuous of art critics for the rest of his life.[73] But he triumphed over them when, starting in 1850, the young Kingdom of Belgium agreed to underwrite the Wiertz Musuem, "a space where he could create his huge paintings" and where they and his other work would be displayed in perpetuity. His triumph was limited, however, for the museum could not guarantee universal acclaim. "Wiertz's painting is admired or spurned, judged grandiose or degenerate, full of genius or ridiculous. Wiertz annoys or seduces, but never leaves one indifferent," the assessment concludes.[74]

---

[71] Brita Velghe, "Antoine WIERTZ (1806–1865)" (Brussels: Royal Museums of Fine Arts of Belgium, 2000), 1–4.
[72] Velghe, 4–5.
[73] Velghe, 5, 6, 7, 11, 7.
[74] Velghe, 1, 3, 11.

John said his Wiertz introduced him to another side of life, one that was bohemian, iconoclastic, and often impoverished. He told me: "You have to feel good about yourself. Something is not wrong just because society says it is." Interpreting his stories about life with Wiertz, I suspect John experienced several intense episodes as a solitary artist, the stereotypical starving artist, episodes characterized by deprivation and the imaginary companionship of the defiant and grandiose Wiertz.

***

After the circus and living with Ko and Frie's family for a time, John returned to Hilversum and presumably lived with his family or in a boardinghouse. According to the distorted narrative he told me, he biked almost every day, sometimes through snow, to Amsterdam for lessons with his Wiertz. At some point, Wiertz supposedly advised him to apply for the National Art Academy (Rijksakademie van Beeldende Kunsten). John said he did and was accepted and started classes in the early summer of 1934. The opportunity to devote himself exclusively to art suited his temperament. He said he really found his niche at the academy, he worked very hard and did very well. Art, he implied, was everything. From the school's perspective, he reportedly showed promise.

Life was good. Not only was John receiving accolades from his teachers and others at the academy, he was also intermittently dating Frie. He told me the crowning glory of this happy time came after his first year when he was informed that he was to be awarded the Prix de Rome, a bursary to complete his studies in Italy. He said it was a great honour.

But this prize brought John's career at the school to an abrupt end. The bursary required that he sign a contract with the academy. He said that one of its stipulations was not to become engaged or to marry. Even though he had no such plans, John felt he could not give such a promise. He said he felt it was wrong to be told you cannot fall in love. So, he refused to sign. This was a monumental and extraordinary decision, a grandiose act. He said the school authorities felt insulted and called him a disgrace to the academy. He described them as very puritanical and rigid about it all. Their response was to expel him, which meant, he said, that no other Dutch school would accept him.

John spoke of this event on several occasions. He maintained his decision was a matter of principle. "What was your mother's reaction?" I asked him in the 1980s, fully expecting that he would tell me that she had been as upset with him as when his sea career came to an end. He said his mother felt his decision was reasonable and that she never scolded him about it. The explanation for this remarkably different reaction is simple: John was neither offered the Prix de Rome, nor was he a student at the academy, points confirmed by the Rijksakademie van Beeldende Kunsten.[75]

In retrospect, John said little about his time at the academy. He never spoke of a teacher or another student there. Yet he was steadfast in his story. Susan's understanding was the same as mine, except in one aspect. She believed he had attended the school and been offered a bursary but had turned it down to marry Frie. John told me he had not really thought about proposing to Frie when the bursary was offered.

The fraudulent and comforting story about John being a student at the National Art Academy and being offered the bursary presumably dates from the late 1930s when he and Susan became a couple, although it is possible that these tales, along with the emergence of Wiertz, coalesced earlier, in conjunction with John's relationship with Frie. In this fantasy, he defies an institution and sacrifices a wonderful artistic opportunity to stand up for principle. He clearly preferred this grandiloquent version of events; he stuck to it for the rest of his life.

John said he was repeatedly drawn to Amsterdam by lessons with Wiertz. These trips were likely also motivated by the possibility of

---

[75] Emails of April 22, 23, and 26, 2004, from Tinie Kerseboom, Head of Collections, Rijksakademie van Beeldende Kunsten, to the author.

seeing Frie and the opportunity to sketch and paint on his own. If there were lessons, were they with Pouwels or at an art school other than the National Art Academy? I don't know about Pouwels or another art school, but I believe we can accept that John made frequent daily commutes and, on some occasions, stayed over at Ko and Frie's mother's place or elsewhere, sometimes for several days. Work projects with Ko were undoubtedly an additional motivator for these trips.

John maintained that about two months after his imaginary expulsion from the National Art Academy, he once again started biking almost daily for lessons with Wiertz. This would have been toward the end of the summer in 1935. Around late September or early October, Wiertz's marriage apparently broke up. According to John, Wiertz's wife had had enough of his bohemian lifestyle. And he and John teamed up about October when the weather was changing. They moved into a studio above a bicycle shop in central Amsterdam, which they occupied for a couple of months.

A strike against Pouwels being John's Wiertz in this instance is that Pouwels didn't get married until August 1942. What is more likely is that Wiertz emerges from psychological forces pressing in on John. My sense is that his relationship with Frie was an on-and-off affair, the status of which was determined, in part, by whether he had any money to take her out. My interpretation of Wiertz's marriage breaking up is that John and Frie broke up. John told me that when he was with Wiertz, he didn't see much of Frie because Wiertz did not like her. He said that his time with Wiertz was an important period in his life and that Wiertz would not prostitute his talents despite his near constant need for money. He also said he and Wiertz were together for about two years, which was also the length of his marriage to Frie.

It may have been while John and Wiertz supposedly lived and worked in the studio that John started drawing and painting art cards that he wholesaled to stores. He said he could only afford half a loaf of bread a day, nothing else. This went on for days, perhaps weeks, and he got physically weak. I have a recollection of him telling me that Wiertz was away at that time. John told me that one day after he left the studio, he collapsed in the snow and was hospitalized. He spent a week in the hospital and another week or two recuperating at his mother's. He said while he was in the hospital, he and Wiertz were evicted from the studio for not paying the rent.

When John told me about his collapse, he also said he threw off his artist inclinations because he didn't want to live in the impoverished way Wiertz lived, that he didn't want to live on what Wiertz made from his paintings. It was probably while he was recovering at his mother's that he received a visit from a friend who was the local district manager for the Holland Life Insurance Company. What started out as a pitch to sell John a policy led to an aptitude test and an informal offer of work selling insurance. "Try it out on a part-time basis and see if you like it," the manager told John. "If you have good leads, I will close the deals," he added. And this is what they did. The manager, a very high producer, according to John, closed several deals and gave John half the commission in each case. John also completed some sales on his own. In addition to discovering he had a knack for the work, John said he made a lot of money. Compared to his previous work history, life insurance was the first job he held for a long period. He believed in the product and never oversold it. He claimed his honesty and nonpressure tactics were the reason he became the company's "second highest salesman … within a year."

This is typical hyperbole because, within six months, John was an unemployed insurance agent. But he may have enjoyed a period of initial success that enabled him to acquire a car, as he claimed. There are two photos of him and Ko with different vehicles.

Figures 17 and 18. John and Ko with vehicles. Petersen family photos.

According to my notes, John's relationship with Frie intensified now that he had money in his pocket. He said his job was not too taxing. This and having a car set the stage for an incident that may have occurred in February or early March of 1936. On this occasion, John drove Ko and his girlfriend from Hilversum to Ko's family home in Amsterdam where Ko was going to visit his mother, John was going to see Frie, and they were all going to spend the night. John's preamble to this story included the statement that Ko "slept with his girlfriend and anyone else he could," while John "had not slept with anyone yet." There were two bedrooms upstairs. One belonged to Frie, the other to a sister who was also still living at home. Between the two bedrooms was a wide hall that accommodated another bed, an ancient, oversized, canopied affair. John said the sleeping arrangements called for Ko's girlfriend to sleep with Frie, while John and Ko were to sleep in the hallway. But Ko had other ideas. Once lights were out, he would join his girlfriend and Frie would join John in the hallway bed. Ko apparently revealed this to John at the last minute. John said he didn't want to do it.

"Tell my mother if you want," Ko replied, perhaps as he got out of bed and headed into Frie's room.

Not too long after Frie had joined John, disaster struck. Their old bed collapsed, the canopy too. The noise of the crash brought Frie and Ko's mother upstairs in a rush. John and Frie were caught red-handed, he said. Sometime later, Frie told him she was pregnant.

John's ownership of the car, if that is what it was, didn't last long. Perhaps it was repossessed after he could no longer make payments. The loss of the car may have prompted another of John's re-imaginings of reality. He told me that when he and Wiertz were together and the weather was good, they spent much of their time sketching in the countryside, which they accessed on their bicycles except for a brief time when they had a car. It was a Model A Ford, which they first saw one day as they rode toward the countryside. It had been adorned with a For Sale sign, which is why it caught their attention. They saw it for several days. It sparked a fantasy: It might become theirs. How easy it would make their travels! They would no longer have to struggle with the supplies they carried, particularly their awkward easels. Eventually they resolved to buy the car. They went door to door selling some of Wiertz's paintings, which, according to John, is what Wiertz did when he needed money. But on the first day the car was theirs, as they drove back from the countryside at dinner time, John said they picked up a barefoot hitchhiker, a door-to-door salesman who told them how hard he had it. So, Wiertz and John decided to give the hitchhiker the car. The man didn't believe them at first; John said he thought they were crazy. And afterward, Wiertz and John's act of spontaneous generosity made them very happy. They spent nights thinking about how much easier life was for the salesman. They didn't think of their own previous dreams and desires for the car.

John's claims about his many jobs and how hard he worked during his marriage appear to be as outlandish as the story about him and Wiertz giving their car to a barefoot hitchhiker. He and Frie were married on June 17, 1936, at Hilversum's city hall.

Figure 19. John and Frie on their wedding day. Petersen family photo.

Figure 20. John's mother; sister, Miek; and Uncle Jan de Ridder, June 17, 1936. Petersen family photo.

Figure 21. Constant in his nautical school uniform with his future wife, Ellie, June 17, 1936. Petersen family photo.

Figure 22. Wim, age 15, June 17, 1936. Petersen family photo.

The run-up to the wedding was a contentious period. John said that many people tried to deter him, and friends told him that Frie slept around and not to marry her. Some of their concerns likely related to questions of status and class, subjects John repeatedly raised when recounting his life in the mid-1930s. His stories in this regard are, once again, unverified and some are more plausible than others.

The earliest of these is about a young man of John's age who I will call the snob. John said this fellow lived with his family for approximately a year prior to the time John went to nautical school. This arrangement was due to the young man's estrangement from his own well-to-do family. The period apart helped to heal the rift, enabling the youth to rejoin his family. John lost track of him after this until one day when he was working at the circus. While selling coffee in the stands, he came upon his old friend who was sitting with a girlfriend. John greeted him with hearty enthusiasm, but the fellow looked him directly in the face and pretended not to know him. According to John, the man could not admit that he had once lived with him and been his friend. He was "above that now." When John told me this vignette forty years after the fact, it still upset him. The experience cut deep and continued to carry an emotional charge. He said it opened his eyes to the fallacy of status.

John also told me about a prostitute and a smuggler. In contrast to the snob, John's stories about them had a patina of innocence and kindness. He said he knew them when he and Wiertz had the studio above the bicycle shop, which Toon, the smuggler, ran. Toon was called the smuggler because he regularly walked small quantities of sugar across the Netherlands' border with Germany. John described him as simple, very warm-hearted, and not too smart. When John collapsed and was hospitalized and, soon after, was evicted from the studio, a bailiff arrived to impound whatever property he could find. But Toon would not let him up the stairs. When the bailiff returned with three policemen, Toon again occupied the stairway.

"You're not going to take anything unless you kill me," he declared.

A melee ensued. It took all the policemen to subdue Toon, after which they handcuffed him and took him away, only to release him soon after. Toon, John said, was a tremendous friend, faithful and totally unselfish.

John told me that the prostitute loved painting and came to the studio to look at their work. She ate her lunch as she watched John work. In this, she had an ulterior motive. She knew John had little money. She would always say she had brought too much food. "Would you help me eat it?" she would ask. She was "a beautiful person, very loving," John said without a hint of irony. And she spoke freely about her work and felt she was helping a lot of people by what she did. It was just a job. John said he met her through Wiertz.

The problem of status came into focus, John said, when he started selling life insurance and became a promising businessman. The nub of the problem was the expectation that he only associate with respectable folk: people like the snob but not like the prostitute and the smuggler, even though the latter, in his estimation, were more worthy of his respect given their kindness, generosity, and genuine friendship. Reasonable as this story sounds, I suspect it is a bit of misdirection to hide the truth. What is most interesting about the prostitute and the smuggler is the possibility that the prostitute may reflect Frie's mother.

The Elhorst family was "from the other side of the tracks," John's son Hans told me. They were a "rough and ready" bunch from a different class, which was bound to concern Stanni, for whom social standing was important. She never warmed to Frie and perhaps looked askance at Frie's mother. Born in December 1914, Frie was the youngest of nine children, six girls and three boys. Her mother's husband had died prior to the birth of Frie's eldest sibling in 1894. Despite never remarrying, Mrs. Elhorst had eight more children. The possibility that multiple fathers were involved made sense to Hans. He said he had always been struck by the marked difference in appearance of some of his aunts who were Frie's older sisters.

John and Frie lived with Stanni for the first six and a half months of their marriage. This was probably a financial necessity, but it may also reflect Stanni's take-charge bent. When Hans was a month old, they moved, probably at the start of January 1937, to their own place, a single room that rented for forty guilders per month in the house at Hindelaan 14, a short distance from Stanni's home. Stanni and Miek visited frequently, if not daily, to see the baby.[76]

---

[76] While Miek mentioned Hindelaan to me, the specific address and the facts that a single room was rented for forty guilders are referenced in the Hilversum Police Report of May 12, 1937, in the Ministry of Justice case file on John's application for naturalization. Complicating matters, however, is a statement in the report, based on John's declaration, that he'd lived at Hindelaan 14 since July 1933, which appears to contradict some points related to my

The marriage was already in trouble. John said it was only good for about a month. He placed most of the blame on Frie. The main problem, he said, was she wanted to live beyond their means and she was extremely demanding. She wanted to go out on a daily basis. He said he took on extra jobs to supplement his income, but these jobs, which he said included constructing a house and lots of manual labour, offended her "ideas of status." Indeed, she reportedly refused to tell her friends about John's other jobs. One day, according to John, she and her friends were bicycling to a resort outside Hilversum where she went every day and, although he waved, she refused to acknowledge him in his work clothes as he pushed a cartload of bricks to the house he was building. What is more, when he came home late at night after selling life insurance during the evening, he was not able to relax because the house was full of guests. This upset him, but he couldn't say anything because, when he did, Frie "would get very mad." He maintained his only contribution to the marriage's failure was that he spent too much time away. Given this and his supposed workload, it's hard to credit his claim that Frie left much of the baby's care to him as well.

Although there is general agreement that Frie abandoned Hans and the marriage around May 1938, the circumstances of the marriage were, in some ways, notably different from how John portrayed them. After Frie's departure, Stanni became Hans's primary caregiver, which remained the case until Susan took over the role of mother in early 1941. John claimed he was awarded custody of Hans on condition that Stanni continued to share responsibility for his care. In fact, in February 1939, the court awarded joint custody to John and Frie, but Stanni effectively excluded Frie until late 1940 when Hans almost died from a burst appendix and blood poisoning.

---

understanding of his life from mid-1933 to May 1937 and the timeline I've presented. As both John and Miek told me that he and Frie moved to the Hindelaan place about a month after Hans was born, I suspect John was either dissembling when he said he'd lived there since July 1933 or that Hindelaan 14 was where he had a room on a periodic basis from the time his mother kicked him out of the house.

Until that time, "Frie was unwelcome in [Stanni's] house," according to Susan.

In March 1937, John reapplied for Dutch citizenship. According to his 1951 letter, his application was supported "by the Burgomaster of Hilversum Lambooy and the Superintendent of Police, Mr. van Beusekom." There are documents signed by both men on John's naturalization case file in the Dutch National Archives. This file also provides insight into his marriage. Despite his claims to the contrary, documents on the file indicate his employment was meagre. This was also the case at the time of their wedding; their marriage certificate says he was an unemployed insurance agent. Speaking of later periods, Susan told me John "was always without a job." To Miek, he "was a young fellow with twelve jobs and thirteen accidents." She added: "He was not practical. He had his head in the clouds. Certainly, a mother would worry about him." Notwithstanding his extravagant employment claims, John's perspective, on occasion, was not too different from that of Miek. Speaking about his life during these years, he told me he was a dreamer and that in telling his story it was important to "emphasize searching, optimism, imagination."

Various case file documents from early June 1937 note that John had a very modest income, that he had applied for financial assistance from the government but was deemed ineligible because he was not Dutch, and that a decision had been made to defer ruling on his naturalization application until he had demonstrated he could support his family. But a short six weeks later another case file document refers to him as set up in "his green-grocery business," an enterprise that required an investment of three thousand guilders. Given that Wim's collaborator statement of August 3, 1946, identifies their mother as the owner of this "wholesale business [where Wim] worked until the beginning of 1942," it is fair to presume she made this investment. The new business changed John's prospects. In a document of October 11, 1937, an official concluded that John was not going to be a burden on the Netherlands, as he was able to support himself and his family. A draft version of his certificate of naturalization was created that month. It appears that the decision to grant him Dutch citizenship was all but made.[77]

John never mentioned his green-grocery business to me. But he did say, more than once, that he started a wholesale business in food. He maintained he started it from scratch after viewing the operation of a friend of his mother's who was in this type of business. John's enterprise purchased canned and dried goods—but no meat or vegetables—from factories and approached stores, which purchased and resold the product, he claimed. John told me that although the business had a lot of potential, it didn't have enough capital. And having to wait thirty days for stores to pay him limited his ability to purchase additional goods and increase sales. In 1976, he said he sold the business to his friend Veltmeijer, who was an employee. But eight years later the story changed. At that time, John reported that after he had operated the business for a year by himself, Ko not only came in (presumably as a partner or investor) but also "conned John's mother into putting money into the business." This upset John and caused him to leave the business. He added that his mother subsequently concluded that she'd been hoodwinked and, as a result, decided to sell her interest, which was the whole business, to Veltmeijer, but this didn't occur until several years later, the beginning of 1942 being the earliest possible date.

John is dissembling in both his 1976 and 1984 accounts. The fact that the investment of three thousand guilders was needed to establish the grocery business means his claim that he ran the business for a year by himself was a lie. It also appears that his accounts use one of his favourite tricks, namely sticking close to what occurred but changing key details. For example, the green-grocery business became a wholesale food business dealing in canned and dried goods but not, he points out, vegetables. Moreover, Miek didn't remember her mother

---

[77] DNA, MJ 1937–1939: inv. 11681 and 11668 (various documents: June 6, 1937, June 9, 1937, July 22, 1937, Oct. 11, 1937). Attachment to Dr. Maili Blauw's February 7, 2013, email (re: John's naturalization case).

having a friend who had a similar business. She also disputed what John had to say about Ko. "I can hardly believe that Ko conned my mother to put money into the operation," she told me.

By leaving the wholesale business on a perceived point of principle—behaviour that was consistent with a stubborn inflexibility John attributed to himself during this period—he not only sacrificed the relative financial security the business provided but also jeopardized his marriage. What seems likely is that significant financial challenges on top of apparent immaturity and their joint responsibility for baby Hans caused John and Frie's relationship to fray, so much so that Frie abandoned both Hans and the marriage less than a year later.

But it must be stated that the point of principle—John's response to Ko conning Stanni to put money into the business—is hazy. I suspect there's more to the story than what John told me. Indeed, he may have abandoned Hans and the marriage before Frie did. We will return to this momentarily.

John said he wouldn't, couldn't believe that the marriage was over. Three times a week he bicycled to Amsterdam, where Frie had returned, in a vain effort to win her back. When his rescue trips stopped and he finally accepted the finality of the situation, he told me he fell into a depression, "a black emotional space where he did not want to do anything," especially talk to people. He said his nerves were bad, that he stopped working, and that he almost broke. In addition, he likely feared that he had proved his mother correct and become "a good-for-nothing" with a failed marriage and a child born too soon, and that he might not amount to anything. He said he believed it was because of his grief and emotional turmoil that the period of his marriage became a blank.

There may be something to his claim that he lost his memory for the two years of his marriage. In fact, the whole period from 1933 through early 1940 is bedevilled not only by lost and confused memory but also by romanticized invention: untrue stories of additional voyages while at sea, being a student at the National Art

Academy, and, of course, the influential role of the imaginary Wiertz. When he first told me about the wholesale food business, he said he was in it for two years, from 1937 to 1939, but on another occasion, he maintained he started it about March or April 1939. Similarly, his recollection of when he received his German call-up notices was all over the map. In his statement of October 8, 1945, he said he'd been summoned by the German embassy in 1934 and 1936. But according to his 1951 letter, these calls "from the German Consulate ... for militairy [sic] service" came in 1937 and 1939. And he told me in 1976 that they came in 1938 and in 1939 or 1940.

During John's breakdown, he and Hans lived with Stanni. Within days or weeks, she intervened and arranged for John to work at a nearby small farm, which he did during the week for the summer growing season. Throughout that summer, and especially during September, there was great fear of war erupting over Czechoslovakia. John said he received a call-up notice from the German army, which he ignored, but the Dutch authorities apparently did not. They arrived at his mother's home one day and searched his room. He said he felt persecuted, lonely, and confused, and that he trusted only himself.

Broadly speaking, I accept John's emotional upheaval in response to Frie's departure and other developments. But once again I suspect his behaviour is a bigger factor than he admitted. When he left the small farm in the late summer or early autumn, he said he rejoined Ko, and they spent three or four months doing woodwork, cement work, landscape gardening, and painting. But is this plausible given that John blamed Ko for causing him to abandon the grocery business, which appears to have led to the marriage breakup and his breakdown?

This question was the first of two indicators that alerted me to what I suspect is the rest of the story John sought to suppress. The second indicator was his claim that he and Wiertz once again lived together during the summer and into the autumn after Frie had left the marriage, which conflicts with him being on the farm and rejoining Ko. John said he and Wiertz lived and worked in an old, abandoned school in central Amsterdam, which they rented for a small amount. They used all the wood in the school—the baseboards and the trim around the windows and doors—to make frames for their paintings. When they ran out of canvas, they painted on the walls. At night they slept on the floor. They lay down at either end of an old carpet and rolled themselves up in it to stay warm.

It appears to me that John's claim that he overthrew his artistic inclinations when he was hospitalized and subsequently started selling life insurance was not the end of his dream of being an artist. It appears his dream reasserted itself before or during his marriage and contributed to a personal crisis when the grocery business, on top of his marriage, threatened to choke off the dream. Rather than face this prospect, he bolted—probably in late 1937 or early 1938—for the abandoned school with his imaginary mentor. Rather than abandon his dream or put it on hold, he abandoned Frie and Hans, at least until reality set in and, unable to feed himself, he returned home.

John's stark and revealing behaviour is matched by one of his Wiertz stories.

"There are two forces in the world: good and evil," a solemn Wiertz reportedly told John at an unspecified time. "The good comes from God, the evil is just there. You're somewhere between and you're being pulled both ways."

John told me it was good for him to hear such a sober assessment at a time when many considered him a good-for-nothing. He implied that Wiertz's words got his attention and caused him to sit up and, in some fashion, to take notice.

But who really delivered this memorable imputation, the rarity and stunning bluntness of which give it the feel of authenticity? My guess is Timperley.

If it was Timperley, I'm not sure he said these words during the mid-1930s. He may have said them about 1950. If this is correct, John probably relocated the words to the earlier period because he was ashamed of the behaviour of the young man of the 1930s and because leaving them at midcentury would call into question his claim that he was a transformed person after 1952 when he came to Canada.

***

When Frie met Harry Rademaker, who would become her second husband in a long and successful marriage, she asked for a divorce from John. As adultery was the only basis for divorce and it was bad for a woman to be branded an adulterer, John and Frie concocted a scheme whereby he would admit to adultery on condition that she would not contest custody of Hans. They proceeded to court and John falsely confessed to adultery in an affidavit dated August 23, 1938. The truth nevertheless emerged. Frie signed a document admitting that she and John agreed to deceive the court. Then she sought custody of Hans. The divorce was granted on December 22, 1938, and the custody decision was handed down on February 9, 1939.

These legal proceedings had a bearing on John's application for Dutch citizenship. According to a document dated March 15, 1939, his petition was denied because "insufficient grounds have been found for granting the request ..." Correspondence on the case file refers to "new facts" arising from his divorce. Two handwritten notations on the ruling highlight three issues: first, "the divorce has been pronounced on the grounds of adultery committed by the applicant. Maybe made up"; second, "his financial position is more or less precarious"; and third, "in the beginning of the movement he was a member of the N.S.B., resigned later." Regarding John's naturalization, the second notation concludes that "objectively seen one should be against it."[78]

John only knew that his application had been denied. He was not given the reasons. He described the government's decision as a "terrific blow." He said he suffered a terrible feeling of rejection and had a strong sense of being outcast, of not belonging anywhere. The

---

[78] DNA, MJ 1937–1939: inv. 11681 and 11668 (document of March 15, 1939). Attachment to Blauw's February 7, 2013, email (re: John's naturalization case).

anger and resentment he felt stayed with him. "I accuse those, who exterminated me from their community, to which I belonged by Human rights," he wrote in his 1951 letter. "I accuse those, who, perhaps thinking, they did their duty, ruined my rights on a human existence, as I saw it." The decision's unfairness still festered in 1976 when he spoke to me about it on several occasions. He noted with some acrimony that Prince Bernhard of Lippe-Biesterfeld, a German with a playboy reputation,[79] was immediately granted Dutch citizenship upon marrying Princess Juliana in January 1937.

***

When John and Ko once again teamed up to do odd jobs during the latter months of 1938, Ko suggested that John apply his drawing talent to commercial advertising. This led to a project with a Jewish druggist named Olsman. I presume John proposed the idea of a boy riding a bottle of Jecovitol health tonic, which he and Olsman developed into a wooden stand to be displayed in store windows. They pitched the display stands to the company that produced Jecovitol. The company ordered one thousand. John said he and Olsman would have been fine if they'd simply sold the concept to the company, but they decided to also manufacture the product despite lacking any ability to mass produce the display stands. This work fell to John. He made a template to trace the design onto wood and told me that all the work was done by hand and it was very tedious.

---

[79] John Spurr quoted in *A Liberation Album: Canadians in the Netherlands, 1944–45*, Michiel Horn, historical text, ed. David Kaufman (Toronto, Montreal, New York: McGraw-Hill Ryerson, Ltd., 1980), 71 (playboy reputation).

Figure 23. John working on Jecovitol display in 1939. Petersen family photo.

He said he produced half of the ordered quantity before throwing in the towel and he ended up losing money. The project was, in his words, a disaster and a debacle.

John said he returned to the insurance business. This probably occurred during or after the Jecovitol project. Whether he devoted himself exclusively to selling life insurance or did it alongside other work is not known. But it is known that he started working in a photography shop sometime in 1939. He added that he didn't like Ko at this time because Ko was always trying to cheat people. He said he kept Ko from going too far several times. He also attributed a spectacular scheme, an outright swindle, to Ko. A lot of planning and preparation went into it. Ko supposedly put the deception into motion one day when he drove a car onto a service-station lot. The con apparently unfolded something like this.

"Fill it up with water, please," he asked.

"You can't drive on water!" was the predictably incredulous response.

"I can with these special tablets," he replied, holding up a package of small white tablets. "Fill it up with water and I'll prove it to you," he added with fanfare, so that others could hear.

A small crowd of interested onlookers assembled for the demonstration. Ko had pre-selected only the largest gas stations for his visits, all of which took place on a single day.

In went the water, followed by several of the tablets. Then Ko started the engine and drove the car slowly around the lot like a magician performing a marvellous feat. People were amazed. They thought it was great. When Ko stopped the car, he was greeted by a small torrent of questions.

"What's the status of the invention?"

"Has it been sold yet?"

"When can the tablets be purchased?"

Ko said he planned to mass produce the tablets himself as soon as he raised the required capital, which would be soon. People were excited by the prospect of easy money and offered to invest. If they were serious, Ko said, he would meet them at a designated location later that day. According to John, by early evening Ko had raised thousands of guilders. The next day he was in Belgium, along with the car that had been outfitted with two gas tanks: one for water; the second, the secret one, for gasoline. His special tablets were ordinary aspirin.

John said Ko was charged when he returned to Holland in early 1940, but when the German invasion and occupation happened, the matter never went to trial. However, no evidence of such a charge or of the preceding alleged fraudulent activity has been found. In June 2004, when I was in the process of pinning down that Ko was the fellow John had identified as "Joe," Miek told me, via Constance, that the man "who built the bunkers for the Germans" was also the man "who got in trouble with the law." Whether this latter phrase is a reference to Ko's 1936 conviction or to his being charged for the double-gas-tank scheme or to both is, unfortunately, not clear, although I suspect Miek was speaking about the more spectacular escapade.

In June 1940, Ko started working as a land surveyor for the Naarden-based Fokkens building firm, which did construction jobs for the German Wehrmacht. Ko worked for Fokkens until the end of 1940. On October 10, 1940, he established his own building contracting firm, Jac. Elhorst. Most of his firm's work was also for the German military. On September 23, 1948, he was convicted of helping the enemy in times of war and sentenced to eighteen months in prison.[80]

John said Ko tried to get him to join his business during the war and never understood why he declined.

---

[80] Files on Jacobus Hermanus (Ko) Elhorst, DNA, CABR 64049 and NBI 75853. Attachment to Blauw's July 10, 2009, email.

8

SUSAN AND THE GURU

When John rejoined Ko doing odd jobs, he said it was because he wanted to minimize his contact with people, which ruled out selling insurance. This was probably sometime during the autumn 1938. About the same time, he began venturing out evenings and weekends. He took up sailing again and he made frequent visits to a dance studio. One evening, he was upstairs at the studio playing cards. The woman who owned the place asked him to go down and invite the new girl to dance. This was Susan, age twenty. She was "all dressed up in white," she recalled. A few months earlier, she had returned from France where she'd gone after high school to work as an au pair for a Jewish family that had homes in Paris and Le Havre. John and Susan knew each other slightly. The youngest of three sisters, Susan's middle sister, Jouk, was John's age. All three of them had attended the same school.

Like John, Susan had a troubled upbringing. Born in Haarlem, North Holland, on January 28, 1918, she grew up with servants in a well-to-do but turbulent family. Her parents divorced in the mid-1920s. Her father, Sijbrandus Posthumus, was a senior engineer for the Netherlands Railways Company. A stern Frisian, he saw things in black and white. Susan described him as overbearing, very strict, and a despot who had a terrible temper and was hard to live with. Her mother, Anna Suzanna, a petite woman about five feet tall with some

French blood, was completely different. She was a very nervous, teary, emotional individual with no backbone, according to her granddaughter, Constance, who, like her mother, often rendered blunt, tough judgments when she gave me her perspective.

There is an oft-repeated story of Susan's enraged father holding a butcher's knife and chasing his wife. Susan doesn't remember who first told her this story. Constance believes that Susan, when she was sick with tuberculosis as a little girl of seven or eight, learned it from her mother who was a frequent visitor at the TB sanatorium. Her father never came. Describing her mother's visits, Susan recalled asking her, "How is Dad? Did he beat you?"

John, in his accepting and insightful way, said Susan's mother was "a little peculiar." She was always seeking love from her daughters, but she "never got it. They all lipped her." He said Susan could be unconsciously cruel to her mother and belittle her. Susan told me her mother never stood up for herself. Referring to the abuse that was heaped upon her, first by her husband and later by her daughters, Susan said her mother just took it.

The girls had been afraid of their father. If they put an elbow on the table, he would take it and bang it down to let them know they'd broken one of his rules. Susan did credit him with being "principled." After the divorce, he ensured that Anna Suzanna and the girls, who had moved to Hilversum, were well looked after. Susan said they were very affluent and continued to have servants. But they also continued to have problems. Their mother had a parade of men friends, many of whom took advantage of her. According to Constance, Anna Suzanna was unavailable to her children. Constance suggested Susan may have had more meaningful contact with the servants. But when I asked Susan about this, she said she had little contact with the servants and that such contact was frowned upon. She also said her mother was good-hearted, always there, and good to her, which is consistent with John's description of Anna Suzanna; he said she was overprotective.

Each of the daughters inherited a forceful personality from their father. According to Susan, while Diel, the eldest, was very outspoken,

Jouk was "very sharp," meaning that she was both intelligent and could say hard things to people. It appears Jouk needed to stand up for herself. Susan said, "Diel called Jouk down. She said she looked like a man." Diel was also judgmental toward Susan. "You're so ugly," she told her youngest sister. Despite this, Susan maintained that Diel was good to her. She said Diel was a lot of fun and she and Susan never bothered much with Jouk. "Diel was really my sister," Susan said.

The first time Susan told me about her sisters she was quick to label Diel a nymphomaniac and Jouk a lesbian. She may have seen herself as a model of moral rectitude by comparison, particularly when she was a young mother raising a seemingly conventional family. Her uprightness could be stern and harsh. It gave her a bearing that her stepson, Hans, said was "very, very authoritarian ... very cold, not very loving" and that Constance said created "a very black-and-white, good-or-bad environment." After re-examining her past over many years with Constance—the two of them would "talk for hours"—Susan came to agree with these assessments. When she was younger, everything had been black or white, right or wrong to her, she told me. It must be added, however, that while Susan had a strong and domineering personality, she also inherited a sizeable measure of her mother's subservience regarding authority figures, most notably John and his mother, both of whom were hugely influential in her life.

One night after John took Susan home from the dance studio, he ran into Jouk. This led to John taking Jouk out sailing a couple of times. John said word soon spread that he and Jouk were going together. He told me this was not the case. "People assume [and] come to a false conclusion," he said. His denial is of interest given his subsequent negative attitude toward Jouk because she was a lesbian—a prejudice that was drummed into him during his SS training. Constance contends that Jouk's homosexuality later became a family secret and that John hated her and would not allow her name to be mentioned. The fact he took Jouk sailing rather than Susan may indicate he was initially more interested in Jouk, whatever the nature of that interest.

During the time John was sailing with Jouk, he was also getting to know Susan better. She said he was very insecure, which she attributed to his upbringing. "You couldn't talk openly with him about things. It would upset him too much," she explained. He was likely still recovering from his breakdown following the end of his marriage to Frie. But what he told me about his early relationship with Susan is remarkable for its misrepresentation. He said Susan had had a tough time in France, especially her initiation into a sexual relationship with a man. She'd been hurt badly and was on the brink of losing all interest in life. The two of them talked a lot. It was perhaps the first time in his life he did social work, he remarked.

The only trouble is, Susan had not had a relationship while she'd been away. Nor was she in any emotional distress, she told me. John was adding some dramatic colour to his telling of this story and he was also reinventing reality by transferring what had been his experience with Frie onto Susan, presumably because he thought it made him look better. I am confident in this assertion for there was at least one other time when he concocted a similar transfer, although in reverse, by claiming someone else's experience as his own.

Despite John's insecurity, he and his family held several significant attractions for Susan. She said her family never talked about deeper things, but John's did. Where Anna Suzanna could talk only about day-to-day subjects, Susan and John would converse about spiritual matters, which fulfilled a need in her. In the later 1940s, John led séances, generally using a Ouija board, with Susan, other members of the family, and some of their friends. He also did automatic writing. One time using the Ouija board, they communicated with a dead German who'd been killed in a war, Susan claimed. He gave them his name and other details about his life, which Susan said they confirmed with someone in Germany. Susan thought they might have been doing these occult activities before the war too, but she couldn't remember for sure. She did say, however, that John was strange and different from the time they first became a couple.

The fact Susan respected John is especially noteworthy. He told me in 1976 that he was particularly aware of this because it was unusual. Few people respected him then, he said. This respect helped forge a new identity for him as a magus and a medium. As he succeeded with this identity, his dream of being an artist became less evident and apparently less important. Members of his family, and especially Susan, were the source of this success; they played key roles in reinforcing this identity.

But Susan's regard was a two-edged sword, for, as John began to feel more strongly for her, her response was less of ardour than it was of deference and esteem. Although John maintained Susan didn't discover her true feelings for him until long after they were married—and although she repeatedly stated in her eighties that she still loved him—it is probably more accurate to describe her feelings for him over the long arc of their relationship as a combination of awe and fascination coupled with frustration and irritation at his neediness and manipulation.

John's family bolstered Susan's ego and self-worth. Stanni, the matriarch of the clan, was a forceful presence with definite opinions and ample backbone, just the opposite of Susan's mother. With her social standing and well-to-do background, Susan got along famously with Stanni, where Frie had not. Susan would help with Hans and often put him to bed at night. According to Constance, Susan's relationship with Stanni is what really appealed to Susan. Indeed, Susan told me the family was as much the attraction for her as was John.

Where John became her spiritual guru, Stanni became her role model. "I learned a lot from John's mother," Susan said. Like Stanni, Susan could be severe. They were both hard workers who did what was necessary to look after their families. When Stanni died on July 7, 1955, at age seventy-one, the family temporarily kept this news from Susan who was pregnant; they didn't tell her until after Onno was born on August 23. "Bul loved her so much," Miek told me, speaking of Susan's relationship with Stanni. "Bul" was Susan's nickname.

Most, if not all, of these dynamics came quickly into play in John and Susan's relationship. John proposed and Susan accepted in the early winter before the end of 1938, just a few months after they'd met. Their decision to marry was like his nationality: Rather than being clear cut, it was fraught with issues that emphasized what was missing. For example, Hans suggested that Stanni may have pressured his father to remarry, and Harald has said both Susan and Miek told him that John remarried because Susan would be a good mother for Hans. While these notions imply John was motivated by more than his feelings for Susan, there are statements from both John and Susan that indicate he was genuinely in love with her. John told Constance that he loved Susan and thought she was beautiful. Susan told me she knew John was passionate for her, especially for her red hair. She added, "I always knew we'd get married." What went largely unacknowledged were the significant areas of incompatibility that existed between them.

Although Susan had many skills, was a practical and highly competent housekeeper, and had a deep sense of responsibility, she was also, for many years, "so unknowledgeable," according to Constance. Miek described her as "simple and naïve." With less self-confidence than her older sisters, Susan admitted she was also self-critical. There were at least two reasons for this. One concerned her education, the other her appearance. Concerned for Susan's health and fearful of a relapse after she was released from the TB sanatorium, Anna Suzanna insisted that her daughter not be subjected to undue pressure at school. Consequently, Susan was shifted away from university preparation and into domestic studies. According to Constance, Susan felt dumb compared to John. Susan admitted as much when she informed me that John often told her she was just as smart as he was, but she didn't believe it. "He was just trying to make me feel good," she said.

While Susan maintained that Diel was good to her, she didn't forget her sister's cutting remarks about her appearance. In photos of Susan as a young woman, she often appears ill at ease, looking down or away from the camera. She didn't think she was attractive despite John's repeated and genuine protests to the contrary.

Figure 24. John and Susan at her mother's home, 1939. Petersen family photo.

Susan had a strong tendency to be swept up and away by subjects that engrossed and tantalized her, like John's reincarnation stories and the automatic writing he did while in a trance. She gave herself over to extremes and vast enthusiasms. She had a need to express reverence. During one of our visits, she told me John had been "her master" in a philosophic and teaching sense. I commented in my notes, she "seems to me childlike, not grown up." Another time, however, the subject of her adoration shifted. "John was smart, but Onno is ten times smarter. He's a genius," she remarked fervently.

Susan lacked agency in important areas of her life. She would unthinkingly parrot what John told her, Constance said. Susan told me on different occasions that she'd been completely devoted to and enthralled by John. She said, "He really possessed me." In 2002, she advised, "If I'd had to choose between John and the children, I'd have chosen John because I could have had more children."

John said their engagement lasted about a year, when in fact it was almost three years before they were married. His statement may be an indication of their original plans, namely, to be married sometime between the latter part of 1939 and the spring of 1940. But these plans were undone by unforeseen events.

In the Netherlands at the time, a woman who was less than twenty-eight required her parents' approval before she could wed. Susan's mother was agreeable, but her father, who John had never met, was not. John wrote to him. This letter, John concluded later, was too thorough and honest. His request for permission to marry Susan was denied because he was "a German and a misfit" (John's words) who had previously been married. This last point seemed to upset John the most because Susan's father was himself divorced and remarried. Susan, however, pleaded with her father, causing him to relent and grant permission.

Describing the protocol for engagement and marriage in the Netherlands, John said the engagement party was a very ceremonial and festive occasion, while the actual wedding was a brief, anti-climatic event in a government office that formalized a couple's new status as husband and wife. John and Susan's engagement party was held at Anna Suzanna's home, probably sometime in the first half of 1939. It is significant for one thing: an unexpected confession Susan made to John.

"I don't know if I really love you," she told him.

He said her words made him feel very sad and confused. She confirmed her remark at least three times. It was characteristic of her to be unguarded and forthright, often gruffly so, but in 2005, given the long lingering effect of her entirely sincere uncertainty, she added: "I probably shouldn't have said that."

Her expression of doubt, which John said hit him like a "thunderbolt," was a fundamental question. That it did not deflect them from their course suggests that necessities other than love were at work—necessities such as her need for the support she found in his family, her perceived need to learn from him, and his need for the esteem she bestowed upon him, as well as his need for a wife to look after his young son. Although John did say Susan eventually came to love him, I think this was a self-protective and ultimately delusional statement. She was certainly deeply committed to their relationship, but what passed for love on her part seems to have been more a mix of reverence and twisted dependency.

"John was not handsome to me. He was too feminine," Susan disclosed a few months after her ninetieth birthday. "Sex was always a trouble point," she frankly admitted. By "too feminine" she was referring to his neediness and the manipulation he used to control her, particularly what Constance termed her mother's "violent temper," which John always wanted to avoid.

"If you go too far, Susan, it will kill me. I will go crazy and it will kill me," is how Constance paraphrased what he would say.

Susan referred to it as "emotional blackmail." On various occasions she quoted John making statements like "If you talk about these things, it will make me sick with upset."

"I always gave in," Susan told me. "I was brainwashed. [John would] tell me: 'You have to stop now because I don't know what's going to happen.'"

"I didn't like the way he acted, threatening, warning that he might go nuts. He was feminine." But, she added, "There [were also] a lot of good things."

Constance reiterated that Susan was not attracted to John and had considerably less interest in sex than he did, and that she was a very detached and angry person who could not give John the warmth, contact, and gentleness he craved. Onno maintained John never felt supported. Not only was he "an individual who had an unusual level of struggle that he never fully came to terms with" but he also longed for "an all-consuming relationship [he] never achieved."

Another complication was John and Susan's mutual friend Jacobus Jan (Koos) Doornbos, who they knew from the late 1930s.

Koos had entered the Model Politie Vakschool (police academy) at Hilversum in October 1938, but his training was interrupted by the general mobilization for war, which in his case lasted from August 29, 1939, to November 1940. When he returned to the police academy, he and two other academy students were tenants at Stanni's home for five months from June 25, 1941, to the end of November. Susan told me she had more of a connection with Koos and would have been happier with him but wouldn't have learned as much. Koos married Door in May 1943, after which they were John and Susan's next-door neighbours in The Hague. The two couples were good friends. Koos remained an issue for the rest of John and Susan's marriage. He was one of the triggers for John's periodic paranoia. John sometimes questioned if he was Harald and Constance's father or if Koos was.

Susan's uncertainty about her feelings for John didn't derail their wedding plans, but something else did. Just prior to the wedding, Susan's father withdrew his consent. (John, with his love of the dramatic, said this happened the day before the wedding, which may be true, but I doubt it.) The date on which John and Susan had hoped to be married is not known.

Their charged engagement party and cancelled wedding were just the beginning of their difficulties. Following the German takeover of the country in May 1940, Susan was ostracized by her father because of her association with John and his family and its ties to Germany. This breach, which was healed after the war, was hardly insignificant, but it was minor compared to other issues related to their union.

"Mom's relationship with Dad was of the mind, with Koos it was of the heart," Onno told me. Susan was attracted to John spiritually rather than romantically. The result was a curious and off-kilter marriage that served many of their varied needs, but also frustrated them in different ways. The foundation of their marriage was compromised from the outset.

***

Although John faced challenges in March 1939—his application for naturalization was denied and he was likely still struggling with the Jecovitol project—the impact of these difficulties was undoubtedly lessened by the fact that Susan was in his life and they were engaged to be married. As a willing resource for Stanni, Susan probably stabilized John's life indirectly as well as directly. Moreover, although we don't know how much selling of life insurance he did that year, my sense is that when, about midyear or during the autumn, he started working at Siewers Fotohandel, a Hilversum photography shop, he entered a rare period of relative job security, one that lasted into May 1940.

Jan Gerrit Siewers (1904–73) was one of two older men who came into John's life during the latter 1930s. The other was Barend van Leeuwen (1893–1981). Both provided housing for Stanni and her family for different periods. From mid-1938 through January 1940, she rented accommodation at three different Hilversum addresses before renting a house at Sophialaan 18, which became the family home for the rest of her life.

Stanni, Wim, Miek, and baby Hans boarded with Van Leeuwen, his wife and daughter, and at least one other person from mid-1938 to mid-1939. They moved to another location from early August until October 11, when they moved into Siewers's home at Ten Katelaan 1a, where John joined them. When the family moved to Sophialaan 18, John boarded at the Van Leeuwens'.

According to John's son Hans, Stanni and the Van Leeuwens were friends.

Figure 25. Van Leeuwens' garden, 1937. Left to right: an unknown young woman (possibly Van Leeuwen's daughter, Dina, or Constant's girlfriend, Elly), Miek, Stanni, John, Constant, Frie holding Hans, Mrs. Van Leeuwen, and Barend van Leeuwen. Petersen family photo.

At some point, John and Barend van Leeuwen, a stevedore, also became friends despite the twenty-one-year difference in their ages. John used the words "stickler," "fussy," and "perfectionist" to describe Van Leeuwen. He said Van Leeuwen had a nervous twitch in one eye that made him appear to be winking at you from behind the glasses he sometimes wore. The two of them shared interests in carpentry, philosophy, and religion. John said Van Leeuwen was strict but also had a good sense of humour, and although he was a member of the Dutch Reformed faith and had strong convictions, he was not a regular churchgoer.

According to John, Van Leeuwen was also an ardent Dutch nationalist who hated the Germans with a passion. In October 1933, he took a twelve-year-old German Jewish boy named Arnold Rothschild into his home. He did this, he said, because of the measures the Germans were taking against the Jews in Germany and because he knew Arnold's father, Josef Rothschild, who asked Van Leeuwen to be totally

118 A SNAKE ON THE HEART

responsible for the boy's upbringing. This information comes from a statement Van Leeuwen made on October 17, 1946.[81] In it, he adds,

> When the boy became part of our family he was raised as our own and he successfully attended secondary High School. Soon after the boy was part of our family, his father in Germany dies, and with great difficulty I managed to get through the German authorities and the boy could attend his father's funeral in Germany.
>
> In the meantime the brother of my foster son Arnold Rothschild, whose name is Werner Rothschild, had been arrested and imprisoned in camp by the Germans. With great difficulty and associated costs I managed to get this boy out of the hands of the Germans and legally got him and his sister Elisabeth Rothschild out of Germany and sent them to England.

After high school, Arnold completed an apprenticeship as an electrician. He planned to join his family in the United States, where he hoped to study electrical engineering. According to information from the "restitution and compensation files" in the archives of the Begegnungsstätte Alte Synagoge in Wuppertal, Germany, Arnold had applied for a visa prior to the German invasion, which prevented his departure.[82] He subsequently had to leave the Van Leeuwen home because the Germans, as Van Leeuwen's statement says, "did not want a Jew living with an Aryan family."[83] But he was still there when John boarded with the family for much of the first half of 1940.

---

[81] Van Leeuwen's statement of October 17, 1946, 1, 2 (DNA, CABR 107966).
[82] Restitution and compensation files, Begegnungsstätte Alte Synagoge archives, Wuppertal, Germany. Attachment to email of February 13, 2006, from Dr. Ulrike Schrader to the author (apprenticeship; travel and education plans and visa), and email of December 10, 2005, from Professor Manfred Brusten to the author (training in "electric-mechanics"; restitution and compentation files in archives).
[83] Van Leeuwen's statement of October 17, 1946, 1, 2.

Siewers's family and Stanni's may have been related. "Momma said somewhere way back the Siewers were family," Miek told me. Such a connection could explain why Stanni occupied the Siewerses' home from October 1939 through January 1940. She may have been asked to house-sit when Siewers, who was in the Dutch army reserve, was called up as part of the general mobilization that occurred a few days before Germany invaded Poland on September 1, 1939. Where Mrs. Siewers and their six-year-old daughter were during this period is not known.

It was either prior to or during this time that John started working at the photography shop. He said he worked there for about a year, up to the German invasion. He told me he learned the whole trade and was happy to be learning. He said he learned a lot about the chemicals and about making super-large enlargements. "It was a good time."

Figure 26. John, a self-portrait, made in 1939 when he worked at Siewers Fotohandel, 59b Kerkstraat, Hilversum. Petersen family photo.

There were also important developments in Constant's life in 1939. On November 20, he married his long-term girlfriend, Elly. He was also "given the position of 4th grade helmsman on the Holland-American ship SS *Boschdijk*."[84] Like John, when he went to sea, it was with a German passport. He noted in one of his postwar statements: "My brother [re-applied] for his Dutch citizenship, but this was not granted, and based on that I did not go to the trouble to try for my Dutch citizenship."[85] He probably would have made a different decision had he known the reasons John's application was denied. Given he had been born on Dutch territory and his record was free of the issues that sank John's case, an application for citizenship from him would undoubtedly have been approved.

Miek maintained the *Boschdijk* was the last ship to make it into harbour prior to the German invasion. "During the night of 8-9 May we entered Rotterdam harbor ... and were given a berth at the Wilhelmina Quay," Constant said in his statement. "On 10 May 1940 [the day the invasion started], I and several other officers of the *Boschdijk* tried to return to the ship, but were forbidden to do so. Our purpose was to try to get the ship out of the harbor."[86] The *Boschdijk* was bombed and sunk the next day.

Had the *Boschdijk* been approaching home thirty or so hours later than was the case, Constant would have had a markedly different war. The *Boschdijk* undoubtedly would have diverted to England. According to Dutch historian Louis de Jong, "When the German attack came, most of our sea-going vessels were on the high seas. They were immediately put at the disposal of the London Ministry of Transport, later of the Combined Shipping Board in Washington."[87] Had this occurred with the *Boschdijk*, many of Constant's Dutch mates likely would have fought on the Allied side during the war. But Constant, as a German, probably would have been interned.

---

[84] Constant's statement of February 14, 1947, 2 (DNA, CABR 70629).
[85] Constant's statement of February 14, 1947, 2.
[86] Constant's statement of February 14, 1947, 2.
[87] Louis de Jong, "The Dutch Government in Exile," *Holland at War Against Hitler: Anglo-Dutch Relations, 1940–1945*, ed. M. R. D. Foot (London: Frank Cass, 1990), 11.

PART TWO

War and Occupation

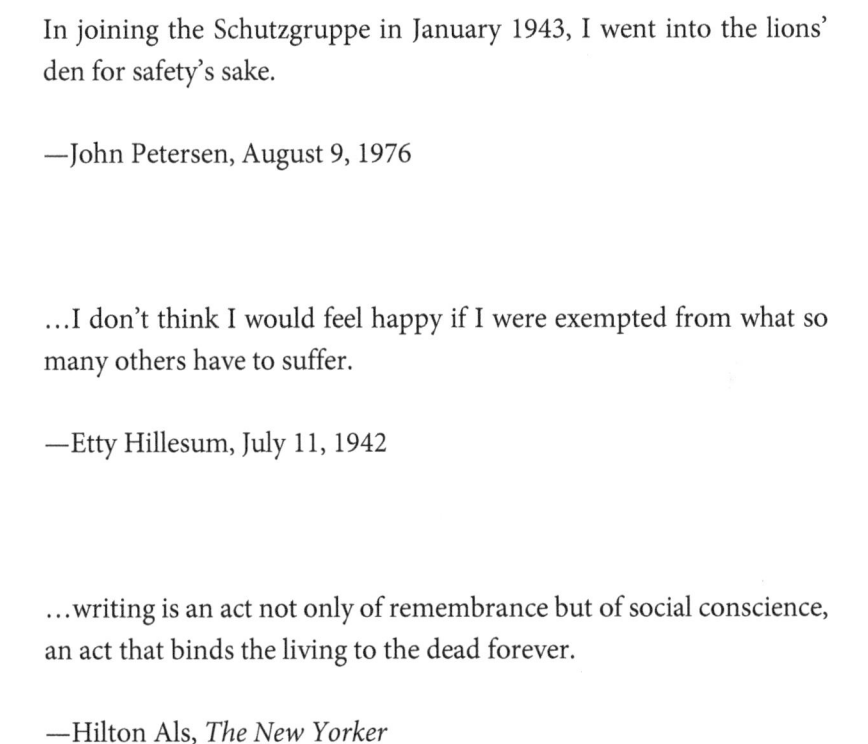

In joining the Schutzgruppe in January 1943, I went into the lions' den for safety's sake.

—John Petersen, August 9, 1976

…I don't think I would feel happy if I were exempted from what so many others have to suffer.

—Etty Hillesum, July 11, 1942

…writing is an act not only of remembrance but of social conscience, an act that binds the living to the dead forever.

—Hilton Als, *The New Yorker*

9

THE GERMAN INVASION AND THE FIVE-DAY WAR

Germany's May 10, 1940, invasion of the Netherlands began at 4:00 a.m. with its troops crossing the border in the east and, in the populous west, the Luftwaffe dropping parachute troops and bombing Dutch airfields—including the one at Hilversum—which were key objectives. A fleet of planes had been reported flying east to west over the country at 1:30 a.m. By 2:45 a.m., it had cleared Dutch air space. Observers presumed the planes were headed for England, but they were wrong. The armada reversed course over the North Sea and headed back to their true targets in Belgium, the Netherlands, and northern France. Historian Walter B. Maass, who lived near Haarlem and witnessed the event, wrote later that the population was awakened at sunrise, 4:15 a.m., by the din of numerous planes overhead and the sound of anti-aircraft guns, and poured out of their houses in their night attire to witness the extraordinary scene against a clear sky. The Luftwaffe had free rein as the Dutch air force was minuscule in comparison.[88] John said the invasion took them completely by surprise.

---

[88] Walter B. Maass, *The Netherlands at War: 1940–1945* (London, New York, Toronto: Abelard-Schuman Ltd., 1970), 19 (Dutch airfields essential), 22 (Belgium, the Netherlands, and northern France; Dutch air force; Luftwaffe; shock), 30 (1:30 a.m.; coordinated attack; 4:00 a.m.; 4:15 a.m.; night attire; clear sky).

124   A SNAKE ON THE HEART

German ground troops punched through most Dutch defences and quickly overran much of the country. The blitzkrieg (lightning war), first practised by the Wehrmacht during the Spanish Civil War in 1937, then used with stunning effect in its overwhelming invasion of Poland eight months earlier, was now being inflicted on the Netherlands. It was a "revolutionary form of attack—with dive-bombers, artillery, and heavy tanks all tied into one consolidated force."[89] By Sunday, May 12, the situation was desperate. General H. G. Winkelman, the Dutch commander-in-chief, advised Queen Wilhelmina to evacuate the royal family. That evening Princess Juliana, Prince Bernhard, and their daughters, Beatrix and Irene, boarded a British destroyer. The queen boarded another British warship the next day. A third British destroyer evacuated the majority of the Dutch cabinet during the early morning, Tuesday, May 14.[90]

Their departure was announced from London during an 8:00 a.m. radio broadcast on the 14th. A proclamation from Queen Wilhelmina was also read. The news was devastating, almost as great a shock to the population as the invasion itself. The people felt deserted. Wilhelmina had wanted to go to a province in the south of the country, but this was not a viable option.[91] German propaganda exploited "the royal family's 'flight' to England."[92] Even thirty-six years later, John was still critical of Wilhelmina for saving herself after she had promised not to leave.

History, however, has rendered a kinder judgment. Unlike King Leopold III, who remained in Belgium and was captured by the Germans

---

[89] Doris Kearns Goodwin, *No Ordinary Times: Franklin and Eleanor Roosevelt: The Home Front in World War II* (New York: Simon & Schuster, 1994), 50.
[90] Louis de Jong, *The Netherlands and Nazi Germany* (Cambridge, Massachusetts: Harvard University Press, 1990), 54–57. Maass, 37. Two members of the Cabinet, the Minister of Foreign Affairs and the Minister of the Colonies, had flown to London on May 10. De Jong, 56–57.
[91] Michiel Horn, *A Liberation Album: Canadians in the Netherlands, 1944–45*, ed. David Kaufman (Toronto, Montreal, New York: McGraw-Hill Ryerson, 1980), 11–12 (broadcast and proclamation). Maass, 37 (population shocked; Queen wanted to go to Zeeland).
[92] Mason, 148.

and forced to give up his throne after the war, Wilhelmina didn't compromise her position. Her timely escape enabled her, via London-based Radio Orange's daily fifteen-minute Dutch-language broadcast at 9 p.m. on the BBC European Service, to rally her people time and again during five long years of occupation and war. She became a redoubtable figure on the international stage and the first woman to address the US Congress. Winston Churchill's remark, "I fear no man in the world, except Queen Wilhelmina," was only partially in jest.[93]

It had been the hope of the "antiquated Dutch army" to hold off the Germans for two to three weeks.[94] Hitler, on the other hand, hoped to conquer the Netherlands in a single day.[95] The Dutch successfully defended three small airfields around The Hague, which foiled German plans to capture the royal family and key members of the government on day one. The Germans also encountered unexpectedly fierce opposition protecting Rotterdam's bridge entrances over the Maas River. A German order issued on the evening of May 13 called for breaking the resistance "at all costs" and, if necessary, destroying the city.[96]

On May 14, at 1:30 p.m., the Germans unleashed a massive fifteen-minute aerial bombardment that flattened the centre of the city.[97] At the time, and for many years afterward, it was believed—due to Allied propaganda—that 30,000 people had been killed and

---

[93] Henri A. van der Zee, *The Hunger Winter: Occupied Holland 1944–5* (London: Jill Norman and Hobhouse, 1982), 89.

[94] Van der Zee, 223 ("antiquated Dutch army"). Robert den Boeft, "The Dutch Armed Forces in Exile," *Holland at War Against Hitler: Anglo-Dutch Relations, 1940–1945*, ed. M. R. D. Foot (London: Frank Cass, 1990), 44 (two to three weeks).

[95] Albert van der Heide, "Timeline of World War II History, December 14, 1931–April 14, 1949," accessed March 7, 2002, www.godutch.com/newspaper/index.php?id=505 (entry for May 15, 1940: "Hitler planned to take the Netherlands in one day"). The pre-1945 portion of this site is no longer available online, but the portion covering January 2, 1945, to April 14, 1949, is. According to Maass (33, 21), a German goal was to arrest the Queen and her family on day one and eliminate Dutch opposition soon after.

[96] Maass, 32–34, 38 (at all costs).

[97] *The SS* (Alexandria, Virginia: Time-Life Books, 1988), 152, 154.

another 30,000 wounded.[98] The actual number was approximately 900 dead, along with several thousand injured, and 78,000 homeless; the homeless became an "endless procession of refugees," many of whom would be relocated throughout the country for the remainder of the war.[99] A German ultimatum followed the raid: surrender or have Utrecht destroyed in the same manner.[100] General Winkelman relented. At 4:50 p.m., he ordered all his commanding officers to stop fighting, and at 7:00 p.m., his message of capitulation to the German ambassador was read over the radio.[101] The bombing of Rotterdam forced the end of the Five-Day War, but it also became a symbol that galvanized and sustained the forces of resistance that would emerge and slowly strengthen over the coming years. Explaining his hatred of the Germans to a downed British airman in February 1945, a member of the resistance referred to the bombing of Rotterdam and said: "We were defenceless then and have since been slaves."[102]

---

[98] The 30,000 dead figure comes from Maass (40) and Gordon A. Craig, *Europe since 1815*, Second Edition (New York, Chicago, San Francisco, Toronto, London: Holt, Rinehart and Winston, 1966), 736, while Louis de Jong and J. W. F. Stoppelman refer to 20,000 dead and 30,000 wounded in *The Lion Rampant: The Story of Holland's Resistance to the Nazis* (New York: Querido, 1943), 10. In *A Liberation Album*, Michiel Horn writes (16): "Allied propaganda would inflate this figure [of the number of dead] enormously."

[99] Maass, 40 (900 dead); *The SS*, 154 (more than 800 killed); Anthony Anderson, "A Forgotten Chapter: Holland under the Third Reich," (a transcript of a lecture presented at the University of Southern California on October 17, 1995, is no longer on the Internet where it was previously available for years), 7 (900 dead, 78,000 homeless, thousands wounded). Lidia Feenstra (a pseudonym) quoted in André Stein, *Quiet Heroes: The True Stories of the Rescue of Jews by Christians in Nazi-Occupied Holland* (Toronto: Lester & Orpen Dennys, Ltd., 1988), 105 (endless procession).

[100] Maass (40); Anderson, "A Forgotten Chapter," (7); and *A Liberation Album* (17) reference the ultimatum threatening Utrecht. But Adriaan J. Barnouw and Raymond A. Wohlrabe, *The Land and People of Holland* (Philadelphia and New York: J.B. Lippincott, 1972), say (105) that the threat was against Amsterdam, while Harry Paape in "How the Dutch Resistance was Organized," *Holland at War Against Hitler: Anglo-Dutch Relations, 1940–1945*, ed. M.R.D. Foot (London: Frank Cass, 1990), maintains (70) "other Dutch towns" were at risk.

[101] Maass, 40. *A Liberation Album*, 13.

[102] Quoted in S. E. Hanson, *Underground Out of Holland* (London: Ian Allan Ltd., 1977), 65.

Despite the German occupation, the Netherlands' legal independence continued thanks to the queen proclaiming that London was now her country's capital, which enabled the Netherlands to fight with the Allies.

***

Like most of the Dutch population, John presumed the Netherlands would be neutral in another European war. Following Germany's assault on Poland, the Dutch government declared its neutrality on September 4, 1939. When Germany attacked the Netherlands, John said he was surprised by the invasion and "very mad at the Germans."

"Why the hell did you have to occupy Holland and betray my high view of you?" was the question he wanted to put to Germany.

According to his personal mythology, when he'd needed a passport to go to sea, the Germans had helped him when the Dutch and British had not. He said his German passport really meant a lot to him. It said he was accepted by at least one country. Indeed, despite "his philosophy against killing," a part of him "wanted to fight against the injustices [that had been] inflicted on Germany." Yet, when his German call-up notices came, he ignored them. He said the second one, which apparently arrived sometime between 1936 and 1940, prompted him to pursue British citizenship. Although he thought the requirement to produce three affidavits from people who could attest to his birth in British North Borneo was an impossible task, his mother apparently proved him wrong by tracing people she had known a quarter century before at Lahad Datu. Miek confirmed their mother's part in this project. John said he received the third affidavit the day before the Germans invaded. This claim is likely another of his tall tales, particularly given what he said happened next.

John maintained he was so incensed by the invasion that he "volunteered for the Dutch army without ever thinking that he wasn't Dutch." This is what he told me in 1976. He told the same story to the

Dutch authorities in October 1945.[103] In his 1951 letter, he described volunteering as a "spontaneous act." He didn't say where he volunteered, only that he had to wait an hour or two at that location, after which he was arrested. During the interval he was quickly investigated, he said. A woman who lived on his street, according to his version of events, told the investigators that he had a German flag and had given directions, via a special radio, to attacking German planes. This, the authorities supposedly told him, was their basis for arresting him. He added that "anyone could be arrested then—just on rumours."

Indeed, rumours and nervousness were widespread due to radio warnings about disguised German parachute troops and fifth columnists.[104] One consequence was a Dutch curfew imposed "on all enemy aliens. Germans, even if they were refugees, were likely to be arrested if found on the street."[105] Approximately 10,000 people—"native National Socialists [or] suspicious German civilians [viewed] as a putative 'Fifth Column'"—were swept up in a wave of "mass arrests."[106] None of the reports of Fifth Column activity "were ever substantiated."[107]

There is little question that John was arrested and interned, but he was not arrested after spontaneously volunteering for the Dutch army. Miek clearly recalled he was arrested at Siewers Fotohandel. She said municipal records were used to identify and round up German nationals. The foreign-national work permits held by the local police could certainly have identified where he was. "When the war broke out on May 10, 1940, I was immediately detained as a German," he admitted in his statement of October 29, 1946.

---

[103] In his statement of October 8, 1945, John says: "In 1940 I volunteered for the Dutch army, however was interned because I was a German citizen." This story is also referenced in the 1946 prosecution document (DNA, CABR 109786) related to his case.
[104] Maass, 32.
[105] Moore, 215.
[106] Hirschfeld, 15 (Fifth Column; arrests), 266 (arrests; 10,000).
[107] Mason, 20.

Sometime after his arrest, he and other detainees were transported under guard to the west. Their destination, he said, was The Hague, specifically a school gymnasium that was to serve as a makeshift concentration camp. It was the start of a seven-day nightmare, "a very painful and cruel experience." John told me that in the gymnasium there was enough room to sit on the floor but not enough to lie down; it was that crowded. Men, women, children, and babies were all housed together. There was no food or exercise. A single toilet served them all, he claimed, and they numbered in the hundreds. And there was a lot of crying. People were going insane. The guards did little, if anything, to help. They were cruel.

The prisoners were freed on May 16, "when the Germans had taken over," John said. Some hours before the end of their captivity, guards entered the gym and picked out by name twelve adult male prisoners, including John. They were taken outside to a recreation field and lined up in front of a deep ditch. On the other side, a short distance away, a mounted machine gun faced them. No one said anything. John said he was frozen by an indescribable fear. An official-looking document was produced and read aloud. It said they'd been found guilty of treason and had been condemned to death. They were asked if they had any final words. No one spoke. A man took up position behind the machine gun. He commenced firing. The men on either side of John fell, but he was still standing. His first thought was that the bullets had missed him. Then he thought he was dead, that *this is what it is like to be dead*. Moments later, he surfaced from the depths of his fear and confusion when he heard the guards laughing. He realized the others who had fallen around him had fainted. The guards told them they were preparing them for what was going to happen.

How much, if any, of this mock firing squad incident is true? John said it occurred on the fourth day. Given his frequent questionable claims, we must treat this story with skepticism. Some details, like the single toilet, are suspect. Yet, the story is not without a degree of plausibility. The guards may have been exacting a measure of revenge while they could for the bombing of Rotterdam and the German ultimatum, two acts which did more than anything else—except the invasion itself—to upend Dutch reality and which were consequently seared into Dutch consciousness. Although the fourth day was May 13, and Rotterdam was bombed on the fourteenth, I believe—given John's normally inaccurate estimates of time—that this discrepancy is less important than the clear indication that the alleged firing squad, if it occurred, likely did so later, on the fourteenth or on the fifteenth.

Notwithstanding this plausibility, I view the firing-squad story as the last in a series of lies intended to evoke pathos. The first lie was his claim that he volunteered for the Dutch army. The second concerned the affidavits, which he told me he had with him in a pocket when he volunteered. He said he could use them to vouchsafe his loyalty to the Netherlands, which, of course, contradicts his claim that he volunteered without ever thinking he wasn't Dutch. He spoke often about the affidavits. They became a symbol of his piteous predicament. I don't doubt that an effort was made to acquire them, but I wonder if they were ever, in fact, obtained, as he claimed. The third probable lie was the alleged extremity of conditions in the gym.

After being freed on the sixteenth, John said he walked the seventy-four kilometres back to Hilversum because there was no transportation. Physically and emotionally exhausted, he said it was quite a trip. Despite his fatigue, his senses were on high alert. He startled himself, first by remembering he still had the affidavits in his pocket, second by realizing he would undoubtedly encounter German roadblocks on his way home. He told me he dealt with the affidavits by tearing them up and eating them. His son Hans heard this story, too, but he understood that John ate the affidavits prior to his release. Harald, however, heard a different version. Rather than eating the affidavits, Harald said John put them through a mail slot in a door when he saw some soldiers coming. According to this version of events, John tried to retrieve the affidavits a day or two later but without success. The roadblocks he met didn't present a problem. He simply told the soldiers he'd been in a German sympathizer camp and they let him pass. When he finally made it back to the Van Leeuwens' home, he found his mother and the rest of the family there. They'd moved in for safety during the fighting.

Despite his fabulist claims, John's experience of the invasion and the first days of the occupation featured a range of powerful and unusual influences, from being interned by the Dutch, to being freed by the Germans, to living at the home of a future resistance leader who hated the Germans, all of which foreshadowed the extraordinary nature of his life during the remainder of the occupation and the war in Europe.

10

ADAPTING TO CHANGED CIRCUMSTANCES

John's sense of not belonging, of not being accepted, of being something of a fish out of water for much of the 1930s, was exacerbated when the Germans took over the Netherlands. He felt even more at risk because of the German call-up notices he had ignored. He told me that he lived in fear of being found out by the Germans. So, he didn't go back to his old job at the photography shop, but instead "went sort of underground." He claimed he did a lot of small jobs during the six weeks that followed the invasion, but Susan said he wasn't working.

Throughout the war, John feared being shot by a firing squad for having ignored his call-up notices. Perhaps he'd learned through connections with the NSB or others that, in Germany in September 1939, during the first weeks of the war, men were regularly imprisoned and executed as war saboteurs or for refusing call-up. In a lecture of September 3, 1940, Theodor Eicke, a key SS official in the development of the Nazi concentration-camp system, told SS officers in that system that "a revolution as in 1918 is out of the question. Every enemy of the state, every war-saboteur is to be liquidated. The Führer desires from the SS that they protect the homeland from all hostile intrigues."[108] More likely, John learned of these consequences in the latter half of 1940 during his SS training in Germany, most of which took place at the Dachau SS training facility next door to the concentration camp.

John said he felt torn by loyalty to the Netherlands on one hand and to Germany on the other. Although upset by the invasion and fearful of being found out, he said his sympathy for Germany was enhanced by his negative feelings for the Netherlands. In addition to his internment and the treatment he had received from "the Dutch in that camp," he also referred to his continual rejection in Holland on personal and governmental levels, going back to when his mother had first applied to have him and Constant naturalized. He told me that people who knew him but didn't know his nationality would often disown him when they found out he was German.

The day Germany invaded the Netherlands and John was arrested and interned, a letter appeared in his mother's mailbox. I heard about this from both John and Miek. The letter was from a member of their mother's bridge club, a lady who'd been a friend since their days together in Java. As you have two German sons, it said, it is better that we not see each other for a while. The estrangement turned out to be permanent. Miek was furious when she saw the letter, which she later described as "unforgiveable." It was an example of what John referred to as his mother's "phony-value friends."

Like John, Constant also faced a dilemma after the Five-Day War. But typical of the brothers, his was less dramatic. He continued working for the Holland-America company keeping watch on the vessel *Veendam*, but he was only paid "a reduced salary of 90 Guilders per month," he said in a postwar statement. "I could not make things meet with that, especially since I had gotten married only six months previously."[109]

---

[108] Peter Padfield, *Himmler: Reichsführer-SS* (London: MacMillan, 1990), 268 (refusing call-up), 267 (Eicke quote).
[109] Constant's statement of February 14, 1947, 3.

A whirlwind was reordering their world. In less than three months the Nazi colossus had rolled through and taken command of much of Western Europe—Denmark and Norway in April; Belgium, Luxembourg, and the Netherlands in May—and led to the evacuation of British troops at Dunkirk in late May and early June and the capitulation of France on June 22.

"The cause of the Allies is lost," King Leopold decided a few days before Belgium surrendered unconditionally.[110]

"The tide of the German motorized armies had swept on so overwhelmingly, so irresistably, the confusion in the minds of the people was so general and the feeling of powerlessness so crushing, that for the great majority of the Belgian population, the Third Reich had irretrievably won an ultimate and total victory," wrote Paul Struye, a postwar Belgian minister of justice. There was "a general desire to normalize the *fait accompli*."[111] Moreover, according to historian Gerhard Hirschfeld, these conclusions were applicable to all the vanquished and Nazi-controlled countries of western Europe.[112]

In the Netherlands, Dr. Arthur Seyss-Inquart was appointed *Reichskommissar* of a German civilian government. As with the other Low Countries and France, it was vitally important "that the occupation of [Holland] use as few German resources as possible."[113] In a meeting on May 25, Hitler gave Seyss-Inquart the additional objective of winning the Dutch people to the German cause. This led to the policy of the "gentle hand" that was operative through early 1941. In a communication of January 7, Heinrich Himmler, *Reichsführer* of the SS, refers to Seyss-Inquart's "historically vital task of reclaiming [the Dutch] … and leading them back to the Germanic community with a firm but very gentle hand."[114] Next to Hitler, Himmler became a second boss to Seyss-Inquart as the war went on,

---

[110] Shirer, 517.
[111] Mason, 1.
[112] Hirschfeld, 57.
[113] Moore, 42.
[114] Hirschfeld, 46.

an indication of the central role the SS was to play during the occupation. Indeed, Seyss-Inquart would adopt "an increasingly conciliatory stance and [rely] on his rank as *SS-Gruppenführer* and good relationship with [Himmler] to maintain his own position."[115]

Numerous authors have commented on "the relatively mild nature of German rule in 1940."[116] Writing during the war, Louis de Jong and J. W. F. Stoppelman noted that "the Germans tried to impress upon the Dutch that nothing had changed." They referred to the Germans' "impeccable behavior" and said, "The military, from the highest officer to the common soldier, behaved correctly and showed remarkable respect for women and children."[117] The only violence John saw during those first six weeks involved a German army contingent marching through Hilversum. He claimed that a soldier reached out and took an apple from a fruit cart. The man's commanding officer shot and killed him on the spot. Any violation of conduct was not tolerated. The good behaviour of the occupation forces was so different from Dutch newspaper reports the previous September about German atrocities in Poland that many Dutch turned "skeptical and believed such stories wildly exaggerated."[118] The Dutch press contributed to this change; "most newspapers [now displayed] an overcautious, uncritical and almost sympathetic reaction to the German occupation."[119]

The "gentle hand," in combination with Holland's stunning change of circumstances, led to a widespread attitude of collaboration. The secretaries-general, the most senior appointed officials in the Dutch government, retained control of their departments but did so under the authority of Seyss-Inquart. They apparently agreed "to set

---

[115] Moore, 191.
[116] Moore, 150.
[117] Louis de Jong and J. W. F. Stoppelman, *The Lion Rampant: The Story of Holland's Resistance to the Nazis* (New York: Querido, 1943), 13 (tried to impress; impeccable), 335 (behaved correctly).
[118] Maass, 44.
[119] Hirschfeld, 124.

aside Dutch law in the interests of executing German wishes."[120] Soon after the defeat of the Netherlands, several of them "had let it be understood that they would be prepared, in certain circumstances, to cooperate with the German (military) authorities in a 'most loyal' way [but] would 'not comply with the instructions of an NSB government.'"[121] For example, the secretary-general for the Ministry of Economics, whose guiding principle was "to avoid chaos," encouraged cooperation and the coordination of economic interests. A National Committee for Economic Cooperation was established "under the chairmanship of F. H. Fentener van Vlissingen, a big industrialist and long-time president of the International Chamber of Commerce in Paris." He said in a communiqué of June 15, 1940, that the committee's most important tasks would be "improving contact with the [Dutch and German] administrations" and "assuming practical leadership of the accommodation which has become necessary in the economic sphere."[122] The population generally didn't object to these adjustments.

Dr. Hendrik Colijn was the dominant figure in Dutch politics between the world wars.[123] Leader of the orthodox Calvinist Anti-Revolutionary Party (ARP), he served as prime minister five times between 1925 and 1939. At the end of June 1940, he argued in a widely distributed pamphlet that "a defeat of the Germans [was] no longer possible" and maintained that the Netherlands had no option but to accept "a German master in political, economic and social questions, even if this should mean that we must copy him."[124]

In August, Dutch writer Johan Brouwer urged his countrymen "to yield to the inevitable, to practice obedience and to wait trustingly." He accepted Seyss-Inquart's conciliatory words as "proof

---

[120] Moore, 201.
[121] Hirschfeld, 133.
[122] Hirschfeld, 205 (avoid chaos), 223 (H.M. Hirschfeld), 224 (improving contact; practical leadership). The Secretary-General, Ministry of Economics, was Hans Max Hirschfeld, a different man to Gerhard Hirschfeld, the historian, sometimes quoted in the text.
[123] Maass, 18.
[124] Hirschfeld, 57, 60–61. Mason, 3.

of respect for a defeated small nation."[125] However, Brouwer would show himself to be typical of a tiny portion of the Dutch population. He would change his opinion of the German occupation, join the resistance, and ultimately give his life for it.[126]

One of the tools for leading the Dutch people into "the Germanic community" was the creation of the Nederlandse SS (Standarte "Westland"), which Hitler authorized on May 25. This entity, which in June 1942 was renamed the Germanic SS in the Netherlands, would solve John's and Constant's immediate problems but irrevocably tie them to the German side for the remainder of the war.[127]

SS Standarte "Westland" was to consist of Dutch and Flemish, as well as German, recruits. Between June 1 and September 11, 1940, 2,448 Dutch volunteers (likely including several dozen Flemish men) were medically examined, according to the SS recruiting office in The Hague. Approximately half were approved and sent for training.[128] According to N. K. C. A. in 't Veld's history of the SS in the Netherlands, "30-40% of the total number of volunteers" were members of the NSB or other collaborating parties. He adds that a "love of adventure, professional failure, improvement in pay, a criminal past ... were probably amongst the most important" reasons that motivated the other 60-70 per cent to sign up. Recruitment offers of "athletic or police training, or for a series of political lectures" were also highly influential in getting young men to sign up.[129]

John needed a job and a means of surviving under the new regime. He also needed to remain undetected as a German who had ignored his call-up notices. And he wanted to avoid the military or, at least, the front lines. An apparent answer to his dilemma presented

---

[125] Hirschfeld, 61.
[126] Hirschfeld, 323. Hirschfeld points out (323) that Brouwer had also fought on both sides during the Spanish Civil War.
[127] Hirschfeld, 46–47, 46n–47n, 276, 276n.
[128] N. K. C. A. in 't Veld, *De SS en Nederland: documenten uit SS-archieven, 1933–1945* (The Hague: Martinus Nijhoff, 1976; two volumes, including an English Summary in Vol. 2), 316–317.
[129] In 't Veld, English Summary, 1523, 1518 (training or lectures).

itself in a roundabout way. He ran into Klein, a friend, who was a member of the NSB. John told me Klein was someone he could trust. When Klein learned of John's predicament, he apparently introduced him to a German army officer. John said the officer, who he referred to as both a commander and a colonel, had taken room and board with Klein. He also said the officer was a very nice man who tried to make things as easy as possible for the Dutch population. While the officer was pro-German, he was also anti-Nazi. John was consistent in this latter description; he said the same thing on two occasions, nine years apart.

The officer, who John saw only once, told him there was no organization to find draft dodgers. The army had neither the time nor the interest, he said, adding that John probably would not be discovered. He suggested the best thing John could do to remain in the Netherlands and stay out of combat was to volunteer as a Dutchman to become a policeman for the occupation authorities, which would require training in Germany. John said this was "good advice, although it did not turn out that way," meaning that while the officer was well-intentioned, his recommended course of action had unanticipated consequences. Rather than an officer in the German army, Susan thought John was advised by a senior NSB official. Whomever John consulted, he accepted the proffered advice. He said he quickly volunteered *as a Dutchman* to be trained for police work.

Constant, once again, followed John's lead. He told Dutch officials after the war that, on the advice of "a man who was a friend of my brother," he volunteered for the SS Standarte "Westland" on June 25, 1940, at Amersfoort.[130] According to what the recruiters had told him, "people in my position would have the opportunity to practice their trade. Since I was a helmsman by trade, I might be able to take a course to become an inland ship's helmsman."[131]

---

[130] Constant's statement of February 14, 1947, 3. Attachment to researcher Dr. Maili Blauw's email of February 14, 2007, to the author notes that Constant's Waffen-SS registration is dated June 25, 1940.

[131] Constant's statement of February 14, 1947, 3.

But Constant, like John, had been misled, which became apparent a few weeks after they arrived in Germany. "Not infrequently the Germans tricked their victims into accepting military service."[132] The tactics of deception were authorized at the top. Due to competition with the army for recruits, Gottlob Berger, the SS's chief of recruitment, felt compelled "to use subterfuge and [tricks] ... to build up the Waffen-SS and reserves."[133] In 't Veld points out that in mid-1940, "the letters 'SS' still had little or no meaning for the great majority of the Dutch population."[134]

As John and Constant were sorting out their futures, there were two notable developments in the country. On June 22, the day that the French surrendered, the NSB held a "Festival of Liberation," which was "organised on the lines of the Nuremberg rallies." Intended as a prelude to a membership drive, the festival "involved a public declaration of solidarity with Hitler" and a tribute to Hermann Göring who, according to NSB leader Mussert, was "the creator and protector of the German Luftwaffe." Given the Luftwaffe's devastating bombing of central Rotterdam less than six weeks before, the tribute was extremely ill-timed. Moreover, rather than demonstrate NSB party unity and its readiness to govern, the festival instead revealed "the enormous gap between the NSB and the majority of Dutch people."[135]

Mussert was in an impossible situation. His twin objectives of being loyal to the German Reich and winning the support of the Dutch people were untenable. The NSB's "open approval of the expansionist foreign policy of the Third Reich" after 1935 alienated the vast majority of Dutch citizens, with the result that the party spent much of its time defending itself against charges of treason.[136]

One week later, on June 29, there was quite a different event. It was Prince Bernhard's birthday, which sparked a fervent

---

[132] Mason, 22.
[133] Padfield, 279 (competition; subterfuge), 297 (chief of recruitment), 316 (tricks).
[134] In 't Veld, 1513.
[135] Hirschfeld, 272, 272n.
[136] Hirschfeld, 263, 264.

demonstration of Dutch patriotism. In The Hague, thousands of citizens marched silently in the streets and many of them wore white carnations, the prince's favourite flower.[137] The day became known as *Anjerdag* or Carnation Day. It enraged Hitler. He ordered Seyss-Inquart and some other senior officials in the Netherlands to report personally to him. In an early contradiction of the "gentle hand," the occupation authorities dealt harshly with the situation. The Hague's mayor was dismissed, General Winkelman was interned, and security measures and arrests were increased.[138]

Two months later, on August 31, the queen's birthday, the first major underground newspaper, *Vrij Nederland* (Free Netherlands), was launched. Other illegal bulletins had already started publishing—the earliest appeared in mid-May in response to the bombing of Rotterdam—and by the end of the year there were approximately sixty.[139] When the war ended, 1,200 different underground papers had collectively produced more than 70,000 issues. And the five largest of these newspapers "appeared in editions averaging 600,000 copies in 1943."[140]

John's friend Johan Veltmeijer was apparently responsible for one of the smaller illegal bulletins. John said Veltmeijer would print little newspapers to inform the populace of what to do, what signals would be used, and so on. It was John's task to distribute several hundred of these bulletins. He said they contained information from Britain, and that Veltmeijer was one of the middlemen between England and the underground. Veltmeijer acknowledged John's help

---

[137] De Jong and Stoppelman, 27, 26.
[138] Hirschfeld, 35, 35n, 36n.
[139] Maass, 75 (earliest bulletin; *Vrij Nederland*). Harry Paape, "How Dutch Resistance Was Organized," *Holland at War Against Hitler: Anglo-Dutch Relations, 1940-1945*, ed. M.R.D. Foot, (London: Frank Cass, 1990), 71 (response to Rotterdam bombing), 91 (sixty underground newspapers by end of 1940). Van der Zee, 114 (earliest illegal paper on May 15). De Jong and Stoppelman, 287-9.
[140] Hirschfeld, 122n (1,200; 600,000). De Jong, *The Netherlands and Nazi Germany*, 46 (over 1,200; 70,000). Van der Zee, 115 (1,200).

"spreading newspapers."[141] Whether this took place in Hilversum, another location, or in multiple locations is not known, but given John's initially pro-German attitude, I presume it didn't occur until mid-1941, at the earliest. John said the fact that he had a German uniform helped in many respects, such as distributing the bulletins and carrying messages.

Notwithstanding the birth of a rudimentary underground press and several displays of support for the royal family, the primary sentiment of most Dutch people was "to be and remain ourselves."[142] Despite the shock of the invasion and the occupation, "everyday life quickly regained its normal rhythm [and] very little seemed to have changed."[143]

Like Veltmeijer, Van Leeuwen was part of the tiny minority that not only recognized that things had changed fundamentally but joined the resistance in response. Van Leeuwen did this "soon after [the Dutch] had lost the war with the Germans." As he "had the task to look after the people in hiding," he obtained milk and butter from a farmer but found the prices "ridiculous." At some point—whether in 1940 or 1941 is not known—he decided to have a few cows himself. According to his police statement of October 17, 1946, "The proceeds were almost entirely used to look after the people in hiding."[144] John and Constant's brother, Wim, went to work for Van Leeuwen's cattle business in early 1942. Wim subsequently became engaged to Van Leeuwen's daughter, Dina, and married her in 1944. Included with Wim's statement of October 23, 1946, is a witness statement from Hans Alexander Friedheim that says that Wim, on behalf of Van Leeuwen, "often brought food to my people in hiding at 6 Schutterweg in Hilversum."[145]

Meanwhile, in the immediate aftermath of Germany's triumph over the Netherlands, Constant and 250 others left for Germany at the

---

[141] Veltmeijer's testimonial letter of June 23, 1951.
[142] Hirschfeld, 13.
[143] Historian J.C.H. Blom quoted in Moore, 51.
[144] Van Leeuwen's police statement of October 17, 1946.
[145] Hans Alexander Friedheim's witness statement within Wim's statement of October 23, 1946 (Dutch original), 20–21.

end of June, while John travelled with a group that departed on July 1, according to statements they each gave to Dutch authorities after the war. In conjunction with John's departure, Susan moved in with the family. Constance said this broke Anna Suzanna's heart, but she nonetheless agreed to pay Susan's room and board. Susan told me she came to feel bad about leaving her mother. Sometime before leaving for Canada, she apologized to her for this. She also apologized for how she had treated her when she was growing up. Having made this apology was a comfort to Susan; she mentioned it to me several times.

11

SS TRAINING

The SS School at Dachau, like the adjoining concentration camp, was established in 1933, shortly after Hitler came to power.[146] The facility that John and Constant attended was part of "an enormous S.S. centre."[147] Much of it had been built in 1937 and 1938 with slave labour from the concentration camp, which comprised approximately a quarter of the area and the "vast complex of buildings."[148] In addition to the training school for professional soldiers, the SS centre housed the *Kommandantur* and its services, as well as the barracks for the concentration camp's officers, staff, and sentries.[149] It also served as home base for the SS-Standarte "Deutschland"[150] and was the storage centre for the SS's loot taken from occupied countries.[151]

---

[146] *The SS* (Alexandria, Virginia: Time-Life Books, 1988), 59. Marcus J. Smith, *The Harrowing of Hell: Dachau* (Albuquerque: University of New Mexico Press, 1972), 186.
[147] Paul Berben, *Dachau, 1933–1945: The Official History* (London: The Norfolk Press, 1975), 36.
[148] Berben, 3 (1937 and 1938; vast complex), 9 (SS camp "much larger" than prisoners' camp), Appendix 3 (diagram of the Dachau SS centre).
[149] Berben, 9.
[150] *The SS*, 147. "Ernst-von-Bergmann-Kaserne," Wikipedia, accessed May 16, 2021, https://en.wikipedia.org/wiki/Ernst-von-Bergmann-Kaserne.
[151] Berben, 36.

John told me they arrived late at night and that the whole camp had been cleared out in preparation for them. He said thousands of Dutchmen went to Munich for police training and he arrived with a group of two thousand. As In 't Veld says "fresh groups of volunteers [were] always" arriving, the figures John cites may be his estimate of the total number of Dutch volunteers.[152] John also said the parade square could hold about a thousand people, which, based on photos of that capacious area, seems a low estimate.

John and some new friends he met during the trip had resolved to stay together during training. But these plans were thwarted the next day when they mustered onto the parade square, which was enclosed by buildings on all sides. The first order of business was to sort the recruits by height. At six foot two, John was selected for the company of tallest men. They were then issued uniforms and weapons. They were also subjected to some sort of examination or inspection because, John maintained, some of the men were rejected at this stage and sent back to the Netherlands.[153] Most, however, were accepted. At this point, John continued to believe he would be trained for police service. He said they still didn't have any real idea of what was in store for them. Information from Constant contradicts John on some points. "After a few days in Munich I was issued a grey uniform with black patches on the collar," he said. "We did not get any weapons until later. Also we were given another contract to sign which guaranteed work for us."[154]

Soon after, the situation started to unravel. John said he and the other Dutch recruits didn't know why they were being trained in an SS camp and with German SS trainees. He told me that the trainers

---

[152] In 't Veld, 1518.
[153] In 't Veld notes (1518) that one of the recruits was "a Dutch veteran who had joined up for the express purpose of learning the military trade better than the Dutch army had taught him. When he refused to swear an oath of allegiance to Hitler, he was sent back to the Netherlands, together with a host of other rejects. He eventually became the leader of a resistance group responsible for many armed attacks on the Germans."
[154] Constant's statement of February 14, 1947.

thought the Dutch were just more SS recruits, and the Dutch started asking questions, which produced confusion rather than answers. This apparently led to some pressure being put on them to sign up rather than go back to Holland. John said this was the beginning of the pressure, which was "sort of persuasion" at the outset. Then, prior to the end of July, each trainee was taken separately into a room and informed that recruits could not be released from the SS. They would either sign up for the duration of the war or they'd be sent to a concentration camp. Most chose to sign up, John said. He and Constant did not. John said fighting was against his philosophy. Summarizing his situation, John wrote in his 1951 letter: "I found myself in Munich in an SS centre, where I had to sign as a volunteer for military service. I refused. Result: Concentration camp Dachau." Constant was also confined.[155]

John told me he did hard labour for three months, but he told Dutch officials after the war that he was "transferred to the concentration camp 'Dachau'" for "about four weeks."[156] Constant said he was sent to a barracks for three weeks "as a threat." Another time he said the reason was "for reflection."[157] In 't Veld maintains that only a few of the recruits were put in the concentration camp.[158] However, Dr. Hans de Vries of the former Netherlands Institute for War Documentation advised that In 't Veld's statement is in error and should have referred to "the SS Straflager Dachau" rather than to the concentration camp.[159] Constant's statement of February 14, 1947, lends support to de Vries's assertion. "Since there was considerable resistance to signing this [new] contract [for military

---

[155] Constant's statements of September 14, 1945, and February 14, 1947. Attachment to Blauw's email of February 14, 2007.

[156] John's statement of October 29, 1946.

[157] Constant's statements of September 14, 1945, and February 14, 1947. Attachment to Blauw's email of February 14, 2007 (threat; reflection).

[158] In 't Veld, 319.

[159] Hans de Vries's letter of April 5, 2004, to the author. Following a merger with the Center for Holocaust and Genocide Studies, the Netherlands Institute for War Documentation or Nederlands instituut voor oorlogsdocumentatie (NIOD), became the NIOD Institute for War, Holocaust and Genocide Studies.

service]," Constant said, "they transported us to an armory in Dachau [where] we only engaged in some sporting activities."

John could not resist playing up the concentration-camp angle when he told me his story. No doubt his ego contributed to this fabrication, but bitterness was also a factor. He said he was treated better when he was jailed at Dachau than when he was in the various collaborator camps where he served seventeen and a half months after the war. (He was interned for nineteen and a half months but was hospitalized for the last two after being injured in a munitions explosion.) He acknowledged his confinement at Dachau was undoubtedly influenced by the Germans' hope that he might yet agree to join the SS. Still, in typical fashion, he bent the truth beyond the breaking point, claiming his time as a prisoner there was "hard due to the hard labour."

The Dachau concentration camp was classified a "Grade Ia" camp for those "in need of consideration," as well as for "prisoners with good records who are definitely capable of improving" and for "special cases and solitary confinement." The largest segment of the camp's population consisted of political prisoners. Many of them had been denounced by a neighbour, colleague, creditor, student, or even a family member. They were charged with "insulting the Fuhrer," "defamation of the swastika," "behaviour prejudicial to the state," or something similar. By comparison, Auschwitz was a Grade II camp "for those likely to benefit from education and reform," while Mauthausen in Austria, which would soon become a much-feared destination for Dutch political prisoners, was Grade III for those who could not be re-educated.[160]

John and Constant were held for three to four weeks. We know this because Reichsführer Himmler, who made frequent visits to Dachau, spoke to the prisoners on August 21 and broke the impasse.[161] John gave me a detailed account of this meeting and what

---

[160] Marcus Smith, *The Harrowing of Hell: Dachau* (Albuquerque: University of New Mexico Press, 1972), 158, 234.
[161] Berben, 20 (visits), 80 (visits). In 't Veld, 321, 1518 (August 21).

Himmler said. His account matches what In 't Veld says about this event. John said Himmler and his entourage arrived for a three-day visit and that the Reichsführer addressed them on the last day.

Himmler spoke on race and German successes. He said he would give them a second chance. If they agreed to sign up for the duration of the war, they would be rewarded with land in the east for farming. He also provided a second option: sign up for two years, after which they would be free to do whatever was available to them, including re-enlist. Questions were permitted. Several of the Dutch recruits protested they had contracts for police training, which would be followed by police service in the Netherlands. Himmler seemed prepared for this. He granted a third option. Complete the necessary training, then return to the Netherlands for some sort of vague police work under the auspices of the SS. When they sought clarification, the Reichsführer gave them a fourth and final choice—outright release—which was really no choice at all.

"You can go back to Holland"—this is John paraphrasing Himmler—"but you will probably end up back in a concentration camp because you're obviously anti-German." Emphasizing the point, Himmler added: "You'll be watched very carefully." He also told them they "would never have a proper job in government service."

With his checkered employment history, this point may have influenced John. He took the third option. He felt it was his only choice. An additional factor loomed large in his decision. A postwar prosecution document quotes John: "Since I am there as a Dutch person [and not as a German citizen] ... and did not want this [falsehood] to be made public, I took the SS course. I was afraid that I would be called to do D [German] military duty."[162]

Constant also took the course. He signed a new contract in September 1940; it included an agreement to serve in the military.[163] Some of the others signed up for the duration. No one, according to John, took the fourth option.

---

[162] Prosecution document of November 14, 1946.
[163] Constant's statement of February 14, 1947, 3.

The episode of being confined at Dachau is unique in that it involved both John and Constant, and we have multiple statements about it from them. Constant referred to it in two of his postwar statements; John mentioned it in one, as well as in his 1951 letter and in three of the sessions he had with me in 1976. Where John claimed emphatically that he was jailed in the Dachau concentration camp, did hard labour, and even stretched the period of his imprisonment from four weeks to three months, Constant talked of being confined to barracks as a threat and "for reflection," but also said they participated in some sporting activities. Compared to John's typical hyperbole, Constant's descriptions are matter of fact and contrast sharply with those of his brother. I find Constant's words easy to trust.

***

Despite his confinement and the misrepresentation that led to it, John spoke highly, even fondly, of his SS training. He described it as "incredible" and "very thorough." He spoke of both physical training and classroom lessons. He said the physical training was almost cruel at times. It was intended to break the man so he would not question authority and would follow orders regardless of circumstance. Initially John viewed the trainers as sadists, but he soon concluded their tough methods were for the recruits' own good. The classroom training was quite different. He said it made you think so you would be able to take over in a crisis.

"Most of the raw recruits were completely taken aback by the strict discipline of the German SS," according to In 't Veld.[164] Their instructors were unrelenting. Great stress was put on drilling and precision. To do the goosestep effectively, they regularly paired off and did exercises, John said. One man held another man's leg waist high and pushed down at the knee. After the required time, they did the other leg. Then they reversed roles. John spoke of the tremendous

---

[164] In 't Veld, 1518.

emphasis on precision. He'd never seen anything like it. In addition, the men were repeatedly drilled to have a symbiotic relationship with their rifles. These semi-automatic weapons were precision made, not mass-produced like those of other armies. They could not easily be replaced and had to be exceedingly well cared for. John said their rifles "were almost sacred."

The most frequent drill John and his mates practised was to immediately hit the ground, simultaneously protecting their rifles. They had to lie as flat as possible, legs spread, heels down. Their rifles had to be tucked by their side, the muzzle slightly elevated, held by a hand or resting on a wrist. If a heel was up, a trainer would stomp it down to help the recruit remember for next time. A lot of men had been shot in the heel and lost to service in past wars. Once when John had to hit the dirt, he jumped over a puddle rather than lie in it. He was royally chewed out and only escaped punishment because it was early in the group's training.

Another area of tremendous emphasis was cleanliness. Their principal nightly chores were to clean the barracks, clean and stack their clothes, and, of course, thoroughly clean their rifles. Their work in each area was closely examined. The inspecting officer wore white gloves and ran his fingers along windowsills and the tops of doors, looking for dust. He also examined their clothes to ensure they were folded and stacked in the prescribed manner. After their rifles were inspected, the men had to hold them with outstretched arms for longer and longer periods of time. The objective was to maintain a ramrod posture for the duration. Inevitably, as the rifles were quite heavy, a recruit would bend his back to help support the weight. This would earn the observation that he "looked like a question mark of shit in the sky."

According to John's stories—all of which are unverified—the six months he spent in SS training provided him with opportunities for clowning and outlandish behaviour. He said that while the Dutch recruits could see the value in their training, there were also times when they could not give the myriad requirements imposed on them

150   A SNAKE ON THE HEART

the seriousness the Germans demanded. One night when it was John's turn to report to the officer in charge that the room was clean, the men were in bed, and all was sound, he made a joke of it.

"All clean, men snoring, and dust evenly spread throughout," he said. Clamourous laughter erupted. The men could not contain themselves. He told me that the officer also appreciated that spirit. But when things quieted down, he advised John what his punishment would be that weekend.

John and his platoon mates were punished on a regular basis. They lost most of their weekends. John was out of circulation even more than the others. He said he had only one Sunday to himself. Sometimes their punishments were for unacceptable performance, but more commonly they were for youthful exuberance and chafing at the extremes of German order and discipline. John said the Germans quickly came to regard John and his cohort as "the crazy Dutch." Their antics were as much a surprise to the Germans as the Germans' endless regimentation was to the Dutch. One day when a high-ranking officer came to inspect the Dutch recruits, John's platoon was ordered to "present arms, eyes right." They presented arms, but instead of looking smartly to the right, they mockingly peeped around their rifles like a bunch of vaudeville comics. This buffoonery cost each of them three days in solitary and four weekends of free time.

In the Netherlands, the spirit of the Dutch would increasingly exasperate and confound the Germans, whose policy of the "gentle hand" did not last long. By mid-March 1941, Reichskommissar Seyss-Inquart was complaining about "the peculiar make-up of the Dutch"[165] and calling for a hardline policy of "for us or against us."[166] Thirty months later, Joseph Goebbels, Hitler's minister of propaganda, fumed to his diary, "The Dutch are the most insolent and obstreperous people in the entire world."[167]

---

[165] De Jong and Stoppelman, 243.
[166] Hirschfeld, 80.
[167] Joseph Goebbels, *The Goebbels Diaries* (New York: Doubleday, 1948), entry for September 10, 1943.

The Dutch recruits' clowning was in sharp contrast to the rigours of their physical training and the concerns some of them doubtless harboured as to what they'd gotten themselves into. Often at night, they didn't get the sleep they expected. Sometimes they were called out for a special exercise and driven in enclosed trucks miles into the countryside, dropped off one by one, and told to make their way back to camp while negotiating various obstacles in a simulated war situation. The task was made considerably more difficult by the fact they were wearing full equipment weighing thirty-five to forty pounds. The shortest of these endurance treks took four hours and even then, upon their return, they still had to clean their rifles and uniforms. John said he "literally crawled up the stairs" when he got back from the first of these special night exercises. He knew he had chores to do, but he was too tired and was past caring. He stumbled into the shower, turned the water on, and stood there with his uniform on and his rifle at his side. It was not the act of a thinking person. He said he spent a week in solitary on bread and water.

Sometimes he had nightmares. One night his mates found him sound asleep, sitting atop the cupboard that was attached to the end of the set of bunk beds that he shared with another man. They woke him and had a laugh, then all went back to bed. Although John had no idea how he'd gotten on top of the cupboard, he knew he'd been having a nightmare. The story became a great joke. John remembered both the joke and the nightmare.

Despite the suppressed anxiety and frequent punishments, John looked back on his months of SS training "as a pleasant time." There was much that impressed him and that he admired. He said it was a great period of development of body and mind, mostly of self-discipline, and noted he learned to do a full day's work. But most important was the feeling "he belonged," which he attributed to two things. First, there was the sense of brotherhood that had arisen from the intense, shared experience of their training. Second, the contrast to the sense of not belonging and of periodic outright rejection he had

152 A SNAKE ON THE HEART

felt for much of his life. To feel you belonged was a good feeling, he said. He was twenty-five at the time.

John claimed that while he trained at the München-Freimann barracks, Hitler made an inspection tour. He also claimed he had a "personal meeting" with the Führer during this chimerical visit.[168] John said that Hitler spoke on two occasions to some of the men individually, once while inspecting the troops and also while inspecting one of the barracks. As John had room duty at the time, he said it was his responsibility to call the men to attention and report to the senior officer. He told me Hitler shook his hand and spoke to him. A "great power came out of Hitler," John claimed. He described it as a "magnetic power, power that you could feel in his handshake." Hitler asked John his name and where he came from and he spoke of the places John had lived. He didn't talk ideology. He said he admired the Netherlands for its cleanliness, its racial purity, and the fact that it had not been in a war for a long time.

"It's sad that Germany has to go to war again," Hitler reportedly said.

The Führer "felt Germany had to be fighting." Germany only invaded the Netherlands because it was necessary, Hitler maintained. He said the Netherlands made it necessary by making a pact with England to allow British troops to attack Germany through Dutch territory. (Seyss-Inquart had made this claim on May 25.)[169] John said

---

[168] Although Hitler was frequently at his Berghof retreat on Obersalzberg mountain near the town of Berchtesgaden and stayed at least twice at Munich during these months, I have found no evidence that he made a tour of inspection at the Dachau SS training facility. See Nicolaus von Below, 66–77.
[169] Quoting and paraphrasing Seyss-Inquart's May 25, 1940, public statement, de Jong and Stoppelman write in *The Lion Rampant* (8) that no one believed "the German fairy tale of an Allied invasion of the Rhineland via Holland, a plan which—supposedly—had been frustrated by the German attack on the Netherlands." Strategic necessity was the real reason for the German invasion of the Low Countries. Sir John Peck, "The Dutch Government in Exile," *Holland at War Against Hitler: Anglo-Dutch Relations, 1940–1945*, ed. M. R. D. Foot (London: Frank Cass, 1990), points out (14–15) "that at the time of the Munich Agreement, the German Luftwaffe did not have a single bomber

Hitler struck him "as a strong and kind man [who was] also very honest [and who] believed in what he said."[170] But he also noted that Hitler's words "weren't that impressive," despite the great power that came from him.

Hitler believed Germany's survival depended on its military strength. The battle with the Soviet Union—suspended by the two countries' Non-Aggression Pact of August 1939 until it was repudiated by Operation Barbarossa (the German invasion of June 22, 1941)—was to be an all-or-nothing struggle, an ideological and military fight to the finish. "A victory of Bolshevism over Germany would not lead to a Versailles Treaty but to the final destruction, indeed to the annihilation of the German people ... In face of the necessity of defence against this danger, all other considerations must recede into the background as being completely irrelevant," the Führer explained in 1936. His goal, therefore, was to make the German army the best in the world in terms of training, equipment, and especially "spiritual education."[171] In addition to personally drawing up "detailed instructions for officers about taking an interest in the personal problems of their men," he also saw to it that officers and men received the same food.[172] Addressing 3,600 young officers on January 18, 1939, he said "a deeply soldierly spirit" permeated Germany.[173]

Interwoven with John's experience of belonging and brotherhood was what he termed "great platoon spirit." It was a mystery to him.

---

capable of dropping bombs on London from bases then under German control, and it was not until Hitler had overrun most of western Europe that he was in a position to bomb London at all." Peck references a memorandum of May 23, 1939, in which Hitler tells his Chiefs of Staff: "Dutch and Belgian air bases must be occupied by armed force.... We must aim at securing a new defence line on Dutch soil up to the Zuider Zee."

[170] At the time John told me this, I would have described him the same way he described Hitler. In fact, like Hitler, John was a man who believed he was privy to special cosmic guidance and lied with abandon.

[171] Ian Kershaw, *Hitler, 1936–1945: Nemesis* (London: Penguin, 2000), 20.

[172] Shirer, 548 (personal problems). Kershaw, *Hitler: Nemesis*, 404 (same food).

[173] Kershaw, *Hitler: Nemesis*, 167.

He marvelled in 1976 that he still didn't know how this spirit was instilled. It is a matter of record that morale in the German armed forces was exceptionally high during the early part of the war. American journalist William Shirer said it was one of the reasons "for the incredible German victory in the West" in 1940. Speaking about "this entirely new esprit," he remarked, "It was based on a camaraderie between officers and men that would have shocked the old Prussian generals and surprised the French, the British and even, I think, the American military."[174] According to British General Sir John Hackett, "the German Army ... was to the end of the war the most highly professional of any in the field."[175]

John said the German officers received no special privileges. They had to carry the same weight and perform the same routines as the enlisted men. If an officer's men had to walk, the officer walked too. Officers were expected to lead the charge into battle, to be the first ones out of the trenches. John said that if an officer gave an order but didn't lead, the men didn't have to obey. The Germans, he added, lost a great many officers during the war as a result. The recruits were told repeatedly that they had to do well for their comrades and their platoon. Prior to long marches or field exercises, it was stressed that the objective was not to finish first or to be judged the best. The vital thing was to get the whole platoon back, even if it meant carrying a comrade's equipment for him or carrying the comrade himself.

SS recruits pledged "obedience unto death." The organization's motto was, "My honour is loyalty."[176] Loyalty, John said, meant implicit trust among the members of a platoon, and it followed that

---

[174] Shirer, 548.
[175] Sir John Hackett, "Operation Market Garden," *Holland at War Against Hitler: Anglo-Dutch Relations, 1940–1945*, ed. M. R. D. Foot (London: Frank Cass, 1990), 162.
[176] *The SS*, 38 (obedience), 31, 40 (honor is loyalty). Paul Berben, *Dachau, 1933–1945: The Official History* (London: Norfolk Press, 1975), 35 (honour is loyalty). Felix Kersten, *The Kersten Memoirs: 1940–1945* (London: Hutchinson, 1956), 169 (honour is loyalty). A second motto of the SS was: "Be more than you appear" (Kersten, 303).

complete honesty was expected throughout the ranks. Himmler told his doctor, Felix Kersten: "No cupboards are locked in the Waffen SS. None of them would even dare to take a cigarette belonging to his comrade." Himmler went on to say: "Plunder is certainly not a gentlemanly crime … I have had a special 'Notice on the Confiscation of Enemy Property' published, which every member of the Waffen SS has to carry in his pay-book." After giving Kersten a copy of this document, Himmler read aloud: "To take the goods and chattels of the unarmed civilian population is unchivalrous and unworthy of the SS. The Reichsführer SS's orders on the 'sanctity of private property' also apply in time of war even to the enemy."[177] But while Himmler "sounded like the stoutest crusader for decency, cleanliness, and justice," these apparent qualities were "all histrionics," according to Hans Gisevius, who called the Reichsführer SS "the greatest actor of his time."[178]

John said the punishment for stealing was death. During his training, one man stole two packs of cigarettes from another man. Everyone was required to witness how such matters were handled. All four companies were called out to the parade ground and lectured on how the thief, who stood before them, had let them all down and disgraced the uniform he was wearing. Honesty, they were told, was part of that uniform, and someone who would steal from his comrades would also steal from conquered people, and that would not be permitted. German conduct in occupied countries was to be beyond reproach. The man didn't have the honour to wear the uniform, even in death, so one by one insignia were torn off the man's uniform. Then he was put before a firing squad and shot.

According to Himmler, it was "essential that every man be committed to the very roots of his being."[179] Such commitment would work both to the positive and the negative. It would support both acts

---

[177] Kersten, 240.
[178] Gisevius, 141.
[179] *The SS*, 38.

of selfless heroism and cold, soul-denying evil. The SS insignia included the skull and crossbones that meant, John said, they would not be taken alive, if possible. They were instructed to always keep one bullet for themselves. Himmler had said as much in a speech in 1938.[180] The practical effect of this was that the men would make every effort, often at great danger to themselves, to save a wounded comrade. But this loyalty to each other was to be matched by loyalty to the cause—by "obedience unto death."

"Comradeship can become the means for the most terrible dehumanization—and it has become just that in the hands of the Nazis," observed Raimund Pretzel, a final-year law student, in a 1939 manuscript, which he wrote after attending a proto-military training camp for several weeks. "They have made all Germans everywhere into comrades. Comradeship relieves men of responsibility for their actions, before themselves, before God, before their consciences. Their comrades are their conscience, and give absolution for everything, provided they do what everyone else does."[181]

John admired the German emphasis on ethical behaviour, but he would learn time and again of contrary German conduct. When he was back in the Netherlands, he would witness the escalating violence of the German reprisal strategy. Multiple sources agree with John that if the resistance or an unaffiliated group ambushed and killed German soldiers or assassinated one or more of their officers, and the Germans could not find those responsible, they would execute ten or so randomly selected men from the street or town in question or arrest all the men and deport them to labour camps in Germany. Violence was always met with greater violence; the harshness of the

---

[180] In his Reichskristallnacht speech of November 8, 1938, Himmler said (Padfield's paraphrasing, 239) that members of the SS "should never be taken prisoner"; rather they should kill themselves.

[181] Lauren Kramer, "Witness to the rise of Nazism," *Vancouver Sun*, Saturday, January 11, 2003, D19. Raimund Pretzel was a post-World War II "journalist renowned for his political analyses." After his death in 1999, his son discovered the manuscript and published it as *Defying Hitler: A Memoir* by Sebastian Haffner (the pseudonym Raimund had chosen to use).

reprisals increased as the war went on. According to Nicolaus von Below, Hitler's Luftwaffe adjutant, "It had always been [the Führer's] principle to retaliate like for like or worse."[182]

Equally disturbing was what Rudolph Höss, the future Commandant of Auschwitz, referred to as "the continual demands [on SS men] for self-conquest and uncompromising hardness."[183] Himmler could not have agreed more. When he observed the liquidation of one hundred people, many of them women, at Minsk in August 1941, "he began to feel ill. He reeled, almost fell to the ground, and then pulled himself together," an eyewitness, who had stood next to him, reported. But Himmler's physical revulsion didn't deter him. He simply wanted the killing to be cleaner, more efficient.[184] Almost two years earlier, following the invasion of Poland, Hitler had said at a meeting on October 17, 1939, that their work—what decades later would be called "ethnic cleansing"—would not be restricted by legalities or "our normal principles."[185]

The foundation of Nazi ideology was hatred of the Jews. This hatred necessitated a fight to the finish. In mid-1941 Himmler said: "The Jews are the eternal enemies of the German people and must be exterminated.... If we do not succeed in destroying the biological basis of Jewry, some day the Jews will annihilate the German *Volk*."[186] This extreme perspective, which originated with Hitler, justified any excess, and it frequently encountered circumstances that prompted the final choice: with us or against us. There was no middle way. Indeed, devotion to the Final Solution was such that it would undermine the German war effort by diverting scarce resources and destroying much-needed manpower.[187] Had the Nazis been somewhat less fanatical and more flexible in pursuing the Final

---

[182] Von Below, 153. See also Kershaw, *Hitler, 1936–1945: Nemesis*, 519.
[183] Padfield, 274.
[184] G. S. Graber, *History of the SS* (New York: David McKay Co., 1978), 157, 160 (clean, efficient).
[185] Kershaw, *Hitler: Nemesis*, 245.
[186] Padfield, 334.
[187] Maass, 125.

Solution they might have prolonged the war and murdered even more of those they characterized as subhuman.

Ideology was central to the last stage of John and Constant's SS training, which took place in December but may have commenced some weeks earlier. Constant, according to his statement of February 14, 1947, began this part of his training in mid-November when he returned from a ten-day leave in Rotterdam. "I was transferred to Berchtesgaden where I would complete my theoretical training," he said. Constant and John were likely at the same place. In 't Veld refers to "Oberau bij Berchtesgaden" (Oberau near Berchtesgaden). This construction of the place name is used to distinguish it from other Oberaus in the region. John said he went to Oberau with "three or four hundred others" and with "several hundred," but In 't Veld gives a precise number: 132.[188] As this number represents just 10 per cent of the approximately 1,224 men approved and sent for training from the SS recruiting office in The Hague by September 11, it may suggest that John and Constant were considered part of the cream of the crop and subjected to special expectations and training.

According to John's statement of October 29, 1946, he and the other Dutch SS trainees "who had followed the course [were] sent back to the Netherlands" on December 24, 1940. Although In 't Veld is less clear about the date of return, he does describe the general role these men were to play: "In December 1940, a number of Dutch recruits to the *SS-Standarte 'Westland'* were sent back to the Netherlands, where they were intended to provide the Dutch SS with a trained nucleus. The Dutch SS as a whole was expected to be a political-cum-military elite of gainfully employed men from all walks of life, prepared to devote all their free time to serving the SS ideal. In theory, the candidates were expected to be of good character, in prime physical condition and of 'Aryan descent'.... The volunteers were expected to spread German ideas, more specifically followed by SS

---

[188] In 't Veld, 321. Constant's statement of February 14, 1947. In 't Veld (321) uses the phrase *"ideologische vorming"* (ideological formation) for this part of their training.

ideas, in their own homes and circles." John was aware of this. He told me that upon return from Germany he chose to train other Dutchmen for the SS in Holland. This claim was not true, but his statement that "these people were to be a postwar elite" was entirely on the mark.[189]

---

[189] John's statement of October 29, 1946, 1. In 't Veld, 1513 (political-cum-military elite), 1509 (spread German ideas, SS ideas).

12

MUDDLED AND MYSTERIOUS, JOHN MAKES HIS OWN WAY IN THE SS

John started work for the SS in Utrecht in January 1941. Constant did the same in The Hague. While the basis of this information is straightforward in Constant's case, it is typically convoluted in John's, featuring layers of invention and cover-up.

After spending the Christmas period with his wife in Rotterdam, Constant reported in early January, as instructed, to "the recruiting office in 's-Gravenhage" (the site of the Dutch royal residence in The Hague and the defacto capital in the western part of the Netherlands), which posted him to the nearby Reich Commissariat. He said his "work was to deliver mail to the various departments and receive and direct visitors."[190] After "about 6 weeks," his boss found him a position in Rotterdam so he would not have to commute each day. Although there is some confusion when he changed jobs, it appears he moved "about mid February."[191] Located at the SD office on the Westplein, "I was

---

[190] Constant's statement of February 14, 1947.
[191] While Constant's statements of September 14, 1945, and February 14, 1947, say he was at the Reich Commissariat in The Hague for "1½ months" and "about 6 weeks" respectively, it is uncertain when he started in Rotterdam. His statement of January 7, 1946, says it was February 1, 1941, but his statements of February 14, 1947, and October 24, 1946, say it was "about mid February" and March 1, respectively.

stationed as an interpreter," he said, "but also continued to do the work as porter and orderly. Later I was transferred to the S.D. office [at Rotterdam's] Heemraadssingel.... I was assigned to the 'Press' division, and was required to translate Dutch newspaper and periodical articles into German, and the purpose of this was to gain control over what was being written in the Netherlands daily newspapers."[192]

The Heemraadssingel was known as the home of the *Aussenstelle Rotterdam*, "the local office of the *Sicherheitspolizei* (German Security Police)." According to historian Frank van Riet: "The stronghold of the Rotterdam *Aussenstelle* in the Heemraadssingel soon became a feared and hated institute. Under the supervision of H.J. Wölk and with the help of informants, staff members and their Dutch assistants acted ruthlessly against those who refused to contribute towards building a New [Germanic] Europe, and against those who were already being continually hunted."[193]

John claimed he experienced considerable anxiety and upset during both his return trip to the Netherlands and upon his arrival. He told me he was emotionally conflicted; he didn't want to do the work to which he was to be assigned. He and other Dutch recruits who had agreed to police work following their session with Himmler in August knew they would soon be working with the SD. John said they were going to serve as a supplement to the SD and the Gestapo, two groups, he said, that worked very closely. Indeed, the SD would become "almost omnipotent [in the country] … with its ubiquitous spies and informers."[194] John became part of this vast network. He admitted it after the war, saying he became involved in early 1944. Although there is no definitive proof, I suspect his involvement may have begun in August 1941. But it appears he sought to cover this up.

---

[192] Constant's statement of February 14, 1947. Attachment to Blauw's email of February 14, 2007.
[193] Frank A. M. van Riet, *Enforcement under the new order: The political history of the Rotterdam police during the Second World War*, PhD thesis, Amsterdam Institute for Humanities Research, 804, accessed June 5, 2021, https://dare.uva.nl/search?identifier=78ea43ea-1b64-4567-a646-528c92b313c0.
[194] Maass, 123.

John told me the train home from Munich was destined for The Hague where all the new Dutch SS men were to be dispersed to different areas. But he didn't make it that far. Prompted by his anxiety, he said he "jumped train" at Arnhem, after crossing the German border. He went home to Hilversum where, as the story goes, he was arrested a week later and taken to SS headquarters at Utrecht. He successfully "spun them a line" to the effect that he had mistakenly thought they were free to go home until they were called up.

The idea of a dramatic, Hollywood-style jump from a moving train was rendered ridiculous when, in 2005, Hans told me that his dad had arrived home with a new (and undamaged) peddle car for his Christmas present. A couple of years later, when I had John's statement of October 29, 1946, translated, I learned that he had told Dutch officials basically the same story he told me, except for two details. First, there was no jump. "I got off the train at Arnhem, even though this was illegal," he said. Second, there was no arrest. Instead, he claimed he received "a written enlistment" from the SS a "few weeks later," which instructed him to report to Utrecht where he "was appointed to be the typist. After 14 days I was moved to ... The Hague."[195] It is an open question if he was at The Hague "from January 15, 1941" as his statement says or if he arrived there sometime closer to the end of the month.

This uncertainty is minor compared to the false victimization he sweepingly claimed he suffered by taking the "illegal" step of leaving the train at Arnhem. "All the boys that were in the proper train were appointed to a good post," he maintained in his statement, "but because I was not part of the division, I missed out and I did not get a post." He went on to claim that he worked at The Hague "as an office assistant till August 1941," an intentionally misleading and conveniently ambiguous role.[196]

Thus, John was posted to The Hague from mid-January or soon after. Susan recalled that she and Hans joined him there in March.

---

[195] John's statement of October 29, 1946, 1.
[196] John's statement of October 29, 1946, 1.

They lived in a "crappy" one-room apartment on Koningin Emmakade, close to Prins Hendrikstraat. It was their home for the next eight to ten months.

***

The latter half of January through February 1941, the time when John was on his own in The Hague, is an important period during the occupation. Despite the German policy of the "gentle hand" and the widespread Dutch desire for normalcy, various acts of the German authorities had started to reveal their true disposition, especially regarding the Jews. This sparked resentment and would soon lead to resistance and the remarkable anti-pogrom strike of February 25 and 26, 1941, in Amsterdam, an event John never mentioned to me. Whether this omission is an indication of non-involvement on his part or of cover-up is not known. What is known is that the *Ordnungspolizei* (Order Police), of which John was likely a member, was on average "made up of three to four battalions stationed in Amsterdam [and] The Hague [in the provinces of North Holland and South Holland, respectively] and in Tilburg" in the southern province of North Brabant. Their "purpose was to suppress mass agitation and opposition and to control the Dutch police." They "were thrown in during the strike in North Holland in February 1941." But they had little to do in The Hague compared to Amsterdam where most of the action occurred.[197]

Soon after John and Constant had departed for their SS training in mid-1940, the Germans began a slow introduction of anti-Jewish measures, the number and impact of which increased during the autumn. By early winter, every Jew in the country was affected. On September 30, provincial and local officials were given the definition of a Jew: "anyone with one Jewish grandparent who had been a member of the Jewish community."[198] By October 26, all civil servants

---

[197] In 't Veld, 1507.
[198] Moore, 55.

and teachers had to complete a Form A (Aryan) or a Form B (non-Aryan), thereby identifying their racial origin. A month later, government departments, educational institutions, and local authorities were instructed to dismiss their Jewish staff members because of the "action of world Jewry against the occupying authorities."[199] Some 2,000 Jewish state employees, or about 1 per cent of the Dutch public sector, lost their jobs.

These actions turned Dutch law on its head and demonstrated Dutch impotence when confronted by the increasingly apparent demands of Nazi ideology. Things only got worse in early 1941. On January 10, a new law required all Jews to register with the government by February 24. The incidence of noncompliance was negligible. Approximately 160,000 registration forms were submitted. They identified 140,000 full Jews, 15,000 half Jews, and about 5,000 quarter Jews.[200] This was a critical development: "the first step to isolation and eventual deportation and extermination."[201]

Compared to the German military regimes in Belgium and France, the structure of the Netherlands' civilian occupation government allowed "greater scope ... for the SS, German police and the Nazi Party to operate unhindered." Not only was there a bigger German police presence in the Netherlands than in France—approximately 5,000 compared to less than 3,000—but more of the Netherlands' Jews died: 102,000, or 73 per cent, compared to 40 per cent in Belgium and 25 per cent in France. Seyss-Inquart and Hanns Albin Rauter, the Higher Police

---

[199] De Jong and Stoppelman, 213.
[200] Hirschfeld, 145n, 145–146. Moore, 64 (high compliance), 65 (140,000 full Jews). Anthony Anderson, "Anne Frank Was Not Alone: Holland and the Holocaust," (a transcript of a lecture presented at the University of Southern California on October 24, 1995, is no longer on the internet where it was previously available for years.), 13 (140,000, 15,000, 5,000). The Nazis' Law for the Protection of German Blood and German Honour of September 15, 1935, also known as the Nuremberg Laws, in Matthew Hockenos's words (118), "divided Jews into three categories: those with three or four Jewish grandparents were full Jews; those with two Jewish grandparents were 'first-degree half-breeds'; and those with one Jewish grandparent were 'second-degree half-breeds.'"
[201] Moore, 65.

and SS leader and Generalkommissar for security matters, were in almost constant conflict, especially "for primacy in control of Jewish affairs," a clear indication of its importance to their superiors. Although Rauter was officially junior to Seyss-Inquart, he frequently "overshadowed" the Reichskommissar because of his wide-ranging authority that was answerable only to Himmler.[202]

When the Dutch civil service was being purged, signs saying "Jews not welcome" or "Forbidden for Jews" started appearing in windows of restaurants, cafés, and coffee houses, particularly those in large cities where most Jews resided: 77,252 in Amsterdam; 13,829 in The Hague; 11,006 in Rotterdam; and 1,908 in Utrecht.[203] The signs were the result of intimidation by pro-Nazi paramilitary groups such as the NSB's *Weerafdeling* (WA), or Defence Section, and the NSNAP's *Sturmabteilung* (SA). These actions, which provoked public protest, were sanctioned by senior occupation officials and supported by the *Sicherheitspolizei* (Sipo) and the SD. At one point "nearly every café and restaurant" in Amsterdam displayed such signs, but most were quickly removed by the business owners. When the campaign in support of these signs began again in early February, violence erupted.[204]

To defend against Nazi attacks, members of the Jewish working class organized Jewish action groups called *knokploegen* (KP).[205] On

---

[202] Moore, 2 (percentages), 9 (greater scope), 74 (primacy in Jewish affairs), 193 (number of German police). Maass, 57 (overshadowed). Hirschfeld, 24 (far-reaching autonomy; officially subordinate). Moore (140) writes: "the SS had the upper hand in the Netherlands. The fact that the country was under civilian rather than military control gave the SS leadership and its representatives much more leverage in the various power struggles that took place, and led to the ideological aims of the regime taking precedence over economic necessity."

[203] Attachment to Frank van Riet's email of July 5, 2009, to the author: "Persecution of the Rotterdam Jews," 3.

[204] Moore, 59, 89, 66, 67. Van Riet, 3, 4. In reference to the 1930 census, Moore states (25) that "80 per cent [of the country's Jews] lived in the seven largest cities with a further 10 per cent in the smaller towns and 10 per cent in the countryside." Moore also references (66) de Jong who "notes that in December [1940], *Generalkommissar* Schmidt had given permission for the paramilitary NSB *Weerafdeling* (WA) and the *Sturmabteilung* (SA) of the NSNAP to take action against Jews …"

[205] Maass, 64, 64n (*Knokploegen*). Moore, 67, 71.

the evening of February 11, a forty-man WA contingent was beaten back by one of these groups. During this battle, Hendrik Koot, a Nazi, was badly hurt and died three days later. These were pivotal developments. The Germans characterized the Jewish fighters as terrorists and justified their response on that basis. The day after the Koot incident, German officials summoned Amsterdam's Jewish leaders and demanded the creation of a twenty-member Jewish Council. Abraham Asscher, an important diamond merchant, became one of two co-chairmen. Addressing 3,000 Jews in the Amsterdam Diamond Exchange's great hall on the thirteenth, he announced the council's formation and "insisted that, on account of the recent disturbances, all weapons held in the Jewish quarter be handed in to the police." This was the start of "the self-appointed elite of the Jewish Council acting as a conduit for Nazi demands."[206]

Amsterdam remained tense, notwithstanding Asscher's call to disarm. Although smaller in size, there were more incidents and clashes on Saturday, Sunday, Monday, and Wednesday the nineteenth. Himmler approved a massive escalation in the German response. On Saturday, February 22, the old Jewish quarter was sealed off by six hundred regular German police. That afternoon, four hundred young Jewish men were arrested, publicly mistreated, and sent to Buchenwald concentration camp, where forty of them died by June. The survivors were moved "to the extermination camp Mauthausen and before the end of the year only one remained alive."[207] According to one historian, the term "'Mauthausen' became synonymous with certain death."[208]

The arrests and brutality caused Amsterdam to seethe "with indignation, fury and yet a feeling of impotence."[209] An outlet for the people's anger was quickly provided when the Communists called for

---

[206] Moore, 69, 70 (weapons; conduit).
[207] Harry Paape, "How Dutch Resistance Was Organized," *Holland at War Against Hitler: Anglo-Dutch Relations, 1940–1945*, ed. M. R. D. Foot, (London: Frank Cass, 1990), 76.
[208] Maass, 114–115.
[209] Paape, 65.

a strike. They'd been publishing the underground newspaper, *De Waarheid* (The Truth), since November, so were able to quickly mimeograph thousands of pamphlets calling for a one-day strike in response to the persecution of the Jews.[210] Following a mass meeting on the evening of Monday, February 24, the strike began on Tuesday morning with the streetcar drivers and quickly spread to other parts of Amsterdam, and within a few hours assumed "a general character" involving "between 200,000 and 300,000 out of a total population of not quite 800,000."[211]

The Germans were stunned. Strikes were anathema and unknown to the Nazi regime. De Jong states it "was the first and only antipogrom strike in human history." But historian Bob Moore concludes, "while the heroism of the strikers and the 'particular dignity' of the action cannot be denied, it has to be said that it failed to deflect the Germans from their task."[212] The strike was quickly suppressed. Approximately two hundred strikers and strike organizers were arrested. On March 13, the day after Seyss-Inquart called for a policy of "for us or against us," fifteen members of the Geuzen, one of the first Dutch resistance groups, and three of the strikers were executed by firing squad in the dunes near Scheveningen, just north of The Hague.[213]

According to Hirschfeld, the February strike was "a caesura in the history of the occupation [and] had an important catalysing effect on both sides." Maass calls it "the point of no return." True as these conclusions are, they do not tell the whole story. Moore adds: "The responses to German actions against the Jews ... were not repeated.... The civilian population [did] not have a particularly good record.... Only a minority organised themselves into formal resistance groups

---

[210] Maass, 65.

[211] Paape, 76 (general character), 77 (200,000 to 300,000).

[212] Maass, 66 (no German strikes under the Nazi regime). De Jong, *The Netherlands and Nazi Germany*, 8. Moore, 73.

[213] Paape, 76 ("strike collapsed rapidly"), 77 (strike "completely fizzled out"; 200 arrested), 78 (executions). Maass, 66–67 (strike suppressed). Hirschfeld, 80 (for us or against us).

to help those in hiding and in a few cases to take direct action against their German oppressors."[214]

***

From what I can tell, John made no attempt to cover up any involvement he may have had with the Order Police during February in The Hague or elsewhere. This is in marked contrast to the evening he told me he "jumped train" at Arnhem, for, in addition to that misleading term, he told two tall tales meant to hide what he really did in the SD.

In his second story, he twice emphasized that he and the other new Dutch SS men, upon completing their training in Germany, had changed from their green wartime SS uniforms to their black peacetime SS uniforms—the uniforms the SS wore before the war. Where I had been naïvely captivated by the idea that John had "jumped train," his repetition about the change of uniforms affected me in the opposite way. It caused that information to jump out and alert me that it was important, even though I would not understand how for a quarter century, until I started studying the occupation much more intensively. Although I don't know if such a change of uniforms took place, I strongly suspect that John's statements were intended to insulate and distance him from an odious fact. The SD's green-uniformed *Ordnungspolizei* (Order Police) would become known as the notorious *Grüne Polizei* (Green Police) for their central role in the roundup and deportation of the Netherlands' Jews.

John's third story was a wholesale fabrication he told me about his job in the SS. According to this yarn, sometime after his arrival in The Hague he encountered one of the officers who had instructed him at Oberau. He maintained that this officer had been tasked with establishing a training program for Dutch SS volunteers. The officer supposedly asked John what he wanted to do within the SS and gave

---

[214] Hirschfeld, 80. Maass, 67. Moore, 257.

him options that the other men did not receive, which contradicts John's claims that he missed out on a good post and, as a result, was a lowly office assistant. John told me he chose to train other Dutchmen for the SS. He put this in the best possible light, describing the SS as "a peace corps" and "a protection corps" dedicated to safeguarding Germany, the Führer, and Nazi ideals. He also said he held the rank of lieutenant and that his training job was "sort of an honour position" and only part time.

But the Netherlands Institute for War Documentation advised there is no evidence "for the existence of [SS] training programs in The Hague" and, as was the case with John and Constant, all SS recruits "were transported for their training straight to Germany." The only training facility for the Dutch SS in Holland was the SS-Schule Avegoor, which was founded in the spring of 1941 and located in Ellecom, near Arnhem. It was for members rather than new recruits. While John took obligatory courses at the SS-Schule Avegoor for several weeks on two occasions, there is no evidence that he was an instructor there.[215]

In claiming he was a trainer for the SS, John may have appropriated the core of this story from the work history of his friend Koos Doornbos. After graduating from Hilversum's police academy as a candidate police inspector, Koos was accepted into the *Politie Opleidings Bataljon* (police training battalion) at Schalkhaar where his course ran from January 12, 1942, until August 1942. He became the "Watchcommander" at the Buitenhof police station in The Hague on September 1, 1942. Six weeks later, on October 15, 1942, he was appointed drill master and teacher for special laws with the 1st Police Company in The Hague. He was selected for this position by Captain Kohlbrugge, who had been his commanding officer at Schalkhaar and was now in charge of the 1st Police Company. Koos served in this position as a lieutenant until the

---

[215] Netherlands Institute for War Documentation – attachment to Hans de Vries's email of August 4, 2005. John's SS card (DNA, CABR 109786) provides the dates he attended the SS School at Avegoor, as does his statement of October 29, 1946.

end of the war when he was arrested and jailed as a collaborator. He was imprisoned for six and a half months.[216]

Rather than being anxious and upset during his trip home from Germany, I suspect John's spirits were buoyant and his outlook optimistic. He was full of the sense of belonging and brotherhood that had been instilled in him during his SS training. He was confident Germany would win the war. He told me Hitler was creating a broader confederation based on the idea of brotherhood and he saw a "home for himself" in that confederation.

To these points we can add the perspective of two of his children. Hans said his father liked being in the SS; he liked the power and authority of it. And, of course, there was the uniform, which—at least at the outset—was an overt expression of his new sense of belonging. After being viewed as a stumblebum and potential good-for-nothing for much of the 1930s, to now be seen as a success, as someone intimately connected with the winning side, must have been a heady experience, indeed. Hans said John spoke "with positive energy" about being in the SS. Constance told me John loved the framework the SS gave him, the companionship, and the feeling he belonged.

But all was not sunshine and roses. John's situation was also fraught with prickles and barbs. When he told me about Hitler's broader confederation and his place in it, he also said he sometimes felt guilty because he'd ignored his call-up notices and he wasn't fighting for the ideals he saw Hitler standing for. This guilt was the lesser of two prods, for had he acted differently, such action would have conflicted with his philosophy against wars and fighting. This conflict would recur and come to a head several months later.

He was also confronted by a more immediate issue: ostracism. It caused the anxiety and upset he genuinely experienced upon his return home. He told me old friends turned on him overnight, he was met with extreme anger and rejection, which greatly affected him, and there was

---

[216] Dutch Central Bureau for Genealogy *Persoonskaart* for Jacobus Jan (Koos) Doornbos. Attachment to Dr. N.C.H.M. Heitman's letter of November 30, 2005, to the author.

incredible mistrust and no moderation or tolerance. It was not unlike the more widespread hostility directed at collaborators immediately after the war, he added. What is surprising is John's surprise. It is a glaring example of him not being prepared for the consequences of his actions, and it suggests he sometimes functioned at a certain distance from reality, that "he had his head in the clouds," as Miek said.

***

During the latter stage of their training in Germany, John and Constant likely met an important Dutch SS officer. This man was to influence John in at least a couple of notable ways: one, triggering compliance and conformity; the other, just the opposite. Johannes Hendrik (Henk) Feldmeijer visited Oberau in December 1940 to meet the Dutch SS trainees who would soon be under his command and who were to be the nucleus of the SS's "political-cum-military elite" in the Netherlands. Described as "unscrupulous and cold-blooded,"[217] "the typical *Kämpfer*, the fighter who lives for the struggle,"[218] and "one of the worst criminals of the Nazi Party,"[219] Feldmeijer and his mentor, Meinod Marinus Rost van Tonningen, were the two most important Dutchmen at the ideological core of the Nazi power structure in the Netherlands. A lawyer, financial expert, and representative of the League of Nations in Vienna, Rost van Tonningen had connections with German and Austrian Nazis. One of these, Franz von Papen, the former German Chancellor and current Ambassador to Austria, helped arrange a private meeting for him with Hitler on August 20, 1936. Rost van Tonningen and Feldmeijer subsequently bonded in the NSB over their opposition to Mussert and their support for the Netherlands being part of a Europe dominated by National Socialist Germany. When, three weeks prior to the German invasion, the Dutch government declared a state of

---

[217] De Jong quoted in Hirschfeld, 324.
[218] In 't Veld, 1512.
[219] Van der Zee, 106.

emergency, it arrested and interned twenty-one pro-German Dutchmen, including Rost van Tonningen and Feldmeijer. The two men shared a cell at Fort Ooltgensplaat before they were moved to France where they were later freed by the Germans. They arrived back in The Hague on June 2. That evening Rost van Tonningen met with Himmler and Seyss-Inquart. Soon after this meeting, Rost van Tonningen introduced Feldmeijer to Rauter. Rauter appointed Feldmeijer to establish and lead the Dutch SS. Rost van Tonningen would go on to serve as president of the Netherlands Bank, head of two ministries, including Finances, and chairman of the Dutch East Company, among other roles. While Himmler referred to him as his "oldest confidant in the Netherlands," Mussert, after the war, bitterly viewed Rost van Tonningen as "'the' man for the Germans. In their patronage he was well ahead."[220]

Feldmeijer was fanatically devoted to the Nazi cause. The "*Silbertanne Aktion*" of September 1943–September 1944 occurred "largely ... under his leadership." Innocent citizens held as hostages were murdered in reprisal when resistance groups attempted to kill Dutch Nazis. Feldmeijer's value to the Nazis was such that despite criminal offences for embezzlement and theft, Rauter advised Himmler on April 30, 1942, "Feldmeijer is not to be replaced at present."[221] After Feldmeijer was killed on February 22, 1945, when his car was strafed by an Allied plane, Himmler told Rauter in a telegram, "I am very sad over the death of Feldmeijer.... Don't bother to offer my condolences to Mister Mussert, as he never knew what kind of man he had in Feldmeijer."[222]

By 1940, Rost van Tonningen was Mussert's "arch-enemy," yet that September, at Seyss-Inquart's insistence, Mussert was grudgingly obliged to appoint Rost van Tonningen to be one of two deputy leaders of the NSB. Mussert was also adamantly against the creation

---

[220] Hirschfeld, 269 (oldest confidant), 271 (patronage).
[221] Hirschfeld, 324 (his leadership; criminal offences; not to be replaced).
[222] "Henk Feldmeijer," Wikipedia, accessed October 22, 2018, https://en.wikipedia.org/wiki/Henk_Feldmeijer.

of the Dutch SS but was forced to relent on that subject as well.[223] Despite his relatively weak position, Mussert unrealistically sought to become Hitler's top deputy in the Netherlands and to have the whip hand, especially after the war was won. But the SS also wanted this pre-eminence and power; it was not only better positioned but also considerably more successful in this struggle. This NSB-SS conflict was a situation of "fierce if covert political infighting."[224]

Mussert was a "cocky little man who resembled Mussolini" and who, late in the war, became "convinced that the Führer was held prisoner by Himmler."[225] In 1944, Anne Frank would refer to Mussert as "that fat pig," while Hirschfeld sums him up as a colourless and naïve individual who over-estimated his own abilities; nonetheless, NSB members had a "strong fixation … on their *Leider*" and, in the eyes of the public, the NSB was the "Mussert Movement."[226] Contemptuous of Mussert, Rauter referred to him as 'that little Philistine.'"[227]

When Mussert and the SS again locked horns in early 1941, it was over "the introduction of non-active 'Supporting Members' (*Begunstigende Leden*)" of the Dutch SS.[228] The BL initiative was Feldmeijer's attempt to emulate Himmler who, as In 't Veld says, "tried to infiltrate the State, the party and society in Germany by granting selected individuals honorary SS titles."[229] The opportunity to be a supporting or beneficial member was intended to make the SS "more attractive to the middle classes and other sectors of the population who were opposed to the NSB." Such members were expected "to provide material and spiritual support."[230] Although the

---

[223] Hirschfeld, 278 (arch-enemy), 279 (bitterly opposed).
[224] In 't Veld, 1514.
[225] Van der Zee, 102, 104.
[226] Anne Frank, *The Diary of a Young Girl: The Definitive Edition* (London: Penguin Books, 2001), 322. Hirschfeld, 261 (naïve; over-estimated), 308 (colourless; naïve; strong fixation; Mussert Movement).
[227] Maass, 57.
[228] Hirschfeld, 287, 287n. In 't Veld (257) says *Begunstigende Leden* memberships "probably" became available during spring 1941.
[229] In 't Veld, 1514.
[230] Hirschfeld, 287.

initiative was only marginally successful (memberships peaked at about 4,000 in August 1944),[231] female memberships were permitted, and one of these, dating from 1941, belonged to John and Constant's mother. This fact, which Wim revealed in his statement of October 23, 1946, surprised Miek when I informed her of it in 2007.[232] "She was not a fanatical person, not at all," Miek said of their mother. "She was not interested in politics, no more than the usual person." But their mother did hate the NSB, Wim said in his statement.

Miek believed it was likely that John, rather than Constant, had convinced their mother to become a supporting member of the SS. John had a marked ability to influence people, she said. Moreover, Susan once told me that John could persuade anyone to do anything. This enlistment of John and Constant's mother was entirely consistent with the expectation that SS men would disseminate German and SS ideas "in their own homes and circles." What is more, in January or February 1944, Wim, with John and their mother's assistance, also became a supporting member of the SS.[233]

Presuming John was responsible for his mother joining the SS, this is the example that shows him in compliance and conformity with Feldmeijer's goals. Where John was not compliant was in response to Feldmeijer's expectation that his men would be "a reservoir for the Waffen-SS" and would volunteer to serve on the front lines.[234] Replenishing these lines became an ongoing priority following the watershed launch of Operation Barbarossa, Germany's invasion of the Soviet Union along a 2,000-kilometre front on June 22, 1941. It began history's most devastating and brutal war, according to Kershaw, what Hitler regarded as an existential, no-holds-barred confrontation with the Bolshevik ideology.[235]

---

[231] In 't Veld, 1514 ("just under 4,000"); Hirschfeld, 287 ("barely 4,000").
[232] Wim's statement of October 23, 1946 (DNA, CABR 107966).
[233] In 't Veld, 1509 (homes and circles). Wim's statement of October 23, 1946.
[234] University of Groningen biography of Feldmeijer, accessed October 22, 2018, https://www.rug.nl/research/biografie-instituut/knomhout?lang=en.
[235] Kershaw, *Hitler: Nemesis*, 357 (Barbarossa), 579 (2,000 km), 388 (most barbaric), 466 (life-and-death; not European rules).

Feldmeijer led by example. He served at the front in Yugoslavia and Greece in April and May 1941 and in southern Russia from June 1942 to March 1943. He "exerted great moral pressure on the [Dutch SS] members to report to battle units of the *Waffen-SS*," according to In 't Veld. In fact, "members of the Dutch SS were constantly siphoned off by the *Waffen-SS*."[236] Speaking of himself as an SS training instructor, John told me that all SS instructors had great pressure put on them to go to the front. We know John was neither an SS instructor nor an office assistant, but there is nothing definitive regarding his specific role with the SD at this time, except his rank: he was promoted from *Rottenleider* to *Onderschaarleider* on April 16, 1941.[237] As noted earlier, he was probably a member of the Order Police. A story he told decades later lends weight to this supposition, as will be discussed.

Insight into John's attitude and response to the pressure to go to the front can be found in his statement of April 22, 1947. In it he expresses his feelings about Pieter Schelte Heerema, a member of the Dutch SS (and one of John's superiors) who claimed to have "switched sides and joined the resistance in 1943." Heerema is of interest for several reasons. Chiefly, when John worked for the Dutch SS's Intelligence Service, he wrote a report on Heerema. The report, which contains new information on Heerema's life and his service in the Dutch SS, is dated April 26, 1944. It says Heerema "was a member of the N.S.N.A.P., but joined the Dutch S.S. after it was founded" in May 1940.[238] Details in the report indicate that John knew Heerema, just as he knew Heerema's sister, Tine. For example, the report states

---

[236] "Henk Feldmeijer," Wikipedia, accessed October 22, 2018, https://en.wikipedia.org/wiki/Henk_Feldmeijer (tours of duty). In 't Veld, 1514 (moral pressure), 1513 (constantly siphoned off).
[237] John's SS card (promotion). For information on *Onderschaarleider*, see footnote 3 in the Prologue.
[238] John Petersen's report on Pieter Schelte Heerema is in the Dutch National Archives file CABR 91103. It was translated for the author by both Léon van der Hoeven and Elisa Goudriaan. I melded and modified their translations for clarity; the report as quoted in these pages is not a literal translation but is consistent with the meaning and spirit of the original Dutch text.

that Feldmeijer sent Heerema to Munich at the end of 1940 "to appraise S.S. trainees [possibly including John] slated to become officers." When Heerema returned to the Netherlands, he "became 'Standaardleider' of the 'Standaard 4' [in which John served. Standaard 4 was one of five Standaarden (regional districts) into which the Dutch SS was organized. Standaard 4 covered the provinces of South Holland and Zeeland and had its headquarters at The Hague.] During this period, [Heerema] occupied himself with gathering information about Mussert,"[239] an activity that may also have involved John who, in 1944, tracked popular opinion—particularly hostility—regarding the NSB. (See Appendix 1 for more on Heerema.) Speaking about Heerema's pro-German period, John made the following personal declaration in his statement: "Piet Heerema filled me with huge aversion because he had incited and even forced many—very many—boys to go to the front, whereas he himself had gone to extremes not to be sent to the front."[240]

I suspect the pressure John felt to go to the front was most acute in mid-1941 and in 1944. I also suspect this pressure, in the first instance, provides much of the context for the mysterious change that occurred in his SD status in August 1941.

***

August 1941 was the month John started working part time for the Centrale Arbeiders Levensverzekeringsmaatschappij (Central Labourers' Life Insurance Company), known as De Centrale, at

---

[239] John Petersen's report on Pieter Schelte Heerema. According to sources I've cited, both Feldmeijer and Heerema were sent to Germany in late 1940 to meet the Dutch SS trainees who were soon to return to the Netherlands. Although the thought has occurred to me that Feldmeijer may have delegated this responsibility to Heerema and may not have gone himself, I have no proof of this.

[240] John's statement of April 22, 1947 (DNA, CABR 91103), 7. Translations per Dr. Maili Blauw (attachment to email of December 9, 2009, to the author, and Haydee Oord (email of December 21, 2009, to the author).

Rijnstraat 24 in The Hague. How and why did this happen, and who in the SS approved this change in his status? I don't have answers for these questions, only inferences.

In his statement of October 29, 1946, John makes several remarkable assertions about the June–August 1941 period. "In connection with the increasing persecution of the Jews I asked to be dismissed from the Germanic S.S. in June of 1941," he says. "At that time I informed them that I was not allowed to serve as a State German in a Dutch formation. They never accepted this resignation.... In August 1941 I was asked if I wanted to join the Sicherheitsdienst [SD]. I did not feel anything for that, so I declined. In response I got an assignment to go to the concentration camp in Ommen as a trainer. I refused this as well. As a result I was marked a conscientious objector and they threatened to send me to a concentration camp. I stood behind my refusal, which resulted in my full dismissal from the S.S.... When I got my full dismissal from the S.S. I went looking for a regular job."[241]

He goes on to say that he was "employed as an office worker" at De Centrale from "August 1941 to December 1943" and that from "October 25, 1941 till December 1, 1941" he "attended compulsory retraining" at the SS-Schule Avegoor. These latter statements are true, but why would he mention the five weeks of retraining, which contradicts his claim about receiving a "full dismissal from the SS"? (Although previously he had also stated, "They had never accepted [his SS] resignation.")

In addition, two of his other claims are implausible. First, the Ommen concentration camp (also known as Camp Erika) was under construction and would not receive its first prisoners until June 19, 1942, more than nine months later. Second, it is extremely unlikely that he would have revealed his German citizenship to his SS masters. His SS card gives his nationality as *Nederlandsche*, which is consistent with how he represented himself to the SS and how they, in turn, regarded him. I believe he was lying in his statement when he said he tried to resign from

---

[241] John's October 29, 1946, statement.

the SS on the grounds that "a State German" could not serve in a Dutch formation. This lie was intended to present him in a more positive light to the Dutch officials, both those who were questioning him and those who ultimately would rule on his case. Admitting in mid-1941 that he was German could have led to the discovery of his Wehrmacht call-up notices, which was something he deeply feared; and, one way or another, it could have led to him being assigned to the fighting forces, something he consistently sought to avoid.

It appears he employed a similar ruse in his statement of April 22, 1947. Indeed, the first thing he says in it is, "I am a German citizen." He goes on to explain why he agreed to work as an informer for Feldmeijer's Intelligence Branch in 1944. "Seeing the situation wherein I found myself *as a German citizen* [my emphasis], ... I did not dare turn down the request," he told them, "and all the more because I saw nothing sinister here."[242]

John's 1947 statement also says that he met G. A. Scholte, his Intelligence Service supervisor, through the Dutch SS in the Netherlands "in early 1944"; Scholte "had gotten me interested in the Intelligence Service."[243] This wording suggests a certain willingness on John's part and is different to the duress implied by his previous statement: "I did not dare turn down the request." But what if John's work as an informer really began in August 1941 when he started with De Centrale? In the unclear and undoubtedly complex circumstances that led to his working for that company, it's not hard to imagine him experiencing duress regarding some scenarios and willingness to accept others.

In 't Veld tells us the German SS conducted "espionage activities against the NSB" from the beginning of the occupation and, when it

---

[242] John's statement of April 22, 1947, 1. In the same statement, John noted (1): "The goal of this Intelligence Service was the gathering of reports of a political nature. It was to include summary reports of the reactions/opinions of the people of the Netherlands generally, and in particular, the reactions of the people of the Netherlands to the measures and regulations imposed by the Occupying Forces."

[243] John's statement of April 22, 1947, 1, 2.

became possible, implanted Dutch members of the SS "within the NSB." He adds, "Both organisations [the Dutch SS and the NSB] formed their own intelligence agencies. The 'Centrale Inlichtingen Dienst' (Central Intelliegence Agency) of the NSB was disbanded in 1941 on the orders of Rauter." In 1942, when he learned that the Dutch SS was also running its own intelligence agency, he ordered it shut down as well. But "Feldmeijer ignored the order and let his subordinates continue their work," which, according to In 't Veld, is "a clear indication of the standing" of the Dutch SS compared to the NSB.[244] In due course, Feldmeijer's Intelligence Service earned "Rauter's agreement" and "co-operated closely with the German *SD* in the Netherlands ... in spying on the *NSB*."[245]

In his 1947 statement, John says that the information he collected for Scholte "concerned the general moods and casual conversations of the Dutch people, and especially about the issues which inflamed the hatred of the average person for the N.S.B." Kershaw refers to this activity as SD "soundings" of public opinion. John adds, "I was asked to specialize my reporting and to focus on people in the commercial sector."[246] I suspect John's statements may also apply to possible work he did with or for Heerema during the first eight months of 1941 and to his work at De Centrale starting in August 1941, although there is nothing more than circumstantial evidence to support this assertion. This evidence includes the fact that De Centrale had recently been "transformed into a *'deutschfreundliche'* [German friendly] and to some extent NSB organization." Fewer than half a dozen Jewish employees had been "laid off on 4 March 1941." A new board was put in place when "De Centrale started a new company" on January 15, 1942.[247]

---

[244] Attachment (quoting In 't Veld, pp. 249–250) to Frank van Riet's email of August 23, 2018, to the author.
[245] In 't Veld, 1513.
[246] John's statement of April 22, 1947, 2, 1. Kershaw, *Hitler: Nemesis*, 596.
[247] Jacques van Gerwen emails to the author of September 14, 2005 (re: company transformation and layoffs) and August 25, 2005 (new board; new

The postwar prosecution document about John's collaboration case says he worked at De Centrale as an administrative assistant.[248] He told me he calculated rates of risk to develop premiums, which was work he had not done before. He claimed he was hired because he knew the head of the company, a Dutchman who'd supposedly taken SS training with him at Dachau and Oberau, and who was excused from regular SS duty because of the importance of his job. On August 8, 1940, Rost van Tonningen appointed Jan Antony Hendrik van der Does and Jonkheer J. van den Bosch to De Centrale's Board of Directors and, on May 1, 1941, elevated Van der Does to chief executive officer. Both men served in these positions until the end of the war, and both had notable connections to their benefactor. Rost van Tonningen and Van der Does were old friends; Van den Bosch, who was in the SS, was Rost van Tonningen's nephew. These appointments can "be seen in the light of the assignment given to Rost van Tonningen in June 1940 by Himmler and Seyss-Inquart to further the nazification of different organizations."[249]

Did John, in fact, know the head of the company, Van der Does and, if so, did Van der Does hire John? Given John's "best lie" theory and Van den Bosch's SS membership, the latter seems the more likely candidate to have enabled this move for John. But Feldmeijer or his second-in-command, Willem Heubel, or one of their subordinates, such as Standaardleider Heerema, are also candidates. The context for John's move could have included some or all of the following factors:

---

company). Van Gerwen is the author of *De Centrale Centraal* (his doctoral thesis). In the latter email, he advised that *De Centrale* or *De Centrale Arbeiders Levensverzekeringsmaatschappij* were shorthand for *De Centrale Arbeiders-Verzekerings- en Depositobank NV* and that the "translation of *Levensverzekeringsmaatschappij* is life insurance company." The address of the company was Rijnstraat 24-26-28 in The Hague.

[248] Prosecution document.

[249] Jacques van Gerwen email to the author of August 23, 2005 (board and CEO appointments; Van den Bosch in SS and nephew). Hans de Vries letter to the author of August 5, 2005 (Van der Does's appointments; nazification assignment). In 't Veld, 338 (old friends). "Jonkheer" (or young lord) is an honourific in the Low Countries denoting the lowest rank within the nobility.

John resisting pressure to volunteer for the Waffen-SS; John manipulating one or more of his Dutch SS colleagues to find him a suitable assignment or otherwise assist him in this regard; and one or more of John's resource-strapped superiors being open to finding a mutually beneficial solution, one that would look after a member of the brotherhood, a member who was thought of highly enough to have been promoted a few months before.

***

Rauter wanted the approximately six hundred members of the Dutch SS to swear their oath to Hitler in a ceremony during the summer of 1941. But Mussert caused what Himmler called "nauseating difficulties." The issue this time was whether the NSB or the SS would control the police in the country.[250]

Meanwhile, John and Susan, possibly with Stanni's help, completed what Susan called "all those papers." Prospective brides of SS men had "to prove that they were of pure Aryan blood, uncontaminated at least since 1750 by the presence of any Jewish, Slavic, or similarly inferior ancestors."[251] They were finally married on October 24, 1941, at the German embassy, not at city hall, as John told me. Their landlord was their witness. Susan recalled that she was "really pregnant." According to John, young Hans, who was close to turning five, publicized the wedding by announcing to all the neighbours: "Mommy and Daddy are getting married." Sometime between the marriage and Harald's birth on January 18,

---

[250] Hirschfeld, 302–303 ("about 600 members"; NSB-SS conflict; nauseating difficulties). In 't Veld, 1516 (NSB-SS conflict). While Hirschfeld says there were "about 600 members of the Dutch SS," In 't Veld (1506) maintains there were "no more than a few hundred ... Dutch collaborators" in the *BdS* (*Befehlshaber der Sicherheitspolizei und des SD*). The *BdS* consisted, in part, of Section III – Intelligence, Section IV – Gestapo, Section V – Kripo (police departments). The Gestapo and Kripo together were the *Sicherheitspolizei* or *Sipo*.
[251] *The SS*, 29.

1942, they moved to 293 Waalsdorperweg in the Clingendael area at the north end of the city.

The day after the wedding, John and Constant attended what Constant termed "refresher courses" at the SS-Schule Avegoor. If the dates given in their respective postwar statements are correct, Constant, who was a *Rottenführer*, was there until December 12, almost two weeks longer than John. He had been the Commandant of the Dutch SS's Rotterdam "Storm," a unit of perhaps several dozen men, since August.[252] That Christmas, he participated in a march sponsored by the NSB's WA.[253] He remained commander of the Rotterdam "Storm" unit until October 1942.[254]

The long-delayed oath-swearing ceremony was finally held on May 17, 1942, at The Hague. Witnessed by Himmler, Mussert administered the oath. "I swear to you, Adolf Hitler, as Germanic Führer, loyalty and bravery!" the troops repeated aloud. "I promise you, and the superiors appointed by you, obedience unto death! So help me God!"[255] Not to be outdone, Mussert required three thousand

---

[252] Constant's statement of February 14, 1947, 4 (Avegoor refresher courses), 5–6 ("'Storm' Rotterdam"). The Dutch SS was organized into five regional *Standaarden* (regiments). In theory, each *Standaard* was sub-divided into groups of four men, troops of forty, and storms of 125 (including the commander and deputy), with a total of three storm units plus staff, comprising about 375 men. But in practice, according to In 't Veld (1513), "Dutch 'standards' were considerably smaller than German *SS-Standarten* … on average they numbered 130 men," or about one-third the size. Thus, noting that Rotterdam and The Hague were *Standaard* IV's largest cities, Constant's Rotterdam Storm may have been a quarter to half as large compared to the storm benchmark of 125 men.

[253] G. M. van Veen's report (Rapport) of March 26, 1946, on Constant (DNA, CABR 70629).

[254] Constant's statement of February 14, 1947.

[255] John's statement of October 29, 1946, 2. Hirschfeld, 302 (date), 294n (oath; Mussert conducts swearing-in; Himmler present). In 't Veld, 1516 (Mussert conducts swearing-in). Immediately after the oath ceremony, John was at the SS-Schule Avegoor for more "compulsory retraining" for the May 18–31 period, according to his October 29, 1946, statement, 2.

NSB officials to swear an oath to him in a ceremony on June 20, to which the SS was not invited.[256]

In an environment of clashing egos and power struggles, it may have been John's good fortune to have received modified status in the SD. Starting in August 1941 or before, he presumably had a hand in creating the circumstances by which he came to divide his time between the SD and De Centrale Life Insurance Company and had desks at both organizations. In the view of Adriaan Korteland, an insurance industry colleague and long-term member of the NSB who John met in February 1942, John was "not strongly German oriented." At the same time, according to Korteland, John adhered to the SS perspective in that his "contempt for Mussert was apparent."[257] In 1944, Korteland joined Feldmeijer's Intelligence Service where he worked with John.

There are two pieces of evidence that indicate John maintained a desk or an office with the SD. In the first, the office is an incidental or background detail in a story he told me about a laundrywoman who worked for his German detachment and was having an affair with one of the detachment's officers. The story includes the words, "The next day at the office."

The second piece of evidence is more interesting, for it lends weight to my speculation that John may have worked for Feldmeijer's Intelligence Service prior to 1944. It concerns Piet Heerema's sister, Tine, who gave a witness statement in 1947 about John's work with the Intelligence Service. Tine, like her brother, was initially pro-Nazi but later changed her views, worked against the Germans, and ultimately went underground to avoid capture.[258]

"The Dutch are only used during the war, however after it, they will be a subordinate people. The authority of the National-Socialism

---

[256] In 't Veld, 1516.
[257] Korteland's statement of April 14, 1947 (DNA, CABR 91103/PRA The Hague, dossier 21717). Researcher Dr. Maili Blauw's attachment to her email of December 3, 2009, to the author.
[258] Tine Heerema's statement of January 25, 1947 (DNA, CABR 91103). Attachment to Blauw's email of December 3, 2009.

in Germany is only based on violence," John quoted her as saying in a report he allegedly wrote on April 5, 1944.[259] In his statement of April 22, 1947, John claimed he "did not compile the report on Tine Heerema, although I recognize that is my signature at the bottom of the report. I do not remember how or when my signature was attached to the report."[260]

Shortly after Piet joined the resistance in the spring of 1943, Tine received a request from him that she should stay with the SD to collect information for the resistance. About June, she got hold of a file on her brother, after which she said she wanted to leave. She intentionally misbehaved toward Hauptsturmführer Eggerstadt and was assigned to another department as a result. She then asked to be dismissed from her service with the SS. Her request "was granted on 1 September" 1943. Five months later, on February 1, 1944, she went underground for the duration of the war. During this time, Dutch detectives undertook an intensive search for her.[261]

It is noteworthy that the critical report John supposedly filed against Tine was dated April 5, 1944, more than two months after she had gone into hiding. This report reads in part:

> She is said to have been fired due to the situation with Obersturmführer Gerhards, in which she played a role. As from that moment on she became dead set against the SS and

---

[259] John's alleged report of April 5, 1944, on Tine Heerema (DNA, CABR 91103). Attachment to Blauw email of December 9, 2009, to the author.
[260] In his statement of April 22, 1947, John says (2): "After SCHOLTE and I talked about Piet HEEREMA and Tine HEEREMA, SCHOLTE came to me with someone from the S.D. The S.D. man asked me to go with him to Binnenhof 7 in 's-Gravenhage [the SD office where Tine worked as a typist from the autumn of 1941 through August 1943] to gather more information about Piet Heerema. This I did and compiled a transcript of the conversations. In these conversations Tine HEEREMA was mentioned, but I did not compile the report on Tine HEEREMA, although I recognize that it is my signature at the bottom of the report. I do not remember how or when my signature was attached to the report."
[261] Tine Heerema's statement of January 25, 1947. Attachment to Blauw's email of December 3, 2009 (September 1, 1943; February 1, 1944; detectives).

Germany, which became clear from her conversations.... Although the aforementioned miss Heerema feared possible measures from the SD against her, or as she said it "she could not tell everything, otherwise she would be in trouble," in spite of this fear she expresses herself everywhere in a [sic] anti-German and anti-National-Socialism way. As such she is a danger for the SD and her deportation from the Netherlands would be desirable. It may also be expected that she is in touch with her brother.[262]

Tine was shown a copy of this report when she made her statement on January 25, 1947. In that statement she said she made a concerted effort to conceal her antipathy to the Germans while she worked for the SD. But she made one exception and that was with John, who she said she trusted completely.[263] Upon reviewing John's alleged report, she commented: "The—for me—incriminating passages in the letter that you show me, indeed represent the content of a conversation that I had with Petersen. I have not considered Petersen to be capable of such a thing. Any link between him and some sort of intelligence service I have never suspected."[264] She refers to a single conversation, but I presume that she and John conversed on multiple occasions for her to have come to trust him as fully as she says she did.

As Tine worked as a typist with the SD Gruppe III B office, Binnenhof 7, The Hague, for twenty-two months, and as her employment ended on September 1, 1943, her start date would have been November 1, 1941. But the fact that she was assigned to another department toward the end of her employment may mean, if that department was at another address, her employment was

---

[262] John's alleged report of April 5, 1944, on Tine Heerema. Attachment to Blauw email of December 9, 2009.
[263] Heerema's statement of January 25, 1947. Attachment to Blauw's email of December 3, 2009 ("fully trusted").
[264] Heerema's statement of January 25, 1947. Attachment to Blauw's email of December 3, 2009.

longer than twenty-two months and, therefore, began before November 1, 1941.[265]

Thus, the referenced conversation between Tine and John took place sometime between the autumn of 1941 and August 1943. Presumably, it also occurred at or in proximity to an SD office where they both worked or at least frequented. It also tells us something about John's relationship with the Intelligence Service, although it does not necessarily prove that he worked for that organization during this period. What it does demonstrate, if John's work for the Intelligence Service only occurred in 1944, is that he sometimes offered up information he was privy to from pre-1944.

---

[265] Heerema's statement of January 25, 1947. Attachment to Blauw's email of December 3, 2009 ("22 months"; "another department").

13

JOHN, CONSTANT, AND WIM

THE HOLOCAUST IN HOLLAND AND THE DUTCH RESISTANCE

John's son Hans turned six on December 2, 1942. He remembers travelling by train with his family from The Hague to Hilversum, where the extended family would gather at Oma Stanni's at least several times each year. He mentioned Easter, Stanni's birthday in October, St. Nicholas Eve and Day on December 5 and 6, Christmas, and New Year's Eve. They would sleep over on some of these occasions. This is important, for it means John, Constant, and Wim had at least this much contact and opportunity to discuss the war and the occupation and their respective and diverse situations. While John and Constant, as SD policemen, were involved in the roundup of the Jews starting in mid-1942, Wim was working for Barend van Leeuwen's cattle business, which was directly connected to his resistance work of feeding people, including Jews, who were in hiding. Wim and Van Leeuwen's daughter, Dina, became engaged in 1942, cancelled the engagement the following spring, but got together again in late 1943 or early 1944 and married that March.

The intention of the invasion of the Soviet Union in mid-1941 was to win *Lebensraum* (living space) for the new thousand-year German

Reich. Hitler had written about it in *Mein Kampf*; Himmler promised it in the form of farms for SS service, including when he spoke to John, Constant, and the other unhappy SS recruits in August 1940. Coupled with the invasion were "the first stages of the war of annihilation against the Jews in Eastern Europe," which, in turn, "brought the possibility of deporting the Jews from the Netherlands that much closer."[266] From the start of 1941 to the middle of 1942, the Nazis "moved from the vague and ill-defined notion" of a Final Solution to resolve the Jewish Question to the promulgation of the Commissar Order that sanctioned the murder of partisans and civilians to the policy of mechanized genocide enunciated at the Wannsee conference of January 1942.[267]

Annihilation and liquidation were even mentioned in several important public statements such as "The Jews Are Guilty," an article by Propaganda Minister Joseph Goebbels, which appeared in *Das Reich* on November 16, 1941. After referencing Hitler's January 30, 1939 "prophecy" of the "annihilation of the Jewish race in Europe," Goebbels declared: "We are experiencing right now the fulfilment of this prophecy."[268] Hitler himself, in a speech to a full house at the Berlin Sportpalast on January 30, 1942, the ninth anniversary of his assumption of power, spoke of "the annihilation of Jewry."[269] Ten days later, in "a hysterical broadcast," the Führer added that "the Jews will be liquidated for at least a thousand years!"[270]

During this same period, however, the Nazis decided that public statements on extermination could prove counterproductive. They could prompt protests and increase resistance in the countries of occupied Western Europe. For this reason, the Nazis would promote the euphemism of Jewish resettlement.

Mass deportations of Jews from Germany to Poland began in October 1941, nine months before similar deportations began from

---

[266] Moore, 77.
[267] Moore, 62.
[268] Kershaw, *Hitler: Nemesis*, 482. John Cornwell, *Hitler's Pope: The Secret History of Pius XII* (New York: Viking Penguin, 1999), 278.
[269] Kershaw, *Hitler: Nemesis*, 494.
[270] Cornwell, 281.

the Netherlands. Senior German occupation officials had held meetings in May and October 1941 to work out the mechanics for removing the Netherlands' Jews. In addition, Jews were increasingly isolated by new regulations. Starting in February 1942, their identity papers had to bear a stamp indicating they were Jews. As of early May, they had to display a six-pointed yellow star on their outer clothing.[271]

When, on German instruction, Dutch officials placed "Forbidden for Jews" signs in restaurants, cafés, and other public places that spring, they encountered virtually no resistance, unlike the situation that prevailed during the winter of 1941. The muted response of the public didn't change once the deportations began in July 1942, although the underground press did encourage protest, and Protestant and Roman Catholic church leaders sent a petition to Air General Friedrich Christiansen, German military commander in the Netherlands, urging more humane treatment of the Jews. Deputy Reich Commissioner Fritz Schmidt responded that "the Jews cannot stay in Holland …. They will return to the place they came from, … covered with lice." He added that people who sympathized with the Jews would "be treated in the same way."[272]

It was a restatement of Seyss-Inquart's policy of "For us or against us."

***

All was in readiness. The machinery was in place. The vast action that lay behind John's subsequent cover-up and false claims—of jumping train at Arnhem, of changing from his green SS uniform to his black one, of being a trainer of SS recruits—was about to begin.

---

[271] SHOAH Resource Center, "Order to wear the Jewish Star, The Netherlands 29 April 1942," accessed May 19, 2021, https://www.yadvashem.org/odot_pdf. Moore, 89 (identity papers; star; "after 4 May … rigorously enforced"), 264–5 (identity cards; "3 May - Introduction of the Jewish Star for people and houses").

[272] De Jong and Stoppelman, 290 (underground press), 192 (Schmidt quote). Moore, 266 (protests).

In the autumn of 1941, Amsterdam's Jewish Council had had its responsibilities expanded to represent Jews throughout the country, although Jewish Councils continued to function in other cities. A few months later, the Germans began removing all non-Dutch Jews to Westerbork, a concentration and transit camp in the northeast of the country, while relocating Dutch Jews from the provinces to Amsterdam. Westerbork had originally been built by the Dutch government in 1939 to house Jewish refugees. In early 1942, the Germans commissioned the construction of twenty new barracks at the camp.

On June 22, 1942, Adolf Eichmann, the Berlin-based SS *Obersturmbannführer* (lieutenant colonel) responsible for executing deportation and extermination policies, advised the German Foreign Office of plans "to 'evacuate' 40,000 Jews from occupied France, 10,000 from Belgium and 40,000 from the Netherlands to Auschwitz at the rate of 1,000 per day."[273] On June 26, Amsterdam's Jewish Council was told of Eichmann's order. On July 4, the *Zentralstelle für jüdische Auswanderung* (Central Office for Jewish Emigration), which had been established in Amsterdam in March 1941, generated letters for the first 4,000 Amsterdam Jews, many of them refugees, selected for deportation. The letters, which were delivered the next day, required the recipients to report to the Zentralstelle on July 13 for transport between the fourteenth and seventeenth. When many didn't report, "some 700 Jews were taken from the streets in all parts of the city and held at the German Security Police Headquarters as hostages against the appearance of those called-up [sic]. The threat was that they would be sent to Mauthausen if the quotas were not met. The Jewish Council ... sent out a circular to all those called up, 'we feel obliged to impress on you the gravity of the situation. Think carefully. The fate of 700 fellow-Jews is at stake.'" The tactic worked; 962 people reported and were transported to Westerbork. But the number collected was "considerably smaller" than the Germans

---

[273] Moore, 77 (execution of policies), 91 (advised Foreign Office of quotas).

wanted, and it had to be supplemented with other Westerbork inmates to fill "the quota of deportees sent to Auschwitz" on July 15 and 16.[274]

There were seven more middle-of-the-night transports from Amsterdam to Westerbork before the end of the month. During the same period, "a further 3,948 people" made the three-day train trip from Westerbork to Auschwitz. "These first call-ups and deportations set the pattern for … the next 15 months."[275]

The start of the roundup of the Jews in Amsterdam set the stage for similar roundups in Rotterdam and The Hague. The mechanics and the results were similar, particularly the problem of large numbers of summoned people not reporting. The process in Rotterdam began in late July when 6,000 Jews from the ages of sixteen to forty received summonses sent by registered mail from the Zentralstelle.[276] The summons directed them to report to Shed 24 at an out-of-the-way port in south Rotterdam. This shed, which was enclosed by a two-metre-high wall, was used as the assembly point from July 30, 1942, to April 10, 1943. The summonses were phased in three blocks of 2,000. Compliance dropped with each block. Of the first 2,000 summoned, 1,020 reported; but from the second and third groups, only 800 and 520, respectively, arrived at Shed 24, yielding a total of 2,340 of the 6,000 summoned. In The Hague, the result was even worse. Four thousand Jews were summoned in mid-August to report to Staatsspoor Railway Station, but just 1,200 were transported to Westerbork on August 18.[277]

---

[274] Moore, 91 (Jewish Council advised), 75 (*Zentralstelle* created), 93 (July 4 letters; 700 Jews; other quotes).
[275] Moore, 94 (transports; set the pattern).
[276] Attachments to Frank van Riet's email of July 5, 2009, to the author: "Summary," 2 (6,000 Jews), and "Persecution of the Rotterdam Jews," 7 (ages sixteen to forty; Zentralstelle).
[277] Attachments to Frank van Riet's email of July 5, 2009, to the author: "Summary," 2 (Shed 24), and "Persecution of the Rotterdam Jews," 7 (Shed 24 assembly point; high wall), 9 (blocks of 2,000; compliance). Van Riet's email of August 23, 2018, to the author notes that roundups in The Hague were

One of several methods used to address these shortfalls was to arrest "the families and dependents still at large" of Jewish men being held in Dutch work camps.[278] In late August, the SD ordered Group 10, the Rotterdam police force's "political branch," which was responsible for undertaking most of the measures against the Jews, to pick up Jewish families in several locations. Group 10 consisted of "nearly all pro-German members of the NSB."[279]

In The Hague, the roundup process was modified on the evening of August 22 when the target was Scheveningen. Instead of summonses, the police resorted to direct arrests of Jews named on a list from the Zentralstelle. The Jews, who had their house keys confiscated, were held at the Academy for Visual Arts on Prinsessegracht until they were sent to Westerbork via Station Staatsspoor. Soon after, the temporary collection point was changed to the Jewish House at Paviljoensgracht 27. The Sipo and The Hague police conducted night arrests of a group of Hungarian Jews on September 16 and of the families of Jewish men in Dutch labour camps on October 2.

These latter arrests were part of "a series of mass raids which took place [in Amsterdam, Rotterdam, and The Hague, as well as in the provinces] on 2–3 October" and resulted in the apprehension of 13,000–15,000 Jews. According to Moore: "The only Jews safe from this action were those with exemptions, baptized Protestants, and people suffering from diphtheria, scarlet fever or typhoid." He also

---

organized "in the same way as in Rotterdam." "The Neighbourhood Speaks: Walk through 'the vanished Jewish neighbourhood' in The Hague" (see: https://izi.travel/nl/2dc2-the-neighbourhood-speaks/en) provides updated information to an earlier booklet of the same name published by The Hague's city archives (Haags Gemeentearchief). "Station Staatsspoor" was replaced in September 1973 by Den Haag Centraal Station, which was built on adjacent land.

[278] Moore, 98.
[279] Frank A. M. van Riet, *Enforcement under the new order: The political history of the Rotterdam police during the Second World War*, PhD thesis, Amsterdam Institute for Humanities Research, 242 (ordered by SD; anti-Jewish measures), 802 (political branch; pro-German), accessed June 5, 2021, https://dare.uva.nl/search?identifier=78ea43ea-1b64-4567-a646-528c92b313c0.

observes that the scale of the operations "required the services of all the available agencies. German and Dutch police, NSB, Dutch SS and German Nazi Party functionaries and the personnel of the *Zentralstelle* were all drafted."[280] This fact is one of several pieces of circumstantial evidence that points to John's involvement in at least some of these roundups.

***

"Himmler and Rauter aimed at the complete militarization and Nazification of the Dutch police." When a program of compulsory ideological training at police stations produced inadequate results, Rauter, in October 1941, "ordered the creation of genuine Nazi police schools or training battalions," which resulted in the establishment of the police academy at Schalkhaar. "Dutch police officers … received six months of 'intensive training'.… They were instructed by German and Dutch SS and police leaders and subjected to a mixture of Prussian barrack drill, Nazi ideology and practical training in the struggle against organized resistance."[281] Graduates became known as "Schalkhaarders," and "the name Schalkhaar soon became a synonym for police terror and the worst form of collaboration with the occupying power."[282]

This was the situation that faced John and Constant. It trapped them, but, after different lengths of time, they both broke away, Constant completely, John less so.

I have no evidence for this, but I wonder if Constant was relieved of his command of the SS "Storm" Rotterdam in October 1942 because his superiors thought he lacked ardour or stridency regarding the roundup of Jews? I pose this question based on what we know about the occupation authorities' expectations of the German and

---

[280] Moore, 98.
[281] In 't Veld, 1507 (militarization and Nazification). Hirschfeld, 168, 168n (date of Rauter's order).
[282] Moore, 200 (Schalkhaarders). Hirschfeld, 168 (synonym).

Dutch police and about Constant's involvement with the Rotterdam raids to round up Jews.

In March 1943, Constant made a courageous decision. He volunteered for the Russian front. The decision was remarkable because it meant leaving his wife, who was seven months pregnant, and their eighteen-month-old son, as well as putting himself in much greater danger than if he remained in Rotterdam. Although Constant may not have fully appreciated it at the time, the recent German defeat at Stalingrad in late January and early February was a watershed event. It shifted the war's forward momentum to the Russians and their allies and ratcheted up the likelihood that German soldiers would be wounded or killed.

Constant addressed his decision in all five statements he made while imprisoned as a collaborator after the war. He was clearest in the fourth of these, on November 26, 1946: "I had to choose either to take part in the raids on Rotterdam or to serve at the front. I chose the latter because I did not agree with those raids." His fifth statement adds two important details: first, "because ... I already had a difference of opinion about my duties, I answered [Hermann Göring's] call for military service"; second, he was also promoted that month to *Unterscharführer*.

Constant was not the only member of the Rotterdam police establishment to undergo a change of status. The whole organization went through a general shakeup. At the beginning of March, Major H. G. Scholz, Commander of the Order Police in South Holland and Zeeland, relocated his office from The Hague to Rotterdam. "He ordered, supervised, and interfered in promotions."[283] Perhaps Constant's promotion was an inducement to volunteer. The increased pay would help him support his growing family. If the promotion was an inducement, perhaps it was viewed by Constant's superiors as a way

---

[283] Frank A. M. van Riet, *Enforcement under the new order: The political history of the Rotterdam police during the Second World War*, 804 (Scholz moved office; interfered with promotions), accessed June 5, 2021, https://dare.uva.nl/search?identifier=78ea43ea-1b64-4567-a646-528c92b313c0.

to relocate someone who didn't possess the right attitude and who had had, in Constant's words, "a quarrel" with the SD. Speculation aside, two final points need to be mentioned. First, at the time of Constant's decision, most of the raids to round up Rotterdam's Jews had been completed. Second, we do not know how far back his "quarrel" and the "difference of opinion" about his duties went.

John would have agreed with Moore's assertion that a Dutch policeman had "few logical choices if [he] was ordered to participate in actions against the Jews."[284] He wrote emphatically in his 1951 letter: "Know Henry, that whatever I did in the war, it was always a result of a position, into which I was forced, and <u>that I have always tried to choose the least worse of the two</u>!" I sense that this is an acknowledgement that circumstances sometimes trapped him in awful situations and, try as he "always" did, he could not always escape or even mitigate the appalling actions to which he was "forced" to be a part. But he did change his general circumstances when he joined the Schutzgruppe at the start of 1943.

Membership in the Schutzgruppe was a requirement for German men living in the Netherlands who were not in the regular army due to age or disability. John said these people were forced to join. Despite this, he told me he volunteered. I suspect, however, that what he really did was manipulate the situation to serve his own ends. In his statement of October 8, 1945, he said he obtained "a certificate from a heart-specialist which certified that I was unfit for active military service."[285] He told me that there had always been something wrong with his heart. It had been discovered, he said, during a checkup prior to his going to nautical school. This interpretation of events could also explain the reference in his 1951 letter to him receiving a third call-up notice "from the German authorities," presumably meaning the Schutzgruppe.

He maintained he joined the Schutzgruppe as a cover; it was a matter of "going into the lions' den for safety's sake." But safety from

---

[284] Moore, 200.
[285] John's statement of October 8, 1945, 2 (medical certificate).

what? In his statement of October 8, 1945, he said, "During the war I did not wish to be involved with the German army. I avoided that by means of a certificate from a heart-specialist … " But it is possible that an additional motivating factor was a desire to minimize his availability for raids to round up Jews and others. To what extent, if any, this reduced his availability for such raids is unknown.

John claimed he also resisted and tried to undermine these raids in more direct ways. With a desk at an SS office, he was well placed to know about raids. He told me about one instance when he, wearing his SS uniform, went around a neighbourhood, warning residents of an impending raid. But at one house he was too late; the police were already there; they were breaking down a wall. He claimed he arrested them at gunpoint for unethical conduct, for destroying property. They said they were following orders. As he didn't know what to do with them, he let them off.

Like many of John's stories, this one is unverified and may simply have been told to make him look good. But there is a postscript that adds to the story's plausibility. The father and son whose home it was sought him out afterward and thanked him for his intervention. After the war, however, when John was interned and they were contacted to stand up for him, they declined to do so. They were probably influenced by the toxic postwar environment of hatred and recrimination directed at collaborators, many of whom had slipped away like floodwater through floorboards, adding to the atmosphere of poisonous mistrust. The father and son probably preferred to avoid any possibility of being tainted by association. Not without bitterness, John observed that perhaps twenty individuals were contacted on his behalf, but only three agreed to help: Siewers, Van Leeuwen, and Veltmeijer.

All Dutch police were not Schalkhaarders; far from it. There are examples of police refusing to obey orders, warning "potential victims of forthcoming raids," and turning "a blind eye to forged or invalid documents." Moreover, although "the Dutch police had more men involved [during the massive countrywide raids on October 2–3] than any other agency, they managed to arrest a mere 700 people. This suggests that they warned many of the intended victims or gave them time to escape if this was practical."[286]

"From July 1942 officers who had been guilty of an 'offence' against the occupying power, or had refused to undertake a task assigned to them, had to answer for their conduct before a special German SS and police court," Gerhard Hirschfeld notes. "This fact alone throws revealing light onto the extremely precarious situation of the Dutch police."[287] Indeed, many Dutch police "paid for their resistance to the Germans in front of a firing squad or by perishing in concentration camps."[288]

***

John carried legacies from his SS training and Nazi indoctrination. In the late 1950s and the 1960s, different members of his family would suffer because of his views on homosexuality, racial intermarriage, and possibly racial superiority. During one of our sessions he spoke about an international business conspiracy and the role played by armament producers in deciding "where to have wars"—a conspiracy led by a cabal of "maybe seven people," which he equated with "the seven-headed dragon" in The Revelation of John. It was coincidental, he said, that these seven men "are probably Jews." He noted that "Jews go to war too and are killed." Referring to the Final Solution, I remember him saying on one occasion, "They did not deserve to die."

I didn't think it possible at the time that he might have been a participant in the process that led to millions of murders. My innocence and ignorance, our bond and friendship, simply didn't allow for that. But when I hear him repeat that short sentence in my memory now—"They did not deserve to die"—I hear regret, guilt, and shame underlying those words.

---

[286] Moore, 200 (potential victims; blind eye), 98 (arrested a mere 700).
[287] Hirschfeld, 173.
[288] In 't Veld, 1523.

198   A SNAKE ON THE HEART

It took me a long time to put together the puzzle pieces that identified him as a participant. Different pieces were suggestive, but I couldn't see the whole picture. Aspects of the story remained unknown to me. These included aspects of John's life. What did he do for the SD, particularly after he returned to the insurance industry in August 1941? While ultimately there are several indicators that he maintained a desk with the SD after that date, the one that enabled a breakthrough on this point was his friendship with Tine Heerema. Other unknowns included aspects of the Holocaust in Holland. Acquiring an understanding of the roundup process in The Hague was critical, but it didn't come until late in the day.

The puzzle pieces were varied. There were the cover-up clues: John's false claims about what he did upon returning to Holland after his SS training in Germany. There were hints in a trio of documents, including his remark in his 1951 letter that he "always tried to choose the least worse of the two" when he was "forced" into some situation.

The second document is his collaborator statement of April 22, 1947. In it he refers to his "sense of guilt towards the people of the Netherlands." It is why he volunteered as an internee for the dangerous work of dismantling bombs, he said.[289] (But he may have been playing for sympathy with his reference to dismantling bombs, for, at the time he made this statement, he was still recovering from the severe injuries he had sustained when he was blown up in October 1946.)

The third document is an untitled 1974 composition dated December 2. This composition is one of four he wrote during the time (the months just before and after he left his marriage to Susan) when he was crazy—at least that is how he described his behaviour when he discussed it with Harald about nine years later. Harald used the phrase "wet in the head" to describe his father's mental state in late 1973 and throughout 1974. The compositions, which range in their ideas from the curious to the crackpot, clearly show the influence of the spiritual teacher Jiddu Krishnamurti. John not only mimics

---

[289] John's statement of April 22, 1947, 10.

Krishnamurti's speaking style, he also discusses similar concepts but without Krishnamurti's clarity or incisiveness. Here is part of the December 2, 1974, composition:

> Time is yesterday, today, and tomorrow; there is the fear that tomorrow something will happen—the loss of a job, death, that my wife or husband will run away, that the disease and pain that I have had many days ago will come back again. This is where time comes in. Time involving what my neighbour may say about tomorrow, or time which up to now has covered up something which I did many years ago. I am afraid of some deep secret desires which might not be fulfilled—and they will not as long as we have these fears. So time is involved in fear, like the fear of death, which comes at the end of life, which may be waiting around the corner, and I am afraid. So time involves fear and thought. There is no time if there is no fear. Thinking about that which happened "yesterday," being afraid of what may happen "tomorrow"—this is what brings about time as well as fear.

What did he mean by the words "time which up to now has covered up something which I did many years ago"? Was this a hypothetical statement or did it pertain to something he did during the war? His preceding phrase, "what my neighbour may say about tomorrow," brings to mind a private investigation into his wartime past supposedly undertaken in the 1950s or later by his former friend Hans Roelants (the recipient of his 1951 letter).[290] But just as he didn't

---

[290] I spoke to Hans Roelants by telephone in November 2002. He advised that he and his family had done some research into John's wartime activities sometime after John had come to Canada. Roelants did not say what motivated this investigation. He said they had contacted the "War Documentation Bureau," a predecessor of the Netherlands Institute for War Documentation (*Nederlands Instituut voor Oorlogsdocumentatie*) or NIOD, which is now the NIOD for War, Holocaust and Genocide Studies. He also said the War

elucidate either his sense of guilt that, he claimed, caused him to volunteer to dismantle bombs, or the nature of the compromising situation "into which [he] was forced" during the war, John also didn't leave answers to these questions.

I acquired part of what became the critical puzzle piece at Susan's memorial service in August 2009, where I met Al Wagstaff, a friend of Harald's from Alberni who, after an extended stay at Vancouver General Hospital for tuberculosis, boarded with the Petersens in 1959 and 1960. Al told me about a meeting he and Harald, along with Constance, Ann, and possibly Harald's friend McDiarmid, attended with John when he told them what he did during the war.[291] I had two subsequent telephone conversations with Al about the meeting and what precipitated it, and I also spoke to Harald about these events.

The meeting was triggered by an incident with McDiarmid. The particulars of the incident are somewhat confused, but the outcome is clear. McDiarmid came to the house wearing a black shirt, black pants, and a yellow tie. Harald said he was fooling around praising the Italian fascists. But John didn't know McDiarmid was jesting.

"Dad went berserk. He went wild. He physically threw him out of the house," Harald recalled.

Al didn't witness this but added some details based on what he was told at the time by Harald. These include McDiarmid calling John a Communist, John telling McDiarmid to get out, and McDiarmid returning later wearing his reserve-army uniform to demonstrate that he was a good Canadian. Despite their varied recollections, both Harald and Al agree that the upshot of the confrontation was the

---

Documentation Bureau sent them a letter in reply that has since been lost. Based on my inquiry, the NIOD's Dr. Hans de Vries reviewed the institute's correspondence files for the 1950s and advised in an email of November 26, 2010, "that no correspondence has been carried out between the institute and the Roelants family." Perhaps the alleged exchange of correspondence occurred in the 1960s.

[291] "McDiarmid" is a hazy figure, less a friend of Harald's than an acquaintance or a friend of a friend. It is uncertain if I am using the correct spelling of the name or even if the surname is correct.

meeting, convened by John, after supper that evening or on a night soon after.

On the rare occasions when John lost his temper, he would often try to recoup the situation afterward. He would say something like "I behaved badly there," according to Harald. Then he would provide an explanation. This is what he did at the meeting following the McDiarmid incident. Al concurred, saying that it appeared John thought he had "stepped too far" and needed "to cover [his] ass."

The meeting lasted at least an hour. The kids sat and John stood. As he spoke, he put cigarettes into his cigarette holder, as was his habit. The essence of Al's memory of the meeting was that John talked about his childhood in the Far East and said that during the war he'd been a policeman who had processed people (he never mentioned Jews) in a segregation area, which determined if they were sent away on a train or were set free. Based on research Al undertook into John's wartime past after he left the Petersen home in December 1960, he learned that John had been in the Dutch SS and concluded that the people being processed had been Jews.

But I was skeptical of Al's interpretation. For the better part of a decade, I thought he'd jumped to a conclusion and that it was more likely John had been describing an August 1943 Schutzgruppe assignment at Amersfoort when he subverted his orders at every turn by issuing exemptions from forced labour to numerous, probably hundreds, of veterans of the Dutch army. My perspective shifted in 2018 when my understanding of the roundup of The Hague's Jews increased substantially thanks to information I acquired from the city's archives and from historian Frank van Riet. Based on the new information, it seems apparent that what John referred to as a segregation area was either the Academy for Visual Arts on Prinsessegracht or the Jewish House at Paviljoensgracht 27 or both, which were used as successive collection points for The Hague's Jews prior to sending them to Westerbork via the Staatsspoor Railway Station. Two points were decisive in shifting my view. First, John was acting as a policeman not as a member of the Schutzgruppe. Second, unlike arrested Jews, veterans of the Dutch army subject to forced labour were not held in segregation areas.

John's admission that he'd been a policeman who processed people in a segregation area, prior to many of them being sent away on a train, is a key factor in my conclusion that he was likely a member of the German Order Police.

***

John told me Barend van Leeuwen confided in him about his resistance work, and as a result, John got involved. If true, this may have occurred during the latter months of 1942 or in early 1943 because notable assistance John claimed he gave Van Leeuwen happened at the same time that, John said, the underground was being organized throughout the country. Although there were some early resistance groups, and Van Leeuwen opted in almost immediately, the Dutch resistance "did not develop into a full scale movement until mid 1943."[292] John claimed his underground work was going on constantly.

Is this one of John's hollow boasts or is there something to it? On one hand, Van Leeuwen wrote two testimonial letters on John's behalf after the war. In the first, he describes himself as an "old illegal worker," a reference to his resistance work. In the second, he explains that John had asked him to provide "a declaration about [John's] behavior as a German in wartime." Van Leeuwen says: "I don't often do this, but in this case I will be very pleased to oblige. It is easy to understand that people, like ex illegal workers, are very much against Germans and the German regime at that time.... I experienced that Mr. J. J. Petersen as an S.S. man, has taken our side totally during the

---

[292] Anderson, "Anne Frank Was Not Alone: The Holocaust and Holland," (a transcript of a lecture presented at the University of Southern California on October 24, 1995, is no longer on the internet where it was previously available for years), 26 (full-scale movement by mid-1943).

war."[293] He added in his earlier letter that "Petersen had knowledge the undersigned worked illegally and hid Jews in his home, and also helped other people."[294] On the other hand, while Van Leeuwen says John "had knowledge," he does not indicate that John was actively involved or did anything to help, which John claims he did. This remains an important unresolved question. Although it is possible John deserves more credit than I can give him based on what is known, his record of false claims must work against him until we learn more, and it lends weight to his version of events.

Fear of a Mussert government spurred the growth of the Dutch resistance. Likely motivated by his unhappiness with the SS's increasing power in the Netherlands, Seyss-Inquart proposed "the possibility of a Mussert government with Hitler" in October 1942. Hitler rejected the idea, but made some concessions. In December, when he met with Mussert and Seyss-Inquart, he awarded Mussert the title "Führer of the Dutch People" and declared "the occupying power would henceforth govern *im Einvernehmen* (which could be interpreted as 'in agreement with,' but also as 'after deliberation with') with the NSB." Mussert was permitted to create a National Political Secretariat to advise the Reichskommissar.[295]

Hirschfeld says, "these German concessions were purely nominal and had no political significance"; but to the NSB at the time, they "seemed a great victory," writes In 't Veld. Seyss-Inquart announced the changes in the Netherlands on December 13 as part of the eleventh anniversary celebration of the founding of the NSB. The National Political Secretariat, or Mussert's shadow cabinet, was formally established with eighteen deputies on January 30, 1943.[296] "The great majority of the Dutch people no less than the SS believed

---

[293] Van Leeuwen's letter of June 17, 1951. See footnote 4.
[294] Van Leeuwen's letter of October 28, 1946 (DNA, CABR 109786).
[295] In 't Veld, 1516 (possible Mussert government; leader of the Dutch people; *Einvernehmen*). Hirschfeld, 305 (meeting details; *Führer* of the Dutch people; National Political Secretariat).
[296] Hirschfeld, 305 (purely nominal), 305n (January 30), 306 (Shadow Cabinet). In 't Veld, 1516 (thirteenth anniversary; great victory).

with the same dismay—but quite wrongly—that Mussert was about to seize power," according to In 't Veld. "The consequences," Hirschfeld adds, "were increased unrest and the growth of organized resistance."[297] Indeed, on February 5, the same day that the Dutch press published the names of Mussert's shadow cabinet, one of its members, Lieutenant General Seyffardt, the deputy for national defence, was assassinated. Within days, the new secretary general for propaganda and the arts, Herman Reydon, was also shot; he would succumb to his injuries a few months later. A telegram from Rauter to Himmler said these events were the direct result of the "very heavily proclaimed introduction of the NSB into the administration."[298]

All of this occurred while the Netherlands' Jews were being rounded up. The assassinations of Seyffardt and Reydon happened on the heels of the German defeat at Stalingrad. Despite the arrest of five thousand student hostages, the number of assassinations increased; forty Dutch Nazis were murdered through August. Other forms of attack also took place. In March, the Labour Exchange and the Population Registration Office in Amsterdam were both set on fire, and on April 11, the RAF, with help from the resistance, bombed the State Inspectorate of Population Registers in The Hague.

Arnold Douwes, an underground leader in Drenthe province, contended that "those who are most active in the resistance, those who achieve the most and who give the most help to *onderduikers* [people in hiding] are found primarily among the extreme right-wing and left-wing elements of the population, that is to say, the anti-revolutionaries [Calvinists] and the communists.... People [in southern Drenthe] who hide fugitives or help in one way or another [were] nearly all *Gereformeerden* [orthodox Calvinists]."[299]

This notion of the activist involvement of extreme elements also applies in a broader context, namely to the resistance on one side and

---

[297] In 't Veld, 1516. Hirschfeld, 306.
[298] Hirschfeld, 306, 306n (telegram). Maass, 141 (growth of opposition).
[299] Quoted in Moore, 164.

the much-hated NSB on the other. The resistance had about 74,000 members, about 0.8 per cent of the Netherlands' wartime population of nine million, while the NSB had a membership of 100,894 (including 19,854 sympathizers) that "comprised no more than 1.25 per cent of the Dutch population" in 1942.[300] Of the full- and part-time resisters, 40,000 supported the 300,000 who went into hiding. More than 25,000 produced illegal newspapers and bulletins, forged identity papers and ration cards, and helped Allied pilots escape; while 4,000 worked as spies; only about 5,000 belonged to fighting units.[301]

In his career as a manipulator and liar, John achieved dual high points. One was with the Schutzgruppe, the other related to the front he presented to his family and possibly others. What he called his "reckless game" and his "double game" reached its apogee when he joined the Schutzgruppe, which knew he was German, while the SS understood he was Dutch. He played "the German authorities against each other," he said.[302] I also strongly suspect that he would have agreed with Hans Bernd Gisevius, who wrote in his memoir, *To The Bitter End*, that "in such dangerous times there is only one relatively safe refugee—in the lions' den."[303] But he paid a price for the paradoxical safety of such a refuge.

He told me he constantly felt pressure from all sides, he was "never ever" able to relax, and he used words like "manipulation," "alertness," "fear," to describe his situation. He said he trained himself to be alert even in his sleep. And he had a recurring nightmare in

---

[300] Hirschfeld, 285.

[301] Van der Zee, 109 (citing "an estimate from the Netherlands Institute for War Documentation."). De Jong in *The Netherlands and Nazi Germany* (47) says the resistance had 50,000 to 60,000 members.

[302] John's June 1951 letter to Hans Roelants.

[303] Gisevius, 585. It appears the phrase "the lions' den" was commonly used by German critics and opponents of the Nazi regime. In addition to Gisevius's use of the phrase in his memoir, the draft or original title of *Defying Hitler: A Memoir* by Raimund Pretzel (using the pseudonym Sebastian Haffner) was *Dance in the Lions' Den*. (See page 157 herein.) In addition, on August 9, 1976, John told me that in joining the Schutzgruppe, he went "into the lions' den for safety's sake."

which he fought a huge tank that had all sorts of hidden guns as well as binoculars and cameras. In this nightmare he was always lying low, trying to stay beneath the guns, trying to figure out where their blind spots were. In one scenario he was lying in front of the tank as it approached. He said he was trying to remember what each gun could do, trying not to forget so he could take the tank out single-handedly, which was his task. But the dream never resolved. He repeated this statement: The dream never resolved.

The pressure he was under—both the general pressure of his "double game" and the concentrated, laser pressure of being "forced" into a position with which he apparently disagreed—ramified onto his family, for it appears he likely misled his mother and brothers about some of his feelings and activities. He certainly misled Susan. To protect the family, he said he never spoke against the Germans or their regime. Instead, he always made a point of mentioning the good things they did. Regarding the resistance, this stance was a matter of two-way protection, he maintained: protection for Susan and the family on one hand, and for the resistance on the other. "The underground had very strict rules," he said. "You couldn't tell anyone what you were doing. If you did, there was no pardon—you were killed."

According to Harald, John made Susan into the collaborator she was. John acknowledged this. He said she never forgave him for not telling her about his secret activities. He told me she didn't know what he was doing at all. Later in the war when he arrived home with food, she didn't know where it came from. For her part, Susan contended that John always told her, "The less you know the safer you are." She added, "I never asked questions." I suspect, however, that her former statement may have been influenced by what she learned from John after the war.

John liked to be an authoritative or compelling or admired figure. He could be full of big talk to act these parts and draw attention to himself. I suspect this tendency was operating in March and April 1943, from the time Constant decided to volunteer for the Waffen-SS until April 29 when he left for training in Germany. I suspect John was saying he wanted to do what Constant was doing. I suspect this is the background to Constant's remark in his June 1944 letter to his wife, when he understood there was a good chance John was to be sent to the eastern front: "Well, he always wanted this, so now he gets what he wants."

Given the pressure of his circumstances, John may have considered going into hiding. He probably would have quickly dismissed this option for it would have imperilled Susan, Hans, and Harald. As Gisevius says, "Everyone has the moral right to risk his own life, but can he justify himself before God and man if he also hazards the lives of his wife and children?"[304] The idea of going into hiding was problematic from another standpoint: a potential unflattering comparison to Constant and Wim, who, in the latter half of 1943, were both serving the German cause in the east.

Constant had been sent to the front in July. "From Charkow we retreated, fighting all the way," he said. In late August or September, he was wounded at Cherkasy in Ukraine when a piece of grenade shrapnel lodged in one of his lungs. He was treated at several field hospitals before arriving at a hospital in Ibbs near Vienna where he remained until being discharged at the end of January 1944. Unable to return to the front, he was assigned to work in supply depots, first in SS Camp Heidelager, in Poland, and later in Graz, Austria. According to his statement of February 14, 1947, he was returned to the rank of corporal in July 1944 because his "previous promotion was declared invalid due to the fact that [his] documentation had been lost."[305]

John's history with his mother and family was probably an effective counterweight to any temptation he felt to go into hiding. How would it look if he became an *onderduiker* and Constant and Wim did not? (Van Leeuwen said Wim did go into hiding late in 1944.)[306] For John, hiding would have meant giving up his insurance work, which could,

---

[304] Gisevius, 590.
[305] Constant's February 14, 1947, statement, 5.
[306] Van Leeuwen's statement of October 17, 1946, 5.

in turn, resurrect the characterization that he was a good-for-nothing who didn't know how to succeed. There may have been psychological dimensions to his feeling of being torn that had nothing to do with conflicted loyalties between Germany and the Netherlands.

While Constant's June 1944 letter provides the basis for my discussion of what may have occurred between Constant and John, Wim does not provide a similar piece of evidence. On the other hand, Wim and John shared a strong connection with Barend van Leeuwen. What is more, Wim's personal views evolved in a highly provocative way during the war and may have been influenced by views expressed by John—for example, never speaking against the Germans and always stressing the good things they did.

During his imprisonment after the war, Wim told Dutch officials in his statement of October 23, 1946, that he knew his father-in-law and wife did illegal work during the occupation, but he didn't like it.[307] He said he'd been apolitical when the occupation began but became pro-German in 1941 and 1942 and was fully aware of his "true Nazistic disposition" by the first half of 1943. "Already before the war I had a strong racial awareness," he added. "I felt a strong aversion to half-breeds and I felt antipathy for Jews in general, although I did not hate them personally." He and Dina had frequent arguments about his political views, which contributed to him becoming involved with another woman in the spring of 1943 and led to the cancellation of their engagement. Dina's father didn't learn of Wim's pro-German disposition until October 1944.[308] Prior to his statement of October 23, 1946, Wim had made another statement on August 3 of that year in which he claimed he had hidden two Jewish children in his house

---

[307] Wim's statement of October 23, 1946 (15). According to the attachment to Blauw's email of February 14, 2007, to the author, Wim maintained (11) "that he actually did no underground/resistance work, and that he did not like the idea of doing so. He knew very well about the underground/resistance work of his father-in-law ..."

[308] Wim's statement of October 23, 1946, 14, 15, 17. Blauw's email of February 14, 2007, attachment, 11 (Nazistic disposition; strong racial awareness; engagement cancelled).

and had two German half-brothers in "German service" who he mistrusted. He revoked these claims in his statement of October 23.[309] Other parts of the earlier statement may be true, however. In finding and expressing his "true Nazistic disposition" was Wim, to some degree, acting upon what he heard from John? Miek said she never noticed Wim's anti-Semitism.

When John told me about his identification with and idealization of Germany because it "was the one country that allowed him into its family," he said this identification forced him into a great personal crisis, what he called "this deep fight." On one side was his wish to help Germany, on the other was his philosophy against killing. Although he said he went with his philosophy, he also noted that he felt he was being untrue to Germany, which had been so good to him. He added a few moments later that he "felt torn," that although he ultimately sided with Holland, he always had a certain loyalty with Germany. Then he deployed a strikingly provocative simile, saying the internal conflict he experienced was "like having to kill your brother to save your father." He went on to say, "Every time I had to trick the Germans … as to my nationality, I felt shame." He felt the Germans had to do what they were doing because of what the world had done to them. Despite this, he said he had to be true to his philosophy.

"Every day I would wish that something would happen, so I wouldn't have to carry on this double game that I was playing," he told me.

He said he had an image in his mind of people holding a snake to their chest—a snake, he said, that was him. Undoubtedly, the people he had in mind included Susan, his mother, Constant, and Wim.

There is one more inconclusive piece of information to add to the picture or puzzle of John's life from mid-1942 to mid-1943. It is a story Hans tells about his father. Hans, who was five or six years of age, was walking with John one day. It was fall or winter. John was wearing his SS uniform. Hans was definite about this. He said a Jew

---

[309] Wim's statements of August 3, 1946, 1 (German service), and October 23, 1946. Blauw's email of February 14, 2007, attachment, 11 (mistrusted brothers; revoked parts of earlier statement).

was standing on the sidewalk next to a building ahead of them. The Jew was identifiable by the yellow star on his heavy overcoat. John told Hans to stay where he was. John went forward and spoke to the Jew, after which the Jew departed. Hans had no idea what John told the man. Presuming Hans was correct about the time of year, this event would have occurred during the autumn of 1942 or the winter of 1942–43. We can deduce this from two facts: first, the wearing of a six-pointed yellow star on outer clothing didn't become mandatory until early May 1942; second, the roundup of Jews in the Netherlands was largely complete by September 1943.

Although this story suggests clandestine activity, we cannot be sure what it tells us. This uncertainty reflects a truth about the resistance, which, of necessity, was a partially false world where many didn't use their real names. S. E. (Stan) Hanson helps us put what might be called the anonymity of the resistance into perspective. He was a navigator on a British Lancaster bomber shot down during the night of February 7–8, 1945, "in the absolute south-eastern corner of [the province of] Gelderland." Hidden by the underground for two months that "felt like at least two years," he observes in his memoir, *Underground Out of Holland*, "the superb Dutch capacity to be tight-lipped when they chose, whilst ideal in the running of an Underground Movement, posed problems of rediscovery later."[310]

***

Next to Anne Frank, Etty Hillesum is the best-known Dutch diarist of the Holocaust. A twenty-eight-year-old employee of the Jewish Council, she volunteered in July 1942 to go to Westerbork to aid Jews in transit. In a letter of December 18, 1942, she described Westerbork as "a camp for people in transit, great waves of human beings

---

[310] Hanson, 9, 159 (navigator); 12, 19 (date); 143, 162 (duration); 35 (Gelderland); 143 (seemed like two years); 191 (problems of rediscovery). Hanson writes of himself during his time in hiding (163): "My mind was clinically active but emotionally dead."

constantly washed in from the cities and provinces, from rest homes, prisons, and other prison camps, from all the nooks and crannies of the Netherlands—only to be deported a few days later to meet their unknown destiny." She wrote of witnessing "the fear and despair of the thousands upon thousands of men, women, children, infants, invalids, the feeble-minded, the sick, and the aged who pass through our helping hands..."[311] This letter and another she wrote on August 24, 1943, were published illegally by the resistance that autumn, the same season she was murdered by the Nazis at Auschwitz. The letters were printed in a disguised manner under the title "Three Letters from the Painter Johannes Baptiste van der Pluym (1843–1912)."

While Hillesum said the "people in transit" were being deported "to meet their unknown destiny," others were writing with more certainty about the situation. A week after the massive early October roundup, thirteen-year-old Anne Frank noted that Jews known to her family "are being taken away in droves. The Gestapo is treating them very roughly and transporting them in cattle-trucks to Westerbork.... If it's that bad in Holland, what must it be like in those faraway and uncivilized places where the Germans are sending them? The English radio says they're being gassed."[312]

Hillesum's reference to "children, infants, invalids, the feeble-minded, the sick, and the aged" is also noteworthy. Historian Bob Moore tells us the fact that the Nazis were targeting these groups "finally gave the lie to the idea that deportees were being selected primarily as a labour force." These groups were increasingly targeted in late 1942 and early 1943.[313] In The Hague, the Rama Clinic in Loosduinen was raided on December 31, eighty patients were removed from the Zuidal Hospital on January 6, and all the orphans and staff at the Jewish orphanage were rounded up on March 5. In

---

[311] Etty Hillesum, *An Interrupted Life: The Diaries, 1941–1943 and Letters from Westerbork,* Foreword by Eva Hoffman, Introduction and Notes by Jan G. Gaarlandt, (New York: Holt Paperbacks, 1996), 246, 247.
[312] Frank, 53–54 (October 9, 1942).
[313] Moore, 98 (gave the lie), 100, 101.

Rotterdam, the Germans, with the assistance "of the voluntary auxiliary police—a National Socialist Organisation—and the WA," collected two hundred patients and residents and sixty-one staff members from the Rotterdam Jewish hospital, old people's home, and orphanage and sent them by truck to Shed 24 on February 26.[314]

It is not known if John and Constant participated in any of these raids, but it is a definite possibility one or both did. In counterpoint to the raids, John maintained that he actively assisted Van Leeuwen with one of the two Jews he hid during this period. The fact John only mentioned one of the two Jews is, I suspect, a red flag. It may indicate he was less close to Van Leeuwen than he implied and that the assistance he said he provided was either exaggerated or entirely untrue.

The two Jews were Van Leeuwen's twenty-one-year-old foster son, Arnold Rothschild, and Johnny Heymans, who turned six in February 1943. Sometime after the occupation began, the Germans had required that Arnold leave the Van Leeuwens' Aryan household. Arnold had since been living with "the Jewish family Lievens" in Amsterdam where he worked as a doorman for the Jewish Council and was one of thousands of its employees who were temporarily exempted from deportation.[315]

After July 30, 1942, M. H. Bolle, general secretary of the Jewish Council, issued safe-conducts to "a list of Council staff and other 'indispensable' people in both Amsterdam and the provinces."[316] A complex system of exemptions covering foreign Jews, baptized Protestant Jews, and others soon sprang up. The largest number of exemptions—17,500—was provided to the Jewish Council.[317] Gertrude van Tijn recalled in her unpublished memoirs, "When the first stamps

---

[314] Attachment to Frank van Riet's email of July 5, 2009, to the author: "Persecution of the Rotterdam Jews," 15 (auxiliary police; Rotterdam Jewish hospital). Attachment to Van Riet's email of August 6, 2018, to the author, 3 (Rama Clinic; Zuidwal Hospital; Jewish orphanage).
[315] Van Leeuwen's statement of October 17, 1946, 1, 2.
[316] Moore 95, 355 (Bolle's initials).
[317] Moore, 95–96.

were issued, the scenes at the Jewish Council were quite indescribable. Doors were broken, the staff of the Council was attacked, and the police had often to be called in ... The stamps quickly became an obsession with every Jew."[318] In due course, Seyss-Inquart required "that all exemptions should be rescinded by the end of May" when the size of the Jewish population would be much reduced.[319]

According to Van Leeuwen's statement, he decided "it was time for Arnold Rothschild to go into hiding" when the Germans "started to arrest the 'spared' [formerly exempted] Jews in Amsterdam." This was probably in late 1942.[320] As a doorman, Arnold would have been especially vulnerable to early cancellation of his exemption because it could not be argued that his position was indispensable. Van Leeuwen, with the help of Officer Van Oort of 's-Graveland in Hilversum, moved Arnold to Van Oort's home. "After that," Van Leeuwen's statement continues, "I was asked to move the boy to different addresses several times because he had such an anxious character. After the boy had been in hiding at my home for a while, he ended up at the home of the Pijl family who resided at the Elleboogstraat. I could not keep the boy at my home because the Germans kept a special eye on my residence. The boy was once again very anxious at the Pijl residence and one day he walked away, which caused the residence to be in danger of exposure. I addressed this to him afterward and also asked the doctor for advice[;] he had already warned the Pijl family to keep an eye on the boy, as he was so stressed he was capable of doing anything.

"Shortly after the doctor had visited the boy, Pijl came to me visibly shaken and told me that the boy had killed himself by hanging."[321]

---

[318] Presser, J., Ondergang. De Vervolging en Verdelging van het Nederlandse Jodendom 1940–45 (The Hague, Staatsuitgeverij, 1965) cites Gertrude van Tijn-Cohn, Bijdrage tot de Geschiedenis der Juden in Nederland van 10 Mei 1940 tot Juni 1944 (unpublished), 48. Moore, 96, 285.
[319] Moore, 100.
[320] Van Leeuwen's statement of October 17, 1946 (Haydee Oord translation), 2. Moore, 99 (toward the end of the year; starting in November 1942, the Germans took steps that forced "the gradual reduction of exemptions").
[321] Van Leeuwen's statement of October 17, 1946 (Haydee Oord translation), 2.

Some of John's claims do not tally with Van Leeuwen's information about Arnold. John knew Arnold's age, that he had come from Germany, and that his family had moved to the United States. But this is to be expected as they both lived with Van Leeuwen's family for approximately the February–June 1940 period. John indicated that Arnold was a musician, describing him to me as "very gifted, always studying and playing piano." He also said that Arnold had studied music before the occupation. He said nothing about Arnold's electrical apprenticeship or studies, which is noteworthy given John's interest in building radios. Perhaps Arnold was both an electrician's apprentice and a pianist. Perhaps John gave Arnold relatively little attention, which would not be surprising given the six-and-a-half-year difference in their ages. John did say that Arnold was "very emotional and child-like [and] didn't have much contact with people; he stayed indoors ... before it [was] necessary." It is possible that John's description of Arnold is another case—like those of Ko and Wiertz—where he obfuscates; although Arnold is different from the others in that John used his real name. Nonetheless, the discrepancies in John's portrait of Arnold are such that we must treat his claims of involvement in Arnold's story with skepticism.

In the spring of 1943, according to Wim, Van Leeuwen received an anonymous letter warning him that the Jews he was hiding were in danger. As a result, Arnold Rothschild and Johnny Heymans were moved to other locations. Heymans said his move occurred unexpectedly and without explanation three or four months after he had arrived at the Family Van Leeuwen in late 1942.[322] When Arnold was relocated from Van Leeuwen's place, it was to the Pijl home on Elleboogstraat in central Hilversum.[323]

John said he was involved in moving Arnold to the Pijl home and in subsequent developments. "We had to do something for the boy to

---

[322] Attachment to John Heymans's email of March 18, 2019, to the author.
[323] Wim's statement of October 23, 1946, Dutch original, 16, and 4 of Haydee Oord's translation notes. Van Leeuwen's statement of October 17, 1946, Haydee Oord's translation, 2.

protect him from the Nazis," he told me. "We put him in an attic in a home in the middle of Hilversum." He also said he took food and books to Arnold, who was extremely scared during this period of about two months when he was in the attic. According to information from the Begegnungsstätte Alt Synagoge in Wuppertal, Arnold committed suicide on March 9, 1943.[324] Wim said Arnold cut his wrists and hanged himself. John said Arnold was found hanging from the ceiling. Based on Arnold's date of death, it seems evident that the anonymous warning letter arrived during the winter, not the spring as Wim recalled in his October 1946 statement.

"When Jews died in hiding," Van Riet writes, "it was no easy task to dispose of the bodies and very dangerous for those helping them."[325] John said as much to me, observing that a Jewish corpse was "a dangerous thing to have." He claimed he helped Van Leeuwen dispose of Arnold's remains. He said they wrapped the body in canvas, tied it to a plank, and placed the plank between two bicycles, which they quietly wheeled down back streets well after dark to a heather field on the edge of town. There they dug a grave as quietly as possible and buried the corpse. John described all this as "exceedingly dangerous." He said that he and Van Leeuwen had to exhume and rebury the body four to six months later. According to John, the resistance had acquired a copy of German plans to excavate an anti-tank trench through the heather field. Van Leeuwen had seen the plans, which convinced him that the body would be disturbed.

Did John really help move Arnold to the safe house, bring food and books to him, then help bury and rebury him? All we have are John's claims that he did these things. There is no third-party corroboration. According to John's rendition, he and Van Leeuwen

---

[324] Restitution and compensation files, Begegnungsstätte Alte Synagoge archives, Wuppertal, Germany. Attachment to email of February 13, 2006, from Dr. Ulrike Schrader to the author (date of suicide; by hanging), and email of December 10, 2005, from Professor Manfred Brusten to the author (date of suicide; by hanging).

[325] Attachment to Frank van Riet's email of July 5, 2009, to the author: "Persecution of the Rotterdam Jews," 22.

used bicycles to transport the body, but many bicycles—especially men's bicycles—had been confiscated starting the previous summer.[326] Other bicycles were still in use, however. In addition, permits were sometimes granted that allowed selected people to retain and use bicycles and it is known John at least once provided such a permit.[327] Moreover, it seems likely that work of this nature, particularly the initial transport of the body, would be accomplished more readily and safely by two people rather than one.

There are additional questions. If John did everything he claimed with respect to Arnold, he would have been in Hilversum on a regular basis. In addition to his work for the SD and the Central Labourers' Life Insurance Company, he was also by this time a member of the Schutzgruppe. Although he never directly explained how he was able to get away so frequently from these three different organizations, several postwar documents do touch on this subject. In his statements of October 8, 1945, and October 29, 1946, he said his Schutzgruppe responsibilities and the related time requirements were minimal initially: "a few exercises for a few hours once a month as a first aid attendant." Decades later, he told me basically the same thing, commenting that at first his Schutzgruppe obligations only occurred during the weekend. But he also said that his work with the Schutzgruppe took up more and more time as the war progressed, and, in 1985, he added that it subsequently became "full time," and he "could only devote part time to his insurance job."

As to the nature of the work, John didn't tell me about his initial responsibilities as a first-aid attendant. Rather he focused on having

---

[326] Moore writes (90): "The expropriation of bicycles was extended [from just the Jews] to the entire population in [July 1942] as the Germans attempted to turn the Dutch 'from a cycling nation to a walking nation.'" Van der Zee adds (73): "Before the war the ... Dutch owned four million bikes, but intensive use and constant raids by the Germans halved this number" by mid 1944. But Maass (18) points out that women's bicycles were often not seized.

[327] In late 1944 or early 1945, John granted a permit to a man authorizing him to use a bicycle. Smit statement (DNA, CABR 109786). Attachment to Blauw's email of December 3, 2009, 2.

to supervise, stand guard over bridges, and inspect trucks for contraband. He implied that he was the leader of the unit. This stands to reason given that he was an Onderschaarleider in the SS. He told me he was in his SS uniform at least some of the time. And when he was not, when he was in his Schutzgruppe uniform, he was able, when necessary, to influence people by showing them his SS papers. What we don't know is whether this activity had commenced by the time of Arnold's suicide on March 9. Based on what John told me, it was certainly underway by June or July 1943, at the latest.

The ten-man guard units had duty at certain hours and on certain days. He said they were on duty for four hours then off duty for four hours, working twelve hours in a 24-hour period. Sometimes, during a four-hour off-duty period, he would go to the insurance company office and do a couple of hours of work. Sometimes he was away from the insurance office for a couple of days at a time. He also worked part time in an SD office, but this connection may have started to taper off at some point. Based on potential information-gathering opportunities at the insurance company, he may have convinced his SS superiors to give him more leeway as to where he spent his time. (Hirschfeld has a low opinion of the Dutch SS's professionalism, noting "its lack of competence and originality were remarkable.")[328]

Moreover, John said he was feared within the Schutzgruppe because he let on that he had a special task, which was secret. This ruse helped to shield his various activities and prevent people from questioning why he—who appeared completely healthy and was in SS uniform—wasn't at the front. It also allowed him to take time off and not be questioned. Although his secret-assignment story was undoubtedly another of his tall tales, his history of making false and audacious claims lends an ironic credibility to this contrivance.

Thus, it appears he may have had the flexibility with his diverse roles to play them off against each other when he needed time for something else, such as helping Van Leeuwen. Nonetheless, no

---

[328] Hirschfeld, 287.

verification exists for any of his claims regarding Arnold. He did know that Arnold had been hidden and died at a safe house in central Hilversum, but this knowledge does not prove he helped move Arnold there or that he brought him food and books. It is possible he simply injected himself into Arnold's tragic story to beef up his resistance résumé.[329]

Van Leeuwen implied that he buried and reburied Arnold on his own.[330] In his statement he is always careful to name the individuals who were involved with him, such as Inspector Van Es, Pijl, the doctor, and others. If John had helped with the burial and reburial, wouldn't Van Leeuwen have mentioned his name? Perhaps not. Van Leeuwen's statement, which was made a full eighteen months after the war, describes the lengthy, contentious, and ongoing relationship he, Dina, and Wim had with two pro-German Dutch police officers, Barend Den Hartog and Van den Elsakker, and

---

[329] John concludes his statement of October 29, 1946 (Dutch original, 11), with three assertions, the second of which is "I also have never had anything to do with the people in hiding or prisoners." But the truthfulness of this assertion is doubtful given his likely involvement in the roundup of The Hague's Jews, some of whom may have been in hiding and all of whom were prisoners. His first and third assertions were: "I have never served on the frontlines.... Besides my household effects I have no personal belongings."

[330] Van Leeuwen's statement of October 17, 1946 (Haydee Oord translation), includes this (2): "After I had been convinced that Pijl had not discussed [Arnold's suicide] with anyone and told him specifically not to expose this any further, besides the doctor, I went to see Police Inspector Van Es, who I knew to be a Dutchman who could be trusted. I discussed the matter with Mr. Van Es and he agreed with me that the boy had to be buried in secrecy until the end of the war at which point the story could come to light. I continued to handle the matter and got permission from Mr. Hermsen, who resided at Kerkelanden [on the southwestern outskirts of] Hilversum, to bury the remains of Arnold Rothschild on his property. About three months after I had buried the boy's remains, Hermsen informed me that the Germans were digging a tank trap around Hilversum and that this trap would be dug right through his land and by the spot where the boy's remains were buried. Hermsen informed me that if the Germans found the remains and he would be questioned about it, he would tell them what had happened. It was clear to me that the remains of Arnold Rothschild had to be dug up and I went that night, while the Germans had security around the tank trap, to dig up the remains and to bury it about 100 meters further on Hermsen's land."

appears intent on protecting Dina from possible recriminations during that toxic time. It is possible Van Leeuwen concluded it would be imprudent to admit to an alliance with John, a member of the SD, who at that time, was still interned as a collaborator, as was Wim.[331]

Compared to Arnold Rothschild's story, that of John Heymans and his family has greater clarity and, in repeated defiance of desperate circumstances, a happy ending. For a long time, all I knew about this story was what Wim and Van Leeuwen revealed in their postwar statements: a Jewish child named Johnny Heijmans stayed with Dina and her parents. Van Leeuwen said Johnny "was the son of the Jewish family Dr. Heijmans of Haarlem." Wim added that Johnny's stay was approximately five months from late 1942 to the spring of 1943. I learned much more in March 2019 when, not expecting much if anything, I searched the name "John Heijmans"[332] on the internet, which led me to an article by John Heymans about his uncle, "The Final Story about Hugo Heijmans."[333]

This enabled me to contact Johnny and to learn the rest of his wartime story. The following information comes from our email correspondence: As a five-year-old, Johnny "had to leave home all of

---

[331] Barend van Leeuwen's statement of October 17, 1946, identifies Barend Den Hartog and Van den Elsakker. Other uncertainties hang over the demise of Arnold Rothschild. In his statement of October 23, 1946 (Dutch original, 16), Wim says: "I do not know for sure if Rothschild passed away by way of suicide because I was not in Holland at the time of his death." This appears to be untrue. Arnold died on March 9, 1943. After volunteering for the N.O.C., Wim, according to Blauw's attachment of February 14, 2007 (9, 11), did not leave the country until July 1943. Moreover, included with Wim's statement is the perspective of a witness who mentioned Wim "in connection with the suspicious death of Rothschild." This seemingly negative interpretation, however, may have been intentional and part of a post-war vendetta against Wim and Barend van Leeuwen, as will be discussed in Chapter 20.

[332] Wim's statement of October 23, 1946, 15. While "Heijmans" is the traditional Dutch spelling of this surname, Johnny's father, David, switched to "Heymans" at some point, although David's older brother, Hugo, continued to go by "Heijmans."

[333] John Heymans, "The final story about Hugo Heijmans," accessed March 7, 2019, https://www.joodsmonument.nl/en/page/550398/the-final-story-about-hugo-heijmans .

a sudden, and to live with foreign non Jewish people" because of German reprisals. When two drunk German soldiers drowned in a canal in Haarlem in late 1942, the German authorities said the soldiers had been pushed, which justified compiling a list of leading Jews to be arrested. Johnny's father, David, a family physician, received a phone call from a patient warning him that he was on the list. David asked that his family be hidden by the resistance, which immediately went to work. According to Johnny, "The arrested Jewish leaders ... were shot dead ... without any delay" by firing squad. He, his twin sister, Willy (Wilhelmina), and their parents were separated and hidden at three different locations. As for the abrupt upheaval in their lives, nothing was explained to Johnny. "I was a very unhappy child.... My interpretation was, my parents did not want me anymore.... I still remember the concerning period clearly." At the Van Leeuwen farm, he was protected "24 hours a day" by a "very intelligent ... hunting dog" named Peter who had "a human instinct" for the special responsibility he had been given. "Nobody could come near me without [Peter's] permission," Johnny wrote. "At night he was sleeping on my bed or I was sleeping with him in his dog basket, warm and secured."[334]

Johnny told me his parents were betrayed by neighbours at their hiding place, which led to them being arrested and transported to Westerbork. Dr. Heymans went to work at Westerbork's hospital. He noticed that children in hiding were being betrayed and sent to Westerbork, from which they were generally sent directly to the extermination camps. Fearing that this fate could befall Johnny and Willy, he "gave instructions to the underground" to bring his children to Westerbork, which is how the family was reunited toward the end of 1943, after almost a year. On September 4, 1944, they left Westerbork in one of the last transports for the east. They made the three-day journey in a cattle car "without food [or sanitary] accommodation." When they arrived at Theresienstadt, in what had

---

[334] From John Heymans's emails of March 14 and 18, 2019, to the author.

been Czechoslovakia, Dr. Heymans once again went to work as a physician and also an anesthetist, as circumstances required. This was possible because the German camp management had struck a deal with "Prof. Dr. Stein … a well-known eye specialist." Under the deal, Dr. Stein was provided with an ophthalmic clinic with an operating room in return for accepting senior German officers with eye injuries as patients. Dr. Stein was permitted to select and train his medical team.[335]

Dr. Heymans, along with his wife, Sara, and Johnny and Willy, were liberated by the Russian army on May 8, 1945. The main reason they survived was another condition of Dr. Stein's agreement with camp management, namely that the members of his medical staff and their families were not to be sent to the extermination camps. The family flew back to the Netherlands on June 25. (See Appendix 2—The Rest of John Heymans's Wartime Story.)

In contrast to Arnold Rothschild's tragic last months and John Petersen's questionable involvement in them, the unfurling of the rest of Johnny Heymans's wartime story—one of the last revelations of my research—came with a wonderful sense of emergence and affirmation. This speaks to the entanglement of my life with John Petersen's, of part of my story being bound up with his. If his claims regarding Arnold are untrue, as may well be the case, they are a form of pollution, a miasma from the past that forever taints the present, whereas the discovery of what happened to Johnny Heymans was a multifaceted restoration. This discovery not only revealed the rest of the Heymans family's wartime travails, it was also a special acquisition for me, one that was tangential to John Petersen's story and soared free of its sorry contortions.

---

[335] From John Heymans's emails of March 14 and 18 and April 10, 2019, to the author. According to Zuzana Justman's essay, "My Terezin Diary," *The New Yorker*, September 16, 2019, (45): "Among the prisoners [at Theresienstadt] were some of the best doctors from Czechoslovakia, Germany, Austria, and Holland."

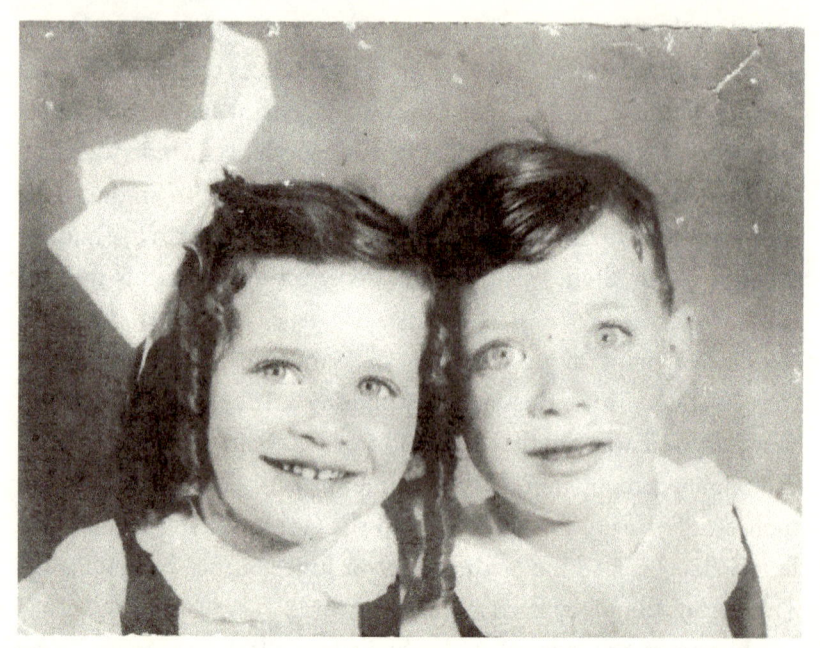

Figure 27. John Heymans and his twin sister, Wilhelmina, when they were three or four in 1940 or 1941. Wilhelmina died in Amsterdam in 2017. John lives in Israel. The photo is reproduced with his permission.

14

THE SCHUTZGRUPPE, THE ECONOMY, AND QUESTIONS OF SURVIVAL AND SANITY

John's membership in the SS and his assignment to the SD were the catalysts that determined his basic circumstances during the war. But his return to the insurance industry, his joining the Schutzgruppe, and, less clearly, his participation in the resistance were emblematic of how he responded to these circumstances and sought more room to manoeuver. These developments appear to have reinforced an independence of perspective and behaviour. They also engaged his skills of deception and manipulation, especially in the Schutzgruppe where he and his unit probably started policing checkpoints and inspecting vehicles for contraband during the late winter or early spring of 1943.

By early that year, the Dutch people, particularly in the major urban centres, were facing hardships. There was a lack of food, clothing, and fuel. Initially, however, there was at least one benefit to the German occupation. Dutch unemployment had dropped from 232,000 in mid-1940 to 103,000 in mid-1941 thanks largely to voluntary labour service in Germany. But in a September 1941 broadcast, Queen Wilhelmina referred to Hitler as "the archenemy of mankind" and accused "his hordes" of looting the Netherlands and delivering "our people to famine." The latter charge was premature, but the former about looting was on point and would only worsen.

The distribution of food, shoes, textiles, and soap had been regulated from the early days of the occupation. Large quantities of a wide range of products were regularly sent to Germany, which caused shortages in the Netherlands and stimulated the black market.[336] Special courts dealing with economic crime, such as black marketeering, violation of price regulations, embezzlement, and economic sabotage, had been operating since April 1941. The number of criminal proceedings had increased from 20,000 in 1941 to approximately 120,000 in 1943, by which time theft of food for immediate consumption had become a common charge. During the roundup and deportation of the Jews in 1942 and 1943, food was used to support that process. Due to a large workload and limited staff, "detectives and traffic police were offered overtime to escort Jews to Westerbork." One of the men who volunteered commented, "It was very worthwhile to take on those extra duties, not only because of the money, but also because on return to the station at Utrecht you were given a bag with well-filled sandwiches. All of that at a time when anything was very useful and when food had become scarce."[337]

While German policies impoverished the country, Hirschfeld observes "there were scarcely any spectacular delays in the production process, or cases of industrial sabotage" during the first three years of the occupation. Even though much Dutch product was being funnelled to Germany, workers wanted to continue working to "avoid being dismissed—a fate which was almost inevitably coupled with subsequent conscription to the German labour mobilization programme," which was now much less attractive. Hirschfeld conjectures that a third of Dutch production was "destined solely for the German economy" in 1943 and that this rose to "almost half of production in 1944."[338] Once again,

---

[336] Maass, 50.
[337] Moore, 201.
[338] Hirschfeld, 190 (conjecture), 191 (scarcely any delays or sabotage; dismissal coupled with conscription), 199 (rapidly impoverished).

Stalingrad is a key demarcation line, for it led to the Nazis' total war policy. Announced in February 1943, it exacerbated the shortages imposed on the Dutch people.

This was the backdrop for John's work in the Schutzgruppe. The truck drivers he encountered while on checkpoint duty were usually transporting more food than was permitted, he said. In some cases, the excess was destined for the black market and huge profits. In others, the drivers were bringing back a little extra for themselves. He claimed he had no mercy for the former but got to know the latter well. He not only let them through, he got them to bring extra back for him. Indeed, he made regular orders and told them what hours he would be on duty. It was apparently understood among the men of the guard unit that they could each keep some of the food, but most of it was for distribution to people in need.

John said he worked his position to the hilt to help people get food. He noted that many people had gone into hiding. He said that they, as well as some members of the resistance, had no means of getting food, so he supplied them as best he could. He claimed that he kept many people from starving.

John didn't mention his checkpoint activities, which are uncorroborated, in any of his postwar statements. I suspect he believed such disclosure could be seen in a negative light. Dutch officials might conclude he benefited at the expense of others or even that he was a war profiteer. This latter idea would likely have been quickly dispelled at the time of his arrest in May 1945 by the facts ascertained by the Dutch Custodian of Enemy Property, namely that his bank account held only a few hundred guilders, his tax return for that year was a mere fifty-five guilders, and he carried with him just twenty guilders.[339] But the notion that he diverted food from the Dutch people for his personal use might have been a problem.

---

[339] John's file with the Dutch Custodian of Enemy Property (DNA, NBI 146868). Transcription (22 pages) of a September 24, 2004, tape recording by Nico van Horn while he reviewed and orally translated information from three collaborator files on J. J. Petersen held in the DNA.

There was the chance his activities could be lumped together with those of another organization, the *Nederlandsche Landwacht* (Dutch Home Guard), which began operation in early 1944. Consisting of NSB men, it operated under the auspices of the German green police. In 't Veld says, "the general view of the Landwacht-man was that of a local Nazi, dressed up in an absurd uniform and armed with a shotgun, ordering passers-by to produce their papers and more often than not relieving them of what little food they had been able to find, and eating it himself later with his comrades." He adds that the Landwacht "at once made itself feared and a source of ridicule." He also says "the Landwacht degenerated more and more into a band of robbers and terrorists," according to "its own Chief of Staff."[340]

John's situation could also have been complicated if either of two incidents he claimed he was involved in came to light. The first occurred during one of his solo expeditions in search of food, something he did increasingly during the latter years of the war. On the occasion in question, he said he compelled a greedy farmer at gunpoint to open one of his pits of potatoes and allow hunger-trekkers, possibly during the Hunger Winter of 1944–45, to help themselves. The other was when he supposedly was accused of theft while on guard duty. This accusation, along with its repercussions, is one of the most fantastic and unlikely stories he told me. He said it led to him being court-martialled and miraculously exonerated. But why, given the guard unit's illegal activities, would his accuser, who was a member of the same ten-man unit, charge John with theft when the same charge might be levelled at him as well? Regarding the food John received from the trucks, he said he always kept for himself a small amount, which he always shared with the other men in the unit. John never indicated what motivated his accuser. He only said that if he were found guilty, he would have been shot for high treason while on duty.

According to John, he denied the charge at his court martial. The other eight men backed him up. He contended that it was a miracle

---

[340] In 't Veld, 1522.

that the other eight were so solidly behind him and always said the right thing and made the story stick. Despite being questioned separately, their stories cohered. John said he didn't know why they stuck their necks out. If they were caught, they could have all been charged with conspiracy, he added. But there is more to this tale, for the man who had charged John was accused of falsely accusing an SS man. John said he didn't want to see this man punished, so he stood up for him. He said his accuser was convinced he had reason to lay the charge and believed he was doing his duty. The other eight men backed this up as well, their story being that the accuser knew John was very thorough when he checked trucks and probably saw John take something out during his inspection that the accuser thought John didn't return, but in fact did. "The accuser was thus let off too," my notes conclude.

Suspect as this account is, it is followed by one of the better-documented episodes of John's life during the occupation. Despite being let off, he said there now was a doubt attached to him that resulted in him being transferred to Amersfoort for a new assignment. He was to be part of a Schutzgruppe team processing soldiers of the former Dutch army who were to be sent to Germany for work service.

Perhaps John really was charged with theft, court-martialled, and improbably exonerated, or maybe there was some other difficulty, after which he was assigned to Amersfoort. But if this is the case, the problem didn't prevent him from returning to Schutzgruppe guard duty later in the war, according to one of his stories. On the other hand, the alleged theft, court martial, and exoneration could be another of his tall tales. Perhaps what happened was ordinary rather than extraordinary. Perhaps he was simply assigned to Amersfoort because it was one of those rudimentary tasks that the Schutzgruppe had been created to perform, thereby enabling the Wehrmacht's scarce resources to be deployed to more important functions. Whatever the case, it is notable that John claimed miraculous events both preceded and followed his time at Amersfoort. Perhaps this is an indication of the stress he was under while he was there, and possibly before and after as well.

John's assignment at Amersfoort was a result of Germany's total war policy. Following "intensive discussions" with his officials in the Netherlands, Hitler ordered the re-internment of the former Dutch army, which in 1940 "had consisted of about 300,000 men," many of whom had been imprisoned for a time following the Five-Day War.[341] Himmler viewed the measure "as a new method to conscript cheap labor" that was to be transported to Germany.[342]

When the re-internment order was announced on April 29, 1943, the Dutch people reacted with shock and considerable resistance. The news provoked an immediate walkout at several factories in Hengelo, in the east of the country, which led to the second of three great strikes during the occupation. "Factories, mines and other businesses emptied, as did municipal installations. Farm-workers left the estates.... On the following morning 18,000 men at Philips [factories] in Eindhoven went on strike, [as did] nearly 40,000 in the mines of Limburg."[343] Close to a million Dutch workers participated; several transport and supply systems were seriously disrupted.[344]

Martial law was proclaimed in five towns on April 30 and "was extended to cover the entire country" the next day.[345] "Riot-act posters, announcing capital punishment for strikers and an eight o'clock curfew, appeared everywhere."[346] On May 1, Anne Frank recorded in her diary that "Holland is being punished for the workers' strikes. Martial law has been declared, and everyone is going to get one less butter coupon. What naughty children."[347] But the repercussions were real. Rauter gave "orders to his SS and police troops to fire without warning on any assembly." Moreover,

---

[341] Hirschfeld, 179 (intensive discussions). Paape, 79 (about 300,000).
[342] Maass, 135 (Himmler). Paape, 79.
[343] Paape, 79, 80.
[344] Hirschfeld, 179 ("Almost a million"; serious disruptions).
[345] Paape, 80.
[346] Maass, 136.
[347] Frank, 99.

according to historian Harry Paape, "Death sentences were carried out after only the most perfunctory hearings." Many strikers returned to work on Monday, May 3. "On Tuesday another 19 executions were carried out."[348] By the time the strike ended on May 7, ninety-five people had been shot and killed in the streets and another four hundred were seriously wounded.[349] Eighty sentences of death had been imposed and sixty people had been executed.[350] And thousands of strikers had been arrested, nine hundred of whom were interned in Holland or Germany. "More than a hundred officials and holders of public offices were dismissed, among them 15 mayors, mainly of towns where the strike had been intensive."[351]

There were additional repercussions. First, "all students who had refused to sign a declaration of loyalty to the occupying power" were to be sent to Germany for work service.[352] Second, all men between eighteen and thirty-five were required to register for forced labour in Germany.[353] In response, many men went into hiding. This fact and the Germans' "increasingly vindictive attitude towards the Dutch civil population," led to significant growth in the organization and activities of the resistance.[354] Despite this, 148,000 conscripted workers were sent to the Reich in 1943. By the end of the war, 550,000 men—or 16 per cent of the male population of the Netherlands—did forced labour in their own country, Germany, or elsewhere in the Third Reich, and 30,000 of them never returned home.[355]

***

---

[348] Paape, 80–81.
[349] Hirschfeld, 179 (May 7, last day of strike). Maass, 137. Paape, 81 (ninety-five killed, four hundred seriously wounded).
[350] Hirschfeld, 179. Paape says (81): "The strike had cost 80 deaths by execution."
[351] Paape, 81.
[352] Paape, 81.
[353] Maass, 137. Paape writes (81) "that all men between the ages of 18 and 35 … had to report for *Arbeitseinsatz*, labour duty in Germany."
[354] Moore, 203.
[355] Maass, 138 (148,000). Van der Zee, 305 (550,000; 16 percent; 30,000).

In addition to what John told me in 1976, there are five documents that attest to his role at Amersfoort processing members of the former Dutch army for forced labour in Germany. These include his statement of October 29, 1946; a handwritten summary of his history and case date-stamped November 14, 1946, which was provided to Special Prosecutor Dr. F. Hollander; J. G. Siewers's testimonial letters of October 26, 1946, and June 23, 1951; and Barend van Leeuwen's testimonial letter of June 17, 1951.

Speaking of the former soldiers he dealt with, John said in his statement, "I was only responsible for checking and stamping their identification. I did send as many Dutch boys home as I could; there were even ones that had no identity cards at all that I sent home as well. I do not know the names of these people anymore, but it was commonly known that I did this."[356]

He told me he and the other members of the Schutzgruppe were each responsible for part of the alphabet; the former soldiers were processed based on the first letter of their last names. They presented their papers, and the Schutzgruppe men had to decide if there was any reason to stamp their documents, thereby providing an exemption from work service. John said only those who had a very good reason were to get stamped. A good reason was "an injury, disability or an important job." He told me he stamped everyone who came to him. Over a two-week period he illegally exempted between 1,200 and 1,500 men; this was about 150 a day, he added. What he was doing apparently became known among the former soldiers who sought to be processed at his station. On a different occasion he told me he stamped the papers of approximately 1,200 former soldiers. He said he had put his life on the line for all 1,200 in an indirect way.

J. G. Siewers owned the photography shop where John worked prior to the German invasion. It is not known how much Siewers was in the shop during this period, however. In his letter of October 26,

---

[356] John's statement of October 29, 1946.

1946, Siewers wrote that he had "to fully thank [John] for my deportation exemption." He went on to say,

> In the last week of the admission, I made my way to Amersfoort. They already told me outside to try to announce myself to a table where a Dutchman was sitting.
>
> Once inside I quickly found out at which table the helpful Dutchman in a German uniform was sitting. Randomly I walked toward him and coincidentally this man happened to be a business acquaintance of mine.
>
> Immediately he said to me: "I will do everything to free you, but this week they are extremely strict. Try first with this stamp and if that doesn't work, come back to me and we will try it through the doctor."
>
> Indeed, because of this stamp I was freed.[357]

---

[357] Siewers's letter of June 23, 1951 (see footnote 4), goes into greater detail. Here it is in its entirety:

During the German occupation years as [an] ex Dutch officer I had to present myself in a centre called Amersfoort.

As my boss at the office at that time was a National-Socialist, I didn't get much help from him, and I had to present myself after [some time] without any valid release permit (*Ausweisz Bescheinigung*).

The chances for me to get deported to a German prisoner of war camp were big. On top of this the measures had been sharpened during the last two weeks rather importantly.

People had told me before I had to report to look out for a fluently Dutch speaking German. As the fatal day for reporting came, I was in possession of a worthless paper called *Vorläufiger Ausweisz*, with which I wouldn't get a release, if there hadn't been special help.

While waiting in line for the office with the letters R.S. on it, I heard the German in the next wicket ask in fluent Dutch: "Are there any people here with the letters T.U."

I thought this is my only chance, so I went to this German and he happened to live in the same town as I did. I knew him slightly before the war. I showed him the worthless paper and he put a mark on it immediately and said: "If this doesn't succeed, come back to me and we will try it with the doctor."

Given John's history of exaggeration and lies, it's easy to dismiss his claims that he exempted 1,200 to 1,500 former Dutch soldiers from forced labour. However, it does appear that his courageous use of the stamp (and other methods available to him) did benefit a considerable number of Dutch men. This conclusion is supported by two sources. Barend van Leeuwen's letter of June 17, 1951, says of John, "In Amersfoort he had to control our soldiers and officers who were to be deported to Germany to the Prisoner of War camps. Personally I know he has helped many men to get a release from this." Moreover, the prosecution summary of November 14, 1946, says that John's liberal use of the exemption stamp enabled "many Dutchmen [to] be sent back home."[358]

As word of what John was doing spread among the former Dutch soldiers, it's not surprising it also came to the attention of the Germans. "Finally the Germans heard of it," he said in his statement. "They did not have proof of anything, but I was shown the door."[359] His statement makes no mention of punishment, presumably because the lack of proof precluded any action. By contrast, he told me he was arrested "for high treason ... on the tenth day by two [German] army officers," which seems more likely than simply being "shown the door." But there is another possibility. Unlikely as it may seem, John may simply have gotten away with it. If so, this is more of a miracle than the miracle he claimed happened next.

After his alleged arrest at Amersfoort, John said he was transferred to German army headquarters at Hilversum, but instead of being dealt with there—"which would have been normal"—he was transferred again, this time to the office of the army commander for the western part of the country, located in The Hague. The

---

It did succeed and although the second control post had much scruples, I got my release.

I herewith declare according to the truth and with the greatest conviction that thanks to Mr. Jan Jurgen Petersen ex-German soldier of Hilversum I got released then from deportation to the German prisoner of war camps.

[358] Prosecution document of November 14, 1946.

[359] John's statement of October 29, 1946.

commander, according to John, was a general, but the Netherlands Institute for War Documentation has stated that the position of *Ortskommandant* "was far too modest and too low in the hierarchy of the German army to be executed by a *General*." The institute also pointed out that the three men who served in the position of commander between February 1941 and August 1943—Boese, Creuzinger, and Steigerthal—were all majors.[360]

This is the first of several facts that contradict John's claims about the commander, who appears to be a Wiertz-like figure in a make-believe world. Just as Wiertz is introduced to the story after the debacle of John's sea career, so the commander first appears following the extended crisis of John's Schutzgruppe assignment at Amersfoort. Moreover, John may have had more on his mind than what was going on at Amersfoort. He may have been worried about his brothers, both of whom were serving the Germans in the east.

Wim, who had attended the horticultural school at Boskoop, had wanted to join the Netherlands East Company to put his agricultural training to use and to support Germany in its fight against the Russians. The company had been established by the Nazis that June in support of their goal of *Lebensraum*, or living space. Wim did not join in 1942 because of Dina's objections. However, after their engagement was cancelled, he volunteered for the Netherlands East Company in July 1943 and, after training at Hoofddorp, was sent later that summer to Rowno in Ukraine where he joined the German equivalent of the company. He managed a sheep farm for about four months in Askania-Nova near the Isthmus of Perekop, which joins the Crimean Peninsula to Ukraine. Meanwhile, Constant was wounded in late August or September and spent the rest of the year in recovery. When John told me he felt guilty because a German commander he knew had four sons fighting on the eastern front, I suspect he was really expressing how he felt about Constant and Wim.

---

[360] Attachment to Dr. Hans de Vries's email of August 4, 2005, and letter of August 5, 2005, to the author. According to Van der Zee (292), the commander of German army headquarters in Amsterdam was Major Körner.

234   A SNAKE ON THE HEART

John said what happened after his arrest was highly unusual. First, his transfer from Hilversum to The Hague was "mysterious." Second, he met with the commander alone; the commander sent the two guards out of his office. Third, the commander invited John, a subordinate charged with high treason to sit down. Fourth, the commander reportedly astounded John by telling him he was a clever man he'd heard about who he knew had a lot of connections.

The commander, according to John, was a short, heavy-set, gracious man who was a real charmer with the ladies. Indeed, he had a lot of girlfriends, many of whom were taking advantage of him. John called him a good soldier, saying he was not a Nazi but believed in the German cause. If the commander were told certain people were in need, he would provide for them. John said he did a lot for the Dutch people, some of whom were in the resistance—these were the same people who shot and killed the commander when he tried to escape back to Germany at the end of the war. Some years later, John added—by way of clarification to a question I had asked—that the commander had been head of the judges during his court martial for theft.

As a result of John's private meeting with the commander, he was exonerated of all charges and transferred to his command, or so John claimed. John supposedly worked for the commander until early February 1945. But information from the Netherlands Institute for War Documentation indicates that Major Steigerthal served as German army commander in The Hague through August 1943 and was replaced by a man named Modrow (rank unknown) in September. Moreover, Modrow was replaced by a new commander about June 1944 who was followed by Commander Zimmerman about September 1944.[361] Thus, the only question regarding John's story about the commander is this: Is it a complete fabrication or are aspects of it, other than the commander, true?

According to one of his postwar statements, John worked at German army headquarters in The Hague from mid-December 1944

---

[361] Attachment to Hans de Vries's email of August 4, 2005, and letter of August 5, 2005.

to May 1, 1945. In his letter of June 1951, he wrote that in conjunction with his Schutzgruppe service he worked as a "clerk at the Wehrmacht Kommandantur in the Hague [sic]."[362] Perhaps he also had occasion to spend time at German army headquarters prior to the last four months of the war. Given the Schutzgruppe's connection with the army, perhaps he developed useful army contacts starting in 1943. Perhaps these contacts helped him in the same manner he claimed the fictional commander did.

John told me that when he was with the army in The Hague, supposedly working for the commander, he managed to have a large printing press placed in a safe building where it could be used by the resistance on certain nights. John said that safe nights were those when he knew the Gestapo and SS would be searching elsewhere. Perhaps this story is more make-believe. Or perhaps John was taking credit for something he'd heard about. Or perhaps it's true.

Some of his claims are more grandiose and clearly more suspect. He said he was in a very responsible position when he worked for the commander, and that his new position coincided with what the underground wanted him to do, which was to infiltrate a high German office. He mentioned three functions he performed in his sensitive position. Two of these—the opportunity to continue to stamp people's papers to exempt them from forced labour in Germany and travelling to the east of the country to pick up items that were scarce or nonexistent in the west—may have been things he did to some degree. The third function—to maintain contact with other branches of the German army in the western half of the Netherlands, Belgium, and northern France on behalf of the commander—is much more of a stretch.

John said he received reports from as many as three hundred different outfits via their field-army phones. Each of these outfits had a code name that changed every day, and John said he had to know them all. He told me that his remarkable memory enabled him to do

---

[362] John's statement of October 29, 1946. John's 1951 letter, 4.

this and implied that he advised the resistance of the location of some or all these units, but he stated that this knowledge was put to little use except on a few occasions when it didn't help much because of the stupidity of the English Secret Service.

He also said he served as a courier for the German army and claimed he carried information for the underground at the same time he was carrying messages for the Wehrmacht. He told me he was valuable to the underground because of his SS uniform and papers and being able to speak German fluently. (He told the Dutch authorities after the war that he did not speak German.)[363] According to John, the information he carried for the underground was coded documents from one cell to another, which he placed in his army courier briefcase. He did this even though army couriers generally worked in pairs. As he and the other courier, who didn't know about John's underground work, rode their bicycles through part of The Hague, they were ambushed. John's companion was killed. He said he found the episode difficult and emotionally isolating. It made him very lonesome.

"Why don't they know I'm on their side?"

He said he knew he could not say, "Hey, stop it! I'm on your side. I've got papers here, papers for our side." But he also said he was strongly tempted to do so.

The men who carried out the ambush were unaffiliated members of the resistance, he said, adding that such attacks often happened. He described these assaults as "stupid," saying they could serve no really good purpose and caused hardship for the underground and the community. In this case, the entire male population of one side of the street where the attack took place was sent to work camps in Germany. John would have agreed with a member of the resistance, quoted in Hanson's *Underground Out of Holland*, who maintained that the resistance should do its work surreptitiously, producing "the most harm" without the enemy "knowing that he had been hurt."[364]

---

[363] John's statement of October 29, 1946, 3.
[364] Hanson, 74.

John categorized the opportunity to work for the commander as a "miracle," which is not surprising given there is no corroborating evidence for this relationship. He added that he didn't become aware of how his life had been guided until he was imprisoned in a concentration camp after the war. This guidance steered him, he implied. When he was in difficulty, he would always know what to do—like someone was sitting on his shoulder giving him advice and crucial warnings.

While John's Schutzgruppe assignment at Amersfoort is probably the best documented episode of his wartime activities, his claims he was court-martialled before that episode and arrested and exonerated after it are unsupported, although other events later in the war, which will be discussed, raise other possibilities. Nonetheless, based on what is known, his claims appear to be after-the-fact fantasy overlays, which call into question not only how he recalled the war when he told me about it, but his mental health as well.

15

ANAK, THE INTELLIGENCE SERVICE, AND PRIVATE FOOD FORAYS

The notion John overlay parts of his story with fantasies decades after the fact begs the question, What was his life really like toward the end of 1943 and into 1944? There are several pieces of information that help us form a picture of this period. Perhaps the most notable is his move from De Centrale to the Algemeen Nederlandsch Assurantiekantoor or ANAK (the General Dutch Insurance Company) in December 1943. Was this move simply a better job opportunity or was there some manipulation involved, either on John's part or that of the SD? It's a fair question given John said his work with Feldmeijer's Intelligence Service began the next month and much of it took place in his ANAK office where Scholte, his Intelligence Service supervisor, and Korteland, an Intelligence Service colleague, came to see him.

"At regular intervals," according to John's statement of April 22, 1947, "Scholte would come by and ask me where my reports had gone. They were not ready. Then Scholte would sit at my desk and type the report I dictated to him." John's statement goes on to say: "KORTELAND visited me frequently.... he asked me to take notes of what he had told me, and these notes stayed on my desk until SCHOLTE came to my office, took them, and then used my typewriter to write a proper report. I did not pass these reports on to anyone else since SCHOLTE was to pass these on to the Intelligence Service who would circulate them."[365]

I have the impression that John's life now revolved primarily around two poles. One was the Schutzgruppe and his private activities in pursuit of food, the other was his ANAK office, where both insurance and Intelligence Service work occurred. Although he was still attached to the SD, it would not surprise me if he operated at a certain remove from it, at least when he could manage it. This supposition is based on other aspects of his life at this time. He continued to wear his SS uniform on occasion, and he made use of the SD when it served his purpose. How much he was involved with it as an SD policeman during the last two years of the war is unknown. This is a pregnant unknown. For the four months from July 1944 through October, every aspect of due legal process was eliminated on direction from Berlin. German police shot saboteurs in the act or subsequently executed them without trial.[366]

John never told me he worked for De Centrale for approximately thirty months compared to less than eighteen months at ANAK. Yet he spoke at greater length and with much more enthusiasm about his role at ANAK, which he said had grown during the war from one office in The Hague to seven offices throughout the country by 1944. He implied he was responsible for much of this growth. ANAK was in bad shape when he became its manager, he claimed. He said he was the youngest director of an insurance company in all of Holland and, while he enjoyed the challenge of the work, he felt the burden of his responsibility, partly because of his youthful age. (He turned twenty-nine in March 1944.) The Board of Directors looked upon him "as a miracle worker," he added.

This bravado and boastfulness is typical John. His claims are undoubtedly inflated and may be largely untrue. What is more useful are statements made about him by two of his ANAK colleagues.

---

[365] John's statement of April 22, 1947, 1, 3.
[366] Maass, 181–182.

Jacobus Theodorus van Schouwen was an ANAK inspector and the chief of personnel. Antonius Johannes Grootveld was an accountant who served as ANAK's interim director from July 15, 1943. Both men gave statements about John on October 28, 1946.

Van Schouwen joined ANAK in February 1944. He had frequent conversations with John and sometimes saw him wear an SS uniform. He said John felt betrayed by the SS and was neither an advocate for the occupation nor for the Germans. Nor did he, to the best of Van Schouwen's knowledge, ever trouble or betray anyone. In fact, he helped Van Schouwen when he was in trouble with two SD men. The issue involved a female ANAK employee who was romantically involved with one of the SD men and frequently wanted time off to be with him. When Van Schouwen denied her a leave of absence it led to him being confronted by the two SD men. John spoke to them on behalf of Van Schouwen and defused the situation.[367]

Grootveld also saw John wearing an SS uniform as well as a German Wehrmacht (i.e., Schutzgruppe) uniform. He and John worked together for about two months. They talked about politics and their different attitudes to the occupation. John told Grootveld he'd been raised in the Netherlands and felt Dutch, but as a German, he also felt obliged to serve in the SS and the Schutzgruppe. At the same time, he said he could understand and approve of Grootveld's negative attitude toward the occupiers. While they didn't agree politically, this didn't lead to any animosity between them, according to Grootveld. Indeed, John knew that Grootveld was involved in illegal activities and kept an illegal radio at the ANAK office, but he did nothing about it. Grootveld added John neither pressured him to join a political party nor, to the best of his knowledge, ever caused trouble for any of the other ANAK staff.[368]

According to these accounts, John was hardly a Nazi ideologue or a hardline member of the German establishment. Although he "felt

---

[367] Van Schouwen's statement of October 28, 1946 (DNA, CABR 109786). Attachment to Blauw's email of December 3, 2009, 3–4.
[368] Grootveld's statement of October 28, 1946 (DNA, CABR 109786).

torn," he told me he tried to deal with situations he encountered more in terms of people who needed help rather than different nationalities. When he helped people, he did it for them as people, not against Germany. He carried on this "double game" both to maximize his independence and to avoid being sent to the front lines.

December 1943 was also the month Wim returned to Holland. He had not enjoyed managing the sheep farm at Askania-Nova, a small place in a hostile region. When the Germans withdrew, he said he delivered the sheep to Odessa as ordered, then returned via Rowno and Germany to the Netherlands on medical leave. Van Leeuwen's statement says, "after four months he came back from Germany on false papers."[369] In January or February 1944, Wim became a BL or supporting member of the SS. John and their mother served as his guarantors. Although there is no proof, it is hard not to see this development as anything but Wim's acceptance of a recommendation from John, a step meant to demonstrate Wim's loyalty and to help protect him. Dina and her father learned of the membership that October.[370] That John had not consulted Barend van Leeuwen about this step is possibly another indication that their relationship was not as close as John led me to believe. On the other hand, such consultation may have been precluded because Wim and Dina had not yet reconciled. They married on March 23. Wim remained on medical leave from the Netherlands East Company until April, after which he made two midyear trips to Lemberg, Poland; the first for six weeks when he worked on a farm; the second for three weeks when he worked in an office.

***

---

[369] Van Leeuwen's statement of October 17, 1946, 4.
[370] Wim's statement of October 23, 1946, 19–20 (January or February 1944; guarantors or sureties; Dina did not know until October 1944). Dr. Blauw's report on Wim of February 14, 2007, p. 11 (Van Leeuwen did not learn of Wim's "true disposition until October 1944").

Much of the Netherlands was in considerable distress during the gloomy winter of 1943-44.[371] Civilian needs were, at best, an afterthought as the war steadily deteriorated for the Germans. The circumstances of daily life were grim and would only get grimmer, culminating in the awful misery of the last four and a half months of the war—the Hunger Winter of 1944-45—and the starvation for some during the early spring that followed.

Always a highly sectarian country, the Netherlands was now deeply fissured in new ways.[372] There were those who were in the German camp, those who opposed it, and those who simply sought to keep a low profile and survive. All were under increasing duress. Fearful of the anticipated Allied invasion, the Germans were hard at work on their Atlantic Wall. They were also threatened internally by the resistance, which sought to hinder and sabotage German interests. The resistance, meanwhile, was subject to the ever-present threats of German infiltration, capture, and execution, as well as reprisals against third parties held as hostages, "the so-called *Todeskandidaten* (candidates for death)." The NSB's concerns largely mirrored those of the Germans. Prominent among these was the possibility of being attacked by the resistance, which led to the creation of the *Landstorm*, an NSB defense force, in the spring of 1943, and the Landwacht (Netherlands Home Guard) in January 1944. The Landstorm became a regular Waffen-SS unit, while the Landwacht was soon taken over by Rauter and employed as a quasi-police formation.[373]

The different camps suffered varying degrees of duress. Some were better positioned to dish out abuse than others. The Landwacht, the members of which were little more than untrained, undisciplined goons, has been called Mussert's "most contemptible" creation. In

---

[371] Maass, 150.
[372] Maass, 52.
[373] In 't Veld, 1506-1507 (candidates for death). Hirschfeld, 309n (Landstorm, self-defense force, spring 1943, Waffen-SS). Van der Zee, 105 (Landwacht – Nazi Home Guard, "officially recognized" January 1944). Maass, 153 (Landwacht – Netherlands Home Guard), 154 (Rauter, auxiliary police).

addition to robbing "hunger-trippers of their precious foodstuff," its members also helped the Germans search for people in hiding and to round up men for forced labour.[374] Those in hiding were reduced to "balancing on the edge of the abyss," Anne Frank wrote on May 25, 1944. Their survival depended on outside helpers and not being betrayed. "We're going to be hungry, but nothing is worse than being caught," she concluded the same entry. Slightly more than two months later, on August 4, she and the rest of her family, as well as the other four people hiding in the secret annex at 263 Prinsengracht in Amsterdam, were arrested. Of the eight of them, only Anne's father survived the war.[375]

John was often away, according to Hans. When he came home, he never stayed long, only a day or two. "He often came at night and left the next morning before [I was] up," Hans recalled. Both he and Susan told me John sometimes brought food home. Susan told me about vegetables "obtained with danger" due to the possibility of being shot by the Germans. She also made a hesitating, uncertain reference to untended vegetable gardens, which reminded me of a story John had told me thirty-two years earlier.

Many of the country's railways are built on a kind of dyke, John said. The rails sit atop triangle-shaped earthen embankments. The slopes on either side of the rails generally range from ten to twenty feet in height, he told me. Prior to the war, these fertile areas were leased to citizens to grow vegetables. But when the occupation began, one of the first German edicts was to prohibit people from coming within a specified distance of the tracks, thereby putting the former vegetable patches off-limits. Manned watchtowers enforced the prohibition.

When John noticed that the vegetables were seeding themselves and continuing to grow, he decided to start harvesting them. He said he did this by putting his SS combat training to use. There were

---

[374] Maass, 153 (untrained, undisciplined; most contemptible). Van der Zee, 105 (robbed hunger-trippers, helped on roundups/razzias, searched for "divers").
[375] Frank, 304.

ditches full of water at the base of the slopes. "The hard thing was to get to the ditch unseen," he noted. Always at night, he would use methods of camouflage he had been taught and crawl on his stomach to the ditch. Several times the guards heard something and opened fire, but they never came to investigate, "most likely out of fear," he speculated. The bullets struck the ground or the water close to where he hid. Sometimes he was on the ground, sometimes he was in the water. He said he discovered "you can sweat in water." He would wait until the guards started to talk or there was a shift change, at which point he would get out of the ditch and onto the slope and start picking vegetables and filling his sack. Then he would crawl back to safety. While "filling the sack would take fifteen minutes at most, the whole exercise would take at least four hours." There were times when he had to get back into the ditch with an empty or only partially filled sack. But his successes kept him going back. It was a "glorious moment when you got home with a full sack of vegetables," he said. In addition to his family, he told me he also distributed vegetables to those in need. He said he collected vegetables in this manner throughout the war.

Another gambit he employed was to ride around trying to get extra food from farmers. He said he used his identification papers and his uniform—he didn't specify which one, but it was undoubtedly his SS uniform—to get through checkpoints and help him get what he wanted.

He had other food sources available to him. As a German, he was entitled to receive food coupons. But he claimed he never used them because he thought it unfair to the Dutch people. Did he mean he never used the coupons personally or that he never used them at all? Tempting as it would have been to use them, I suspect he eschewed the coupons because accepting or using them might reveal to the SS that he was German and not Dutch, as they believed.

He maintained he also earned extra food late in the war by volunteering to run messages by motor bike between army headquarters in The Hague and army headquarters at Utrecht, sixty kilometres away. There was heavy reliance on these couriers. Allied bombing was causing significant damage, and John said that German communications were in a bad state. It was risky work. The couriers, who frequently travelled at night in the complete dark, couldn't see the bomb craters that pockmarked the road. John told me many riders were killed. The worst he experienced was to be strafed a couple of times. He was getting very little sleep then, he added.

16

JOHN IS INVESTIGATED—OR SO HE CLAIMED

"Discoveries" made by Feldmeijer's Intelligence Service "were trivial in the extreme," according to In 't Veld.[376] But this was not always the case. A point of friction between Korteland's statement of April 14, 1947, and John's of eight days later provides an example. It focuses on serious issues and contemplates significant consequences—forced labour in Germany—for those being investigated.

John's statement says he was receiving reports from Korteland who "travelled all over the Netherlands and ... had all kinds of connections in all sorts of circles." Korteland's information concerned sabotage against the Wehrmacht "in the district of Roosendale, the smuggling of weapons from Belgium to the Netherlands, underground members working in a grass-drying plant in Krimpenerwaard [south of Gouda], and of an underground group in de Peel (N. Ba.) [on the border between the provinces of North Brabant and Limburg]." Regarding the underground group in de Peel, both John and Korteland appear to be at pains in their statements not to incriminate themselves.

John asked Korteland to investigate the de Peel group and, according to Korteland, "insisted on more and more specific

---

[376] In 't Veld, 1513.

information." Korteland says although he put some information in writing, "he avoided mentioning names and addresses [and otherwise] found excuses not [to] deliver."[377] John's statement provides a different picture. While he admits he asked "KORTELAND for updates on the reports re the underground organization in de Peel, after SCHOLTE had repeatedly asked [him] to get more information," he also claims he suggested to Korteland that he suppress key pieces of information. "I pointed out to him that he should not pass on reports of members of the underground to SCHOLTE, as there may be complicated and mitigating circumstances for some of the individuals involved, which would make them not want to be in Germany," John said.[378] According to John's statement, "KORTELAND'S reply to this was, 'Either you are a National-Socialist or you are not; even a surgeon cuts out the rotten flesh.'"[379]

There is a second subject on which John and Korteland's statements disagree. Korteland says John told him and Scholte he was to be drafted and this occurred "about June 1944 for the Wach- und Schutzdienst."[380] John disputed this. He maintained in his statement, "It was not in May–June 1944, but rather the evening before 'Dolle Dinsdag' [Crazy Tuesday] (4 September 1944) that I told SCHOLTE that I was called up to serve with the 'Schutzgruppe' and that I could no longer provide reports of the 'Intelligence Service.'"[381] Perhaps Korteland mixed up the names of the two organizations as well as misremembered the time period when John was "drafted" or called up. The two organizations were similar in that both were staffed by *Rijkduitsers* (foreign Germans) and were adjuncts to the Wehrmacht, performing rudimentary and repetitive functions on its behalf. According to Louis de Jong, the Wach- und Schutzdienst was

---

[377] Korteland's April 14, 1947, statement. Attachment to Blauw's email of December 3, 2009, 3–4.
[378] John's statement of April 22, 1947, 3, 4.
[379] John's statement of April 22, 1947, 4.
[380] Korteland's April 14, 1947, statement. Attachment to Blauw's email of December 3, 2009, 3–4.
[381] John's statement of April 22, 1947, 4.

established by a private company and worked under contract for the Wehrmacht to provide security at airports and other infrastructure.[382]

Nonetheless, I wonder if John was dissembling by making a truthful statement about what happened in early September to hide something else that occurred in the spring. After all, it was not just Korteland who understood John's life was to change in a significant way about June. Constant's letter of June 14, 1944, also anticipated a major change—that John could be sent to the eastern front:

> Mother wrote that [John] passed again and that he was to leave early in June. Did he really leave or did it fail again; with him you never really know. Well, he always wanted this, so now he gets what he wants. But it won't be easy for him. I wonder if he will be hard enough for it. If he is not, he will break here and that would be such a pity for him.[383]

In 1976, John told me he was investigated toward the end of the war by the German army and the SS, and that these separate investigations occurred about a month apart. It was my understanding these alleged investigations occurred between November 1944 and January 1945. There is some modest corroboration for this understanding. In December 1944 or the next month, Susan, Hans, and Harald took the train from The Hague to Hilversum. While at Stanni's home, Susan and John put blackout paper on the windows of the top-floor room where the boys were to sleep. While they were doing this, John was called downstairs and outside. Susan told me the authorities had come for him. "He was

---

[382] Blauw's report of December 9, 2009, says the Wach- und Schutzdienst, based on the prosecution document on John's case, was a semi-military organization for "foreign Germans" (*Rijkduitsers*) who were not in the active military. See Louis de Jong's *Het Koninkrijk der Nederlanden in de Tweede Wereldoorlog 1939–1945*, DEEL 6 eerste helft, 435 (attachment to Frank van Riet's email to the author of December 30, 2018).

[383] Constant's letter of June 14, 1944, quoted in Blauw's report of February 14, 2007, 2.

called away," she said. She thought it likely this had to do with one of the investigations John claimed to have undergone.

But what if one of these investigations occurred approximately a year earlier, in the latter months of 1943 or the early months of 1944? Writing about the autumn of 1943, Hitler's Luftwaffe adjutant, Nicolaus von Below, said that the Führer "regularly issued instructions to comb through the support services and reserves for young men to put at the front."[384] Although John didn't say what caused the investigations, the idea that one of them occurred during the earlier time frame could tie in with the information from Korteland and Constant. It also begs other questions. Might there be something to John's claim that he was court-martialled for theft prior to his August 1943 Schutzgruppe posting at Amersfoort or his supposed arrest during that assignment? Might one or both of those possible events have precipitated an investigation during the earlier time frame? This scenario, in conjunction with John's version of the SS investigation, could easily have created the expectation he would be going to the Russian front.

As with most of John's claims, his stories about these investigations contain much that is suspect and unverified. These stories also represent opportunities for him to indulge himself and to entertain. Moreover, their outcome does not line up with the hypothetical scenario I have put forward, for John said the SS investigation followed that of the army; but to make the scenario's timing work, I believe the SS investigation had to have happened first. This is one more illustration that what we don't know is much more than what we do, that John's stories can do at least as much to muddy the waters as to bring clarity to them, and that in trying to find the truth about aspects of his life, we sometimes find ourselves in those waters in the same way others have found themselves through the looking glass.

Notwithstanding my speculation that the SS investigation may have happened first and as much as a year or more earlier, what

---

[384] Von Below, 181.

follows is what John told me about the two investigations, starting with that of the German army. He said he received a notice directing him to report to Army Head Command in Amsterdam. He knew he would be questioned, that he was pretty well caught. He was interviewed, he claimed, by the Commander's adjunct who wanted to know why he was not in full uniform. Why was he only in the Schutzgruppe? As a German, he must have been called up by the army. John lied, saying he had never received a call-up notice. He then showed the adjunct his release from the SS, which greatly startled the man. The adjunct had not known John had been in the SS. He knew only of the conscription records and where John worked.

"That's impossible," the adjunct said. "Nobody is released from the SS."

John agreed with him but added he'd been released from active duty in order to conduct a special mission.

"What is it?"

"I can't tell you. The only way you can find out is to contact Hitler's headquarters. I'm under his special command." John was counting on the army's fear and jealousy of the SS; he told me the gambit worked. The adjunct was apparently not prepared to check John's story with the SS and instead dropped the matter.

John said he was called in and investigated by SS headquarters a month later. He maintained the SS was unaware of his earlier interrogation by the army. Still there were several things in his SS file that struck them as highly unusual. Why, they wanted to know, was he in the Netherlands and not at the front? And why had he been released from the SS?

"How am I to know?" John responded. "I was a volunteer."

"And I don't suppose you know how you came to be listed as a Dutch rather than a German volunteer?" he was asked.

"No, I don't," he lied.

Beyond this, he was truthful, he told me, which was a compound lie. He claimed he told his interrogator that he instructed SS trainees and worked with the army in The Hague. While the latter may have been true in some manner, the claim that he instructed SS trainees, as we know, is refuted by the available evidence.

John invited the interrogator to check the truth of what he was saying with his superiors. The man assured John he would. He also told him it was highly likely he would be going to the front. The official was good to his word. John said he received a notice ten days later advising him he was being sent to the front and directing him to report to an SS office in The Hague for a medical examination.

What are we to make of his purported release from the SS? Although he referred to it several times when he told me his story, examining what he said produces more questions than answers. Given he continued to wear an SS uniform after August 1941 and he continued to work part time in an SD office, he obviously had not achieved his outright release from the organization. The SS may, however, have given him some sort of document in conjunction with his return to the insurance industry and he may have been able to use it to his advantage in different situations, as he claimed, but we'll never know for sure if such a document existed and, if it did, what it said.

Another issue: If John had a certificate from a heart specialist declaring he was unfit for active military service, or if he had filed such a certificate with the Schutzgruppe, why did he not use this information in the interrogations to support his case? Or, if he did, why did he neglect to include this point when he told me about the investigations? This information may have exempted him from both the medical exam and serving at the front with the SS. On the other hand, given the urgent need for men, perhaps the SS overrode John's medical certificate or, alternatively, wanted to test its validity by seeing if their doctors would come to the same conclusion.[385] Only two things are certain about the purported medical exam. First, John did apparently have something

---

[385] According to John Spurr (quoted in *A Liberation Album*, 73), "Towards the end of the war, the Germans sent into battle both the very young and the very old.... men who were deaf, or ... who had stomach ailments." This suggests that physical fitness was not a primary concern for the German authorities. However, as a member of the SS, John was likely treated with greater respect (e.g., the apparent requirement to be medically examined).

wrong with his heart, discovered during a checkup when he was sixteen. Second, it's a fine example of his penchant to tell an amusing tale. But we don't know how much, if any, of what he said about the exam is true.

The night before the physical, he claimed he stayed up all night drinking very bitter coffee extract and chain-smoking. His intent was to exacerbate and highlight his existing minor heart condition. The next morning, when he was to be examined by a series of doctors, each one dedicated to a different part of the body, he didn't get past the first one, who dealt with the heart.

"Do you have anything wrong with your heart?" the doctor asked, after listening to it with his stethoscope.

"No, not that I know of," John replied, neglecting to mention the aforementioned irregularity or his alleged medical certificate.

"Well, you better see your own doctor because your heart sounds like an alarm clock."

"I hope this doesn't mean that I can't go to the front?"

"It certainly does. If you don't attend to it, you won't live long."

John said he was terribly sick for the next two days. His heart would alternately race then beat very slowly. He was dizzy, nauseous, and hyperactive. He thought he'd done himself in, he said, but he didn't mind: "It was much better than killing people at the front." But his heartbeat gradually returned to normal. The report of the doctor who examined him led to a follow-up examination by a specialist. This took place over two days, three hours each day, with the conclusion that John's heart had an untreatable nervous condition. Thus, he didn't have to go to the front. He told me he returned to his work with his fictitious commander at the *Ortskommandantur*, the Wehrmacht's local headquarters at Lange Voorhout 38 in The Hague.

Constant's letter says John "passed again." There is a chance this is a reference to a medical examination. We can only guess at what might, in fact, have occurred and at what John might have told their mother. Our inability to know, while frustrating, is to be expected given John's dedication to manipulation and the solitary way he, apparently, often practised it.

17

THE TIDE OF WAR AND THE TSUNAMIS THAT NEARLY DROWNED THE NETHERLANDS

While Korteland and Constant thought June 1944 was a month of some significance for John, it was certainly a month of decisive consequence for the war. D-Day, which saw an armada of close to 3,000 vessels land American, British, and Canadian troops at contiguous beaches in Normandy, finally arrived at 6:30 a.m. on Tuesday, June 6. Sixteen days later, on the third anniversary of Hitler's invasion of the Soviet Union, Stalin launched an enormous offensive. Involving 2.5 million men, 5,300 planes, and more than 5,000 tanks, it was meant to beat back and eventually crush Germany and its Axis partners. These were the grip points of a massive vice—the Red Army in the east and another 2 million Allied troops in the west—that would squeeze and strangle the Third Reich over the next ten and a half months until it surrendered unconditionally in early May 1945.

On June 15, the V-1 flying bomb, also known as the buzz bomb or doodlebug, had its major introduction when 244 of them hit London. On July 20, Hitler miraculously survived an assassination attempt, which an SD report said stoked "mystical, religious notions" many

254   A SNAKE ON THE HEART

Germans had for their Führer. Between these dates the conditions in some parts of the Netherlands "approximated civil war." As unrest grew, so did the occupier's terror tactics and the Allied bombing, while the ration of potatoes was reduced. Conditions were also brutal in Germany where many of its cities were being pulverized by Allied air raids. The full name of the V-1s, *Vergeltungswaffe-1* or Retaliation Weapon 1, spoke to this larger context.[386]

By August, the Germans were largely vanquished in France. In the Netherlands, the prospect of liberation produced widespread talk of a looming "Hatchet Day" when "Blitz-Justice" would be administered to collaborators. The Dutch government in London ordered some of their trusted contacts in the Netherlands "to convince the population that 'private justice' would be unDutch and anti-Democratic." In a confidential letter of September 5, 1944, the Dutch Roman Catholic church instructed "all parish priests ... to exert their influence to avoid lynchings in the days to follow. The priests were to hold open church buildings as places of refuge for Quislings [traitors]." Indeed, "many observers believed that [upon liberation—which was expected within weeks] the pent-up hatred of the population against the Quislings was such that only mass arrests of all suspected collaborators would prevent mass lynchings."[387] September also saw the government publish a list of collaborator crimes called the *Besluit Buitengewoon Strafrecht* (BBS), which created "a semblance of [a] legal framework" for what was to come— just not as quickly as many expected.[388]

When British troops roared into Belgium on September 3, capturing Brussels the same day and Antwerp on the fourth, there were major repercussions in the Netherlands. Seyss-Inquart ordered a state of emergency and, on the fifth, which became known as *Dolle Dinsdag*

---

[386] Kershaw, *Hitler: Nemesis*, 642 (244 hit London), 645 (Vergeltungswaffe-1 or Retaliation Weapon 1), 699 (mystical notions). Maass, 157 (civil war; German terror; Allied bombing; potato ration).
[387] Mason, 41 (Blitz-Justice; convince the population; parish priests; prevent mass lynchings).
[388] Mason, 43 (legal framework), 44 (BBS).

(Mad Tuesday), false rumours created a surreal atmosphere of exhilaration in which people in The Hague believed Rotterdam had welcomed the Allies, while others in Amsterdam celebrated the presumed liberation of The Hague and Haarlem. In Leiden, an underground newspaper printed thousands of "Liberation specials." Elsewhere, Dutch police accepted the surrender of German soldiers, a Nazi mayor gave his pistol to his secretary, and a resistance group commandeered a school.[389] The excitement was such that "many people who had been in hiding came out, thinking that salvation was at hand … a few [Jewish *onderduikers*] certainly fell into German hands."[390] On the other side, the NSB, fearing Hatchet Day, was overtaken by panic. A few apparently committed suicide, a grisly counterpoint to the more widespread suicides that took place among Jews, first at the end of the Five-Day War, and later during their roundup and deportation. Many, many more NSB members, including spouses and children, reacted in another way. Over 30,000 fled to Germany, among them Constant's wife, Elly, and their two young sons.[391] As it turned out, Maastricht, the first Dutch city to see the Allies, was not liberated until September 13, more than a week after the chimera of Dolle Dinsdag.

There was a second brief period of misplaced jubilation during September. It occurred with Operation Market Garden, launched by the Supreme Allied Commander, General Dwight David (Ike) Eisenhower, on September 17. It called for parachute troops to capture and hold the bridges over the Maas, Waal (Rhine), and Nederrijn (Lower Rhine) rivers and the five minor waterways

---

[389] Maass, 160 (Allied advance), 164–165 (wild rumours; unreal atmosphere; Dolle Dinsdag). Van der Zee, 21 (underground newspaper; soldiers surrender; Nazi mayor; resistance group), 23 (state of emergency).

[390] Moore, 226.

[391] Hirschfeld, 310 (more than 30,000). In his statement of February 14, 1947 (translation by Harry Eerkes), 5, Constant said his wife "fled the Netherlands in September 1944" (DNA, CABR 70629). A neighbour quoted in the same document (1) says the same thing. However, according to the attachment (3) to Blauw's email of February 14, 2007, a report of April 18, 1946? (the year is illegible) in DNA, NBI file 146852 says that Constant's wife left for Germany in July 1944.

between Eindhoven and Arnhem in the eastern Netherlands, while infantry, which would fight their way north on the highway between the two cities, would provide reinforcements for the newly acquired territory. The whole operation "was to be completed in two days and would be followed by an advance to the Zuider Zee [in the west] and a right wheel into the Ruhr."[392] According to one historian, "hundreds of thousands of people in the Netherlands were surprised by the squadrons of British and American aircraft on their way to Arnhem. Their great number, the routes they flew and their low altitude, all seemed to point to one conclusion: the hour of liberation was near."[393] Once again, people "in hiding appeared in the streets."[394]

The same day as the air assault on Arnhem, the Dutch government called a long-planned national railway strike to support Operation Market Garden. The third of the three great strikes of the occupation, it was an immediate success. In little more than twenty-four hours it "assumed a general character," with all but 1,500 to 2,000 of the 30,000-member workforce participating.[395] In some places the resistance made threats and brought pressure to bear on workers, which contributed to the high level of compliance. Not only did the trains stop running, virtually all communications were cut off: "Horse-pulled barges would only later come back in fashion—there was hardly any mail, only a few telephones still worked, and the radio and newspapers, under German 'protection,' wrote no word about [the strike]."[396] Public transport soon came to a standstill too.

"Whoever goes on strike will be shot," the Germans warned.[397] But, desperately short of manpower, they didn't have the resources to

---

[392] Hackett, 158.
[393] Paape, 82.
[394] Piet Kamphuis, "Caught Between Hope and Fear: Operation Market Garden and its Effects on the Civilian Population in the Netherlands," *Holland at War Against Hitler: Anglo-Dutch Relations, 1940–1945*, ed. M. R. D. Foot (London: Frank Cass, 1990), 171.
[395] Paape, 85.
[396] Van der Zee, 39.
[397] Paape, 85.

track down the strikers, although a small number of them were found and executed. Most of the strikers went into hiding.

The Germans had to bring 4,000 to 5,000 railway personnel from their own country to get the Dutch system running again, which took "approximately ten days."[398] And once it was back on track, they "dealt solely with their own needs." According to historian Henri van der Zee, the Germans "warned the Dutch food authorities not to count on them for any help as long as the strike continued. 'On the contrary,' they told The Hague, 'we will hinder you as much as possible.'"[399] Moreover, the German railway men "assisted in the plundering of the Netherlands; a massive quantity of trams, trains and factory installations were shipped to Germany."[400]

Although the railway strike was judged to have been "an unmitigated success"—which Van der Zee said "was the grand gesture against Nazism that the Dutch people needed to restore their national pride"—it came at a fearsome cost.[401] The Netherlands was descending into one of the darkest parts of its collective dark night of the soul, which is what the occupation by Nazi Germany was. That descent was aided and abetted by the failure of Operation Market Garden, the initial success of which could not be sustained due to bad weather, inadequate leadership and preparation, and insufficient resources, particularly air support. That failure ended the hope for the imminent liberation of the Netherlands. Although the Allies gained territory, they did not secure the Lower Rhine, which remained an imposing obstacle for another six months.[402]

At the end of September, both the Dutch and the Germans made pivotal decisions, which had profound consequences. A telegram of September 27 advised the exiled Dutch government, "In Amsterdam ... we still can count on five weeks' bread, three weeks'

---

[398] Kamphuis, 175 (ten days).
[399] Paape, 83 (their own needs). Van der Zee, 31 (Germans warn).
[400] Paape, 83.
[401] Kamphuis, 175 (unmitigated success). Van der Zee, 310 (grand gesture).
[402] Maass, 174.

potatoes and butter, and nil weeks' meat ..." Another telegram, this one "sent through Underground channels," said, "The production of gas will stop between 1 and 15 October, the supply of electricity not much later." Dr. J. W. Albarda, the Dutch Minister of Roads and Waterworks, wanted to end the strike, but Prime Minister Pieter Gerbrandy, with backing from the Minister of War, Otto van Lidth de Jeude, rejected the proposal. On September 30, the government announced that "military interests demand that the strike goes on— till the day the enemy leaves the country."[403]

On the same day, the Germans, in retaliation, imposed "an embargo on all inland shipping," effectively shutting down all barge traffic on the Netherlands' vast network of canals and waterways. As a result, food piled up in the east, leaving the populous western part of the country without. "German military reports ... warned of hunger revolts."[404] In normal times the Dutch railways would use the autumn months to transport "fuel and winter supplies of food for the west of the Netherlands."[405] When Seyss-Inquart acceded to the insistence of two senior Dutch officials and lifted the embargo on November 8, it was too late: "Organizational problems and early winter weather prevented the laying in of sufficient supplies for the winter. The results were disastrous."[406]

By October, the widespread elation experienced on Dolle Dinsdag and at the start of Operation Market Garden had, in the words of Frank van Riet, "disappeared like snow in summer." In the big cities of the provinces of North and South Holland, the extremity of the war, its cruelty and wretchedness, was biting harder and deeper, its poison spreading out like the intentional and increasing inundations that flooded vast tracts of land, eventually covering "eight per cent of the country, one-third of that with salt water." In addition to the flooding,

---

[403] Van der Zee, 33 (in Amsterdam), 35 production of gas), 35–36 (Albarda's proposal).
[404] Van der Zee, 32 (embargo). Kamphuis, 175 (revolts).
[405] Kamphuis, 174.
[406] Kamphuis, 176.

the destruction of power and pumping stations affected the availability "of fresh water, sanitation, lighting and heating" in some areas.[407] Moreover, "immediately after the railway strike started the Germans … turned to scorched-earth and terror tactics [as well as] manhunts."[408] The destruction of the Netherlands' ports began in Amsterdam on September 22. "More than 6000 German explosives experts" were sent to systematically destroy Rotterdam's great port.[409] Revenge and reprisal were the watchwords.

***

John and the "Schutzgruppe of The Hague" were "assigned to quarters in a school in Voorburg," a part of The Hague, on September 6. "There I served as a medic until the first half of December of 1944," he said in one of his collaborator statements. "I was then posted as a writer to the headquarters of the German armed forces … in The Hague." He also says he continued working at ANAK "till the surrender," but Van Schouwen's statement says John was ANAK's director "until the end of 1944."[410]

If John was able to carry on at ANAK, why was he not able to continue with the Intelligence Service? Perhaps he viewed being assigned to quarters as an opportunity to further distance himself from the SD. Or perhaps he had presumed he would be under greater restriction than proved to be the case. He told me at least one unverified story about his Schutzgruppe unit being away on assignment after it had been posted to quarters in Voorburg. This and

---

[407] Frank A. M. van Riet, *Enforcement under the new order: The political history of the Rotterdam police during the Second World War*, PhD thesis, Amsterdam Institute for Humanities Research, 804, accessed June 5, 2021, https://dare.uva.nl/search?identifier=78ea43ea-1b64-4567-a646-528c92b313c0. Van der Zee, 13 (intentional flooding), 306 (8 percent), 38 fresh water, etc.).
[408] Van der Zee, 38 (scorched-earth and terror), 53 (manhunts).
[409] Van der Zee, 38 (Amsterdam), 38–39 (Rotterdam).
[410] John's statement of October 29, 1946, 2. Van Schouwen's statement of October 28, 1946. Attachment to Blauw's email of December 3, 2009, 2.

the fact that he was still working at ANAK suggests he had some flexibility and freedom.

What is also true, I suspect, is that through manipulation and circumstances, he'd managed to insinuate himself into a relatively safe and peaceful situation where he simply had to wait things out. Although there are indications that he worked with the resistance during the last months of the war, the details—if this is true—are hidden from us. He spoke with contempt about the "September Warriors," the disdainful name, according to Van der Zee, given "by the old hands" to those who suddenly joined the resistance during that remarkable whipsawing month.[411] John told me these late-in-the-day volunteers had previously been safely "glued behind the wallpaper" where they'd done nothing.

Maybe he'd achieved a relatively safe situation for himself but also worked for the resistance. Of these two possibilities, I have more confidence in the former, and for an odd reason: John liked aphorisms. When he told me his story, the expression I heard him use the most was a supplication: "Please God, don't let the pages of my book be blank." I suspect some of his tall tales about his alleged wartime experiences were exercises in compensating for uneventful periods when he was simply waiting things out. A lengthy, grandiose chronicle he spun about the February–April 1945 period is a case in point. The irony is that with this extraordinary string of lies, he was trying to impose himself on history, even though a central tenet of his version of his story is how he had been a victim of history with his German nationality imposing upon him, as he wrote in 1951, "a direction that was not mine." Moreover, if he was active with the resistance during the war's final months, why did he not highlight this in his collaborator statements? If anything, these statements lend support to my sense that he was largely waiting things out. "As a German citizen I was forced into service with the Germans from … Jan 1 to May 1, 1945," he says in his statement of October 8, 1945.

---

[411] Van der Zee, 113.

During this period, he worked "as a writer" at the local headquarters of the German Army, according to his statement of October 29, 1946.

Leaving aside John's penchant for reinventing reality, the sense of being imposed upon by history and by war is a fitting representation of what the people of the western Netherlands experienced during the last seven months of the occupation. For many, the hope for liberation fought against the near stranglehold of despair. The sense of imposition, the images of deluge, and the dwarfing of ordinary life reflected the general diminishment of individual lives, which too often were like so much flotsam and jetsam carried hither and yon on ceaseless, uncaring flood waters. As for John, his brothers, their families, and those attached to them, we now only get glimpses. Like the brief sighting of Constant's wife escaping the Netherlands with their two small boys, it is as though the people we are following bob into view on a swell then disappear again.

***

On September 7, the day after John and his Schutzgruppe unit were assigned to quarters, Wim left the Netherlands East Company. Upon returning from his second work assignment in Poland, he quarrelled with his director, which led to him tendering his resignation on August 4. The company asked him to stay until October, but he departed on September 7, on the pretense he was joining the SS.[412]

There is no hard evidence that these developments are connected to the trouble that befell Wim and Dina in October. But given the generally heightened anxieties in the country and the tendency of the Nazis and their sympathizers for reprisal, it is certainly possible that they are linked. The trouble began when two officers for the *Crisis Controle Dienst* (CCD), Barend Den Hartog and Van den Elsakker, searched Wim and Dina's residence "in connection with the sale of illegal meat," according to Barend van Leeuwen's police statement of

---

[412] Blauw's report of February 14, 2007, 9 (based on Wim's statement of August 3, 1946).

October 1946. In the process "all the documents of illegal [resistance] activities in 's Graveland" were discovered. Not only were Wim and Dina arrested for "illicit slaughtering," but on October 29, Den Hartog and Van den Elsakker searched Van Leeuwen's home and interrogated Van Leeuwen based on information that he "occasionally had helped with hiding people."[413]

"I did not trust Den Hartog and Van den Elsakker," Van Leeuwen said in his statement. Despite this, he asked them if they were "good Dutch citizens." They, of course, said they were. As Dina was apparently released soon after her arrest, Van Leeuwen asked the officers to release Wim, explaining to them that Wim "had just escaped out of Germany on false documents and if this would come out in the open the Germans would lock him up in a concentration camp." If the references to having "just escaped" and "false documents" relate to Wim's return to Holland from Ukraine in December 1943, Van Leeuwen was using an elastic interpretation of the term "just" ten months after the fact.

This looseness of language is consistent with the cat-and-mouse game he was playing with his CCD adversaries, which explains why his statement is not always truthful. It states, for example, "At that time my son-in-law had the son of the Jewish family Dr. Heijmans of Haarlem in hiding," which was not the case. To protect Dina from possible reprisal, Van Leeuwen altered the time periods and declared that Wim had done things that Dina, in fact, had done (with her parents) in late 1942 and early 1943. Van Leeuwen not only protested Dina's arrest, he claimed she "had nothing to do with the case."[414]

Van Leeuwen "tried to hint to" Den Hartog and Van den Elsakker about "the illegal documents which were found at the home of my son-in-law in 's Graveland." He told them that if that

---

[413] Wim's statement of August 3, 1946. Attachment to Blauw's email of February 14, 2007, 9 (illicit slaughtering). Van Leeuwen's statement of October 17, 1946, 3 (Den Hartog and Van den Elsakker, house search, illegal meat, documents of illegal activities), 4 (October 29, hiding people).
[414] Van Leeuwen's statement of October 17, 1946.

material fell "into the hands of the Germans that there would probably be more casualties." His statement also says, "Nobody else but Den Hartog and Van den Elsakker knew that my son-in-law escaped from Germany on false documents.... Instead of letting [him] go ..., [they] handed him in to the Germans." Wim was released six weeks later, after what Van Leeuwen says was "an intensive investigation." While the charge related to "illicit slaughtering" could not be proved, Wim was held for as long as he was because he was not working in Germany.[415]

Starting in early December, Wim was required to work transporting ammunition at Lage Vuursche near Hilversum. He did this for four or five days until he acquired a document stating that he worked there, after which "he ran away." Van Leeuwen said he "went into hiding," doubtless to avoid the *razzias* (forced labour manhunts), which had intensified through the autumn. When Den Hartog and Van den Elsakker learned of Wim's disappearance, they "were so mad," according to Van Leeuwen, "that they said to [Wim] 'We will get you for this after the war.'"[416] Van Leeuwen didn't explain how they were able to make this threat given Wim had disappeared.

Although we don't know what John was doing when Wim was locked up, there's a good chance he did what he could, likely in consort with their mother, to have Wim released.

***

On October 18, an Amsterdam man who'd managed to escape to freedom in the south told Radio Orange about conditions in the country's largest city. "There is no electricity," he reported. "A large part of the population is hiding. Part of the surrounding country is

---

[415] Van Leeuwen's statement of October 17, 1946, 4–5, 3. Blauw's report of February 14, 2007, 9 (not proven; held because he was not working in Germany).
[416] Blauw's report of February 14, 2007, 9, (based on Wim's statement of August 3, 1946). Van Leeuwen's statement of October 17, 1946.

flooded. There is hardly any food ... and in the evening the Amsterdammers stay in their unheated houses round a candle or oil-lamp. Thousands of them never come outdoors. Life in the once so-busy city has come to a standstill." Circumstances were no different in Rotterdam, which ran out of gas on October 25. As a conservation measure, lights went out throughout the provinces of North and South Holland at 9:30 p.m.[417] While "Amsterdam was still getting some food supplies from the tip of Noord-Holland, and Rotterdam from the islands in the south, ... The Hague ... had no 'hinterland' and many, in despair, began to loot" in November. Its communal central kitchen tried to feed 350,000 people a day.[418]

Starting that month, the weekly food ration consisted of bread (three pounds), potatoes (four pounds), a small amount of sub-standard cheese, a few vegetables, and, for the first time, sugarbeets. There was no meat, eggs, milk, sugar, or fat.[419] During the winter "140 million [tulip bulbs] were consumed.... and dogs and cats were widely hunted.... and cats were sold as 'roof rabbits.'"[420] Hans said he looked after Harald when Susan was away all day trying to find food for the family. She told me she had coupons for sugarbeets—their nutritional value was extolled in the newspapers—and that she went to a designated location to line up for them. At Stanni's house in Hilversum, it was Miek's job to take the sheet of coupons they received once a month and obtain the bread, soup, and other items to which they were entitled. "You had to line up for everything," she recalled. But they were also in the fortunate position of being able to barter, swapping bedsheets for butter, eggs, and the like from farmers. "Despite all the misery, a lot of people were very strong and healthy," she said.

In late November, Prime Minister Gerbrandy and four of his ministers flew across the North Sea and returned to the Netherlands for the first time in four and a half years. They landed near Breda and

---

[417] Van der Zee, 49 (no electricity), 50 (no gas, conservation measure).
[418] Van der Zee, 69 (Amsterdam, Rotterdam, The Hague), 50 (350,000).
[419] Maass, 205.
[420] Van der Zee, 150.

proceeded to make a firsthand appraisal of the situation in the three liberated provinces in the south of the country. When they reported back to Queen Wilhelmina on potential problems once the country was fully liberated, their findings noted "the considerable mental instability of our people after all that has happened." Years later, Wilhelmina commented in her memoirs: "We could not have suspected how widespread the destruction would be at the end of the struggle and how tired and physically weakened, and in what psychological condition our people would return to freedom."[421]

Desperate measures took many forms during the last months of the war. Given their ages at the time, Harald could recall much less than Hans. Where Harald's memory was limited to a few isolated instances, Hans's recollections were numerous, vivid, and sometimes startling, for there were times he acted like a combatant, which will be described later. In mid-1991, at a United Church of Canada men's retreat at Camp Homewood on Quadra Island, Hans gave a personal testimony, which was tape recorded and later transcribed, producing a 20-page document. Speaking about the last year or two of the war, when he was seven and eight, Hans said of his father, he "taught me everything that he could about Germany. He taught me German songs, which to this very day I can remember. He taught me always how to be self-sustaining to make sure that I could survive no matter what situation would happen." A dozen years later, Hans repeated much of this to me, adding that John made him sing the songs over and over upstairs, so he'd memorize them. This was an effective strategy on John's part for it helped Hans obtain food from the German soldiers at their army compound located behind the woods on the other side of the street from where the Petersen family lived. Hans told me his first trip to the compound was prompted by the need for food. On another occasion he said that while he sang for the German soldiers quite a few times, he didn't do it every time. Such behaviour was not always welcomed. Sometimes, while the soldiers were eating, he was told, "Go away kid" or "When we're finished."

---

[421] Van der Zee, 161 (visit to liberated provinces). Gerbrandy and the Queen quoted in Van der Zee, 162 and 306.

According to Hans, he sometimes had to wait two or three hours to get some of the food that was left over. "That would feed our family, maybe for two days." Both Hans and Harald tell a story about spilling some precious soup obtained from the German soldiers that was being carried home in a bucket or an open container. Harald has twice told me that he was carrying the soup, tripped, and spilled it all, and that he was absolutely devastated and carries with him still a sense of the world's unfairness that a three-year-old should feel such tremendous responsibility and guilt.

But Hans contends this was not Harald. "I got the soup," he told me. He was coming back with it through the woods at night, he said. It was dark. He suddenly encountered a cow or a bull—which "scared the shit out of me"—and he dropped the container of soup. Harald may have been accompanying him. Or perhaps one or both of them were severely chastised for coming home empty-handed. Whatever happened, it made a particularly strong impression on Harald, indicative not only of the importance of the food but also of the depth of his disappointment at having to go without.

Some of the bicycling around that John did to obtain food from farmers undoubtedly occurred during the war's last autumn and winter. He illustrated these forays with a tale worthy of Robin Hood. It contains at least one embellishment. He said one farmer made him "furious" by offering to sell him potatoes at a guilder a piece. "A lot of farmers were that way in the west," he explained. Despite having huge quantities of potatoes buried in great pits (to protect them from frost), many farmers refused to part with them at a fair price, choosing instead to exploit their advantageous circumstances by charging exorbitant amounts. Van der Zee describes a "farmer near The Hague [who] refused to sell his potatoes by the kilogram, cruelly admitting that he was waiting until he could sell them one by one."[422]

When John was unable to persuade the farmer to compromise, he decided to make a return visit, this time wearing his uniform and

---

[422] Van der Zee, 75.

carrying his gun.[423] On this occasion, John told the farmer he had two choices: sell his potatoes at a fair price or be turned over to the authorities for dealing on the black market. The man, who John said had three pits of potatoes, would not hear of selling them at a reasonable price. Rebuffed again, John upped the ante. He said he drew his gun and told the man he would be shot if he didn't open one of his pits. The farmer complied. When the pit was open, John said he invited all the people from round about to come and help themselves. Presumably, many of these people were hunger-trekkers. He also said that as a German officer he had the authority to shoot the man, but he would never have done that. He contended that if this incident had come out after the war he could have been tried as a war criminal.

John told two other unverified food-related stories that, if they did occur in some manner, would have taken place during the autumn or later. The first likely happened after the September railway strike, while the second features the launch of a V-2 supersonic rocket, which didn't come into use until September 8. The V-2s had the appearance of "a long torpedo-shaped monster with a long fiery tail"; soundless in full flight, they made "an indescribable noise, shrieking and thundering" upon launch, according to one observer, and sounded like a huge train rumbling loudly across the sky, according to another.[424]

Back in mid-1943, due to "mounting unrest," Generalkommissar Rauter had prohibited travel to the five eastern provinces. In normal times these provinces were a poorer part of the country, but as the occupation went on, they became better off than the big cities in the west. John indicated that he drove to the east with some frequency, supposedly to obtain "special things the commander wanted for his women." John, presumably, also brought back food, fuel, and other scarce items. He said the farmers in the east gave willingly, in contrast

---

[423] Presumably, John was wearing the uniform of an Onderschaarleider, the most junior noncommissioned officer rank of the SS. See footnote 3.
[424] Maass, 165 (train; rumbling), 166 (soundless); Van der Zee, 186 (monster; indescribable noise).

to their generally more miserly cousins in the west. His trips were enabled by a permit that allowed him to get gas at any time, despite it being severely rationed. In due course, however, gas was no longer available to him, but this didn't put an end to his trips.

Unable to drive and with few trains running at the time, John and his three companions from the resistance devised an audacious expedition. The commander John referred to reportedly knew of the plan and that John had helpers, but he didn't know that the others were with the resistance. While John claimed the army commander was a general, we've established that this wasn't the case, that the local army commander was a major, and that, rather than a single individual filling this position for the last twenty months of the war, a succession of individuals did so. The appearance in the story of the Wiertz-like commander is a red flag that compels us to ask what else about the story might be untrue. John and his companions travelled east by bicycle. Their goal was to bring back whatever of value they could find by whatever means were available. They succeeded marvellously, according to John. They found a boxcar in a remote corner of a railway yard and, over several hours, loaded it up with sacks of potatoes, a fair bit of coal, and some sausages, which they obtained from cooperative local farmers and transported by horse-drawn carts. John told me that all of this was quite a job, particularly not being detected by guards. They had to push the boxcar to start it rolling, switch it over several tracks, and hitch it to a train going to Utrecht. At Utrecht, they uncoupled the car and switched it to a train going to The Hague. John told me that the commander was so impressed by what they had achieved that he gave the food and fuel to the local citizens. John said an advertisement to this effect was placed in a newspaper. He and his partners were each rewarded with a sack of potatoes. John said he gave half his sack to Susan's best friend, meaning Koos's wife, Door, and noted he felt a great sense of accomplishment.

The third story had a less successful outcome. One night when his Schutzgruppe unit was on duty, John and two of the others asked a nearby farmer for some potatoes. When the farmer refused, John and his mates decided to steal some of the farmer's chickens. They planned to provide a feast for their ten-man unit. John told this story as a humourous episode, but it has echoes of the notorious, high-handed behaviour of the Landwacht, although the men of that organization were hated for targeting desperate hunger-trekkers, not well-off farmers.

The operation involved putting a plank across an irrigation ditch and venturing back onto the farmer's property. They didn't know that in the interim the farmer had tied up a dog outside. At some point the animal became aware of their presence and started barking. This brought the farmer outside, gun in hand. However, not seeing anything, he told the dog to shut up and went back in, not thinking to untie the animal. John and the others proceeded to the chicken coop, but once they were inside and about to grab several of the sleeping chickens, another surprise occurred. A V-2 was launched from a nearby site. It made an enormous noise and lit up the night sky, waking and scaring the chickens. It also scared the would-be thieves, who hightailed it off the farm. In the process, John missed the plank and fell into the ditch, getting his SS uniform "all dirty." Reminiscent of his misadventures with his nautical school uniform a decade earlier, his tumble into the ditch became a great joke, he said.

This purported comic interlude stands in stark contrast to the manifold dangers and difficulties people in the provinces of North and South Holland faced during these months. But it's also an indication that pluck and resilience persisted in many quarters. As John told me, despite the adversity they faced, people went on with life as normally as possible. They had no other choice.

***

On December 16, the Germans began a desperate, high-risk offensive through the Ardennes Forest in eastern Belgium. The plan was to slice across the country and capture Antwerp, an Allied supply centre, 125 miles to the west. Success would cut off the American First Army, the

British Second Army, and much of the First Canadian Army in northern Belgium and the southern Netherlands. To mount their attack, the Germans had reduced their defences on the eastern front. The offensive, which became known as the Battle of the Bulge, caught the Allies by surprise. It was initially successful thanks to heavy cloud cover that hid the German positions and movements and neutralized the Allies' overwhelming air superiority. But fortunes reversed when the skies cleared on December 24, exposing the Germans to attack. Despite this, the battle continued until the end of January.

Once again, "all hopes of a speedy liberation for western Holland" were dashed.[425] On the eastern front, the Soviets unleashed yet another offensive on January 12. For every two German defenders, there were eleven Soviet soldiers bearing down on them. Germany's urgent manpower requirements spawned the so-called Liese action in the Netherlands to call up all Dutch men between sixteen and forty for work service. The initiative failed. It was met by an intense counter campaign by the resistance. Acknowledging the country's miserable circumstances, one of their rhymes said, "You may think this is a disaster, but the Hun will kill you faster."[426] According to Kershaw, the "savage brutality" wrecked upon the people of eastern Europe now rebounded on much of Germany, which in the war's final months, "reaped the whirlwind of the unconstrained barbarism Hitler's regime had sown." In addition to the crushing force coming from the east, the Allies in the west massively increased the bombing of German cities and their "near-defenceless citizens." Yet, despite inevitable defeat, Hitler would not countenance surrender. "We will not capitulate, ever. We can go down. We will take the world down with us," he told his Luftwaffe adjutant, Captain Nicolaus von Below, in late December.[427]

---

[425] Van der Zee, 80.
[426] Van der Zee, 120 (Liese action; rhyme).
[427] Kershaw, *Hitler: Nemesis*, 762 (savage brutality; whirlwind), 761 near-defenceless). Von Below, 223 (never capitulate). To not capitulate was a consistent theme with Hitler—see Von Below, 37, 185, 207, 212.

In Holland, the "man-made famine" of the Hunger Winter was inaugurated by a brutal and prolonged cold snap that started on December 23. It continued throughout January, ratcheting up the misery. On New Year's Eve, one Dutchman wondered, Will 1945 be "the year of Liberation or the year of our death?" In January, a young engineer hiding in The Hague wrote that "the trio of hunger, cold and darkness ... were terrible ... and the worst is that they intensify each other." According to Maass, "Life seemed like a return to the middle ages."[428] People scavenged wherever they could for wood to burn. Trees in parks were cut down, abandoned houses were ransacked, air-raid shelters collapsed after their supporting beams were removed, and the "wooden blocks between the tram rails" were ripped from the ground in all cities. Amsterdam "lost 22,000 of its 42,000 trees." In Hilversum, the wooded Korversbos area "disappeared in a few weeks."[429]

Susan, Hans, and Harald benefited in several ways from living where they did. They had a ready supply of wood from the small forest opposite their row house. There was little competition for it, as few Dutch lived in the vicinity. Hans said that Susan used the wood he collected to cook sugarbeets on an open fire. In Hilversum, at 5:00 a.m. one day, eighteen-year-old Miek helped Wim illegally cut down a tree about five houses away on the other side of the street from Sophialaan 18. She was terrified by the sound of Wim sawing in the quiet of the early morning. They transported their tree on a sleigh, taking care to erase the sleigh's tracks and their footsteps in the snow. She and her mother generally contented themselves with twigs collected in the woods, which they used to fuel a little burner. It was so cold they went to bed as soon as it was dark. We "spent half the time in bed," Miek said.

**

---

[428] Maass, 205 (man-made), 209 (middle ages). Van der Zee, 87 (Liberation or death), 148 (trio).
[429] Maass, 209 (wooden blocks). Van der Zee, 78 (Amsterdam's trees), 85 (Korverbos).

According to the false epic John spun about his life from February through April, it was during the November-January period that he was supposedly investigated, first by the German army then by the SS. These investigations and the fear and upset they supposedly engendered provide background for John's fantastic claims.

John said he occupied a position where he could help people. The principal way he did this was by stamping their papers to exempt them from forced labour. He was the custodian of a stamp used exclusively for this purpose, which had to be locked in a safe when it was not being used. John said that on the day after the Battle of the Ardennes, presumably meaning January 26 or thereabouts, he received a phone call from the commander, who sounded very stern. In retrospect, John said he probably imagined the harsh tone. But this misinterpretation was enough to cause a critical misstep. He'd been using the stamp when the commander called. Afterward, John realized he'd neglected to lock the stamp in the safe. And now it was nowhere to be seen. He didn't stop to think that the ever-present duty officer, who was responsible for ensuring all was well, would have picked it up. Instead, John told me that, for the first time, he panicked. He said he was very anxious because of the interrogations he'd recently been through. While he survived both investigations, he said he was consumed by alarm and constantly reviewed in his mind questions he might be asked at future interrogations. He feared he would be found out, that the illegal stamping he was doing would be discovered. With terror swamping his self-control, he told me he believed that everything about him would be discovered. He thought he would be sent to a concentration camp or killed by a firing squad. So, he deserted. He took his rifle and gear and he fled.

He ripped and muddied his uniform and went to another army outfit in The Hague—where they would never look for him. He told them he was a survivor of an army section, which he knew had been destroyed by the Allies. They were reportedly quite amazed that he'd been able to travel so far. John said he was with them until two weeks before the end of the war. He also said this interlude was a period of a few weeks, but the available chronological markers, which he himself provided, indicate it was more than three months. Neither Susan nor anyone else knew where he was, he said.

John claimed he was transferred to Haarlem toward the end of April and that shortly after he reported there, he was arrested for desertion; a few days later, he was subjected to a very short trial and sentenced to death. The date of the execution was in early May, two days before the liberation of Holland, he told me. His family still didn't know where he was. He said he felt totally cut off. He sat in his cell and marked off the days on the wall, making "peace with himself to face [the] firing squad." There was a sense of relief, he said. He didn't know the end of the war was near, only that the end of his days had come. He said he thought the end of the war was much further away—perhaps another half year.

The day before the execution, he heard footsteps approaching. He could not understand it. He had one day left. He was angry. When the door to his cell swung open, he saw two Canadian soldiers. "You're free to go," they told him. He was utterly confused. He had been prepared to die the next day. He said he felt no joy, no excitement, no relief—just confusion. Six weeks after he told me this, he added that he found it very hard to understand the war was over. "The feeling," he said, "is that of emptiness, silence—you can't comprehend it. It is as if life has stopped all of a sudden."

None of the major elements of this extraordinary tale—his fleeing, hiding, arrest, trial, death sentence, or liberation—is true. He mentioned none of this in his statement of October 29, 1946. What is more, these dramatic events are refuted by other things he told me. For example, during the time he claimed he was hiding with another army outfit and neither Susan nor his family knew where he was, he was visiting Susan in the hospital on a regular basis after she'd given birth to Constance in early February.

It was not until something Susan told me in 2002 that I realized John's story was an elaborate fabrication. She made two simple points about what really happened in early May 1945, when John, according to his ostentatious tale, was supposedly languishing in jail awaiting execution. First, John broke up his rifle and buried it in their backyard. Second, Susan cut up his Schutzgruppe uniform, dyed the fabric navy blue, and made jackets for Hans and Harald. Had John's story been true and had he been freed from prison by Canadian soldiers, he would not have had his rifle when he returned home. Susan's information was confirmed when I obtained John's collaborator statements, which said that in early May he went into hiding at home where he destroyed his uniform and rifle.

***

What could have possessed John to tell such an extraordinary and elaborate series of falsehoods? His axiom that one's lies should be as close to the truth as possible was decidedly not in play in this case. Much as it looks like this fable was fuelled by his grandiosity and ego and by excessive romanticism running riot on reality, I suspect there was more to it than this. I see three possible explanations: cover-up, compensatory behaviour, or mental health problems.

First, was it another case of misdirection, like his false claim that he trained new recruits for the SS? Was it meant to hide something else that he did? Or, second, is there a simpler explanation, like my earlier suggestion that he was compensating for a quiet period when he was awaiting the war's end? While I stand by this possibility, it is important to qualify it. John may have been waiting things out, but that doesn't mean he had an easy time during those difficult months. The fact that he taught Hans to sing German songs to obtain food for the family was likely a form of insurance in case John was sent away and could not provide for Susan and the children.

This is one of several factors that point to the third possibility: generalized anxiety and uncertainty that may have manifested in subsequent decades as post-traumatic stress disorder and other mental health problems, as well as in misremembering. These other factors include the alleged and possibly traumatizing investigations into his status by the German army and the SS, his recurring nightmare that never resolved, his claim that he worked as an army motorcycle courier at night and was getting little sleep, and the possibility that the fable was a partial conflation with what he experienced and felt when he was imprisoned as a collaborator after the war, particularly during the several weeks he spent in isolation. Did the seemingly heartfelt drama and compelling theatrics of his storytelling—being totally cut off in his cell, experiencing emptiness and silence, feeling as if life stopped all of a sudden, marking off the days, making peace with himself to face the firing squad—speak in some ways to that latter experience? Were some or all of these factors a reflection of "the considerable mental instability of our people after all that has happened" that Gerbrandy saw and reported to the Queen?

***

On February 5, Susan bicycled to the hospital to give birth to Constance. She was accompanied by Door. Both the bicycle trip and the birth were harrowing. Constance "was almost born on the bike," Susan recalled. Hans was with Stanni in Hilversum; Harald was with a neighbour. Susan said she had to stop riding several times because of labour pains. Bombs were falling as they crossed a bridge. At the hospital, Constance was delivered in a tent and without the assistance of a doctor. The afterbirth would not come; Susan lost a lot of blood. She almost died and may have had not a doctor finally appeared. John visited regularly when Susan was recovering. He gave her his Schutzgruppe rations as there was no food in the hospital. He and "a nurse who wanted to leave" the hospital, brought Susan and the baby home. The nurse stayed for a couple of weeks. Susan was extremely weak. She could not get out of bed. And Constance didn't grow. Susan told me her breast milk, although plentiful, probably lacked goodness due to her own malnourishment.

About a week after Constance's birth, the bombing of The Hague escalated when the British began a campaign against V-2 launch sites.

The sites were moved constantly. There were several near Wassenaar close to where the Petersen family lived. Air raids were so frequent that month that few citizens heeded them.

Described as "the curse of the city," many V-2s "exploded in the launching area," while others crashed nearby. They were a continuing threat to residents. There was "constant glass damage," which added to the suffering as "the windowless apartments" could not be properly heated.[430] John, Susan, Hans, and Harald all described V-2 misfires. Hans said the big field close to where they lived was used as a launch site. He described the destruction caused by a V-2 that came down several blocks up the street. It created an enormous crater after demolishing a group of houses and killing some people. Susan spoke of the tremendous sound the rockets made. She said if the noise stopped it indicated a malfunction and that the bomb could fall to earth close by, putting them in great danger. Harald, who turned three on January 18, 1945, has a clear memory of Susan drumming the V-2 drill into him: If you hear it, you are safe; but if the sound stops, take cover fast. Cover meant standing in a doorway, which provided greater protection in the event of the house collapsing. Sometimes the air pressure from misfires blew out windows and doors. Harald recalled their windows being blown out. He also remembered his father going to get doors from evacuated houses to put over the broken windows. Susan confirmed this story, but said it was Koos, not John, who got the doors.

Strafing was another frequent hazard. It, too, had escalated since May 1944, when Allied planes not only attacked anything "on rails," but also "chased trucks or even streetcars," according to Maass.[431] In December or January, prior to Constance's birth, Susan and the boys took the train from The Hague to Hilversum where Susan thought she might deliver her baby. The train was strafed, which forced it to stop. All the passengers got out and pressed themselves flat against the embankment beneath the tracks. Susan recalled that she had

---

[430] Maass, 221 (curse; explosions; crashes; glass damage; misery).
[431] Maass, 155.

Harald beside her, and Hans close by. Hans said it was more frightening than any of the surprisingly dangerous situations he got himself into in his neighbourhood in The Hague.

Both John and Susan said there was a lot of strafing in 1945. John went so far as to say that for a few weeks it seemed to happen every ten minutes. They both mentioned a particular close call John had, although the details they described vary somewhat. Susan said John was strafed as he rode his bicycle over a bridge on his way home; there was a bullet hole through his cap and another through the loaf of bread he had strapped to the back of his bike. John confirmed the bullet hole through the loaf of bread, but didn't mention a bridge or a bullet hole through his cap. He said he was coming home riding on a road through some woods. It was daytime. He said he was in a reverie and heard neither the planes nor the machine-gunning until the last moment when he came to and dove off the bike into one of the manholes on the side of the road that had been dug for that purpose. Afterward, when the planes had gone and he had gotten out of the manhole, he said he saw all the injured and dying.

It was a terrible experience after a strafing, he said. I doubt I will ever forget his graphic description of one alleged occasion. "People who were innocent and uninvolved in war ... were lying around, crying in pain, [some with] dismembered limbs." He equated it to the napalm fire-bombings during the Vietnam War. He spoke of comforting a six-year-old boy whose stomach had been ripped open and who, in shock, watched his intestines coming out. The child, according to John, asked him if he was going to die. John said yes and tried to explain what would happen and "lead him into heaven while he was still alive." To John, it was a horrible thought that all of it was unnecessary.

The strafing, V-2 misfires, and Allied bombing of V-2 sites during February were a prelude to what happened on March 3, when fifty-six RAF Mitchell bombers appeared over the city. Not only did they drop their bombs on the populous Bezuidenhout district, but they returned twice to complete the job. The toll, according to two sources, was more than five hundred killed, "many more wounded,

[and] 3,250 houses ... destroyed," leaving twelve thousand homeless. But a third source maintains the destruction was much more modest: "Several dozen civilians died and were injured."[432]

John said he was standing in the doorway of a house that sustained a direct hit—all that was left standing was the doorway—and it was a pretty ugly situation. He claimed a hospital had also been damaged and that he was one of those who went in afterward to rescue survivors. He said hospitals had red crosses on their roofs to minimize the chance they would be hit. As he went about his work, he was consumed by "the stupidity and senselessness, the evil, the horrendousness" of what had occurred. "How people can't see that is beyond me," he said.

On March 23, Radio Orange reported that the bombing had been an accident. The aircrews had been inaccurately briefed; the horizontal and vertical coordinates had been inadvertently transposed. The actual target was "at least a mile" from where the bombs had been dropped. Goebbels remarked caustically "that when the Germans bombed Rotterdam in 1940 the British had shouted 'Murder,' using it then as an excuse to 'ruin the Reich,' while when they bomb The Hague 'it is just a mistake.'"[433] Although the destruction of the centre of Rotterdam had been intentional and an indication of what was in store for other Dutch cities if their army didn't capitulate, John echoed Goebbels' bitterness when he spoke of the bombing of The Hague. "People conveniently forget the bombing of The Hague by the Allies," he said, "but remember the bombing of Rotterdam by the Germans."

---

[432] Maass, 221 (densely populated; Bezuidenhout; "More than 500 ... killed). Van der Zee, 186–187 (fifty-six bombers; returned twice; 511 killed; many more wounded; 12,000 homeless). *Liberation Album*, 53 (third source).
[433] Van der Zee, 187 (at least a mile), 188 (accident; coordinates transposed; Goebbels). Maass, 221 (faulty navigation).

18

HANS, THE CHILD WARRIOR

We can get an inkling of the hidden parts of John's life during the last months of the war by listening to Hans. We've already heard that John taught him lots of German songs as a hedge against hunger for himself and the family. But John also taught Hans how to disarm a hand grenade and how to break open bullets of different sizes to collect their gunpowder. Hans said John showed him how to use a can of gasoline as an incendiary. Moreover, regarding the German soldiers, Hans told me he was instructed by his father, "If you can set them back, do it." Hans heeded these instructions. He said he single-handedly blew up a large German communications truck on one occasion; on another, he attacked a convoy of German military trucks.

Hans's training appears to have been a priority for John. It seems he devoted more time to it than to anything else he did with Hans during this period. Their only other shared activity, according to Hans, was to cut wood together in the small forest across the street. Beyond this, John was often not around, Hans said.

After the war and in the decades to come, they never discussed what had passed between them during that time nor what they each had gotten up to in their separate spheres.

They both largely kept their wartime activities secret from others. In the 1970s and 1980s, when John told me his story, he never mentioned the training he gave Hans. With a couple of exceptions, Hans never spoke of his training, or what it led to, either. But he did speak of these things to me on at least half a dozen occasions between 2003 and 2008. He also mentioned them in the testimony he gave at the United Church men's retreat at Camp Homewood in 1991.

Although John was a semi-absent father who generally didn't live with Hans when Stanni was Hans's primary caregiver during the latter part of 1938 through 1940, he and Hans shared a close bond. Hans and his dad had always been really close, Hans told me. In his 1991 testimony, Hans said: "I really love my dad.... My dad has always been everything for me. He has taught me to become very competitive.... My positive was always my strength that my dad taught me ..."

Both father and son were abandoned by their mothers, although in John's case it was a form of emotional abandonment, and both had four marriages, although I don't believe Hans has been prone to the same desperate dependency on women. They also shared several psychic experiences when Hans was a small boy. What makes these experiences more interesting is John's claim that he had several remarkable experiences with his father at a similar age.

While there is no corroboration for any of the events John claimed occurred the night his father died, there is corroboration for a supernormal experience John and Hans had in early 1941 and for one of two telepathic experiences that occurred between them in the autumn of 1940 when John was in Germany for his SS training. One day out of the blue, three-year-old Hans exclaimed to his grandmother Stanni, "Oma! Oma! Daddy is dead!" John was not dead, but he had hurt himself. He'd been participating in a training exercise, which required that he jump off a cliff. He cracked his ankle in the process. John, Hans, and Susan all stated on different occasions that Hans's long-distance awareness that something had happened to his father and his related outcry to Stanni did, in fact, occur.

Perhaps a month later, likely in November, Hans became gravely ill when he suffered a burst appendix and blood poisoning. John told me he'd been aware of this situation psychically and that his knowledge included that Hans was ill with acute appendicitis, that his appendix burst while he was on the operating table, and that Hans would recover. John further claimed that he wrote to Susan listing each of these points and that she confirmed them all. Unfortunately, I never asked Susan about this correspondence, so we do not have her confirmation, correction, or outright contradiction.

When John told me of these episodes, he also maintained that, while he was in Germany, he knew what was going on back in Hilversum, that he could follow people in his mind, see what they were doing and even hear their conversations. He added that during the war when he was in difficulty, he always knew what to do. He said it was like someone sitting on his shoulder giving him advice and crucial warnings.

Unlike the earlier occasions of telepathic connection, the third episode was more of a mystical experience and it occurred when John and Hans were together. This event happened to Hans sometime during the early months of 1941. He told me it occurred sometime after his appendicitis. John said he and Hans had been talking about a serious subject when Hans, who was looking at his father, started to shake. According to John, Hans saw two men, one of whom was John "as a person he [Hans] knew in a former life," as well as another man, and both figures had lights around them. John maintained the second figure was a spiritual manifestation of Hans's namesake (his grandfather, who died in 1918). The younger Hans confirmed to me on at least four occasions that this experience took place—but without endorsing John's reincarnation interpretation of it or that the second figure was his paternal grandfather.

That same year, when John, Susan, and Hans lived on Koningin Emmakade in The Hague, Hans, who was not yet five, got into trouble, according to Susan, when John found him playing outside the fence and too close to the canal. Remarkably, about three years later, John was imperilling Hans's life: "If you can set [the Germans] back, do it."

Hans was not the only child John instructed. In his 1991 testimony, Hans said: "I had one friend and he used to always be beside me. There were no other kids there [where I lived] at the time." Hans rode his bicycle a considerable distance from his home on Waalsdorperweg to attend Grade 1 in 1942–43, but after that he didn't attend school until the war was over. Most likely this was because areas cleared of Dutch residents had their schools closed and other schools were too far away. His friend, who was about the same age and didn't attend school either, was often with Hans when he was being trained by John.

Hans said his father asked him to steal bullets and grenades from the German soldiers and to hide them for him. Hans explained that it was comparatively easy for a little kid to sneak into the soldiers' sleeping quarters and steal such items. When he acquired them, he brought them home and put them in a hollow that John had built under the sidewalk in front of their residence. Hans accessed the hollow by levering up a cement paver that was approximately twelve by twelve inches. The entire sidewalk was made of these pavers. John regularly emptied the hollow of its contents. One day when John came home on a bicycle or a motorbike—Hans thinks it was a bicycle—he went over the paver atop the hollow and caused a collapse. It was quickly fixed.

To obtain gunpowder from bullets, Hans most often placed them between a vehicle's wheel rim and tire to pry them open, but on occasion he also opened them by carefully rolling them on a smooth surface. His 1991 testimony includes this:

> Because of the training that my dad had given me, I was very good at—if I now may use the word—infiltrating ... the German army.... I was ... a little guy and the Germans as soldiers had families of their own which they had left back in Germany, so they could relate as men to little children, and again, my dad taught me very well because I knew how to take advantage of that. I could sneak into their bedrooms. I could sneak into their very private possessions without them ever

noticing that I had ever been there. I could steal hand grenades from them. I could steal ammunition. I could steal gas masks. I could steal anything. I was very good. I used to hide it in their own dugouts in the ground. I used to steal it from them and then hide it in their own stuff. I would take the tiles out of the sidewalks. In Holland we had tiles, stones on the sidewalks, that were about this big and that thick. I would rip them out of the sidewalk and I would dig into these dugouts that they had into the side of them and I would make like a cache and I would put a stone in front of it and all of the ammunition would be there. They would be there but they wouldn't know that my stuff was right there. Then my dad would come home on infrequent occasions and I would give him the stuff so that he could, in turn, use it for the Dutch underground so that they could do with it whatever.

I knew how to take the heads off bullets to get the powder out to use the powder to set off an explosion wherever it was needed. As a little boy I could do that, and nobody would take notice of me.

John also taught Hans and his friend how to minimize the chance of being caught in places they should not be.

"The first thing people see is movement," he emphasized to the boys, telling them that they should be very, very still if they were in danger of being detected.

"He'd drill me forever [on this]," Hans said. He added that his father really shaped him. He "knew I'd take direction."

I asked Hans what he meant when he said John taught him to become very competitive. Hans replied, "You're in the game to win. You have to do more than your best. You have to win." Elaborating further, several months later, Hans added his father would often emphasize certain things to him, saying, "You have to learn and remember." Hans went on to say a better explanation for conveying what his father meant is that you have to have the upper hand.

The large communications truck Hans blew up was parked, along with several other German army vehicles, on Waalsdorperweg, one block up the street from where he lived. Some of the adjacent row houses were used as offices by the Germans, while others were used to house some of their soldiers. Some soldiers were on the street working on trucks, but they were several vehicles away from where Hans was. Nobody paid any attention to him. The communications truck he was focused on had large tires that gave it high ground clearance. Hans had put some gunpowder under the vehicle. He then opened two forty-five-gallon drums of gasoline that were close by. One was almost empty. Not thinking of the fumes, he dropped a lit match in. When the fumes ignited, Hans was burned on the face, forehead, hands, and arms. He said he booted the drum under the truck and ran like hell. I asked him how much time elapsed before the burning drum and gunpowder exploded.

"Not very much," he said. "Not enough. It seemed like seconds. Stuff was flying around. That barrel disintegrated."

His 1991 testimony also alludes to this event: "I was always directed by my dad to do this, not directed in an angry way, but it was necessary. I used to blow up stuff like communications trucks with forty-five-gallon drums. Once my hair was burnt, my face was burnt, my arms were burnt because I had done this."

In recent years Hans has reflected on his wartime experiences and the incredible risks and dangers to which he was exposed by his father's teaching and encouragement. In contrast to his 1991 conclusion that "it was necessary," his reaction in 2008 to "how he used me" is more bemused and appalled. He doesn't know if he injured or killed anyone: "One thing I've always wondered about: I don't know if there were people inside that truck."

The Germans were also good guys, he said on another occasion. "When they were marching in formation, they invited you to join their column." He told me that when the Allies were bombing or strafing the area, the Germans would pull people into trenches or allow them to share other relatively safe space with them. And they provided food. As Harald said, "Germans were human beings with families"; of course, some of them also had small children.

I asked Hans if he had any idea of the year or the time of year when he blew up the communications truck. He cited several possibilities that were little more than guesses sixty-plus years after the fact. He was inclined toward an earlier time period because he would have been out on his own and would not have had Harald in tow, as was often the case late in the war. He also told me he thought three or four months elapsed between his attacks on the Germans. The fact that two of the three episodes he recounted featured strafing, which became much more widespread in and around The Hague during the last months of the war, suggests these events happened between the latter half of 1944 and the early months of 1945.

Hans's second attack was against a truck convoy headed into the depot at the army compound. He was holding a can that contained gunpowder. The can had a hole in it that had been filled with a paper fuse and lit. He ran forward to get closer to one of the trucks and threw the can like a Molotov cocktail. A moment later Allied planes started strafing the convoy. Hans said he jumped into a ditch beside the road. The Germans did the same. The fortuitous strafing may have saved Hans from being caught. If the Germans were aware of the initial attack before the strafing began, they apparently didn't connect Hans with it. He suggested the strafing saved his life.

Hans was involved in one other incident, but this time he was just a bystander playing on the street. In those days, the part of Waalsdorperweg where they lived was a dead end. A brick wall marked the end of the road. It was made from the same bricks used to construct the row houses occupied by John, Susan, and their neighbours. There was a large field on the other side of the wall. Scarred with trenches, it was used for German army exercises. It was also used as a launch site for V-2 rockets late in the war. On the day in question, the army was conducting exercises on the field. These attracted the attention of a single Allied plane that attacked with guns blazing. The watchtower returned fire with its anti-aircraft gun, hitting the plane and causing it to explode in midair. Detritus fell to earth throughout the area. A small piece of debris hit Hans in the back of the head.

"I was bleeding like a pig," he told me the first time he referred to this injury.

Of these three incidents, the destruction of the communications truck was the most important for it had deadly repercussions. What is more, Hans and Susan have conflicting recollections about aspects of the event's aftermath. Hans told me that Susan was so concerned about what had happened she would not let him leave the house for a couple of weeks. The clear implication is that he told her something about what had occurred, perhaps in response to being questioned about how he got burned. However, when I asked Susan about Hans being burned during the war, she said: "I don't remember it." Then she said: "That never happened." When I pursued the subject, she said Hans had a history of telling stories and exaggerating "to be important."

"You couldn't rely on him to tell the truth," she told me.

Constance agreed with her mother, telling me that Hans did lie and embellish when he was younger. At the same time, she didn't have an alternative explanation for the hard-to-see burn scars on Hans's face and neck. On another occasion she related an incident from her teens, circa 1963, that links back and lends credence to Hans's claims about his wartime past. She, Hans, and their adopted sister, Ann, were out one night in Victoria when some guys on the street started giving Ann unwanted attention. Hans challenged them, and they backed off and left. When Hans and Constance reviewed what had occurred, he told her he could have killed those guys had he resorted to training he'd received from their father during the war. She inferred that he normally never spoke about that period because it took him to a dark place. Hans said he only spoke to me about it because I asked.

When I followed up with Hans, he found it hard to believe that Susan didn't remember his burns. "She had to dress the wounds!" he exclaimed. "It's come across a couple of times that she can't remember different instances [from the war]," he added a few moments later. But memorable as the occasion would have been, perhaps more pressing matters obscured it in Susan's mind. She didn't lack for stresses and worries during the latter months of 1944 and January 1945, as the occupied parts of the country entered the bitter and painful months of the Hunger Winter. She was pregnant, increasingly malnourished, spent long hours standing in lines for meagre rations, and had two children for whom to care. An additional possibility is that she tended Hans's burns during February or March 1945 when she was very weak and largely bedridden while recovering after Constance's difficult birth.

It is possible that Susan conflated what she experienced during the war with what she experienced, was told, and understood years later. During one of our sessions, she insisted that John never worked in the insurance industry between 1941 and the end of the war. We, of course, have evidence that he did. Another time she told me Constant was not with John in Germany for SS training. "They were never there at the same time," she said with finality.

The issues of whether Hans had been burned in the manner he claimed and whether he was telling me tall tales in the same way his father had decades before prompted me to ask him if he was telling me "the honest-to-God truth." He responded by saying that he was not embellishing, that there would be no point for him not to tell the truth. As an afterthought, he added his father had "a longing to accomplish things and be famous, but it was mostly big talk." Then he frankly admitted that he, too, had the same longing.

I accept what Hans has told me. From 2003 through 2008, he was consistent about the core elements of his wartime experiences, and he said the same things when he gave his personal testimony in 1991. But I also recognize that he is sometimes guilty of enthusiastic storytelling and has exaggerated some points. His claim that Susan would not allow him to go out for a couple of weeks after he was burned is a case in point, for in relating the next part of this story he also said he was out and about as before within a few days.

According to Hans, the destruction of the communications truck created quite a stir. The German reaction is not something he likes to talk about. It probably took place over a couple of days, he said. "They weren't known for dilly-dallying around. It was an act of sabotage and someone had to pay. There was a need for retribution." He also said he and his friend witnessed the executions that resulted. They took place several days after the incident in an abandoned, ransacked church in the neighbourhood. All the pews had been removed. Hans and his friend hid in the balcony. There were two or three men in the firing squad. They used rifles. Five men were executed.

"I didn't realize the atrocity of it as much then as I did later," he told me. "I didn't understand the idea of death." He said he heard the commands and the shots; he saw each of the victims fall and not get up. He also said this experience was tied in his memory to many, many Allied planes flying over The Hague and bombing it (another indication that this event took place during the last months of the war).

Hans told the same story, though with fewer details, when he gave his 1991 testimony: "I used to sneak into churches that they had ransacked. Absolutely everything [was] gone and they would park a tank inside them. They would execute people in a church in the neighbourhood that I lived in. I had one friend and he used to always be beside me."

I asked Hans if there was any chance that the executions were related to an incident other than the destruction of the communications truck. He said it was possible, but unlikely. He believes that the executions were a direct result of what he did. I also asked him where the execution victims came from, given the vicinity had been cleared of Dutch citizens. He rightly pointed out the Nazis kept hostages for just this purpose.

Death was not unknown to Hans. Killing and destruction were matter-of-fact occurrences. Speaking of V-2 rockets that were launched nearby and often malfunctioned, he said in his 1991 testimony that "they would go *poof* and then they would come down and another few houses were gone and stuff like that. The houses that were there were even occupied by the Germans themselves, but they would still be gone and that didn't seem to matter too much."

He described the delayed impact the executions had on him as "very devastating." He said he had nightmares into his twenties and, after that, the memory of it returned from time to time to haunt and depress him.

Hans died on December 1, 2022.

19

THE DEAD CORNER AND ITS RETURN TO LIFE

"We here in Occupied Holland are still no-man's-land," H. Diemer, a Rotterdam journalist, wrote in his diary in March 1945. "It saves us from the destruction of warfare—apart from the air-raids—but the suffering caused by the lack of food and fuel doesn't diminish." Would the country's populous west remain the "dead corner … until the end of the gigantic struggle"? he wondered.[434]

The term "dead corner" bluntly captured their predicament. On February 24, when Prime Minister Gerbrandy pressed for a special military operation to liberate all the Netherlands and provide relief to its people, General Walter Bedell Smith, Eisenhower's chief of staff, said "the necessary divisions and equipment" were not available. According to Van der Zee, Smith "explained that it was not possible to win the war without the Russians, and that therefore it was necessary to advance to the heart of Germany. The liberation

---

[434] Van der Zee, 194 (no-man's-land, dead corner), 50 (journalist Diemer), 322 (initial H).

of Holland was a diversion the Allies could not afford."[435] Simply put, the demands of victory in Europe outweighed the urgent needs of the people of the occupied part of the Netherlands.

In April, the Allies swept through the east and north of the Netherlands. Fighting had been underway in the east and southeast since February 8, when the First Canadian Army directed one thousand guns at the Reichswald forest across the border in Germany.[436] Soon after, American troops were in Germany, reaching Dusseldorf on March 2 and Cologne on March 5. British and Canadian troops, meanwhile, were pushing to the north and west in the Netherlands. On April 14, more than six months after the Operation Market Garden failure, the Allies finally captured Arnhem. Groningen and Leeuwarden, the major cities of the north, also fell in mid-April.

"After a miserable long wait the east and north of our country are liberated," Radio Orange announced on April 22, "but the three hunger provinces in the west are still occupied … the Dutch nation has begun to go under because of starvation." Compared to the months of the Hunger Winter, "April was far worse."[437] Fortunately, Gerbrandy's efforts to get the attention of the Allies were paying off. Churchill, in a handwritten letter of April 19 to the Dutch prime minister, referred to the Netherlands in his sign-off as a "much-harrowed country." Ten days earlier, in another letter, Churchill advised US President Franklin Roosevelt, who would die on the twelfth, "I fear we may soon be in the presence of a tragedy" in the Netherlands. He added, "we must avert [it] if we can." On the twentieth, Eisenhower told the US Army Chief of Staff, George

---

[435] Van der Zee, 174 (liberation of Holland would be a diversion), 329 (General Walter Bedell Smith), 37 (Chief of Staff). The Netherlands, according to Horn in *A Liberation Album* (75), "was less important in military planning than the Ruhr valley; it would have to wait weeks for liberation."
[436] Maass, 219 (Reichswald).
[437] Van der Zee, 223 (east and north liberated, three hunger provinces), 224 (April).

Marshall, that "the advanced state of starvation of the population in the larger cities" demands action, "even though it may be at some expense of our own operations against the enemy."[438]

Meanwhile, Seyss-Inquart, who was under orders to widen the application of the scorched-earth policy, "did not want to inflict any more damage on Holland," according to Germany's armaments minister, Albert Speer. When Seyss-Inquart learned that Speer was ignoring the scorched-earth policy, he decided to do the same. In early April, Seyss-Inquart advised the secretary-general for trade and agriculture of his intention to allow the Allies to "help the starving Dutch," provided they didn't advance beyond the Grebbe Line, a defensive water barrier (based on inundation) where the Dutch and Germans had fought a fierce three-day battle in May 1940.[439] This overture led to negotiations between the Germans and the Allies and, ultimately, to airborne food drops: Operation Manna was carried out by the British, Australian, Canadian, New Zealand, and Polish air forces from April 29 to May 7; Operation Chowhound, by the US Air Force, delivered food from May 1 to May 8. The Allies and Germans agreed the food drops were "the least practical but the fastest method" for delivering food. They were supplemented with relief delivered "by barges ... from southern Holland through the inland waterways, ... by [ships] from Antwerp to Rotterdam [the Germans had "partially cleared" the port for this purpose], and finally by road and by rail."[440]

The first low-flying Operation Manna planes arrived about 1:30 p.m. on approach to four designated drop zones, two for The Hague and the others near Leiden and Rotterdam. There were ten zones in all. A *News Chronicle* reporter travelling in one of the planes reported, "We had thought that the rain would have kept the Dutch inside, but they were waving sheets and tablecloths from the roofs." J. G.

---

[438] Van der Zee, 239 (must avert tragedy), 241 (at expense of our operation), 242 (advanced state of starvation). Maass, 237 (much-harrowed country).
[439] Van der Zee, 231 (Seyss-Inquart and Speer), 232 (starving Dutch, Grebbe Line).
[440] Van der Zee, 259 (fastest method; by barges, ship, road, and rail), 251, (Operation Manna), 242 (partially cleared).

Raatgever, an unemployed journalist in The Hague, observed, "In a flash our whole street was filled with a cheering, waving crowd and the elated people were even dancing on their roofs.... Many had tears in their eyes, others could not utter more than a few inarticulate cries ..." The food, dropped without parachutes from low altitude to minimize damage, was "packed in bags normally used for cement"; another source says "gunny sacks" were used.[441]

One of the drop zones for The Hague was the Duindigt racetrack, which was a short walk from the Petersen residence and a routine destination for Hans, who liked to visit the horses and sometimes watched the harness races. He may have witnessed airdrops on multiple days as Operation Manna flew between 3,100 and 3,300 flights over the ten drop zones. He said parcels from the planes looked like balloons coming down. He found and opened at least one that landed outside the racetrack.

One source says the cement bags held twenty-three pounds of food: "flour, chocolate, egg powder, tea and even salt and pepper"; a second states the dropped food consisted of "tinned food, dried food and chocolate." Between them, Operations Manna and Chowhound used approximately 800 planes to drop "no less than 7458" and "over 11,000" tons of food, according to different sources. Hans spoke fondly of white bread he enjoyed about this time. But it was not part of the airdrops. Rather it came from flour shipped in shortly before from neutral Sweden; the bread was baked locally and distributed to the public.[442]

When Hans accessed the food parcel outside the Duindigt racetrack, he recalled a family member being with him. He thought it

---

[441] Van der Zee, 251 (cement bags), 253 (four drop zones, *News Chronicle* reporter), 253–54 (Raatgever), 75 (Raatgever). Maass, 240 (ten zones). Joe English, "Operation Manna," *Bomber Museum of Canada,* accessed Oct. 2, 2020, https://www.bombercommandmuseum.ca/bomber-command/operation-manna/ (dropped without parachutes, gunny sacks).

[442] Van der Zee, 251 (23-pound packs and food contents), 254, 256 (800 planes, 7458 tons). Joe English (3,100 flights). "Operations Manna and Chowhound," Wikipedia, accessed October 1, 2020, https://en.wikipedia.org/wiki/Operations_Manna_and_Chowhound (tinned food, over 11,000 tons, 5,569 sorties, white bread).

was his father. This may have been the case. Two of John's collaborator statements say that he "was drafted into the German Wehrmacht" and "called to serve with the active troops" at the end of April and that he ignored these orders and went into hiding at his home. He did this despite the warning of General Blaskowitz, who had recently taken command of the German army's 120,000 troops in occupied Holland, that all shirkers would be executed. In this, Blaskowitz was following the example of Himmler, who had established summary courts in 1944 "that had the right to try and condemn any deserter." The Reichsführer SS had also distributed posters throughout Germany that read "Every deserter will find his just punishment. His infamous behavior will entail the direst consequences for his family." Corpses of soldiers hanging from German trees were adorned with signs that read: "I am hanging here because I left my unit without permission."[443]

At about the same time John was getting ready to desert, Hitler committed suicide on the afternoon of April 30. He was still revered in many quarters. Seyss-Inquart, who had continued to hope that the Führer would deploy a secret weapon to turn the tide, issued a statement that Hitler's "spirit will never disappear" and admonished, "Don't cover his picture, but bring flowers to him, who has made our lives proud and worth living."[444]

Although not without significant worries and unknowns, it must have been a brief, happy time for the Petersen family. Not only was John home and food falling from the sky, but Susan was much better too. She had recovered sufficiently by mid-April to be out and about. She told me about warily crossing a bridge on her way to see a doctor. "You stopped on one side, checked for planes, then hurried over," she said. Moreover, while the food drops continued, news of Germany's capitulation in the Netherlands was broadcast a few minutes before 9:00 p.m. on Friday, May 4. The terms of surrender stipulated that fighting would stop on

---

[443] Maass, 223 (shirkers to be shot). Graber, 182–183 (summary courts, try and condemn any deserter, hanging here).
[444] Van der Zee, 269.

Saturday, May 5, at 8:00 a.m. A more comprehensive capitulation covering all German forces in Western Europe was signed at Eisenhower's headquarters in Reims at 2:41 a.m. on Monday, May 7. All hostilities were to be over by the end of the eighth. Churchill proclaimed May 8 as Victory in Europe Day (VE Day).

The Dutch in the occupied provinces "waited nervously, eagerly, impatiently on the morning of May 5 for their first sight of the Allied soldiers." But under the terms of the capitulation, it was agreed that the 1st Canadian Corps would not enter "Fortress Holland" until Monday, May 7. In fact, while the Canadians entered Amersfoort, Hilversum, and Utrecht from the east and were met by adoring crowds on the seventh, the residents of Amsterdam, Rotterdam, and The Hague had to wait until the eighth to greet their liberators.[445]

Saturday the fifth through Monday the seventh was a strange, twilight interregnum. On one hand, church bells rang that weekend for the first time in five years; on the other, the Germans, while acknowledging their capitulation, were still armed, in charge, and giving orders. In addition, joyous celebration was accompanied in some quarters by the revenge and retribution of Hatchet Day. The most prominent of these latter activities was the rounding up and public shaming in town squares of "Hun-girls," Dutch women who had fraternized with German soldiers. Pocket scissors, pen knives, and razors were used to shave their heads, which in some cases were also painted orange. John said these women were often forced to undress in public. Sometimes the treatment was much worse. In Utrecht, John claimed he witnessed pregnant women publicly raped with nightsticks with the intent to kill the fetuses, which were presumed to be German. Similar graphic claims were made by other observers, one of whom regarded shaving heads as a "villainous ritual" that demonstrated "the victors could be just as mean as the losers" and added that gruesome incidents occurred "all over the land."[446]

---

[445] *Liberation Album*, 89.
[446] Salie Bottinga (a pseudonym) quoted in Stein, 296–298, 8 (pseudonym).

"It was one of the most horrible times I've lived through," John said. He added that there was no order in Holland then.

The Hatchet Day incidents largely stopped once the Canadians arrived, after which a new phase of adjustment to changed circumstances quickly began. John said that members of the underground were now acting as a police force trying to find those who sided with Germany during the war. He added, however, that many underground people eschewed this process, while numerous pretenders who *said* they'd been in the underground participated (John's emphasis). Historians agree the process was plagued with problems. Henry Mason states, "Each town had its own arrest-teams under local resistance officers, who interpreted the arrest-instructions as they chose." He refers to "the wild arrests of Quislings by the resistance" and states that "the mass arrests included a considerable number of innocents, or near-innocents, whose crimes of collaboration were trivial." Moreover, this injustice was compounded by the fact that the "pre-trial release of innocents and near-innocents was very reluctantly and inefficiently handled."[447] Maass maintains that the "pent-up hatred" derailed impartiality, while biases and mistakes produced many "unjust arrests."[448]

By comparison, the arrests of the leaders of the occupation—Austrians Seyss-Inquart and Rauter, and the leader of the Dutch NSB, Mussert—were easy and without complication. Soon after their arrival, the Canadians apprehended Seyss-Inquart and Mussert. The so-called Führer of the Dutch People was condemned to death by a special court in December 1945. He was executed on May 7, 1946. During that year's Nuremberg Trials, Seyss-Inquart was convicted as a war criminal and hanged. Rauter was arrested by the British in a German hospital and returned to the Netherlands in an ambulance. He had almost been killed during a resistance attack on his car the night of March 6–7. Known as the "High Lord Executioner," he surprisingly asked that there be no reprisals. Himmler, however, had other ideas. On March 7,

---

[447] Mason, 46 (Each town), 44 (wild arrests), 53 (mass arrests, pre-trial release).
[448] Maass, 187 (hatred, unjust).

he "ordered the execution of at least 500 people." Approximately four hundred people died in reprisal. The killings were "merely a new example of the unparalleled terror to which people in Occupied Holland are now subjected," wrote the *Times* of London on March 28. After a lengthy investigation, Rauter was tried and convicted by a Dutch court in 1948. He was executed in 1949.[449]

Sometime during the first heady days after the Canadians arrived in The Hague, Hans was given a ride to Hilversum by a couple of soldiers in a "huge" Canadian truck. He remembers the ride, and Miek remembers the truck's impressive arrival at the house on Sophialaan. Hans rode in the back; there were blankets in which he wrapped himself against the cold. He saw houses decked out in the Netherlands' red-white-and-blue flag. He was impressed that Hilversum had sustained very little war damage compared to The Hague. Miek recalled that one of the soldiers was somewhat inebriated. They said the rest of the family in The Hague was all right. Miek suggested Hans's relocation may have been to get him back into school, but Hans says he didn't return to school until the new school year started. The more likely reason for sending him to Hilversum was that John and Susan didn't want him to see his father arrested, which they both expected.

While the Netherlands' freedom had been restored and, in the words of Prince Bernhard, the "difficult but gratifying task" of recovery lay ahead for its people, quite a different reality awaited John.[450]

---

[449] Maass, 221 (Executioner). Van der Zee, 183–184 (Himmler ordered executions, the *Times*).
[450] Van der Zee, 285.

PART THREE

Postwar
Internment, Release, and Readjustment

The years lived in terror of the knock on the door in the night, the arrogance of the conqueror, and the memory of close friends who had been taken away to concentration camps and never seen again had left no trace of pity in the hearts of the men who resisted.

—S. E. (Stan) Hanson, *Underground Out of Holland*

The grief done to our nation in war and occupation will not easily be forgotten. Therefore it is easy to understand and justify feelings in this connection against certain Dutchmen. However, we have to realize that sooner or later they too will have to be accepted again by our society.

—Queen Wilhelmina, Proclamation, September 4, 1948

20

THE BROTHERS ARE ARRESTED

Among the democracies of the western world, the Netherlands had endured the most hardship, according to Maass. The Hunger Winter and the starvation spring and the long, difficult months that preceded them "had broken the spirit" of innumerable people.[451] The country was "physically and mentally exhausted."[452]

Although the First Canadian Army transferred responsibility for the relief effort to the Netherlands Military Authority by the end of May 1945, rations were still generally inadequate throughout July. Indeed, bread was rationed until July 15, and Canadian troops, in the words of one soldier, "went on half rations to help feed the population."[453] The black market continued to flourish, "many took to more or less subtle forms of begging from the soldiers," and acts of desperation were not uncommon.[454]

The country required substantial rebuilding. The roads, railways, and many of the ports were in dreadful shape. "By mid-summer rail service was still rudimentary; there was no public transportation by road or highway."[455] Recovery started slowly. The workforce was terribly debilitated. Shortly after liberation, Major General A.

---

[451] Maass, 249.
[452] Mason, 137.
[453] *Liberation Album*, 156.
[454] *Liberation Album*, 131.
[455] *Liberation Album*, 135.

Galloway, the Canadian heading up the relief operation, observed that there were "five times as many males suffering from starvation as females." He added that "the large proportion of the population who were unable to buy on the black market have lost, on average, forty-five pounds in weight.... fifteen per cent showed signs of malnutrition, fifty per cent were definitely under-nourished and thirty-five per cent were more or less normal."[456] Indeed, "many people were too weak to put in a day's work, a state that persisted for weeks."[457]

In September, the country reformed its currency; in March 1946, the state of emergency was lifted, and the military government disbanded; and that May, the first national election since 1937 was held. Despite these stabilizing steps, recovery for the Netherlands was still years away. An extended process, it was at least as long as the occupation, probably longer. There were many tensions and much ugliness. Difficult changes had to be accepted. In 1949, when Indonesia became "a sovereign state united in partnership with the Netherlands," it was the end of the latter's colonial empire but also the period when living standards finally began to rise.[458] By 1952, the country was largely rebuilt.

***

For John and Wim, the weeks after VE Day and before their respective arrests in late May and early June must have been a tense time. Based on what he told me, John visited Utrecht for an unknown reason and an unknown length of time during this period. According to Hans, John also stayed for a while at his mother's home in Hilversum. During this visit, it appears that Susan remained behind in The Hague with Harald and baby Constance.

When John was at his mother's, an incident occurred that I suspect was triggered, at least in part, by the strain he was under. It

---

[456] Van der Zee, 299.
[457] *Liberation Album*, 131.
[458] Craig, 850 (united in partnership), 877 (living standards).

involved a whipping that he and Wim—but "mostly" John—gave Hans in the hallway of the Sophialaan house. Wim had apparently acquired the whip when he had managed the sheep farm in Ukraine. The whipping was precipitated by Hans and a friend jumping off the roof of the garage into the garden. The friend was sent home. But there may have been more to it than this one act of boyish behaviour. Hans told me he had become street smart during the latter half of the war and, not having gone to school for two years, he was rebellious and defiant and resented authority. "I probably needed a lot of those beatings because ... I was probably totally unruly," he stated in his 1991 testimony. He confirmed to me that he received several "beatings" during this period, but none were as severe as the whipping. That experience was such that, sometime afterward, he took the whip and threw it away. "I could still steal," he recalled in 1991, "and to this very day my dad never knew where that whip ... went. But I knew that it would never be used on me ... again."

At 10:00 a.m. on May 22, Wim's father-in-law, Barend van Leeuwen, was confronted by his family's old antagonists, Barend Den Hartog and Van den Elsakker. Van Leeuwen's statement of October 17, 1946, says they "came to my home with 4 BS-ers under the command of Commander Picaulli." BS-ers were members of the *Binnenlandse Strijdkrachten* (BS), or Forces of the Interior, an umbrella organization created on September 5, 1944, which placed the different resistance groups under a joint command. The BS, along with the Princess Irene Brigade, which had landed at Normandy in August, were led by Prince Bernhard. Although Van Leeuwen does not explicitly say that Wim and Dina were confronted at the same time, this was probably the case. Van Leeuwen's statement reads, "Picaulli informed us he came to arrest my son-in-law and daughter."

"I informed Picaulli," the statement continues, "that Rabbi Dasburg, who had come to thank me for the aid I had given to the Jews during the occupation, had just left the home. I refused to go with him and informed him to first do a thorough investigation of the claims against me." Van Leeuwen and Picaulli knew each other, and

Picaulli did as Van Leeuwen asked. However, when he and the others departed, they may have taken Wim and Dina with them, for we know Wim was detained on that date. What is unclear is whether Wim was detained until he was arrested in early June. Property, home furnishings, and other items he owned with Dina, who was living with her parents at Loosdrechtseweg 23 in Hilversum, were seized and inventoried by the government on July 24.[459]

As for Van Leeuwen, May 22 only got more eventful. In his statement, he notes that, not only did Picaulli return "to apologize" and inform him "the allegations of Den Hartog and Van den Elsakker were false," but the latter two, "disappointed" by this outcome, "did not give up." His statement continues,

> I was arrested, based on their information, by BS of the Bussumerstraat at about 3PM that same day and taken to the police station.
>
> When I asked the gentlemen of the BS what the meaning of this was, they said, 'Walk or we will shoot you down.'

According to Wim, in his statement of October 23, 1946, Van Leeuwen had been arrested on this occasion "as a suspect in … the mysterious death of Rothschild." This charge appears to be another dimension of Den Hartog's and Van den Elsakker's vendetta against Van Leeuwen. The "reporting officer" who took Wim's statement notes that Wim had been named "in connection with the mysterious death of Rothschild." In response, Wim states that he was never arrested regarding the alleged connection and clarifies that Van Leeuwen was.

Van Leeuwen's statement continues,

> After I was interrogated at the police station, and after it became clear that the case of Arnold Rothschild had been

---

[459] Report on Wim's property (DNA, NBI 99047). Dina was not interned (email of October 13, 2020, from the DNA to the author).

investigated from beginning to end by Officer Van Oort and Constable Van der Leulen, I was let go.

I was lucky that the gentlemen of the BS did not take me to the N. S. F. as this could have led to a shaven head and imprisonment as an NSB-er for one or more days while they investigated my case. [The N. S. F. was an internment camp located on the site of the NV Nederlandsche Seintoestellen Fabriek in Hilversum.][460]

John was arrested on the twenty-sixth. Susan witnessed it. Their friend and neighbour, Koos Doornbos, was also arrested, but Susan could not remember when this occurred. John said that following his arrest, he was not treated badly initially. He told me that along with about seventy-five others, he was put in a room about twenty by twenty-five feet. At the end of the day, they were taken outside, formed into a column, and marched to the prison at Scheveningen, some four miles northwest of The Hague. As they marched, there were many women along the roadside looking for their husbands. The women waved and shouted, trying to get their attention, but the men ignored them. The prisoners kept their eyes forward and said nothing as they marched by. John claimed they had been told by the guards that they would be shot if they spoke to anyone.

According to what John told me, he was interned at Scheveningen prison until late 1945 or early 1946 when he was transferred to Duindorp. However, in his statement of April 22, 1947, he said "that soon after the capitulation of the German army, SCHOLTE, KORTELAND and I were incarcerated in the prison camp here in Duindorp." John's statement continues:

KORTELAND then came to me saying he had a message from SCHOLTE. SCHOLTE informed me that in case we were questioned about the Intelligence Service, we were not

---

[460] Email of January 4, 2022, from Frank van Riet to the author regarding the N. S. F. interment camp in Hilversum.

to say anything except about the reports on the political situation. According to SCHOLTE, there was no news about any of the other people involved. I can also state that the German people I was in contact [with] showed that they were deeply sympathetic to the German cause. SCHOLTE spoke German most of the time, and if he did speak Dutch, his speech included many German words and phrases. KORTELAND later became anti-German.

Although John's statement says he was imprisoned at Duindorp "soon after" the German surrender, I'm confident that he was initially incarcerated at Scheveningen prison. When visits were eventually permitted at Scheveningen, Susan and Miek visited him there. As there was no public transportation to Scheveningen, they had to walk or hitchhike to the prison. This was chancy because the prison had set hours for visiting and, unless they left early enough, there was no guarantee that they would arrive in time. Miek spoke of a vivid memory: "I can still see Susan running with little Constance under her arm" to get to the prison before they stopped admitting visitors. Miek said the baby was six months old, so this was likely about August. Susan told me that Prince Bernhard stopped for hitchhikers, although she never received a ride from him.

John's April 1947 statement is almost exclusively about his work with the Intelligence Service. I suspect it makes no mention of Scheveningen because it was not relevant: presumably, none of John's fellow SD members were housed at Scheveningen with him. I also suspect that his statement jumps ahead to Duindorp because that is where he found himself in the same facility as Scholte and Korteland. He told me a lot of former SS men were prisoners at Duindorp. The contradictory information as to where John was first imprisoned was resolved in late 2009 when I received the results of further research into files at the Dutch National Archives. A card in CABR file 91103 shows that John was transferred to Duindorp on January 18, 1946.[461] Thus, John's imprecise phrase "soon after the capitulation" was, in fact, more than eight months after VE Day.

Constant was not arrested until July 16. He had fled Graz, Austria, on May 8, just ahead of the advancing Russians, and made his way to Dermbach, Thuringia, in Germany, where Elly and their two young sons were located. At Dermbach, he identified himself to the mayor, who surrendered him to the Americans. He was a prisoner of war for fourteen days, then released. When the Russians occupied Dermbach, he, Elly, and the boys left for the Netherlands. He was arrested on the German-Dutch border, near Roermond in the province of Limburg. Elly and the boys lived at the Sophialaan house for a time before moving to her parents, who also lived in Hilversum.[462]

***

During the last years of the occupation, "women had become the providers, hunters for food at a time when many men were in Germany or dared not show themselves for fear of being sent into German war service." Van der Zee writes that "life revolved around [women] and they had by far the most difficult task."[463] Queen Wilhelmina acknowledged this in a speech of November 28, 1944, when she thanked "all those housewives who lack absolutely everything to keep their households going. My thoughts are constantly with them."[464]

While Stanni was one of these women when Wim was in hiding at her home from December 1944, she also endured a second and rarer experience when her three sons were interned in mid-1945. Her

---

[461] Dr. M. Blauw's report of December 3, 2009, 4; her report is based on DNA, CABR 91103/PRA The Hague, dossier 21717.
[462] Constant's statements of November 1, 1945, and February 14, 1947 (DNA, CABR 70629). Blauw's report of February 14, 2007 (3, 6).
[463] *Liberation Album*, 137 (women had become the providers). Van der Zee, 152.
[464] Van der Zee, 152.

daughters-in-law shared these experiences with her, although Elly was out of the country for the last eight months of the occupation and didn't return until July. Stanni, who turned sixty-two later in 1945, worked very hard, according to Miek, taking in boarders when she had extra room, which was the case before John's family moved in during the latter half of 1946 and before John and Wim were released. Once back in Hilversum, Susan, for her part, worked as a housecleaner to earn money for her family. While she regarded Stanni as a second mother, she also observed that Stanni—prompted by necessity—had "changed a lot" since the affluence and privilege she had enjoyed as a young woman at Lahad Datu with John and Constant's father and later during the first years of her marriage to Wim and Miek's father. Susan, in turn, "learned a lot" from Stanni's strong example.

"The war," according to historian Michiel Horn, "had affected traditional notions of right and wrong, had undermined parental authority, had thrust younger women into positions of unusual importance" such as couriering messages for the resistance on their bicycles. It was not feasible "to limit their freedom ... in the euphoria of that liberation summer"—what one Dutch writer termed "the wild, crazy summer of '45."[465]

"Life was messy, unsettled, full of goodwill, and, not surprisingly, we were celebrating every night," writes Van der Zee. "Every self-respecting neighbourhood organized a street-party and the fraternization [with Canadian soldiers] was general."[466]

Of the 170,000 Canadian soldiers that had entered the country, 65 per cent were still there at the end of August. Those who had served longest were sent home first, but a lack of ships to carry the men was delaying a process that everyone wanted to move faster. Only 16,000 had been repatriated by the end of June, 59,000 by the end of August,

---

[465] *Liberation Album*, 140–41 (traditional notions, euphoria), 131 (crazy summer). Maass, 218 (resistance relied on young women to courier information).
[466] Van der Zee, 297.

and 100,000 by the end of November, with the remainder cleared in December and January.

When liberation came, "many Dutch men were still absent. Those who were around were thin, weak, badly dressed, poor and quite unattractive." One Dutchman, who was nineteen that year, recollected, "We were no competition for the Canadians."[467] But the deck was stacked against them in other ways too. Dutchmen were excluded from Canadian dances and parties, which became a "sore point with many civilians."[468] As soldiers without a date weren't permitted entry, a surplus of Dutch girls would congregate outside hoping "to get picked up at the door."[469]

Canadian soldiers were not only much-admired liberators, they were also rich. They used chocolate bars as inducements, an advantage unavailable to many Dutch men. Soldiers also employed these and other items to ingratiate themselves with a girl's parents.[470] Mothers who needed laundry soap could obtain it by offering to do soldiers' washing.[471]

Stanni's sister, Sjaan, and two of her three daughters, including the eldest, Stan (a diminutive of Constance), continued to live at Sophialaan 18 during this period. Stan had a son by a Canadian soldier. The soldier promised to return for Stan and their son, but he never did.

That autumn, Miek became a professional singer when she replaced one of the members of the Swinging Nightingales, a female trio like the Andrews Sisters. They performed for the Canadian troops in Hilversum several times. By the following spring, the Swinging Nightingales were part of a regular radio program. They had several hit records. Miek said they toured the Netherlands and Belgium and would have gone to Indonesia had not one of their members become

---

[467] *Liberation Album*, 137 (quite unattractive; no competition).
[468] *Liberation Album*, 138.
[469] *Liberation Album*, 147.
[470] Maass, 249. *Liberation Album*, 147.
[471] *Liberation Album*, 147.

pregnant. Miek said singing with the trio was "the nicest time in [her] life" and she "enjoyed it so much." She performed with the group until 1952, when she and her husband, Bob Sundermeijer, immigrated to New Zealand.

But, as with many Dutch citizens, Miek could not shake the war's shadow. In a May 2004 telephone conversation, she told Constance that none of her circle of friends knew she had two German brothers. Constance told me Miek became very distressed when she revealed this. Constance added Miek never had the courage to go to one of the support groups for families of collaborators. The family's allegiance with Germany during the war and the fact she had two German brothers were Miek's "big secret," according to Constance.

Four years later, at Miek's request, I sent her copies of her brothers' collaborator statements, along with some related documents held by the Dutch National Archives. In an April 2008 telephone call, Miek told me that reading the papers "made [her] sick." She cried when she read two letters Constant had written to his wife during the war. "I feel so sorry for *all* of them," she said about her brothers and their families. By emphasizing the word "all," she was doubtless signalling she was including John as well.

21

SCHEVENINGEN PRISON

"The prisons and camps filled up very quickly," John said.

He claimed about 800,000 people were arrested. This figure is typical of his exaggeration. It represents about 8.7 per cent of the country's population, which was 9.22 million on January 1, 1945. The actual number arrested was "between 120,000 and 150,000," although the maximum number interned was 96,044, which was reached on October 15, 1945.[472]

While the cases of those arrested were heard by the Special Courts, another 300,000 to 450,000 were investigated by tribunals for "attitude" and "opinion" crimes punishable by up to ten years in prison.[473] The tribunals were based on a distinction in Dutch jurisprudence between *Strafrecht* (criminal law) and *Tuchtrecht*

---

[472] Hirschfeld, 321 (120–150,000). Mason, 40 (120–150,000; country's population; "The known maximum number of arrestees at one time was reached on October 15, 1945: 96,044 were imprisoned of whom 72,321 were men, and 23,723 were women"). Van der Heide, "Timeline of World War II History, December 14, 1931–April 14, 1949," 19, accessed March 7, 2002, www.godutch.com/newspaper/index.php?id=505 (92,485, including 21,923 women, were interned as of December 15, 1945). See footnote 95 for additional information on the Van der Heide source.

[473] Mason, 139 (450,000 investigations begun), 69 (attitude and opinion crimes), 76 (ten years). Mason adds (175) that "300,000 *dossiers* [were] prepared against non-arrestees."

(disciplinary law); the tribunals were "*Tuchtrecht* organs." They were "people's courts" and functioned as "safety-valves, aiding in the avoidance of lynch justice." They used lay judges who also acted as prosecutors. These "judges always were resistance men."[474]

The "tribunals punished such acts and attitudes as eating with Germans in public places; having German friends; permitting one's minor daughter to go out with Germans; letting one's minor son join the NSB youth movement; giving the Hitler salute; ending a letter with the NSB (*Hou Zee*) salute; having Hitler's portrait in one's room; sending congratulations to Seyss-Inquart on his birthday; subscribing to Nazi newspapers; being proud of one's German origin; calling the Allied fliers overhead 'murderers.'"[475] Tribunal sentences involving punitive measures had to be reviewed and approved by a "High Authority" appointed by the government. "The *Tuchtrecht* concept of the Tribunals has been severely attacked," Mason writes, adding: "Later, when lynch justice did not occur, the Tribunals were largely used as overflow for the overloaded Special Courts."[476]

John's statement that the internment camps filled up quickly is correct. Housing 96,000 men and women was one more huge problem for the overburdened country. This challenge had to be tackled at the same time as camps were being "improvised for the Allied armies and ... for returned slave-laborers and political and racial deportees," including 5,500 Jews.[477]

There were 106 camps for collaborators. Many "were set up in former German concentration camps, Dutch and German military barracks, and labor camps. Other Quislings had to be interned in evacuated monasteries, hospitals, mental institutions, medieval castles, partly destroyed houses, and even in warehouses, stables, and air raid shelters."[478]

---

[474] Mason, 69, (safety-valves), 70 and 79 (people's courts), 70 (*Strafrecht, Tuchtrecht*), 72 (lay judges; always resistance men).
[475] Mason, 75.
[476] Mason, 73 (Higher Authority), 71 (severely attacked), 79 (used as overflow).
[477] Mason, 48. Moore, 232 (5,500 Jews).
[478] Mason, 48–49.

The collaborator camps were fraught with major problems. They were often led by "unsuitable men." The rare capable commanders were put in charge of several camps simultaneously. Consequently, burnout and turnover among camp commanders was high. The issue of suitability extended to the 25,000 guards who staffed the camps. Some were brutal, cruel, and corrupt and "of definitely inferior quality." Overcrowding was commonplace. Prisoners included children, women with babies, and people over eighty years of age. "Murderers, war criminals, profiteers, and N.S.B. youth" were indiscriminately housed together. Men and women were often not effectively separated, which "caused undesirable relationships" and "much evil." Medical care "was often very poor." Tuberculosis was "the 'occupational' disease of concentration camps"; tubercular patients "were frequently not isolated." Arbitrary punishments contributed to the "terrible conditions." Punishments were administered by "guards without knowledge of the camp commander."[479]

A special inspection of the camps undertaken in early 1946 "decried the 'special cells for punishment' [*strafbunker*], a Nazi innovation which the commission found applied in many camps ..." The resulting report stated, "The commission has visited '*bunkers*' which can be described only as inhuman; at Leiden, for example, punished persons had to stand or sit all day on a stone floor. These cells are often unheated in the middle of winter.... In the camp 'De Eeze' this punishment [Strafbunker] was applied for weeks in a row ..."[480]

---

[479] Mason, 49–50.
[480] Mason, 49–50. Moore, 232 ("shortage of space"). Mason notes (54–55, 175) that the corruption problem extended to "some of the POD [Political Investigative Service, which was later called the Political Investigation Departments (*Politieke Recherche Afdelingen* or PRA)] sections. The commission of the Second Chamber which inspected the camps reported that the internees complained above all about irregularities in the pre-trial releases. Those with money and connections seemed to be helped first. Camp officials told the commission that POD (PRA) investigators had been known to arrange

During the war, the large jail at Scheveningen became known as the "Orange Hotel" because the Germans used it to lock up "several thousand resistance fighters."[481] As of May 1945, it became one of the 106 facilities used to house suspected traitors to the Orange state. Officially, it was the responsibility of Canadian Field Security until it was transferred to the military government in mid-July. In practice, however, "the Dutch Military Police and the Forces of the Interior (BS) were in charge" during the initial two-month "wild stage." According to historian David Barnouw and author Gerrold van der Stroom, operations during that period "did not work very well; in fact, it was 'a barbarian regime.' Sunday was 'show day,' when the relatives and acquaintances of the members of the Forces of the Interior in Scheveningen came to 'view' the prisoners."[482]

By the summer of 1945, several church leaders were publicly denouncing conditions in the camps. The first such condemnation appeared in a weekly paper published by the Dutch Reformed Church on June 23. A Protestant minister who published a pamphlet on the conditions in the camp at Vught "cited many severe beatings and cruelties, and noted the general atmosphere of corruption and immorality which affected internees and staff."[483]

In January 1950, the Dutch solicitor general admitted, "Such offensive things happened that they must be considered a black page in our national history. One could hardly believe that Dutch camp guards would be guilty of the same abuses which made the Germans so hated."[484]

***

---

things for 'money, goods, and even women'.... Several POD investigators, and even section heads were convicted of corruption and other crimes."
[481] Maass, 85 (Hotel). Paape, 77 (several thousand).
[482] David Barnouw and Gerrold van der Stroom, "Who betrayed Anne Frank?" Netherlands Institute for War Documentation, April 25, 2003, 19, 20.
[483] Mason, 49.
[484] Mason, 51, 174 (January 28, 1950).

After the marching prisoners arrived at Scheveningen Prison, all their body hair was shaved off and everything was taken from them, except their clothes. John said it was not long before the jail was crammed full; four men were put into each of the cells, which were about four feet by eight feet and meant for a single occupant. The cell to which John and his new companions were assigned contained a cot, a table, a chair, and a bucket that served as a toilet. There was a single window high up on one wall. The thick cell door had a small eyehole for use by the guards.

John said that when that door closed behind them, "it was worse than anything that had happened before."

Perhaps this is a true statement. Perhaps John put some of what he experienced then into his false story of being imprisoned and sentenced to death by the Germans a short time before the end of the war. But there was also melodrama in his account of the beginning of his internment.

"All previous times John knew what he had done and what he could expect," my notes from 1976 read. "This time he did not know anything." None of the internees "knew what they were charged with … or how long they would be there."

Was John being disingenuous or had his recall (thirty years later) of some of the events of this period shifted in genuine and significant ways? On the surface, his professed ignorance as to why he was interned just seems silly. After all, Susan said they both had expected his arrest. And he was certainly familiar with what was going on. "Underground people," he told me, were serving as a posse comitatus searching out "the enemies of Holland." Are some of his tales—such as deserting his unit and being sentenced to death by the Germans—just the spinning of fantastic yarns? Or are they to some extent part of an alternate reality, one he actually believed? At a minimum, he tended to play the victim and sought to make people feel sorry for him. "I'm in need—I'm hurting—poor me," is how Hans described this behaviour.

John said, "All previous times I knew what I had done and what I could expect." This points to the emotional impact of not only what he had been through during the war but also of what lay in store for him as an internee. But it's unclear what events he was referring to when he spoke of "all previous times." Did they include his apocryphal death sentence in late April 1945? Did they include his seven-day internment in May 1940 when he claimed he faced a mock firing squad, which was something he could not have expected? Did they include his dubious court-martial for stealing while inspecting vehicles for contraband at checkpoints, which led to his unexpected exoneration based on the miraculously consistent testimony of his Schutzgruppe mates? Did they include his suspect arrest at Amersfoort in 1943 for exempting former Dutch soldiers from forced labour in Germany and his subsequent avoidance of any punishment—thanks, he claimed, to his unexpected transfer to the staff of a nonexistent German army commander? Presumably, they did include the two hazy investigations by the German army and the SS into his status during the last year or so of the war when he managed to avoid the expected outcome of being sent to the front. Whatever was meant by "all previous times," there is no question that in this new situation he had no idea what to expect or how long he would be interned.

According to John, the three other men sharing his fate (and shoehorned into the same cell) were a scientist who was in his early- to mid-fifties, a flower vendor who was about John's age, and a man in his sixties who "gave the impression of being much older." In due course, John learned more about each of them. He implausibly maintained that the scientist was accused of working with the Germans in their efforts to develop an atomic bomb, a charge the scientist denied. The flower vendor was accused of profiting from the Germans by selling flowers to them, something that required a German licence, John said. The vendor, who also claimed to have been in the underground, said he used his business to get close to the Germans. John thought it was probably true that this man had been in the resistance. The old man was a different case. John said he was "inept ... rather dumb [and] inspired pity [because] he couldn't take care of himself. He had a sad, pouty face like something out of Van Gogh. He was loveable, though." John gave no indication why he had been arrested.

The four of them agreed to take turns using the cot, which meant that the second person was on the chair, and the third and fourth were on the floor. The floor was made more comfortable sometime later when straw was provided.

During their first night, at about 1:00 a.m., John had an encounter with four guards. He said there was a distinct difference between the regular guards and the new ones who were hired in conjunction with the mass arrests. The regular guards behaved in a professional manner; they were "indifferent but not cruel." The new recruits, however, were prejudiced and brutish; they made a point of humiliating and abusing prisoners. John said the prison was staffed by the regular guards, but his description of the guards he encountered that night sounds more like the new recruits. Whatever the case, the guards unlocked the door to the cell. They'd been drinking beer but were not drunk. They selected John and made him come out into the corridor where they all peed into a pail that had holes in it. They told John to pick up the pail. He protested that the pee would drain out.

"That doesn't matter," they said, insisting that John do as he was told.

When he did and the pee drained out, they told him to mop it up.

"There's no mop," John said.

"Use your jacket," they insisted.

John said he had to continue the futile exercise—wiping up the floor, wringing out his wet jacket into the pail, picking up the pail again, and repeating the process—for some time. Those who resisted the guards, he said, received much worse treatment. He didn't see what happened to these other people, but he heard their screams, which always occurred at night. This made John and his cellmates fear the sound of footsteps after dark.

318   A SNAKE ON THE HEART

"I don't know where the law was then," John observed.[485]

He said life in the prison was chaos during their first weeks there. Other than two small dry biscuits a day, there was no food. Corruption was commonplace. Any packages that came for the prisoners didn't make it past the guards. The dry biscuits were among the first extra food provided to the Dutch people as part of the relief effort at the end of the war. The biscuits "contained whale oil and were made especially for people who had vitamin deficiencies."[486] There was water for drinking, but none for washing. And except for a daily visit to the courtyard to empty their toilet, they were locked in their cell nearly all the time and got virtually no exercise. Cleanliness was nonexistent; there was no way to keep yourself clean, John said. He continued to wear the jacket he had used to mop up the pee. Despite it being late May and early June, it was often cold since they were close to the North Sea. Within a week of their arrival, the prison was infested with lice, and sickness was rampant.

The flower vendor got dysentery, but nothing was done for him. He spent nearly all his time on the toilet passing blood. John said it was a miracle they didn't all get it. Perhaps more miraculous was the large, unopened bottle of pills they found on a little triangular shelf in the corner of the cell. The bottle, which was about eight inches tall with a three-inch base, contained about a thousand pills that turned out to be multiple vitamins. John said the bottle was remarkable for several reasons: No one knew how it got there; no one knew why it hadn't been removed before they hid it; and virtually no one took vitamins at that time. They each took a pill a day. John was sure those pills had a lot to do with why they survived the ordeal of that period as well as they did.

---

[485] Mason (135) quotes Professor G. Russel, one of the strongest critics of the Netherlands' postwar handling of collaborators: "After the expulsion of the Germans, the government ... permitted illegal and inhuman treatment of collaborators, members of the NSB, and thousands of others who did not belong to these groups. Practically no police protection was available against actions of the Forces of the Interior, the M.G. [military government], and other sinister forces."
[486] *Liberation Album*, 118 (whale oil).

About two weeks into their stay, the guards started selecting relatively able-bodied men for work detail. John was not chosen right away. Soon after, he decided to volunteer. He said he figured anything was better than rotting in jail. The work was heavy and hard. They cleared the rubble from the war, moved big rocks, scraped the mortar off bricks so they could be used again, and moved the cleaned bricks in wheelbarrows to building sites. In addition to the physical activity and the variation in routine, those on work detail were also fed, although John once said this was nothing more than a slice of bread and water with green leaves in it. Hunger was a constant, gnawing issue. Nonetheless, there was what John described as "a great phenomenon": Those favoured with work would sometimes share their good fortune—namely, the superior rations they received—with their less fortunate, cell-bound mates. Those on work detail also became adept—John called them "great artists"—at smuggling bits of food and tobacco into their cells.

The scientist was also on work detail. He bargained successfully with some of the nonprofessional guards for cigarettes and other items of value, which he shared. Bribery and work-camp transactions of this sort usually involved a third party, an associate or family member of the prisoner on the outside. The prisoner would provide the guard with a signed note, which the guard would take to the third party for payment in return for goods supplied to the prisoner. John admired the scientist's generosity and respected the calm, quiet efficiency with which he did things. The flower vendor, while also generous, was, in John's estimation, "sly." He somehow landed a job in the kitchen. John thought he might have blackmailed some of the guards. John said he "was the sort of person to look for openings like that." The old man, who walked slumped over like a hunchback, didn't go out to work. He stayed behind and would clean the cell, which earned him rewards from his cellmates. He also talked incessantly about food—"When I get out of here I'm going to have ham and eggs"—which, John said, "would drive the others nuts." The old man would say to John, the scientist, or the flower vendor: "If you aren't hungry, I'll eat yours" or "I know you're probably getting fed at work, so if you can spare your evening meal, I would like to have it." He also craved smokes.

John said they were completely cut off from the outside world during their first months of imprisonment. Barnouw and Van der Stroom confirm that correspondence was not permitted at least well into July. Even when the prisoners were working in public areas, the guards made sure they had no contact with civilians. After about two months, they were permitted to send and receive short letters of a quarter-page in length. The letters were censored. The prisoners were not allowed to mention how they were treated or the conditions in which they lived. Susan told me that she was not permitted to visit John for the first several months.

Sometime during the late summer or early autumn—John said it was after about four months—he was moved to the work camp. He told me he'd dreaded this because of stories he'd heard, all of which related to the guards. These guards were nonprofessionals and reportedly treated the prisoners worse than animals. The prison was good in comparison to the work camp, he said. It provided "more security and routine." But he later qualified this, noting that the male prisoners had it better than the female prisoners, who were in a different wing of the prison. Some of the male guards treated this wing as their sexual playground. John said they could rape any woman prisoner and that this was a frequent practice. He added that it was hushed up from the outside world and occurred only within the prison.

According to John, the work-camp guards liked to subject prisoners to a game they called Playing a Record. They did this on the pretext of having found something wrong with the prisoner's work. A walking cane would be produced and set vertically with the bottom tip on the ground. The prisoner had to put his hands on the top of the cane then bend forward placing his forehead on his hands and walk in circles around the cane. He was soon very dizzy and unable to stand. "When you fell down," John said, "this was laziness or insubordination and reason to kick and beat you. This doesn't sound so bad, but it was, especially considering you were already so weak."

There were worse tortures than Playing a Record. They often involved food. At one of the work sites, the guards, who ate well, threw their leftovers into a wooden barrel that was dumped once a week. The barrel was off-limits to the prisoners. The penalty for attempting to breach this rule was to be shot in the act. And many were, John claimed. He never tried to reach the barrel, but one day he did something he came to regard as equally stupid, something that sprang from a similar, although less desperate, need: When the guards were eating, he asked one of them if he could have a slice of bread. Rather than a simple no, he said he received a pitiless, sadistic punishment. They made him get into an empty coal bin and stick his head out the trapdoor at the bottom, which effectively trapped him in that position. The guards then put a plate of hot food—pork, fried eggs, and potatoes—a few inches in front of his face. The wonderful aroma caused him to jolt forward, but no matter how much he strained he could not reach it. That sort of thing, he said, "almost drives you crazy when you are that hungry."

In contrast to such treatment, the prisoners, according to John's stories, were a noble lot. They treated each other with decency and, when they could, they acted in solidarity and even found humour in their circumstances. The following January, John wrote a poem titled "Comrades," which is representative of his attitude and includes this stanza:

Comrades, women, brothers
In this tough battle for life
Let us endure
These difficult times together
Offer our weaker brother
A friendly hand.
Bonded together closely
We stand much stronger.[487]

---

[487] Translated by Haydee Oord.

According to Veltmeijer, John was "reliable" and had "an innate feeling for his fellow human beings."[488]

Sharing was the most common way the internees expressed their humanity. They did this with tools, tobacco, and food—whether it was smuggled or from their meagre rations. Among the tools in John's cell were a tin can that had been smuggled in and a small piece of wood that had fallen off the cot. These items were "real treasures," he said. He and his cellmates shared them with the men in the next cell who they communicated with via a hole in the wall, which they had created by scraping mortar away from a brick. They hid this fact from the guards by putting the brick back in the wall and surrounding it with fake mortar produced by chewing the fine rice paper pages torn from a Bible, which was one of the few standard items in all cells.

One very hot day when John was working outside the jail, he claimed he somehow obtained a pound of margarine. At the end of the day, he wrapped this great prize in a cloth and tied it loose between his legs like a diaper in hopes of smuggling it undetected into the jail and into their cell. He said he was taking a chance because sometimes upon their return they had to strip entirely. Other times they were just frisked. Normally they were transported back and forth between the jail and their various work locations by truck, but on this occasion the vehicle broke down and they had to walk. John said it was about four miles. He was soon concerned that he would be found out, that the melting margarine would come out the bottom of his pant legs. But it didn't get that far. His luck also held at the jail; he and the others were only frisked. Back in the safety of the cell, the precious commodity was carefully "scraped off his legs and penis" with the piece of wood and transferred to the tin can. A splendid victory had yielded a great bounty. John and his mates enjoyed "rather salty tasting margarine for several weeks."

Tobacco in the form of cigarette butts was the most frequently smuggled item. On days when they had had an especially good haul or

---

[488] Veltmeijer's testimonial letter of June 23, 1951 (see footnote 4).

when, over several days, they'd accumulated enough, they would have a smoking party after "lights out" at 8:00 p.m. They rolled their cigarettes using pages from the Bible, which was another of the multiple purposes to which this paper was put.[489] The only damper on these occasions was the need to keep an attentive ear for guards who made periodic checks on some of the cells. One time when John and the others were contentedly sitting back puffing on their cigarettes, they heard the guards coming. It was a long corridor, but John said he knew theirs would be one of the cells to be checked. He opened the little window high up on the wall and they all flapped their jackets and arms to clear the smoke as best they could. The old man, who was starting to go senile, did this as well. In the dark no one noticed he had not butted his cigarette. He still held it between his lips. This was discovered when the door to the cell was opened and the light from the corridor poured in. After their frenetic activity, it was a stupefying moment; John said it was both hilarious and tragic. The guards took the old man away. His cellmates never saw him again.

Their smoking parties, smuggling successes, and other acts of free expression helped them make the most of their sorry situation. There were also rare triumphs of the spirit. The greatest of these was the "orange-bow incident." It involved a cruel guard who was their nemesis. She was the only female guard in the men's prison, and she often required them to strip naked and stand at attention when they returned from work. On the day of the incident, one of the men had found a large piece of orange fabric. Orange being the colour of the royal family, it was an omnipresent part of the celebrations accompanying liberation. The members of the twenty-man work detail tore the fabric into strips, then each man tied a strip into a bow around his penis. And for once they all hoped they would be ordered to strip. True to form, the female guard obliged them. John described her as "a disturbed woman [who] was not liked by the other guards." The prisoners had to strip on command: first their jackets, then their

---

[489] John said they also used pages from the Bible "to make crossword puzzles [and] a checkerboard"; they "played games with it …"

shirts, then their pants. When the denouement came and the twenty decorated penises were revealed, the woman "went absolutely berserk." She "was screaming as if she was going out of her mind."

Too upset to retaliate, she yelled, "Take them away! Take them away!" to the male guards, who thought it was funny.

"She was belittled [and] made a fool of," John said. "Her status was destroyed."

22

THE DARK CELL

John's most notable experience while at Scheveningen began when he and three other internees were sent with a guard to work at the English garrison, probably during September. He said the English soldiers were "really terrible, extremely bad." He told me that he and his mates had to clean up, do household jobs, and wash dishes. When they entered one room, they were immediately confronted by temptation: a large bunch of grapes sat on a table. (Were grapes available despite the postwar shortages? Or are they another manifestation of John's imaginative storytelling? Despite this uncertainty, which could be an indicator of another tall tale, there are a couple of pieces of evidence that tend to corroborate the culminating part of the lengthy episode that supposedly began with the grapes.) Not only was it literally forbidden fruit that commanded their attention, it was also a possible set-up for some "show day" entertainment. As they moved toward it, several things happened in rapid succession.

"Don't touch them," John warned, sensing a trap. But he was too late. One of the men had helped himself to four grapes, which he dropped almost as soon as he took them. He was responding to a sudden noise behind them: an English sergeant major entering the room. The sergeant major went directly to the grapes and counted them. Then he informed the guard outside the room that four grapes were missing.

The guard lined the four of them up in the hallway and questioned each of them in turn. "Did you take the grapes?" he asked the first man.

"No."

"Do you know who did?"

"No."

When they all answered these questions the same way, the guard slapped each of them twice in the face.

"I'm going to punish all four of you seeing that your motto is 'one for all and all for one.'"

He ordered them into the courtyard, which was full of rocks, rubble, broken bricks, and glass. They were commanded to run to the right, run to the left, lie down, crawl on knees and elbows, stand up, run to the right, run to the left, lie down, crawl on knees and elbows. For good measure, the guard also kicked them when they were on the ground. After a while they were told to line up facing a brick wall and bend over with their heads against the wall. The guard walloped each of them on the buttocks with the butt of his rifle, causing them to bump their heads as well. Then he ordered them to stand up and turn around. As this was going on, a crowd had quickly gathered on the far side of the iron gates to the courtyard. John said hundreds of people were watching.

"Are you enjoying this?" the guard asked his prisoners in turn.

"No," came the response from each of them, except John.

"Oh, I don't mind," he claimed to have said, not wanting to give the guard any satisfaction. "If it gives you pleasure, it's okay."

"I guess I'll have to take you a little further," the guard replied, determined to have John submit to his authority.

Once more, John was running to the right, running to the left, crawling on knees and elbows, and receiving kicks from the guard's heavy boots. Only this time there was something else.

"Kill him! Kill him!" yelled rabid voices from beyond the gates. The guard seemed energized by the hysteria of the mob. John said he felt "just like an animal."

Finally, when the guard told him to stand up, John could do no more than raise his chest and head. Exasperated, the guard swung his rifle, hitting John between the eyes with the butt end and knocking him unconscious.

Such abuse was happening everywhere, John told me.

He was unconscious for a long time. When he awoke, he was back in his cell at the prison. He knew this despite having been blinded. A guard, who had been waiting for him to regain consciousness, led him to the warden's office. The guard who had beaten him was also there.

"I hear you stole six packs of cigarettes from the English officers," the warden said. "Do you have anything to say?"

"Yes, I do," John answered. "I didn't steal any cigarettes! We were accused of stealing four grapes."

"Here are the stolen cigarettes," the guard said, apparently producing six packs.

"He's lying," John charged angrily.

"Do you mean to say that this upright citizen is lying, and I should take your word for it?" the warden asked.

"That's exactly what I'm saying."

"Well, I know what to do with liars like you," was the warden's reply, which brought the interview to an end.

John was locked away in a dark cell. In one way, because he was blind, this made no difference. But in other ways, it mattered a lot. He'd heard stories about the dark cells. They had no lights or windows or furniture or heat, just cement floors and brick walls, and prisoners entered them through not one but two doors, wearing nothing but their underwear; John mentioned this last point twice. It was "bitter cold," he said. This factor may explain the inconsistency in his dating of his dark-cell experience. One time, he said it was toward winter, but three weeks earlier, he said the events in question occurred during the first four months of his internment, meaning sometime during the June–September period. (Given what happened after John's time in the dark cell, it appears his confinement there started sometime in September and extended into October. He made his first collaborator statement on the eighth of October.)

The near-barren cell contained three things: a barrel in one corner that served as a toilet; a can of water that was changed daily, provided it was placed by the interior door next to the floor-level pass-through; and a pipe along one wall about three feet off the ground. John said, "When you first go in there you feel as if the last little thread of life has been cut." He emphasized the isolation, the "total seclusion" and that most of the time you couldn't hear a sound. "It really feels like the end—there's nothing. *You know you can't get out.* [John's emphasis.] It's almost as if you can't think anymore. You can no longer see your thoughts. It's too dark. I just wanted to roll up in a corner and die—not because I wanted to die, but because there was nothing and I was naked and so helpless and there was nothing to fight."

As the days passed in pitch-black silence, he lost track of time. The only markers available to him were the water cart and the bread cart, which he could hear coming down the corridor. The water cart came once a day. The bread cart came every second day. It provided two slices of bread. John said he made it a practice to eat his in two sittings. During his stay in the dark cell—which was "at least four weeks and at most five"—he apparently ate approximately twenty-eight to thirty-five slices of bread and nothing else. And, with one exception, his only contact with the outside world was those carts.

One day, after about two weeks, when he heard the cart coming and was expecting to receive his two slices of bread, the cart didn't stop. Perhaps it was not even the bread cart, he said in retrospect. But at the time he was in "a frantic state of mind." He started shouting and banging his fists against the interior door. When he didn't stop, the guards opened the first door and the viewing slot on the second and turned a fire hose on him. The force of the water knocked him down and against the far wall. It quickly cooled him off, he said. The volume of water was tremendous. When the torrent stopped, John was sitting in four inches of water. There was no drain in the cell. The only way he could get out of the water was to sit on the pipe, lean back, and lift his legs, but he could only do that for short spells. He lived in the water for many hours, perhaps more than a day, and he said he had to sleep in it for a time. Eventually it seeped away beneath the doors and through the cement floor. One of the consequences of this experience, he claimed, was the permanent loss of some of the feeling in his feet. In later years he could not distinguish warm and cold with his feet, he said, although he could tell when he was stepping into a hot bath.

There were other consequences. The flooding of his cell was the lowest point in his life. He noted he was almost ready to chuck it and give up. He told me that he started thinking of Jesus and what he had to go through and of others who had suffered greatly. He said he felt a kinship with Jesus, and that Jesus "appeared" to him. He said he didn't actually see him, but it was almost like seeing him. "I could certainly feel him." John told me he felt warm, like someone put a cloak around him. He said Jesus told him that in difficult times ahead, if he thought of him, the hard things would pass more easily, that he would still have to go through them and be aware of them, but he would not feel them.

My notes add: "This is where it all started, and John realized that he knew Jesus and started to get flashbacks."

On at least one occasion, John referred to this event as "a miracle." He told me that it happened between five and twenty-four hours after the fire hose had been turned on him, which was at about the midpoint of his stay in the dark cell. John credits the experience with his survival and the fact he didn't catch so much as a cold. He felt he had received "a strength that could not be beaten," except by himself through lack of faith. He said in the difficult times to come he would specifically be aware of this strength, but during normal times he would not be conscious of it. The experience in the dark cell was "the most important time" of his life. He said it was the basis of everything he did subsequently.

When John came out of the dark cell, he could see; he said his eyes were "completely cured." During his first days in the cell, he thought it was his blindness that was making it so dark, but he came to believe that the darkness was good for his blindness, that the dark and his blindness helped him to see. He was immediately treated for lice and fleas with which he was infested. And he had a shower. "It was a godsend, nice and warm—or I thought it was—and I felt clean and there was daylight. It was almost like I was liberated—and reborn." He said he felt overjoyed.

Soon after, he wrote a poem entitled "Freedom Symphony." It reads in part:

There are sounds of the ages,
A humming melody.
There's a murmur of singing, so beautiful, sonorous,
The freedom symphony.

God grant that resentment and hatred
Be banished from the heart now
Oh, man, leave purified
This place of pain and sorrow.

We've been through so much together
And carried so many burdens
Yet in what must also come to be
We shall never falter.

He gave a handwritten copy of this poem to Constance on her wedding day, April 30, 1966. He appended a note: "Written in 1945 when I had reached the deepest point in my life. Through a miracle I found the strength to let go ... and free myself from the deepest hopelessness I have ever known."[490]

John was returned to his old cell where he received a muted welcome from the scientist and flower vendor. This was due to the

---

[490] Poem and note translated with the assistance of Will Collishaw.

circumstances confronting them. A third prisoner, who had taken the place of the old man, was delirious with dysentery. He suffered seemingly constant diarrhea. John joined the other two in cleaning him up as best they could. John said it was miraculous that none of them got sick. When the man died three days after John's return, they were given Lysol to clean the cell.

23

PLAYING THE FOOL WITH CANADIAN SOLDIERS

John said that a week after his return to his old cell, there was a request for prisoners to work for the Canadian army camp in the middle of town. John volunteered and was one of those selected. It was "the start of a very happy time," he said. The Canadians immediately took a shine to him. Although John's main duty was housecleaning, the Canadians were more interested in fattening him up because he was exceedingly skinny. On his first day, they told him, "John, go into the kitchen and cut some wood." This instruction was really meant to divert the attention of John's guard, who remained outside and who the Canadians preoccupied. Meanwhile, the chef put John in a cupboard under the sink and fed him "white bread covered in lard and salt." But the Canadians' strategy backfired. John's system could not tolerate the rich food and he became sick: jaundice, he said. He had a high fever and had to stay at the jail for the next three days. John told me that he worried he would lose his new job, but the Canadians kept asking for him and held his place even though they had hundreds of potential replacements available to them.

When John returned, he was one of five prisoners assigned to the Canadians. Guards accompanied the prisoners when they were in transit but not when they were with the Canadians, which was something new. When the prisoners were working, they were now under Canadian supervision. This was an easy-going arrangement for John and the others, for the Canadians didn't regard them as prisoners. During these first days, John's new friends told him they trusted him and would try to make life good for him if he behaved himself. In due course, the number of prisoners assigned to the Canadians declined; eventually there was only John. He said he was assigned to them for about three months, which would have covered the period from about mid-October 1945 through to mid-January. At one point he said to his benefactors, "If only I didn't have to go back to the prison, my life would be perfect." This spurred them to action. Soon after, arrangements were made for John to stay with the Canadians throughout the week; he only returned to the prison on weekends. This was the situation during his last three weeks when he lived with six of them in a house, which was also in the middle of Scheveningen.

The Canadians' laxness and the freedom they granted John were typical of their mode of operation and of the widespread "deterioration of the deportment of the troops," which General Simonds, the Canadian commander-in-chief, referred to during a staff conference on October 15.[491] John said there was little supervision from above. Most of the men were corporals and there was one sergeant. Their Dutch girlfriends often slept over. For them, "the wild, crazy summer of '45" stretched well into the autumn. On October 10, General Simonds held a news conference in response to newspaper editorials criticizing the behaviour of his soldiers with Dutch women.[492]

The relaxed environment gave free reign to the carefree part of John's personality. The more the Canadians accepted him, the more

---

[491] *Liberation Album*, 141.
[492] Van der Heide, "Timeline of World War II History, December 14, 1931–April 14, 1949," 19, accessed March 7, 2002, www.godutch.com/newspaper/index.php?id=505. See footnote 95 for additional information on the Van der Heide source.

he felt free to enjoy himself, to be mischievous, and to "play the fool." John told the Canadians how he came to be imprisoned. He said they were not prejudiced and saw the situation for what it was: He "hadn't been found guilty of anything."

But there was also self-interest in their acceptance of him. Although he was there as a housekeeper, they would give him additional tasks—which he happily accepted—that served their unofficial purposes. When one of them wanted to take a day off to be with a girlfriend, they would dress John up in a Canadian uniform and have him attend the gas pump. John claimed he also broke into a large Canadian warehouse on the soldiers' behalf. He said it contained "literally everything"—goods that were to be distributed to people in need. He'd been given a good pair of shoes from this facility soon after his arrival. As the story goes, John was so thin he could climb down the chimney. He did this to obtain things the soldiers wanted for their girlfriends. When inventories were taken and it was discovered that items were missing, it became a great conundrum since the building was regarded as secure. To those in the know, it was a fine trick. Perhaps in return for his assistance, the soldiers gave John time off and money to spend and allowed him to have frequent visits with his family. Once a week he was given a day off and allowed out in a Canadian uniform. On one unverified occasion, when he and Susan were walking in town, he was "absolutely petrified" to see a guard from the prison approaching them on the sidewalk, but the man didn't recognize him and walked right by.

John felt sufficiently comfortable with the Canadians to pull pranks on them. One evening when three of the soldiers had retired early to bed with their girlfriends, he closed the damper on the potbellied stove so the house quickly filled with smoke. "Fire! Fire!" he yelled, causing them to hurriedly depart the building, wearing little if anything. One couple climbed out a window "absolutely naked." John said all this was witnessed by many townspeople. At first, the Canadians were angry. The next morning, they told him he was being returned to the prison. But this mild riposte to his prank was only a joke, they clarified soon after. Their embarrassment was quickly forgotten; they saw the humour in what had occurred, John said.

He relished the acceptance of the Canadians. He appreciated their "unbiased" attitude toward him. He attended a large party thrown by the Canadian army, which included Canadian officers and their wives. Perhaps it was a Christmas party. He said he ate the same food, played records, danced with most of the women, acted the fool, and had a grand time. While living with the Canadians, he said it became clear to him that it was Canada he wanted to adopt as a country, if possible, so he might in some way repay the kindness of the people who had befriended him.

John never got to thank those Canadians or to say goodbye, which he always regretted. One Sunday morning, when he was back at the jail, he and some other prisoners were told to pack up. They were being transferred to another prison camp.

"It sure was a sad day," John said, noting he and the others were once again faced with the unknown. He told me that there were numerous rumours about how bad it would be. They lost several small but precious items, such as tobacco and makeshift implements, and they found this "very depressing."

How much of John's interlude with the Canadians is true is anyone's guess. He was wrong about at least one point. His transfer date to the new camp—January 18, 1946—was not a Sunday; it was a Friday. Perhaps this inaccuracy undercuts everything he said about his purported time with the Canadians. On the other hand, the Canadians were in the process of sending the last of their troops home that month, which means that John's special assignment to them would have drawn to a close prior to or about the same time.

24

DUINDORP

The new prison camp, Duindorp, was not far away. A former fishing village, it was just down the coast from Scheveningen. Like Scheveningen, it was a satellite community of The Hague. John was transferred there on Harald's fourth birthday.

He said the camp was enclosed by several high, barbed-wire fences. The prisoners lived in block-length row houses, most of which had two levels and provided separate main-floor and upstairs apartments. The front doors to these houses, as well as the doors to the main-floor apartments, had been removed. The houses were also bereft of furniture. But they did contain small pot-bellied stoves and large burlap bags filled with straw for mattresses, and there was electricity.

The row houses were remnants of one of the huge projects that were part of the Germans' vaunted Atlantic Wall. In 1943, much of the community had been evacuated on German orders. About five hundred houses were demolished to make way for an elaborate network of bunkers. Built with the help of Dutch contractors, the bunkers consisted of some 350 underground rooms. The whole area was off-limits and fenced with barbed wire. Some of the evacuated houses were never demolished. These neglected buildings were used for accommodation when the area was pressed into service as a prison camp in mid-1945.[493]

Duindorp was run like a hard-labour camp. Everyone had to work. There was strict discipline; roll call was taken three times each day. Unlike Scheveningen, the prisoners never worked outside the camp. John called Duindorp "a world in itself." And although there was not much cruelty or abuse, it was "a very bad world," he said. The reason for this was privation. The food was terrible; they ate weeds to supplement their diet. Each day the houses were supplied with a few large pieces of coal, which would last at most two or three hours in the evening. This and the single blanket provided to each prisoner gave little comfort in their doorless houses against the cold winds that blew in off the North Sea. To compensate, they tended to sleep in threes so they had the benefit of three blankets and each other's body heat. It was not supposed to be like this. The prisoners would learn later that they should have been receiving considerably more in the way of food, clothing, and other provisions, but according to John, these supplies were being largely stolen by officials before they got to the prison camps.

Kamp Duindorp, a television documentary by Hans Polak, was broadcast on Nederland 3 in 1998. Based largely on the recollections of former guards and prisoners, as well as what children of former prisoners learned from their inquiries about Duindorp, it confirms much of what John said. Conditions, according to guard I. Schermer, "were harsh." He said he felt bad for the prison population of about five thousand. The buildings where they lived generally lacked heat, electricity (contrary to what John said), doors, and windows (meaning there was no glass in the frames). Hay was used in the place of mattresses. Guard C. La Lau, a former soldier with the Dutch army, said prisoners died from lack of food.[494]

---

[493] *Kamp Duindorp,* a documentary directed by Hans Polak (Filmed at Duindorp, The Hague, Scheveningen, and possibly other locations: VARA Broadcasting Association and Studios, 1998). *Kamp Duindorp* was broadcasted in 1998 on Nederland 3. See: Afra Botman, "Levenslang bestempeld als 'Fout'," *Trouw,* September 15, 1998.
[494] *Kamp Duindorp.*

The inmates' work was war cleanup, reconstruction, or other work connected to camp operations. As at Scheveningen, one job was to collect bricks from bombed houses, remove the mortar, then wheelbarrow the bricks, often a considerable distance, over gullies and planks, to construction sites where they would be stacked for use. John did this. He also helped restore a church and other buildings. And he worked in the kitchen, the boiler room, and on coal detail, which delivered coal by wheelbarrow to the houses. The boiler room was in a house that had been converted into a bathhouse for the camp. Another house had been converted into the kitchen.

The prisoners also worked in the sewer system, but they did this secretly for themselves. One night, after the possibility was raised that the system might provide a means of connection to the village outside, several men stealthily removed a manhole cover in one of the streets and descended below. It took them some time to learn the network, and they had to be careful of potentially dangerous sewer fumes, but in time they were able to find their way to the village. Thereafter they used this route to bring in much-needed extra supplies. This ended when one of the prisoners used the system to escape. John said he tried to dissuade the man. John argued it would likely forfeit their use of the system, which it did. After the escape, the guards sealed the manhole covers.

The escape was an exceptional occurrence. The prisoners generally functioned in a cooperative manner; they knew it was in their best interest. When a group of prisoners staged a successful theatre production and each of them received an extra loaf of bread as a reward, they shared their good fortune with their mates. Similarly, when there was a birthday, they would celebrate with a party and a cake. Everyone contributed their slice of bread for the day and the small slice of butter they each received once a week. The bread would be mixed, wetted, and kneaded, then put on top of the pot-bellied stove to be browned. The final touch was to spread the butter, which had been whipped, as fancily as possible on the "cake." Once this delicacy had been consumed, the remainder of the party consisted of sitting around the stove and sharing whatever tobacco might be available. The rule, John said, was "three puffs each."

They shared their food in other ways as well. Prisoners with ulcers were given a different diet: a little can of milk along with a small amount of porridge, but no bread. Some prisoners thought this was a better diet. To obtain it, they faked ulcers and the "lay doctors," who didn't have the benefit of an x-ray machine, made their decisions based on the symptoms. John said there was one real doctor in the camp, but they never saw him. Most of the prisoners who switched to the ulcer diet soon regretted it, having discovered they preferred the old diet. But it was easier to get on the ulcer diet than off it. Trading meals, one diet for the other, occurred frequently, particularly among those who remained curious about the ulcer diet.

Sundays were a free day. Despite having none of the right tools, John used this time to build a clock and a little radio from parts. He developed a design and made drawings with measurements for furniture for an entire house. He also participated in various groups that wrote and read poems, drew pictures, and did theatre. There was also a school where lessons in a variety of subjects were provided; they called it Sunday school. It may have been during this period that he carved a cigarette holder for Susan.

When it became known he was an artist, the guards wanted him to draw pictures for them. Perhaps because his furniture drawings had disappeared and may have been stolen, he refused to do pictures that could be taken outside. He did agree to draw murals in their offices and other places for a fee—extra bread—which he shared. The guards provided the crayons. John said he got quite a bit of work this way. His list of his paintings includes this notation: "Prison camp 45-47—Murals—Landscapes."

He also participated with the theatre group in a production of *Peer Gynt*. He claimed that most of the people involved were professionals. When the administrators and guards saw the show, they were sufficiently impressed that they arranged public performances over three nights in the church. This was the success that earned each member of the group an extra loaf of bread. Their triumph was blunted, however, by the hostility the public displayed toward them before and after each performance.

Despite the rewards of extra bread some prisoners received periodically, their life at Duindorp through the late winter and spring and into the summer of 1946 was one of bare subsistence. In "At Home," one of eight poems[495] from the January–February 1946 period, John wrote:

Oh home, if all men were free,
Banding together
In love and affection.
Oh home, promised land.

How I sigh in the chains
Of this prison
While so close, so nearby
Is my home.

How heavy the weight
Of being locked up
Impotent, defenceless, exhausted,
No more than a dirty pig.

The yelling of the guards booms
Hollow through the chilly hallways.
Not even priests talk to he
Who is held fast ... he must hang.

---

[495] John transcribed the eight poems in compressed handwriting onto two pieces of paper, which are now in the possession of his son Hans. Seven of the eight poems are dated, the earliest being January 18, 1946, and the latest February 27, 1946. The only poem not dated is "At Home," but all indications suggest it comes from the same period.

The day goes by so monotonously.
What can you talk about again and again[?]
Life dwindles
In these tortured hours.

Only the rumbling of my stomach
Sometimes breaks the silence.
Slowly, barely moving
From hunger, fatigue, the cold.

And there an hour away
Lives those I love.
There lives my dear strong wife
Together with my children.

They suffer their fate of freedom
That father remains imprisoned
And pray to God every day
For a great reunion.

Oh home, mankind's treasure,
Never so treasured
As when stuck in misery.
Oh home, never so worshipped.[496]

As time passed, the atmosphere in the prison camp steadily worsened and the prisoners became "more and more full of hatred," John said. When they discovered that they were not receiving supplies intended for them, they started demanding them. In due course they supported this demand by refusing to work, which escalated into what John called a "riot situation."

---

[496] Will Collishaw translation.

The documentary, *Kamp Duindorp*, mentions the riot, which probably occurred during the summer, but gives no reason why it occurred. According to La Lau, there was unrest in one of the blocks. There was also a fire. Firemen sought access to the camp, but they never got the chance to fight the fire. Nico de Heijer, a former prisoner, said word spread among the inmates to open all the taps and flush all the toilets, reducing water pressure and hampering the firemen's response. While La Lau said prisoners climbed onto the roof and threw rocks, Schermer described a more serious situation. Prisoners broke into the armory, obtained weapons, and were firing them, which necessitated more guards being called in, he said. It was "a big chaos." The military was soon called in as well, which caused panic amongst the rioters.[497]

According to Schermer, Mr. Pot, the prison camp's director, shouted, "Don't shoot! Don't shoot!" But he was either ignored or overruled, for there was shooting. Schermer said he shot too, and that he killed someone. "There were only a few killed," he added. "Then it was finished."[498]

John said many of the prisoners had SS training and knew how to fight. He also said they breached the armory where the guards kept their rifles and ammunition. Contrary to Schermer's information, John said the prisoners rendered the weapons inoperable by removing their pins. They also locked up several guards in their own quarters. Although John maintained all this was done as a precaution, these developments may well have signalled to the authorities that the prisoners had crossed the point of no return. Possibly, while the prisoners milled about in the streets of the camp, waiting, one of the camp officials alerted the external authorities by telephone regarding what was occurring. The response, according to John, was to send in the Dutch army. The camp was soon surrounded by soldiers and tanks. Machine guns were set up at the end of every street. What came next, John said, was the most horrible two days of his life.

---

[497] *Kamp Duindorp*.
[498] *Kamp Duindorp*.

The prisoners must have taken cover when the army arrived, for once the soldiers were in place, John said they fired at anything that moved. John, his roommates, and most of the other prisoners got back to their respective houses. John's house was at "one of the bad points," namely the T-junction of two streets. It looked across one street and down the length of the other to where a machine gun was situated at the far end. John and the others hid anywhere they could not be seen. After some time, one man stuck his head up slightly to peek out the window—he was shot through the top of the head and killed instantly. John said the man's head "just exploded; brains were splattered all over the walls and ceiling." He had never seen anything like it. The army, he claimed, was using dumdum bullets that expand on impact and leave a gaping wound.

In his unverified and increasingly improbable version of these alleged events, John said he didn't know what was more unsettling, the corpse or the "huge pool of sweetish-smelling blood" it produced. After a couple of hours, the blood began to smell terribly. Perhaps it was this that caused what happened next. For no other apparent reason and despite impassioned pleas from the others, one man started to go down the stairs. The machine gunner at the far end of the street had a clear view of the staircase through the doorless entryway. A long staccato burst sounded from his weapon. The torrent of bullets cut the man's legs off above the knees and he rolled helplessly into the street, bleeding profusely. John said he knew he had to do something. He felt elected by virtue of his training. He tucked himself into a ball and rolled quickly down the stairs and into the street. He was fired upon, but not hit. He lay atop the injured man who, still conscious, hung on to John around his neck as bullets continued to zing by and hit all around them. They were vulnerable from three directions, then two, as John crawled as quickly as possible, dragging the man from alcove to alcove, toward the hospital house, half a block away. He was consumed by the need to get there before the man bled out. He said he was "crying in desperation all the while, as if to say: 'Oh God, let me be on time!'"

He succeeded. They made it, without further injury, to the infirmary where help was available. Presumably, tourniquets were applied to the man's legs and he was given painkillers and other attention. He survived—a remarkable outcome, if true, which is dubious. John stayed there until the siege ended a day and a half later, when the army sent in a team of negotiators. They promised more blankets, better food, and better treatment provided the prisoners surrendered and went back to work. The prisoners had no choice, John said. Nonetheless, they believed their situation would improve. But later, when conditions had returned to normal, they found this was not the case. According to John, the promised improvements didn't occur.

John didn't know how many people were killed during the siege. He claimed he saw some newspaper articles about it long afterward. They said some prisoners had been shot fleeing, but based on John's experience, this was rarely the case. He indicated the true story was not reported.

John said Duindorp was the worst of the postwar camps he was in because of its harsh conditions, the rebellion and siege, and the lack of humourous occurrences. "There weren't that many funny things that happened there," he said.

Early one morning, at around five o'clock, the prisoners were called out and lined up in the public square. It was August 18, 1946.[499] Those whose names were read from a list were to be transferred to another facility. John's name was on the list. He and the others were ordered into the back of a canvas-covered truck, which provided the setting for a couple of his colourful stories. To get as many men in as possible, they sat with their backs to the front of the truck, their legs spread, and the back of the next man touching their chest. Once loaded, the truck started away only to slam on its brakes to compress the men tighter, enabling the guards to squeeze in a few more prisoners.

---

[499] John's internment history card (DNA, CABR 91103/PRA The Hague, dossier 21717).

Although they were apparently travelling less than fifty miles, John said the trip required the whole day because of the bad condition of the roads. And they were not given rest breaks. When John had to pee, he had to use one of his wooden shoes as a receptacle, but as he could not reach the shoe himself, he had to ask the second fellow in front of him to pass it to him. He managed to relieve himself while sitting down and hardly being able to move. The shoe was then carefully passed to someone next to the side of the truck who lifted the canvas and emptied the shoe over the side. This process—with John's shoe—was supposedly repeated as required. (What happened, I wonder, to the good pair of shoes he was given when he was with the Canadians at Scheveningen?) When they finally reached their destination, the small town of Muiden east of Amsterdam, John said they "were terribly stiff."

There is some uncertainty regarding the third postwar internment camp to which John was assigned. Documents for this period indicate that he was in *Centraal Bewarings-en verblijfskamp Crailoo* (Camp Crailoo) in Laren, near Hilversum, presumably indicating that Muiden was a satellite camp to Crailoo.[500]

---

[500] Both John and Wim are identified in official documents as being at Crailoo but were housed at Muiden. See John's release document of mid-December 1946; John's internment history card; Blauw's report of December 3, 2009, 4. Blauw's report of February 14, 2007 (10) on Wim states he was in *Camp Crailoo* in August 1946 (my emphasis), which is the same month John was transferred to Muiden.

25

MUIDEN

They arrived at the Muiden prison camp in the early evening, cold, hungry, and stiff. Once again, not knowing what to expect, John said they were fearful, vulnerable, and at the mercy of the authorities. They were ordered to line up; DDT was pumped down the back of their shirts to kill any lice and fleas. They stank of it for days. They were asked to produce their blankets for inspection, but they hadn't been allowed to bring them. John said this caused a big song and dance, which increased their apprehension. The head guard taunted them. "Do you expect us to provide you with blankets?" he asked. "I suppose you expect us to feed you too."

But they were fed, and things quickly improved. The long wooden barracks, which John said had been used to quarantine sick people during the 1918–20 Spanish flu pandemic, were warm, comfortable, and full of furniture: bunk beds, tables, and chairs. "Having furniture made quite a difference," he told me. Moreover, he described the food as "quite good" and said it was better than anything he had at other camps. Another happy surprise was that Wim was also a prisoner there. Wim knew John was coming, had been on the lookout for him, and may have had something to do with John being assigned to the same barracks as him. For all these reasons, Muiden was the best of the camps John was in after the war. He could be effusive in describing it. "It was heaven comparatively," he said. "I had a real good time there in comparison to the other two camps." But he also said that while it was much better, it was by no means pleasant. There was still a good deal of cruelty. On another occasion he referred to Duindorp and Muiden as "the two worst camps in Holland"; he told me they were "very bad." I suspect these contradictory assessments were the result of emotion and drama overwhelming rationality in his storytelling. Based on his descriptions of camp conditions at Muiden, I also suspect his positive remarks are more accurate.

In addition to his conflicting views, John didn't acknowledge the possibility that the move to Muiden may have been related to the riot at Duindorp and an effort to both improve conditions and relieve pressure on the makeshift postwar internment system. Earlier in the year, March 4, 1946, the Dutch cabinet accepted a Canadian recommendation to release the majority of Dutch Nazi sympathizers—"the so-called light cases"—from internment without trial.[501] This apparently triggered a process whereby cases were reviewed to distinguish those that were "light" from those that were more serious.

John said Muiden was a small camp. It had no streets or halls, just four barracks that surrounded a grass field. Like Duindorp, it was encircled by high barbed-wire fences. Beyond the fences was a large heather field that spread everywhere except for a barren area behind the camp where nothing grew. John said the heather didn't grow tall and the guards could see a great distance over it.

The defining feature of this camp was what John referred to as the "ammunition factory" or "the gunpowder factory '*de Krijgsman*'" (the warrior). Located just outside the town, the factory was where some of the prisoners worked dismantling bombs and other

---

[501] Van der Heide, "Timeline of World War II History, December 14, 1931– April 14, 1949," 20, accessed March 7, 2002, www.godutch.com/newspaper/index.php?id=505. See footnote 95 for additional information on the Van der Heide source.

munitions such as torpedoes, mines, and V-2 rockets. These prisoners, who included John and Wim, were housed in the same barracks. They worked alongside men who were not prisoners. John volunteered for this assignment despite its danger. There were occasional explosions; on January 17, 1947, an "explosion of collected grenades" caused seventeen deaths.[502] The work covered the men in a yellow substance, possibly phosphorus, from some of the chemicals involved. Although the explosive parts of the various munitions were burned under controlled circumstances, explosions sometimes occurred here as well. There were "tremendous flames" from these fires, John said.

He speculated that the prisoners who worked at the factory may have been in a favoured position because of the dangerous work they did. On the other hand, it may simply have been administratively easier to treat them in some of the same ways as the workers who were not prisoners. John said they received lunch and two coffee breaks. They took their coffee breaks at the work site, while lunch occurred at another building where they were permitted to smoke. The other workers often gave them real cigarettes, many of which were smuggled into the prison camp. Another benefit of working in the factory was the leftover parts, such as precision-timing pieces that John and some of the others used to build clocks.

In addition to these perks and the improved food and housing, there were other reasons John said Muiden was the best of the camps. There was an exercise regime; the internees did group calisthenics. And there were much-improved arrangements for visiting. Except for his time at the Canadian army camp in Scheveningen, Muiden's rules for visitors were more relaxed than anything that had prevailed before. Not only was he allowed to visit with Susan through a wire-mesh fence, which enabled a degree of closeness not previously

---

[502] In his statement of October 29, 1946, 11, John referred to "the gunpowder factory 'de Krijgsman' in Muiden," which operated from 1702 to 2001. "Muiden," Wikipedia, accessed October 13, 2020, https://en.wikipedia.org/wiki/Muiden (explosions, deaths).

permitted, he was also allowed to accept gifts like chocolate bars. Visiting at Duindorp had taken place in a church with the prisoners in one row of seats and their visitors in another. John explained that several rows in between were kept empty, where guards patrolled back and forth ensuring nothing was passed to or from the prisoners. Under these conditions, communication was difficult, people had to speak loudly, and there was no privacy. For her part, Susan tried to visit John once a week. She still had to hitchhike since there were no trains and few cars running at the time. At some point, she and the kids relocated from The Hague to Stanni's home in Hilversum. Logic suggests this would have occurred soon after John was transferred to Muiden, which was much closer to Hilversum, a distance that could be covered by bicycle, walking, or hitchhiking.

As at Scheveningen, humour was also a salve at Muiden. One evening a guard, who John described as "nasty," claimed he could not be hypnotized. The discussion had occurred, in part, because one of the prisoners was a good hypnotist. This man proceeded to hypnotize the guard and had him dance on the tabletops. While the prisoners greatly enjoyed this performance, they did so in a restrained manner so as not to attract attention from outside. But as the performance continued, and the hypnotist had the guard behave and sound like a chicken, the men's delight became louder and more uncontrolled. It was not long before the warden and several guards entered the barracks to investigate. The warden ordered the removal of the hypnotized guard, who was subsequently fired. The prisoners were not punished.

Despite the improved conditions, discipline within the camp at Muiden was still strict. And prisoners were far from enamoured with their circumstances. Of several claims John made, most are questionable, and all should be regarded warily. He said there were many attempts to escape by tunnelling out of the camp. None, as far as he knew, were successful. He said the tunnels kept collapsing because of the sandy soil. There were, however, a few successful escapes from the factory, which was surrounded by water. And while there was "no sadistic punishment in this camp," there was cruelty, he said. One night the prisoners from all four barracks were ordered out into the cold and assembled on the grass field where they had to stand for hours. John said the temperature was below zero. They were in their sleeping attire, which usually meant just underwear. Several men collapsed and were left to lie on the ground, and at least one man died, John contended. He could not recall the reason for the punishment, except that it had nothing to do with his barracks. If this dubious event—or even one remotely like it—actually occurred, it didn't happen later than the latter half of September or the first half of October 1946; we know this because of injuries John sustained on October 15, which hospitalized him for the next two months.[503] Given the time of year, the improbable below-zero temperature, and the reported death of at least one prisoner, I suspect this is a highly exaggerated or imaginary account based on similar but more vicious treatment meted out at some Nazi concentration camps: namely using a hose in mid-winter to soak prisoners who froze solid as a result.[504]

John said he and his mates were mindful of the extreme danger of the munitions they handled at the factory, which were delivered by a steady stream of army trucks. By contrast, the soldiers who off-loaded this perilous cargo had little such awareness and "seemed almost to be playing with it." When John was blown up, no one expected him to live, he said. He and another man had been working in a large unheated structure, which John referred to as a barn. They were apparently dismantling airplane bombs that had been manufactured in Czechoslovakia. "About four feet tall and eight inches thick," these bombs didn't require contact to explode. They relied on a timing device in their nose. A vast number of these bombs were stacked against one wall to a height of about four feet, their tipped heads pointing inward as a precaution.

---

[503] John's statement of October 29, 1946, provides the date of the explosion.
[504] This treatment by the Nazis is mentioned in Marcus J. Smith's *The Harrowing of Hell: Dachau*. It is also mentioned in "Stories told by Bert Schapelhouman – a Dutch Survivor of Mauthausen," accessed October 19, 2021, https://furtherglory.wordpress.com/2011/01/16/stories-told-by-bert-schapelhouman-a-dutch-survivor-of-mauthausen/.

The two men were sitting on the bombs. They worked separately dismantling them one at a time, first exposing and deactivating the timing devices, then removing the explosive. The first step was always to remove the two screws that secured the timing device. It was not uncommon for the screws to be rusted from age and weathering. Sometimes in the process of trying to remove them, a screw broke off. When this happened, they used a drill press to drill out the remaining part of the screw. They had been told and knew from experience that it was safe to do this because this type of bomb had been built with two safety devices. But the existence of these safety devices, which were housed in the head of the bomb, could not be confirmed until the head was removed, John explained. What no one knew, he added, was that a later version of the bomb had been built with only one safety device.

John's mate got off the stack and carried the bomb he was working on to the drill press in the middle of the room. For a moment John heard the drill; then there was "a tremendous, absolutely shattering explosion" and a sharp change in air pressure. John said he never lost consciousness. If this was true, he was nevertheless severely disoriented. When he regained his senses, his buddy and the drill press were nowhere to be seen. Then he discovered that he was covered in blood and badly hurt. Somehow, he got himself out of the barn. How he managed this was still a mystery to him when he told me about it. He said he never panicked. Nor did he feel any pain—"probably because of shock." Men were running toward him. As he first sat, then lay down on the ground, he observed a fountain of blood spurting high into the air from his right arm. He learned later that a piece of shrapnel had severed the artery. It was one of the more serious of the numerous injuries he sustained. Wim was one of the first to reach him. John said he told them where to apply the tourniquets. When this was done, they covered him with coats.

This is probably the end, John thought as he waited for the ambulance to come.

It took a long time for the ambulance to arrive. Once it did and he was on his way to the hospital, he was told repeatedly, "It's going to be okay, John."

"Yeah, okay," he replied at one point. "But give me a cigarette." His principal recollection of that ride was his intense desire for a cigarette.

To ward off the cold in the barn, John had been wearing a thick woollen sweater, a coat made from a blanket, and a leather apron. He believed his apparel that day probably saved his life. He'd absorbed metal from one end of his body to the other but primarily in his head, chest, and arms. The most dangerous pieces were the ones in his chest, one of which came to a stop next to his heart but didn't pierce it. He said the barrier of his clothes caused this piece of shrapnel to slow and twist just enough not to kill him. Other pieces penetrated his head but didn't enter his brain. One eye had virtually been encircled by metal, but the eye itself was fine. At the hospital, four surgeons went to work removing shrapnel, resetting bones—John's left arm had been broken in two places—and doing what else they could. When they were finished, there were still thirteen pieces of metal in his body that they had to leave. One of these was embedded in the palm of his left hand where it remained for forty years until advances in surgery permitted its safe removal.

Figure 28. John in mid-1984. The shrapnel in his left hand was removed surgically soon after. Patrick Wolfe photo.

John's most contentious injury was the severed artery. Three of the four doctors agreed that the arm had to be amputated. The fourth doctor—Dr. Schouten—wanted to try to save it. He'd read that blood, when deprived of an artery, had been known to find other ways to feed a limb. The others disagreed. They predicted gangrene if the arm were left on. Dr. Schouten said he would check the arm every fifteen minutes, enabling a fast response to amputate if gangrene did occur. With this, the other doctors withdrew their objections. Dr. Schouten proceeded to save John's right arm, which healed much faster than his left arm and continued to be the stronger of the two. In the years following, John, true to form, enjoyed the extra attention his right arm brought him from nurses and others who tried to find his pulse.

Many months later, probably during the latter half of 1947, John said he returned to the barn. The wall behind where he had sat was, with one exception, pockmarked with seemingly hundreds of holes created by metal fragments that had exploded outward. The exception was a silhouette defined by John's upper body, which had absorbed all the shrapnel that otherwise would have scattershot that part of the wall.

26

THE HOSPITAL

John woke in Diaconessenhuis, a hospital in Naarden, southeast of Muiden.[505] He said he was on his back, both arms were in slings, and he was barely able to move due to the extent of his injuries and utter weakness. He was also in extreme pain. He received morphine every two hours and said that toward the end of those intervals he really looked forward to his next injection. Dr. Schouten was there several times each hour, checking his right arm, looking for signs of gangrene.

In the immediate aftermath of his surgery, John's chances of survival had been rated no better than those for his right arm. Indeed, everyone believed he wouldn't make it. He didn't share this opinion. Against the odds, both he and his right arm recovered, but there were some difficult periods. Bear in mind, however, while there is no question about the injuries he suffered, his stories about his stay in hospital are nearly all uncorroborated.

"The stench in the room was unbelievable," he said. It was the malodor of burnt human flesh. One of his first discoveries upon regaining consciousness was that his buddy from the barn had not been killed instantly. He was there in the room with him. John said he was a terrible sight. Half his face was gone, and he'd lost both arms.

---

[505] Dr. H. Schouten's statement of October 29, 1946 (DNA, CABR 109786). Attachment to Blauw's email of December 3, 2009, 5.

The fetor was from their injuries, especially his friend's. John said the man knew he was not going to make it. John told him about the peace he had found when he'd been in the dark cell. John said he could see that his words helped his friend and allowed him to surrender. As John spoke of Jesus, the man died, he said.

The next morning, John awoke with a very painful stomach, which had become badly distended with gas. He wanted and needed to fart, but he was too weak to do so. He identified the problem to a nurse who remedied it with a rubber tube she inserted up his anus. Relief was almost instantaneous; his stomach deflated like a pricked balloon and released "a sudden swoosh of the foulest-smelling air ever." He enjoyed telling this story. He was still the person who, as a boy, had relished setting off stink bombs in class.

John claimed that later that day or the next, he asked the doctor to take him off morphine. He said he wanted the nurses instructed not to give him the drug even if he asked for it. The doctor advised against this. He said it would be impossible to tolerate the pain. But John was focused on what he'd experienced in the dark cell: the assurance he would be given support, "a strength that could not be beaten," or, as he told me on another occasion, "that Jesus would stand with [him] through anything." Holding this belief in his mind, he used it and "help from the other side" to absorb the excruciating pain. He didn't ask for morphine. After some time, he became delirious. He had burning fevers that came and went. They lasted for four days, he said. During the bursts of fever, small noises seemed tremendously magnified and became almost unbearable. Then the fevers ended. The crisis was over.

I have strong doubts about this story. I suspect it's an example of John ignoring his inner wisdom and higher nature and succumbing to the temptations of glamour and grandiosity. In this case, the wisdom he trampled was the idea that we are not to have expectations of our spirit partners, which is a variation on the stricture that we are not to set tests for God. John earnestly expounded on such expectations several times with me, which is why this tale rankles.

Despite his alleged triumph over morphine, John was still tormented by his demons. While the hospital became a sanctuary and a place of restoration for him, he still had to find a way out of his dark thoughts and sense of inadequacy. When he was moved into a ten-man ward, it was a clear sign his condition had stabilized and he was recovering. But with this came a new problem. He couldn't sleep, neither at night, nor any time. Sleeping pills had no effect on him. "The nights were terrible," he said. Everyone else was asleep, which magnified his isolation and loneliness. He was consumed by thoughts of all the bad things that had happened and wondered if they would ever end. The night-shift head nurse began sitting with him for long stretches of the night. Her presence was a special comfort to him. Alone in the deep quiet, they would talk throughout the night. One night she told him she would help him get to sleep, provided he promised not to tell the doctor. He agreed. She brought him a tall glass—about ten ounces—of straight rum. It did the trick. He had no more trouble after that. The spell of sleeplessness was broken.

John continued to be extremely weak. Close to two weeks after the accident, one of the nurses took him on a gurney to a church service in the hospital chapel, but he was soon exhausted and unable to stay until the end. About this time, government investigators began looking into his case. Two of them arrived at the hospital but were told he was too weak to be questioned. They snuck in anyway. John said it was a real interrogation; they threw accusations at him to see how he would answer; they tried to break him down. John's statement of October 29, 1946, was the result. Its tenor belies any sense of an intensive interrogation. Although the document includes at least a couple of falsehoods, it is John's relatively straightforward recounting of his life, with emphasis on the years of the occupation. One of the investigators concludes the statement with this sentence: "After reading, he stands by his declaration, however due to having his hands in bandage dressings, he cannot sign this declaration." Nonetheless, whether due to grandiosity or his sense of victimization or both, John told me the doctor was furious when he learned that the investigators had disobeyed his instructions. John claimed the doctor wrote a letter of protest to the minister of justice.

John was in the hospital for about two months. He was bedridden; for a long time he could neither use his arms nor roll over. It amused him that a guard was posted outside his ward. He admitted he kept his right arm in its sling longer than necessary. He said he liked being fed and babied and he delighted in the extra attention.

Like his time at the Canadian army camp in Scheveningen, John's stay at the hospital was marked by fun and shenanigans. These occasions nearly always involved one or more of the nurses. He discovered early on that they could give as good as they got and then some. One nurse had a fear of spiders. John didn't say whether she told him this or he learned it inadvertently. One day when she was attending to him, he told her there was a spider on her cap. He anticipated a startled reaction and a few moments of fright but nothing like what ensued. He said the nurse, who had long hair tucked into a bun under her cap, "went berserk." She started "screaming and dancing madly about" causing her cap to fall off and her hair to tumble down and fly frantically around her head and upper body. "It was only a joke," John told her when she began to settle down. She stormed out of the ward. A short time later, she stormed back in, the very picture of resolution. She was carrying a container of ice. "You're never going to do that again," she declared. She kept saying this as she packed his body with ice, placing it under his pyjama top and in his pants. Seeing John's reaction—his helpless, physically shocked, sucking-air response to the biting cold of the ice—she relaxed and smiled. "It's only a joke," she told him.

The nurses were generally indulgent of John, his ward mates, and their tomfoolery. The men regularly took advantage of the dimwittedness of "a dumb boxer" who had had an appendectomy. One of the men would ask him to get out of bed and fetch a glass of water. When he did this, they would all ring their bells, which were soundless in the ward, to bring one of the nurses running. The boxer would catch hell for being out of bed. The men pulled this stunt repeatedly. The boxer never caught on.

The night nurse who had sat with John was a favourite of all the men. At the end of her shift, she would hand out cigarettes and permit the men to smoke even though it was against regulations. In due course, her schedule changed so she worked days and handed out the cigarettes in the early evening. One of the men had to periodically butt John's cigarette for him and put it out when he was finished. But one evening, their smoking and John's dependency landed him in hot water. The new night nurse, who was a stickler for the rules, arrived early. The men could hear her in the adjoining ward, which was separated by a door. They didn't want to be found out by this lady who could be punitive when rules were violated. They quickly butted their cigarettes, all except John's, which he said they forgot; he didn't explain why he didn't call attention to his predicament. It was a replay of what had occurred in the Scheveningen cell approximately sixteen months earlier, only now John had the part of the old man, a repetition, I'd suggest, that is a warning signal, another indication of an attention-seeking tall tale. In his telling, he sat in his bed helpless, condemned by the evidence between his lips. "So, it's you, John," the nurse said when she appeared. "I thought I could smell smoke." He was banished as a result, transferred, he said, to another room.

John didn't say he retaliated for this punishment. But sometime later, when he'd regained some use of his right arm and hand, he somehow obtained a pig's eye. He placed it into "a beautiful ... empty chocolate box," which he gift-wrapped as best he could. He said it was Christmas time, by which he meant Sinterklaas, or St. Nicholas Eve and Day, on December 5 and 6. He could not have meant December 25 because he was released from the hospital in mid-December. John's "gift" was opened by a group of nurses who thought they were about to enjoy some chocolates. Instead, there was, in John's phrase, "a great collective scream." He said they paid him back with ice-water bed baths.

John maintained these antics were all in fun. He described the hospital as a place of good cheer. In the evenings, a nurse would open the door between the main men's ward and the adjoining maternity ward. The men would sing songs for the women. John said this created a lot of good feelings.

December 7—what he referred to as "the day after Christmas"—was an important day for John. He was assisted to a sitting position and permitted to dangle his legs over the side of the bed. This was the first step to getting him ambulatory again. Ever full of bravado, he believed he'd be able to walk right away. He engaged the two nurses with him in a bet. He was confident he could stand on his own and would thereby win the wager. According to his robust storytelling, he managed maybe one step before falling flat on his face, which is the height of improbability. His broken left arm, which didn't heal for many months, would have been in a sling. The nurses, knowing full well that his legs would fail him, would have been on either side of him and would have caught him as he crumbled and shifted him safely back onto the bed, that is, if anything like this episode happened. John told me it took about two weeks to regain the use of his legs. He said he enjoyed learning to walk again.

During this period, John implied that the hospital had been under pressure to return him to prison where he could be kept in sick bay. The doctor used John's broken left arm, which refused to heal properly, as his excuse for keeping John at the hospital. But one morning at mid-month, John was told he was being returned to prison. He said he became "very, very bitter." As he sat in the black prison of his thoughts, a nonconformist clergyman entered the room and sat down beside his bed. No one had seen this man before or knew who he was. He sat there for some time before speaking. "You're pretty bitter, aren't you?" he asked John finally. "If you're angry at God, why don't you tell him you think he's a bastard?" Then he left. He was gone as suddenly as he had appeared. After a while, John followed the clergyman's advice. He told God he thought it was very unfair he had to go back to prison. And he wanted to know why he had to.

John left the hospital early that afternoon. He claimed all the staff came outside to wave goodbye to him as he departed "in a paddy wagon." He was taken to Crailoo rather than Muiden. His return to prison was brief. Once at Crailoo, he learned he was to be released. He said he spent part of the afternoon signing release papers. One of these documents, *Acte Van Invrijheidstelling* (No. 25159/46), says his release was effective December 14, 1946, but where John signed on the reverse, it is date-stamped "17 Dec. 1946."

At the end of the afternoon, John was told he was free to go. But he had no transportation and he was still very weak, barely having relearned how to walk. The doctor had told him he needed to convalesce for another two to three months. He sat outside the gate of the prison camp. He was in a "heather wilderness," and he wondered how he would get to Hilversum, eight miles away. The answer appeared in the form of a truck driven by an old friend who was making deliveries. If John could wait a couple of hours, the friend, who would be returning to Hilversum, said he would give him a lift.

27

JOHN'S CASE

"In 1945 I was interned and have been imprisoned for 19 months," John wrote in his letter of mid-1951. "After I had been there for 17 months my case went on trial and after 2 months I was free. After my release ... there was nothing whatsoever to find fault with my behaviour." This is misleading on at least two points. First, while his case was finally examined in the autumn of 1946, it never went to trial. Second, he neglects to mention he was questioned in April 1947 about his role with the SD's Intelligence Service in 1944, an omission that, to some, could contradict his assertion that "there was nothing whatsoever to find fault with my behaviour."

Despite John's unlikely claim that government investigators snuck into his room or ward on October 29, 1946, and subjected him to a real interrogation, he and his family knew his case was up for review. Susan gave a statement on October 22, and Johan Veltmeijer and J. G. Siewers wrote testimonial letters on his behalf on the twenty-sixth, and Barend van Leeuwen added a third on the twenty-eighth. These letters from men who knew John and interacted with him portray him as someone who, when he could, behaved in an independent-minded or pro-Dutch manner inconsistent with the expectations of the German organizations in which he served. In addition, although Antonius Johannes Grootveld and Jacobus Theodorus van Schouwen, two of

John's colleagues at the ANAK insurance company, saw him at different times wearing his SS and Schutzgruppe uniforms, they said he never betrayed anyone or created trouble for any Dutch citizens as far as they knew. John displayed a philosophic or detached perspective when he and Grootveld talked politics on several occasions. On one hand, John said he felt obliged, as a German, to serve in the SS and the Schutzgruppe, but, on the other, he found Grootveld's hostility to the occupiers to be perfectly natural. Van Schouwen had the impression John felt betrayed by the SS. John helped Van Schouwen when he had a problem with a couple of SD men, and he turned a blind eye to Grootveld's illegal activities, which included keeping a radio in the ANAK office.

Grootveld's and Van Schouwen's statements appear to have carried considerable weight. A two-page handwritten report, date-stamped November 14, 1946, provided to Special Prosecutor Dr. F. Hollander, states John "never propagated" and this was "true, according to witnesses."

On October 30, Adrianus Cornelis Smit also made a statement. Born April 23, 1902, he found himself in need of an *Ausweis* (permit) for his bicycle at the end of 1944 or in early 1945. He was advised to go to the Wehrmacht command post and to ask for John, who was known for his willingness to provide the Dutch with such permits when he could. Smit had never met John before. He said John granted the permit without asking any questions or requiring any payment.[506]

John told me that the same afternoon he was released from internment, he also learned he had been found not guilty. Six months earlier, he claimed his release document said he had been interned in error. He added that he never got any compensation for the time he was imprisoned, emphasizing the unfairness of it and his sense of victimization. Like his claims that his case was decided at a trial that concluded "there has been nothing whatsoever to find fault with my behaviour," his 1976 statements are false and self-serving. I learned

---

[506] Smit's statement of October 30, 1946. Attachment to Blauw's email of December 3, 2009, 2, to the author.

twenty-five years later, upon having his release document translated, that it gives no indication of innocence or guilt.

The report provided to Special Prosecutor Hollander includes the following line: "In my opinion extraj. Settlement." In addition, annotated in the lefthand margin of page two of the report is the following: "Suspect got severely injured at both arms, when he, as a prisoner, did voluntary work in a gunpowder factory. Is still in infirmary." In mid-December, Hollander "ordered the release of Jan Jurgen Petersen." Since the Dutch National Archives' files on John give no indication of a trial, and since a "sentence card" for him has not been found, it appears that his case—like the "overwhelming" majority—was settled in an extra-judicial manner without a verdict.[507]

"Conclusions about the practice of out-of-court settlements are difficult," Mason writes, "for contents of settlements were never published.... an overwhelming number of collaborators were sent home with an out-of-court settlement." He estimates there may have been as many as 100,000 such settlements. "Only 23,000 arrested collaborators had not ... been disposed of by March 1, 1947," he adds.[508]

On April 22, 1947, John was questioned for the last time, the focus being his role with the Intelligence Service. Tine Heerema gave a statement on January 25, 1947, while Scholte and Korteland gave statements on April 8 and April 14, respectively, all of which bear on John's work for the Intelligence Service. It must be pointed out, however, that the latter two statements were given as part of an investigation of Scholte. Although these three statements appear to be more damning than those of earlier witnesses, many of their claims are disputed by John or mitigated by other information presented earlier. Moreover, the claims against John in these statements didn't result in any charges against him.

---

[507] The two-page handwritten report of November 14, 1946, provided to Special Prosecutor Dr. F. Hollander is in one of the collaborator files on Jan Jürgen Petersen (DNA, CABR 109786). Attachment to Blauw's email of December 3, 2009, 4–5, to the author.

[508] Mason, 82, 80.

28

READJUSTMENT AND OTHER CHALLENGES

Susan said it was an adjustment for the family when John came home in mid-December 1946. This change was one of several they and the extended family accommodated over the next five and a half years.

Two months after John, Wim was released on February 13, 1947. The prosecution of his case ceased on condition he pay a fine of 5,000 guilders by May 1. This condition had not been met by July 25 when the amount was reduced to 250 guilders. This amount was paid. I don't know if Wim lived with Dina after he was released or if he lived at his mother's place during 1947 and early 1948. What is known is that he and Dina were divorced on April 8, 1948, a month after state supervision of his property ended. He subsequently lived at his mother's and married his second wife, Rie, on August 10, 1949.

Meanwhile, Constant had been imprisoned in seven different facilities, most of them in Rotterdam. He was ultimately released from Westerbork on March 27, 1948. He went to live with his wife and young sons at his in-laws' in Hilversum. From May 20, he worked at the Avia pastry factory where he earned 40 guilders a week, 25 of which he paid to his in-laws for his family's room and board.

Owing to the housing shortage, "four families lived in the same house," Hans explained. He said that each family had one room that was private. In addition to John, Susan, Hans, Harald, and Constance, there was Aunt Sjaan and her daughters and Stan's young son, Wesley. The third family was Wim and Rie. The fourth was Miek and her husband, Bob, whom she married on July 23, 1947. And, of course, Stanni, the matriarch, was there too.

Figure 29. "New Years Eve supper at midnight 1950" (The caption was written by Susan. I don't know whether this was taken on the cusp of 1950 or 1951.) Left to right. Standing: Hans, Rie, Wim, Susan, Elly, Constant. Sitting: Bob, Miek, Constance, Harald, Stanni, John. Petersen family photo.

The passage of time helped to sort some things out. Sometime in the latter half of 1945, Susan took three-year-old Harald and met her father at a railway station in an attempt at reconciliation. It didn't go well. It was probably too soon; John's internment was a reminder that he and his family had been on Germany's side. Susan and her father tried again a few years later with better results. They re-established their relationship, and Susan's children gained a grandfather. John said his father-in-law turned out to be "a pretty good sort." Indicative of the nature of their contact and the formality of the time, Susan would shake hands with her father rather than hug him. He would use these exchanges as an opportunity to slip her the equivalent of one hundred dollars. "Don't tell Tant Suus," he would whisper, referring to his wife. The cash infusions were much appreciated since John and Susan had little at the time. Susan described her father as "a good grandfather" who regularly sent birthday and Christmas presents for the children, including Onno, Ann, and Philip when they came along.

The passage of time also led to different parts of the family making different choices about the future. John and Susan and their children joined "more than 160,000" Netherlanders who immigrated to Canada between 1945 and 1960.[509] Miek and Bob left for New Zealand. Constant and Wim and their families remained in the Netherlands.

***

Upon his return to the family, John spent long hours in his and Susan's bed convalescing. Their bed was in the sunroom off the living room. Constance, who turned two in February, "was afraid of the man behind the curtain," Susan said. Constance described the sunroom as "a frightening area" and told me John was "an angry man" at this time. Of course, being at home again was also an adjustment for him. He recovered much of his physical strength by March 1947, but it was mid-July—nine full months after his injury—before the bones in his left arm mended; the slow healing was attributed to a deficient diet. After this, other issues persisted. For two years, through the end of 1948, he said he was prone to nightmares and paranoia.

At some point, he returned to work. This may have occurred as early as the latter half of 1947. He had two jobs: one selling life insurance, the other as a salesman for a cork factory, where he met Hans Roelants. It is not known whether he held both jobs concurrently for a time. Despite working, John's tendency to

---

[509] *Liberation Album*, 9, 171.

withdraw was apparently more pronounced from 1947 to 1952. Descriptions of him during this period are of a solitary individual. Hans said his father was not around much and was kind of quiet and not very supportive. Although John found some time to paint, Hans told me his father was "not himself."

Figure 30. John's driver's licence photo, November 1948. Petersen family photo.

There were other problems. Negative patterns in John's behaviour re-emerged. When he was interned at Duindorp, he wrote a poem for Susan's twenty-eighth birthday on January 28, 1946. Titled "Your Eyes," it is a love poem, both a confession and a promise. In it he refers to Susan as "dark eyes" and speaks of her compassion:

> *Your brilliant intellect*
> *Has forgiven*
> *The cowardly gliding*
> *Between unfaithfulness and friendship.*

"I have to look inside / In this richness," he continues. "I have to promise / To never spoil them again." He concludes:

> *I shall be very strong*
> *Be solid as a church*
> *A name in a brand*
> *Of everlasting faithfulness.*
> *And always carry you*
> *Till the end of my days*
> *In the heart that aches of inner remorse.*[510]

But John could not keep his promise "of everlasting faithfulness." In the late 1940s and early 1950s, there were times of notable tension between him and Susan, and he had at least one affair. He told me he was in love with a woman named Jooka, an Amsterdam singer who lived on a houseboat and was also Susan's cousin. I don't know how long the affair lasted. While it persisted until the family departed for Canada, I don't know when it began. Nor do I know how Susan learned of it. John's justification for the relationship was that Susan had a boyfriend, by whom he meant Koos. Although Susan had feelings for Koos, I accept her claim that they never had an affair. According to Constance, "Mom

---

[510] Haydee Oord translation.

thought Dad was faithful. Dad thought Mom was unfaithful. They both imposed their reality on the other." But not everyone in the family sees it the same way. For example, Hans believes Koos gave Susan a piece of jewellery and that this was an indication of the closeness of their relationship, which in his opinion likely included an affair.

One afternoon in March 2005, Susan encapsulated John in a paradox. "He was a man of great inner strength and no inner strength," she told me. Almost sixty years earlier, in "Your Eyes," he had acknowledged his personal weakness with the words:

The cowardly gliding
Between unfaithfulness and friendship.

He resolved to do better:

I shall be very strong
Be solid as a church
A name in a brand
Of everlasting faithfulness.

But he was not strong. He succumbed again and again to "cowardly gliding."

He didn't like to be confronted or challenged. "He was such a chicken with stuff like that," according to Constance. "He was all about avoidance."

Speaking about his affair with Jooka, he told me: "Leaving for Canada was a way to end it without ending it." I remember being struck in that moment by his shirking attitude and his pusillanimity. While that statement conveyed vital truth about him, and while I caught a glimpse of that truth, I was far from grasping its full significance, namely that it was a revelatory snapshot representative of much of his behaviour.

Jooka, he added, wrote him a long letter, but he never answered it. He said he felt very guilty about the relationship, but I suspect this feeling was not about the relationship itself but how he had cravenly allowed it to end. He had, after all, professed to have been in love with her.

***

Hans said he was caught in the middle of the stressed situation between John and Susan, particularly after the decision was made to immigrate to Canada. Leaving meant that Hans, who turned thirteen at the end of 1949, would be separated from his mother, Frie, by an ocean and a continent. Thus, in the years prior to their eventual departure, he spent considerable time with her and her family at Scheveningen. He recalled one visit that lasted two to three months. He told me the atmosphere at his mother's home was more comfortable and accepting. There was talk of him staying permanently with Frie and her husband and being groomed to take over their nightclub business, but it is unlikely this was ever seriously discussed with John or Susan. Hans said he wasn't going to win that discussion with his father. "Remember, son, your mother abandoned you once before," John told him.

Hans said there were often fights between his parents after he came home from visiting his mother. "My stepmother was very jealous … of my mother," he recalled in his 1991 testimony. New clothes Frie had purchased for him were frequently a contributing factor in these fights. Hans told me Susan would take the clothes from him, put them away until he was too big for them, then give them to Harald, who was her favourite (until he was supplanted by Onno). But Hans also mentioned another episode when he showed off his new clothes to taunt Harald. This earned Hans a beating from his father, possibly because Hans's behaviour had upset Susan, who apparently found the situation with Hans and Frie a challenge to her normally tight control over her family.

In her responses to the new clothes, Susan may have been unconsciously penalizing Hans for his connection to Frie, for apparent divided loyalties, and for not being fully part of the Petersen family, which was a view she sometimes expressed. It appears, at least at times, that she was conflicted about her relationship with Hans. She told me once, wistfully: "Hans wasn't my real son." On another occasion she declared with vehemence, "Hans isn't mine!" Yet, she also told me, "[Hans] was John's son, but he was always more my son.... He was my child forever." Constance observed that Susan was very hard on Hans and Phil and regarded them as not fully up to the standard of the family.

Occasionally, during the late 1940s and early 1950s, Frie would visit John's family in Hilversum. Sometimes John and Susan and Frie would go out for a walk, and John would have Frie on one arm and Susan on the other. Susan herself told this story.

It was during this period that Hans, having returned from a visit to his mother's, received "a severe beating" from Susan. She claimed he had changed, which he undoubtedly had, for he had witnessed a death. While with his mother, the two of them had travelled to Amsterdam to stay with members of her family. One of these people, the owner of a watch shop, was part of the extended family and had promised that Hans could stay over with him for a day or two. This man, who had never married, lived with his mother in a small two-bedroom apartment behind the watch shop. There was no extra bed, so this man shared his with Hans. They had done this on several of Hans's previous visits. This time, however, the man died in the middle of the night, which had a marked effect on Hans. "I felt his body getting cold and I didn't know what to do," he recounted in his 1991 testimony. "I was scared. I finally got out of bed and went across to the other room where his mother slept and said, 'I think there is something wrong.'"

Like Hans, Harald was also a source of tension between John and Susan but in a more fundamental way. Where Hans was a reminder of John's life before Susan, Harald was the first to be saddled with the full baggage of his parents' conflicted life together. As John's poem to Susan professed his "everlasting faithfulness," so another poem written the same month for Harald's fourth birthday, is called "To Raldi." It reads in part:

> *I think*
> *Of the Gift*
> *That God has given us.*
> *That young life*
> *That on that long awaited day*
> *Suddenly laid in the crib.*
> *My little son*
> *Here where I live*
> *Behind the barbed wire*
> *Scorned by everyone*
> *I remind myself*
> *Of the hour that you came into our lives.*[511]

But as John failed to be faithful to Susan, he also had trouble adhering to the view that Harald was a gift from God. The key factors underlying this change in John's attitude toward Harald were jealousy and a combination of suspicion and anger: jealousy arising from the love and affection that Harald received from Susan and suspicion that Koos was her lover and Harald's father.

Of all the children, Harald most resembles John physically. He told me that when he was growing up his father always competed with him and sedulously rendered him second best. I suspect such behaviour on John's part was his reaction to semi-suppressed parts of himself he saw in aspects of Harald's personality. Though the evidence is not conclusive, much of it suggests John had been a difficult and challenging child; after all, he did admit to having temper tantrums and anger and frustration during his youth. And later, there was his need to be the centre of attention and his acknowledged tendency to play the fool. In his turn, Harald was also the class clown,

---

[511] Haydee Oord translation.

had a special ability to push buttons and upset people, and spoke of his rage and uncontrollable anger and his cries for help.

About 1983, almost a decade after John left Susan and the family had been sundered by the divorce and related developments, John and Harald reconciled. At least until that time, John had been unable to be the supportive, nurturing father they had both missed. Rather than see Harald as a mirror that revealed important aspects of his own isolation and suffering, John was trapped by the separate and insulated reality he had created for himself. He denied and distanced himself from what he saw in Harald's needy disposition and behaviour.

Figure 31. Left to right: Hans, Constance, and Harald in 1950. Petersen family photo.

***

According to Onno, in the 1960s and early 1970s, John referred most often to writers Kahlil Gibran and Edgar Cayce. John would read aloud from Gibran's *The Prophet*, which, Onno said, represented "the outer beauty he was trying to reach." John was also interested in Jiddu Krishnamurti, the philosopher and spiritual teacher. He gave me a copy of Krishnamurti's *At the Feet of the Master*. Years later, when I learned that Krishnamurti had spoken on numerous occasions in the Netherlands during the 1920s and 1930s, I wondered if John knew of him from this earlier period.

Miek didn't think so when I asked her in January 2005. But my question surfaced a memory for her. During the latter 1940s, she recalled repeatedly seeing John with a particular book; he was very interested in the philosophy propounded by its English author, she said. But she could remember neither the name of the author nor the title of the book. All she remembered was that the book's dust jacket included a photo of the author, his wife, and their two children. (It turned out there were three children in the photo.)

I asked Miek again about the mystery book in a letter of September 2005. She replied, "A few days ago (in the middle of the night) the name of the author of the book came to my mind. It was (is?) Peter Howard. Not a famous philosopher but a journalist (and maybe a famous sportsman). He wrote several books on democracy, Christianity, and materialism. The name of the book is: 'Ideas have legs.'"

Peter Howard achieved fame as captain of England's rugby team and as a champion bobsledder who went on to become a political columnist and the author of numerous books. *Ideas Have Legs* was first published in Britain in 1945 and, soon after, in the United States, India, Denmark, South Africa, Canada, Australia, and the Netherlands. It's not hard to see the book's appeal for John. Like John, Peter Howard was a seeker.

"I was always searching for something," he writes. "What were my deepest convictions?" he asks.

Howard is prodded by a man who tells him "his secret" with the result that Howard's "life suddenly slipped into perspective." Soon after he declares that "the master key [is] the Cross of Christ" and he writes about the "battle between MRA [Moral Re-Armament] and Materialism for the soul of the world."[512]

Moral Re-Armament was a campaign created by an organization known as the Oxford Group, "a Protestant sect that embraced group

---

[512] Peter Howard, *Ideas Have Legs* (Toronto: Longmans, Green and Company, 1946), 64, 66, 85, 91, 80 (Moral Re-Armament).

confession of moral failure as a kind of storytelling that can lead to salvation." It was the Oxford Group, along with an ecstatic experience, that enabled Alcoholics Anonymous founder Bill Wilson to achieve sobriety.[513] The group's ideas as conveyed by Peter Howard didn't have a similar self-disciplining effect on John. Aspects of the group's core beliefs, the "Four Absolutes"—Honesty, Purity, Unselfishness, and Love—may have got in his way.[514]

Although the romantic and questing nature of Peter Howard's idealism clearly held strong appeal for John, he was more interested in spiritualism and the occult. He made frequent use of the Ouija board and automatic writing during these years. Constance, based on what she heard from her mother and Aunt Miek, told me all the members of the family participated in the Ouija-board sessions. She mentioned Stanni, Wim, Susan, and Bob, who she said was very involved. However, Miek told me she would watch, implying she was not an active participant. Susan was devoted to John in his role as leader of their séances and said she was fascinated by what he had to say about past lives. They used the Ouija board and automatic writing with several of their friends but not Koos and Door.

One of these sets of friends was Ge (Gerald) and his wife, Ludz, who John and Susan saw regularly. Ge (pronounced "Hay") and Ludz are notable because both John and Susan spoke to me on separate occasions about them, particularly how John, functioning as a medium, helped Ge with an issue that had been troubling him deeply. John said Ge was a minister who had quit the church because he

---

[513] Gary Greenberg, "Whiskey and Ink" (a review essay on Leslie Jamison's *The Recovering: Intoxication and Its Aftermath*), *The New Yorker*, April 2, 2018, 84–89 (87—group confession of moral failure). Anonymous, "Freedom from Addiction: The Presence of a Moment—The remarkable story of A.A. Co-founder Bill Wilson," *Parabola*, May 1, 2020. Reprinted by DAILYGOOD, May 29, 2020 (influence of the Oxford Group, ecstatic experience), https://www.dailygood.org/more.php?n=8454.

[514] Anonymous, "Freedom from Addiction: The Presence of a Moment – The remarkable story of A.A. co-founder Bill Wilson."

couldn't understand many things. John said he would go into a trance and serve as a vehicle for a high spirit to explain things to Ge. Most of the time, Ge posed questions through John to the spirit, and John voiced the response he received. But sometimes John also functioned as a writing medium, transcribing the responses. John said when he spoke the spirit's words, he was not aware that he was speaking. He said he would quote Bible passages that Ge knew he didn't know, which "undoubtedly help[ed] convince" Ge to return to the church. John said, "Prior to this, I didn't have that much knowledge of the Bible," but he noted that he "learned a lot" from this process, presumably by de-briefing with Ge after the channelling was over.

Susan spoke of these sessions on two occasions, more than a quarter century later. In her version, Ge was studying theology, but never became a minister. She said she and John used the Ouija board with Ge and Ludz and that they contacted one of the "old, old Popes" who "had good advice, especially for Ge."

The Ouija board and séances fed John's ego and his relationship with Susan. These activities played an important role in sustaining them and counterbalancing their problems with sex, John's infidelities, and their laden friendship with Koos and Door. The four of them played cards on a regular basis during these years. For several reasons, I find it hard to believe Susan and Koos could have been lovers at the same time they were playing cards with their spouses. First, there was Susan's personality: very forthright and direct and, unlike John, not given to secrecy and manipulation. Second, she admitted to being very black and white in how she saw the world, which included rigid views on what she felt was morally right and wrong. Third, Koos apparently conducted himself with similar rectitude. Fourth, there was the factor of Susan's loyalty to her good friend, Door. Fifth and finally, there was John and Susan's joint commitment to the occult. It was an area of learning for her, and learning was a subject she identified almost exclusively with John. She said it was "destiny" she was with him and noted she wouldn't have learned as much if she had been with Koos. Furthermore, Miek, who described Koos as "very down to earth," said he would have been skeptical about the séances.

***

Miek and Bob emigrated in March 1952, several months before John and his family departed. She told me there was a lot of unemployment and it was hard to find a good job. The Netherlands' economic recovery was tied to that of Germany, which had been inhibited by denazification measures such as "limiting German steel production to a low level, destroying armament plants and industries with a direct war potential, and dismantling plants and sending them to Russia, Poland, and elsewhere as reparations."[515] Fear of the Russians and of a new war was another factor, she added. This was particularly the case during and after the crisis over Berlin from June 1948 to mid-May 1949, when the Cold War announced itself to the world.

A "sense of inadequate opportunity" undoubtedly contributed to John and Susan's decision to depart, but it was not John's primary motivator.[516] "My greatest and only wish is to be <u>accepted</u> [John's emphasis] by a community of people," he wrote in his letter of mid-1951. The letter goes on: "I wish to build in peace a future for my family and my children.... I'm ready to work and to die for the people, who will accept me and will allow me to live among them." His letter also refers to "the Dutch people, that I loved, although it had exterminated me." From 1933, when he first sought Dutch naturalization, until he came to Canada, he told me he was accepted nowhere and was not able to belong. Constance described her father as "a man without a country," adding that his fear never went away.

The question of acceptance for John was doubtless exacerbated by the treatment Constant received from the Dutch courts. On March 16, 1948, less than two weeks prior to his release, the Dutch Supreme

---

[515] Arthur S. Link and William B. Catton, *American Epoch: A History of the United States Since the 1890's* (New York: Alfred A. Knopf, 1967), 693.
[516] *Liberation Album*, 171.

Court ruled he could be considered a Dutch subject.[517] On June 12, 1948, he was found guilty of having violated article 101/102 of the penal code, namely "as a Dutchman voluntarily joining the army of a foreign power, knowing that this power is at war with the Netherlands."[518] He was sentenced to six months in prison, but this was reduced to three years' probation. He was also stripped of his newly acquired Dutch citizenship.[519] Documents from 1948–50 state that he was "without nationality," had "lost Dutch nationality," and was "stateless."[520] A law to restore Dutch citizenship to those who had been deprived of it was introduced by the government in April 1951.

The decisions of the Dutch courts to first grant Constant citizenship then remove it were cruelly ironic in light of two facts: First, Constant could have applied for and received Dutch citizenship in the late 1930s; his mistaken presumption that the reasons John's application for naturalization was rejected would also pertain to him was why he didn't apply and why he and John, as Dutch residents and German nationals, joined the SS in 1940 (although John lied, claiming he was Dutch); and second, in March 1943, Constant joined the Waffen SS because it was the only practical way he could avoid participating in further raids to round up Jews in and around Rotterdam. In yet another irony, there was a distinction between John and Constant's cases, of which John was likely unaware. "Service in such units as the *Waffen* SS," according to Mason, "was considered

---

[517] According to an interrogator's annotation on page 8 of Constant's statement of February 14, 1947, "both Constant Wilhelm Petersen and his wife were German citizens but viewed as subjects of the Netherlands by virtue of being born in the Dutch East Indies. Also, C.W. Petersen is registered in the population registration records as being German by birth but a Dutch subject." Attachment to Blauw's email of February 14, 2007, 3.

[518] Decision document on Constant's file (DNA, CABR 70629). Attachment to Blauw's email of February 14, 2007, 4, 7.

[519] Attachment to Blauw's email of February 14, 2007, 4. "60,000 Dutchmen became stateless during World War II," writes Mason (66–67). Of these, 40,000 had served the Germans, often in a military capacity, and "20,000 were wives who according to Dutch law automatically follow any change of status regarding citizenship of their husbands."

[520] Attachment to Blauw's email of February 14, 2007, 4, 5.

foreign military service by the courts" and was reason for loss of Dutch citizenship. "On the other hand, membership in the Dutch (political) SS ... was considered foreign 'public' service, not state service, and did not entail loss of citizenship."[521]

***

"I have ... burned all my ships behind me to go to Canada to begin a new life," John told Hans Roelants in his June 1951 letter. But this development was more a continuation than it was a break in pattern or a change of habit. Lies he told in the first of his collaborator statements, in October 1945, were repeated in his letter to Roelants. During the First World War, "the British newspapers were indignant about my father, a German, leading an English venture" is one example; when the Germans invaded on May 10, 1940, "I volunteered for the Dutch army" is another.

In preparing himself for Canada, John devised lies as necessary. If he hadn't already created his fictional artistic mentor, Wiertz, in stories he'd told Susan, logic suggests this invention occurred with the need, during his pre-emigration period, to cover up the pro-Nazi parts of his past, such as his association with the artist Pieter Pouwels. Another probable lie was the claim that the Petersen and Roelants families were related, that John and the Roelants siblings were cousins. This was likely a ruse to enable Marie Roelants to sponsor John and his family during their initial period in Canada. Once this was accomplished, the two families discovered they were mistaken about their relationship.

In doubling down on deceit, the move to Canada was more a tipping point than a turning point for John. It reinforced the false in him—his penchant for deception and manipulation, which he generally found to be the easier road—as well as troubled aspects of his life, which were accumulating and compounding as his children got older, and exposed new areas of tension. These troubled areas—such as his relationship with Susan and his affair with Jooka—were also warning signs that his

---

[521] Mason, 66.

behaviour was encouraging a collection of festering problems. These signs were not heeded, however. They were overwhelmed by the momentum and apparent requirements of the move to begin a new life.

But true as I believe this is, I suspect it was neither this simple nor this straightforward. Although there is no definitive proof, it appears John's behaviour and course of action were fundamentally challenged by an important figure in his life. This was likely his old Sea Scout leader, Timperley, who from 1949 to 1952 was Hans's Sea Scout leader too. Hans told me Timperley would visit John at the house during these years. Miek remembered Timperley as well, referring to him as "a nice man." But John never mentioned Timperley in relation to this period, telling me instead that he had lost track of his old friend around 1943, after Timperley had apparently been interned by the Germans.[522] Given John said he "adored" Timperley and credited him with being a profound and lifelong influence, it's unlikely, under normal circumstances, he would have forgotten the contact he had with this man in 1949 and the early 1950s. So, why the apparent obfuscation? It may be another indication that John was "not himself." Perhaps he had memory gaps during these years, like those he said occurred with the traumatic ending of his first marriage. Or perhaps his memory in this instance was just fine. Perhaps, as with Pieter Pouwels, he was suppressing something that embarrassed him and didn't fit the image of who he wished to be.

According to John, Wiertz told him at a critical juncture in his life, "There are two forces in the world: good and evil. The good comes from God, the evil is just there. You're somewhere between and you're being pulled both ways." But John's Wiertz didn't exist. So, presuming these penetrating words or ones like them were actually spoken to John at

---

[522] William Timperley is mentioned in "Zuiderkruisgroep" (Southern Cross Group), a Wikipedia article about a scouting group with club buildings in Hilversum, Loosdrecht, and Kortenhoef. While the group was founded in 1919, the article says "The man who popularized the originally Catholic group was the Englishman William Timperley. He became skipper of the group in 1927. During the occupation years (1940–1945) scouting was banned by the Germans and Timperley was deported to Germany…," accessed August 8, 2021, https://nl.wikipedia.org/wiki/Zuiderkruisgroep.

some point, who spoke them and when? What I presume to be the *why* of the situation—the circumstances of John's life in the run-up to his family's emigration—helps me to respond to the *who* and the *when* questions. Just as John claimed an unknown iconoclastic minister appeared at his bedside in the hospital at another critical time prior to another transition, my intuition tells me it was Timperley who delivered the searing judgment that John was "being pulled both ways."

In denying Timperley and in doubling down on deceit, John crossed the Rubicon when he came to Canada.

Figure 31. John's German passport photo, April 1951 (in the possession of the Petersen family). Author's note: While reviewing and finalizing the manuscript for this book, I found myself returning to this photograph, trying to interpret it. Is it passivity that we see, a man simply fulfilling the requirement for a passport photo? Or is there more in his expression: a man burdened by past and ongoing suffering? Is that coldness and alienation in his gaze? Is there anger, hardness, and perhaps even cruelty in the set of his mouth? These are qualities at odds with the man I thought I knew in the 1970s and '80s.

PART FOUR

Canada
The Final Chapters

Without mother [Susan], I wouldn't be what I am.

—John's note of April 30, 1966, accompanying his poem, "Freedom Symphony," which he gave to Constance on her wedding day.

John wanted to be master of it all. He'd sense people's dependence; then he'd grab them.

—Miek, January 2005

People who shut their eyes to reality simply invite their own destruction, and anyone who insists on remaining in a state of innocence long after that innocence is dead turns himself into a monster.

—James Baldwin, "Stranger in the Village"

29

THE TRUTH BEHIND THE FACADE

My intention was to focus this biography on the first half of John's life, but there are some events from his latter thirty-five years in Canada that must be noted lest I commit the error of omission and compromise the truth, the pursuit of which has driven the compilation of this record.

***

John and Susan generally put on a good front in their marriage and, in many ways, they succeeded in their lives. Constance told me Susan saved John from being a scatterbrained artist, while he taught her about her soul. Both Constance and Harald said John would have been a good-for-nothing were it not for Susan.

In July 1952, when they immigrated to Vancouver Island, Canada, with three children, they had next to nothing. But they managed to make their way. Taking in foster children and boarders, which started in Alberni and rapidly expanded in Victoria, enabled them to bring in more money and to live more comfortably. Although keeping the house full of foster kids and boarders served worthy and practical purposes, it was also fraught. Harald, Constance, Onno, and Phil all said they felt they lost their family as a result; it was submerged in the larger enterprise. According to Onno, they "lost a sense of identity with what family meant." Susan's rule for her own kids, the foster children, and the boarders was, "We're all equal." But it never quite felt that way.

One of the boarders, Al Wagstaff, recounted that Susan said they were all part of the family, but he knew they weren't. Onno added, "There was an insistence that the [foster kids and boarders] were all brothers and sisters, but I didn't feel that for most of them." There was a lot of guilt in not feeling the required closeness for everyone, he noted. Nonetheless, he said he had a lot of really happy memories. Years later, after she had many conversations with Constance, Susan said all the fostering and boarders were detrimental to her own children and if she were to do it again, it would be on a much-reduced scale.

The foster kids and boarders were emblematic of the Petersen family and of John and Susan's marriage, as was the Ouija board. Both were thorny briar patches that entangled them. I suspect John and Susan's partnership in keeping the house full of foster kids and boarders might have been an unconscious way to avoid dealing with what was really going on between them. According to Harald, "Dad got all the kudos for the foster kids; Mom did all the work." Al Wagstaff said Susan "ran her ass off," and noted that the welfare of the kids was most important to her. He called her "a sweetheart," even though he didn't always agree with her. As for Susan, she said she didn't get much help with the foster kids and noted that John's heart wasn't in it. Constance added that Susan did the day-to-day stuff and John was only involved when there were big problems. "Then he was the hero."

Where Susan was the family's frontline worker spending most of her time on deck and directing the family, John, the patriarch, was more in the background, mostly sitting quietly in the living room. And within this dynamic there was another tighter, testier one. John needed calm and quiet. According to Susan, he cited this need as his reason for leaving her. Before that watershed event occurred, he was always on guard against what Constance referred to as Susan's "violent temper." To avoid it, he would manipulate her. "Dad had a strong control on Mom," their adopted daughter, Kitt, told me. "She pretty well did what Dad wanted."

His infidelities continued in Canada. In Alberni, the family of Jim and Jane Lett (pseudonyms) and their three children became good friends of the Petersens. The Lett family "taught us how to be

Canadian," Constance said. At some point, John announced to Susan, "I slept with Jane." Although John appeared serious, Susan took it as a joke. But she did ask Jane about it.

"That's news to me," Jane told Susan.

However, Constance claimed Jane was smitten with John and that they had an affair right from the beginning. While Susan found John "too feminine," Constance spoke of his prowess and said he always slept around.

John and Susan's problematic sex life was a factor in his infidelities. Their sexual relationship "was horrible," according to Onno. He said he heard this from both parents. I heard similar statements from Constance and Susan.

These problems, along with the deferential reverence Susan accorded John in some areas, enabled more trouble. They were out of their depth, for example, when Ann became their first foster child in mid-1956. Ann was a challenge to Susan, who had no idea of the extent of the abuse her new charge had suffered or of the psychological damage she had sustained. Susan's abrasive parenting did no more than skim the surface of Ann's reality. Emotional and easily distraught, Ann was given to frequent tears. Susan didn't like the bouts of crying and tried to stop them. "I irritated her quite often," Kitt told me, speaking of Ann, her younger self. "I think she thought I was stupid, but I wasn't." Ann was left-handed, but Susan insisted she eat with her right hand because it was good manners to do so. Susan was harsh at times, Kitt recalled. Once, when Susan threatened to strike her, Ann threatened her back: "If you ever hit me, I'll kill you." It was a confrontation they wryly recollected decades later.

Constance and Ann shared a room and a bed. Kitt told me it was not uncommon for her to shake at night because she was so scared. Constance was the family's first responder when Ann was upset. Constance would hold her and rock her and sing her Dutch lullabies.

"I was so mean to [Constance]," Kitt recalled. While holding her, Constance would tell her she loved her, but Ann—who was not used to being held—didn't want to hear it.

Despite this, Constance remained the primary refuge for Ann, whose tendency to shake at night continued for several years. Constance said her parents were generally off duty during the evening. The kids had to fend for themselves for emotional support. "It was too scary to go to my parents' room," she stated. One night when Ann would not settle, when her shaking persisted, Constance did knock on her parents' door for help. Susan told Constance to go back to bed. Susan then told Ann, who turned sixteen in August 1959, to get into bed with John. Then she left the room at his request, so he could talk to Ann in private. "Ann was terrified the whole time," Constance told me, based on what she heard afterward from Ann. "I'd never do it again," she said, referring to going to her parents' bedroom for assistance. "You don't make that mistake twice."

Constance added that Ann was sent to John's bed only the one time. However, Kitt told me it happened more than once. But, on another occasion, she said she has little memory of any of this. She said she doesn't remember being abused, but she doesn't dispute it either. As a child, from the ages of seven to twelve, she would dissociate when she was raped by her stepfather and grandfather. "There's so much I don't remember," she remarked in an abstracted, perplexed way. Another time she asked rhetorically, "How do you make amends when you can't remember?" This reflects the influence of the Alcoholics Anonymous 12-Step Program, which was instrumental in her quitting alcohol in 1979. She said her mother, stepfather, and grandfather were all alcoholics. Her First Nations father, who she did not meet until she was forty-seven, was also "a drinker."

Constance told me that John did not rape Ann. She based this on what was shared between her and Ann at the time and on at least one later occasion when they revisited the event. John "fondled" Ann, Constance said.

In 2003, when I first spoke to Constance, she talked about John's sexual needs, that Susan wasn't attracted to him and "couldn't and wouldn't" oblige him, at least not often enough. Three months later, Constance spoke of their "highly paternalistic family structure." She said Susan was trapped by a model of European paternalism that she passed on to her: "The man comes home and you give him his slippers and dinner and no one speaks until he permits it."

According to Constance, John believed "as a man he was superior." She said he had "this eagle sense of superiority." It manifested in a subtle and distinctive male chauvinism, which permitted him to overstep convention and intrude in the private worlds of young women. These violations appear to have been motivated by his belief in his superiority and special abilities as well as his desire for sexual gratification. As Constance and I discussed this, we used the terms "favour" and "blessing" and acknowledged the absurdity of it. "By fondling young women he was doing them a favour, he was bestowing a blessing on them," I recorded in my notes.

"Yes," Constance agreed when I repeated this back to her.

But absurdity only skims the surface of John's behaviour. Underlying his different motivations in such situations was, I suspect, an addiction to sex—or at least a heavy emphasis on it—that had arisen in response to long-standing, unresolved emotional needs. John himself will speak to this shortly, arguing in an essay that "the only time [man] can be free is in sexual experience."

While I was appalled when I first heard about John and Susan's joint involvement in Ann being sent to his bed, I can't say I was surprised by John's behaviour, for I'd previously heard at least one other story about deeply inappropriate behaviour on his part, which will be discussed. Looking back, what stands out for me are several of Kitt's statements, which are remarkable in a shocking way. Her life was so horrendous from the ages of seven to twelve that she told me she believed then that it'd be better to be dead than alive and that she preferred sleeping to being awake. Another time she said her belief as a young person was that "dying is easy, living is hard."[523]

---

[523] Kitt told me she was with her mother for the first year of her life, but from the age of one until she turned seven, she was raised by Bonnie and Alec, a grey-haired couple with a grown son in the navy. "I grew up thinking they were my parents," she said. About the time of her seventh birthday, she was returned

Despite the sexual abuse, Kitt shared some fond memories of John. She told me she particularly remembered John's laugh. Prior to him, she didn't know men laughed, she said, a simple observation that has stayed with me because of the joyless, compassionless turpitude of the men she'd known previously. Another time she told me—again remarkably, some would say unbelievably—"John really did have my best interests at heart." Repeating these statements is not in any way meant to excuse John and Susan's deplorable behaviour when Ann was sent to John's bed or at least one other occasion of even more egregious behaviour on John's part regarding Ann, which I heard from Al Wagstaff, who had joined the family at the beginning of 1959. He said he never felt close to John, but he respected him at first. Then, during his second year with the family, he started to have doubts.

John maintained a home office for his insurance work. It was on the main floor and off-limits to the family. Al didn't know about this rule when he breached it one day, prompted by unusual circumstances: The phone was ringing, but no one was answering it. John had a second phone in his office, but he didn't pick up. So, Al answered the main phone in the kitchen. It was an urgent call for John. Al went to the office, opened the door, and delivered the message to John, who was facing him, sitting at his desk. As Al did this, he also saw Ann. She was below John's desk. Al saw Ann's head, which was in the area of John's lap.[524]

---

to her mother who Kitt initially thought was an aunt. In addition to being a "raging alcoholic," Kitt said her mother was also very violent. When Kitt was twelve, there was an incident when her mother straddled her on a couch while pulling her hair with one hand and threatening her with a butcher's knife in the other. Her mother might have killed her had not Kitt's younger half-sister run to get Kitt's stepfather to intervene. It was after this that Kitt was placed with the Petersen family. Kitt's stepfather was also violent and would hit her every night, she said. She described herself as "very stubborn"; she wouldn't do what she was asked. She told me her stepfather made her kneel in the corner with her head against the wall and her hands behind her back. She had to stay in that position for extended periods.

[524] In August 2010, Kitt told me, "I talked to [dad] a lot in his [home] office. He could always calm me down."

While Kitt does not recall being sexually abused by John, she does remember being hugged by him "a lot." Sometimes while he hugged her, he would shake and rock back and forth, she told me. Her first instinct was he was attracted to her, but she would try to suppress the thought because it made her feel disloyal to him. "I had such uncomfortable feelings around him."

When Ann became pregnant by her boyfriend in the spring of 1963, John kicked her out of the house. Her move into an apartment was one of the most difficult changes of her life. "I was at a loss," Kitt told me. "I was devastated." As Susan was mom to Ann, John was her dad. Except for some contact with Susan, Ann lost her parents and her home in one fell swoop. She felt betrayed and harboured anger about John's decision for years, and she said she didn't see him for four or five years.

Her anger may have been about more than John's decision. It may have related as well to his subsequent actions, particularly his disapproval of her decision to marry her boyfriend. John refused to attend the wedding and didn't want Susan to attend either. When Ann asked Susan if she could come home on the day of the wedding to get dressed, Susan—likely in defiance of John—said yes. Ann had hoped to see John, but he shunned her by locking himself in the kitchen. When they discussed the situation, Constance advised her mother to go to the wedding without John, that she was entitled as an individual to make her own decision. This was a novel concept to Susan. Up until then, her thinking had been circumscribed by paternalism, deference, and her marked tendency to deify John.

"Mom was his disciple," Constance said. "She idealized him as a spiritual being."

Figure 32. Christmas 1965. John strikes a familiar pose as Susan looks on. Onno is between them. Sandra Roodenburg photo. When Sandra started dating her future husband, John Roodenburg, in late 1963, she became a frequent guest at the home where John had boarded since 1961 or 1962. She said there were always at least a dozen people at the Petersen dinner table, more on Sundays when "it was shoulder-to-shoulder."

***

Like Ann, Phil had a blood parent who was First Nations. Phil suffered more from racial prejudice than Ann. He was a slow learner who had difficulty in the various schools he attended. The Petersens, in Susan's words, were "an intellectual family," and by late 1960, or a few years later, they—especially John—questioned if Phil was a good fit with them. So, a handful of years after Phil had joined them, arrangements were made for him to be sent to a different foster family on a farm. Although Phil's departure had been discussed beforehand, Onno said, "He disappeared."

About four months later, when the new foster family was going on vacation, they didn't want to take Phil with them, so they returned him to John and Susan on a temporary basis. According to Constance, Susan was horrified when Phil came back. He was "so dirty. The dirt was caked on." Susan put him in a bath to soak and soften the dirt before scrubbing him clean. Under the dirt, Susan said she discovered that Phil was covered in sores: mosquito bites that had become infected. While Phil was in the bathtub, she asked him if he wanted to live with them rather than the other family; he answered with an emphatic yes. Phil's recollection was slightly different. He said he pleaded to stay. Whatever the case, he didn't return to the other family. Onno said, "Mom was quite angry." Despite John's objections, Susan resolved to keep Phil.[525]

John's ideological indoctrination by the Nazis in 1940 continued to influence his views on race and homosexuality. He opposed racial intermarriage; I heard him say so. But did Nazi influence extend beyond the subjects of homosexuality and racial intermarriage for John? Was he racist? My answer to these questions is conflicted because the information I can bring to bear on them is mixed. On the first two occasions that I spoke to Constance, she told me her father "believed in

---

[525] Phil died in 2011 at the age of fifty-seven. He is survived by his wife and daughter. A civilian employee of the Canadian Department of National Defence for 37 years, he was the Construction Engineering Works Coordinator. Having been raised in foster care, Phil made a point of hiring Indigenous youth from British Columbia's foster care system. He helped them to become self-sufficient and, in his words, "to have a good life too." He regularly supported Victoria's "Aboriginal Back to School Picnic," helping low-income families with the cost of school supplies and speaking to students in elementary and secondary schools about the importance of education. After his death, the Phil Petersen Indigenous Scholarship was established at the University of Victoria's School of Social Work.

Mein Kampf," was anti-Semitic, and prejudiced against Blacks and First Nations people. I have come to regard these statements as somewhat unreliable, representing a release of pent-up emotion that Constance held regarding her father, a release prompted, at least in part, by an attentive and sympathetic audience: me. While her strong feelings were unquestionably genuine, some of her unequivocal statements were not only inflammatory (and need to be carefully tested), they also reflect a periodic tendency to extremity on her part that I will discuss shortly. Recalling that John spoke to me several times about his friendship with a local First Nations chief, I challenged Constance's assertion that he was prejudiced against First Nations people. She backed off on this point, saying that his perspective changed over time. Years later, John Roodenburg, who boarded with the Petersens from the early 1960s until April 1965 and remained close with the family after that, told me about John Petersen's friend Ozzie, a Black man, who came by the house to visit with him during that period. There is also the significant influence the Indigenous people of Java had on John when he was a little boy, which is something Constance herself recounted. While some of John's personal relationships defy the stereotype of a racist, his attitude and behaviour other times support a different conclusion, as with Phil's temporary expulsion from the family. This inconsistency is typical of John. He sometimes presented markedly different versions of himself depending on the situation and the audience.

Homosexuality was generally regarded as a mental illness into the late 1960s and early 1970s.[526] Speaking about the Nazi antipathy to it, John made several exaggerated statements. He said there was one article in German law that was printed in red to emphasize the crime's heinous nature. The article, he told me, decreed that homosexuality "must automatically be punished by death." He said homosexuality was "the red act" and he maintained "there was no homosexuality in the German army."

---

[526] Homosexuality was decriminalized in Canada in 1969. It was removed as a psychological disorder from the *Diagnostic and Statistical Manual of Mental Disorders* (DSM) in 1973.

The article in question may have been Paragraph 175 of the German criminal code, which outlawed male homosexuality. When the Nazis came to power, they enforced this provision more strictly than previous German governments. In 1935, they amended the paragraph and "expanded the category of 'criminally indecent activities between men' to include any act that could be construed as homosexual. The courts later decided that the intention to commit a homosexual act or even the contemplation of such an act was sufficient."[527]

John's changed view of his gay sister-in-law, Jouk—from a prewar classmate and friend with whom he went sailing to a postwar lesbian he purportedly "hated" and relegated to "a family secret," to quote Constance—is another indication of the anti-homosexual attitude he had absorbed. While many readers may accept that John would hate Jouk, my initial response was to challenge this notion. In disclosing this, I'm hoisting a red flag and admitting I'm still unclear and conflicted in some ways about John. I still have some loyalty to the man I thought I knew. My problem with the idea that John hated Jouk is that it does not align with his general equanimity and his normally gentle and tolerant nature. Moreover, I sense in Constance's characterization an emotional overlay of entirely understandable stridency and anger based on her relationship with her father. At the same time, I recognize there were aspects of John's life that I was not privy to, that were unknown or hidden from me, aspects which seem increasingly to be bearing down and trying to make themselves known to me. This recognition reminds me of my ruminations on John's 1951 passport photo (see Figure 31), namely the possibility that it revealed "qualities at odds with the man I thought I knew." I've had conversations with several people who raised the possibility that John was a psychopath.[528] As Constance told me, there were times

---

[527] "Persecution of homosexuals in the Third Reich," *Holocaust Encyclopedia*, United States Holocaust Memorial Museum, accessed December 30, 2019, https://encyclopedia.ushmm.org/content/en/article/persecution-of-homosexuals-in-the-third-reich.
[528] A person suffering from chronic mental disorder with abnormal or violent social behaviour.

when John behaved in a threatening or warning manner without "a shred of emotion," perhaps the term sociopath[529] may also fit.

What I've referred to as Constance's stridency and anger were rooted in a disastrous episode with her father in 1959. Acting on an overweening presumption of special ability born of hubris and delusion, John intruded where he had no right or business and committed an enormous violation of trust. Constance was fourteen at the time. She seemed, to her mother, different than the other kids in the house, inclined to her Aunt Jouk's orientation. "Our family was very open about sexuality," Constance said. "There was a lot of sexual innuendo amongst the kids." She was the odd one out, "a square peg in a round hole," she called herself. Although boundaries were in place, such as the older girls sharing a top-floor bedroom and the older boys sharing one in the basement, some of the teenage foster kids were having sex, Al Wagstaff said. Susan conveyed her concerns about Constance to John, who set out to "try to fix her."

In describing what transpired, Constance used the term "fix" more than once. She said her father was concerned about how she felt about being a woman. She said it "wasn't a sexual thing as such." In the large kitchen with the lights on, John made her take off all her clothes and sit on his lap. He made her take his hand and put it all over her body.

"It was the most humiliating experience of my life," she said, forty-four years later in 2003. In 2010, she referred to those years as "a very dark period."

I first heard of this incident from Onno in 1995. Susan confirmed it when I met with her at her mobile home later that year. And Constance told me about it on several occasions in 2003 and 2004.

The effect on Constance was profound. Al Wagstaff, who knew nothing of what had occurred, nonetheless observed that "Connie had started to be kind of funny toward the family. She had changed." Constance herself said that she often suffered an upset stomach at dinner

---

[529] A person with a personality disorder manifesting itself in extreme antisocial attitudes and behaviour and a lack of conscience.

and had to excuse herself. She "was very aware," she said, "of all the upset feelings not being expressed." As she went through her mid-teens, there were significant frictions with her parents. She became very hostile and a very bitter, angry young woman, she told me. By April 1964, when she left for a visit with extended family in the Netherlands for about nine months, she was "extremely suicidal" and "at the lowest point in [her] life."

Of the various causes that eventually split the family apart in 1974, what happened between Constance and her father when she was fourteen was, next to John's mental health, likely the most critical factor, for it had cascading ramifications that fed his fears, paranoia, and psychosis. Soon after Constance's return from Europe at the end of 1964, her relationship with her father changed in a notable way.

"Connie was his confidante," Susan told me.

John told Constance not to talk to others about their conversations. "This is very special," he told her. He anointed her with singular responsibilities.

"My role in his life, he told me, was to be a support system, to help him recharge his batteries," Constance explained.

He was struggling in his new circumstances as a social worker. Perhaps he hoped Constance could help counterbalance this. He told her about "marathon weekends"—workshops and social-work retreats—he was required to attend in Seattle. She described them as very confrontational, experiential workshops that were meant to break people down. She said John often had great difficulty coping with them. He called them "horrible weekends." People associated with those weekends told John, apparently based on his performance and behaviour during the workshops, that he should see a psychiatrist. Like his possible confrontation with Timperley before coming to Canada, this advice had the potential to transform and restore his life, but he didn't heed it. Constance said he was afraid a psychiatrist would confirm his psychotic tendencies and prescribe pills that would have the side effect of diminishing or eliminating his psychic abilities. With her dad, she added, it was sometimes hard to tell the difference between the psychic and the psychotic.

In addition to being a classic indicator of an abusive relationship, John, in making Constance his confidante and stressing the need for secrecy, may have expected she would be as compliant as Susan had been in most areas of their marriage. But he was also terrified, according to Constance, that she might betray him. She suspects this fear may have been rooted in the fact she told Susan he had been advised to see a psychiatrist, a disclosure that Susan revealed to him. His fear of betrayal necessitated upping the ante; it appears the danger and extremity of the situation, as he perceived it, spawned extremity in the form of psychological abuse. He infused his relationship with Constance with a powerful religious dimension that called for her adherence to him as a representative of godliness and goodness. He could read her mind and the minds of the other kids, he told her. The control he exerted was intensely fear-based.

"Don't look in my eyes. They can burn your eyes out," he reportedly told her on one occasion.

"The minute I'd see my dad, my thinking would change," she said.

John used a similar approach with Ann. She said he had this "amazing voice." She described it as "a kind of voice I could get lost in." He "seemed to me to be a very sad person inside. He was gentle." But "I also knew him to be really harsh." He could be fun, but he was also "dark and mysterious." He told Ann he could always reach her, even if it meant coming back from the grave. "He always said he could come back." She had nightmares about this after he died. They likely contributed to her decision several years later to symbolically reclaim her life by changing her name to Kitt, which she used until her death in June 2021. When she told Susan about the nightmares, Susan said she, too, believed John might come back and that she had the same dream. This overwrought reaction was typical of the long-standing influence John exercised over Ann, Susan, and, most dramatically, Constance.

I believe the sexual and psychological abuse Constance suffered at her father's hands transformed and supercharged her relationship with him. The extremity of his abuse produced a tendency to extremity in her as well. In this, she is, to some extent, the flip side of her father.

Where he hid many of his emotional scars beneath his affable exterior, his romanticized reinterpretations of his life, and his claims of special ability, she often revealed hers by edgy, provocative, and critical pronouncements. While some of this is likely the same bluntness typical of her mother, a sizeable part is, I believe, from the abuse and the long-lasting pain and anger it sowed, which I will discuss.

Throughout the 1960s, John continued to emphasize that homosexuality was a mental illness. "If I didn't cure myself, I could be committed [to an institution]," is how Constance summarized what she heard from him. It terrified her and caused her to repress her true nature for much of her life. When Constance married her first husband, Henk, in April 1966, John thanked him for saving her, in Constance's words, from "a life of tragic lesbianism." Henk was another of the family's boarders. A Dutch seaman who had broken a leg, which prevented him from departing with his ship, he'd moved in while Constance was in Europe. Before she returned, he would look at a photo of her that was on display and one time told John and Susan that he was going to marry her. On April 30, 1997, the thirty-first anniversary of that marriage, now long over (as was a second marriage), Constance, inspired by the recent example of comedian and talk show host Ellen DeGeneres, declared that she was gay.

Hans and Harald dispute that their father sexually abused Constance. The disbelief is strongest with Hans, who, when the incident occurred, was recently married and had been out of the house for about eighteen months. Harald, however, told me in July 2003: "I'm not sure Con's not right, that dad did molest her." Constance was surprised and moved by Harald's remark when I passed it on to her. But he has since moved closer to Hans's position. "I'm not sure I believe it," he said in 2010. "I don't want to believe it."

Constance said the whole family lined up against her when she went into therapy in the early 1990s. She was the outsider, "an outcast in her family," she said repeatedly. When she started to address sensitive family issues, she felt ostracized by Hans and Harald. Susan would alternate between supporting her and adopting a more neutral position, she said. In Constance's view, the family, except for Kitt, who had seen a psychiatrist for five years starting in the late 1960s, colluded in not discussing the subjects she was exploring. Some members of the family wanted to continue living in a world where John "was a god," Constance said.

Constance's anger and alienation reflect, in part, how isolated she has felt within the family. But what is missing in this is acknowledgement that the others were all aware, in their different ways, of many of John's considerable flaws and failings. Constance's strong feelings reflect her distinct situation: Not only that she was abused and the abuse was a defining reality in her life but also that those facts have rarely, if ever, been acknowledged or accepted by some family members. In 2003, Susan remarked that Hans and Harald didn't really know their sister. About the same time, Constance told me she and her elder brothers had agreed to leave the past in the past so they could have some sort of relationship now, which was very important to her.

Constance's role as John's confidante and being sworn to secrecy by him was doubtless a factor in her distinct and occasionally extreme perspective. Like me, she was bitten and poisoned by the snake of John's falseness. In both cases, deceit and hubris were key factors in the administering of this poison. But it was much more toxic for Constance because it continued to be administered, and in stronger doses, through the psychological abuse that was sustained for two decades.

Constance's sense that her life was *infected* by her parents, particularly her father, is clearly different than the perspective of any of her brothers. Like Constance, Kitt was subjected to physical and psychological abuse by John. But she suppressed the memories of the severe sexual abuse she suffered as a child, before living with the Petersens, and it appears that when she was sexually abused by John, the suppressive undertow of her early life swallowed those events as well.

In the 1970s, Constance had a social worker who had participated with John in the "marathon weekends" of training during the mid-1960s. One day when she was meeting with this social worker, she told him her father thought her husband was psychotic.

"Have you ever considered it might be your father who is psychotic?" the social worker asked in reply. The question surprised and alarmed Constance. Eventually, however, she came to regard it as an important turning point, even though her initial reaction was one of intense fear.

"If I thought that, and Dad was of God, then I was of the devil," is how she recounted her thought process. Even years after therapy and substantial recovery, Constance would suffer panic attacks following conversations in which she revealed to me the twisted nature of this core part of her relationship with her father.

Despite Constance's feeling of being infected, she has other, brighter sides to her. I wrote in my notes following a talk we had in July 2003: "Constance has a very generous spirit. You see it in the understanding and balanced way she sees and speaks of her parents and family, and how she treats Susan. Constance has radiance."

She told me three years later, "Dad never came to terms with his life. I want to come to terms with mine."

***

By the time of Ann's wedding in early July 1963, Susan had already made her first trip back to the Netherlands in January 1962. When she returned from her second trip in April 1967, she found the house in turmoil. The reason for this was that Gail, an eighteen-year-old foster child, had, in Susan's words, "taken my place in bed." Gail had been with the family for about two years. John claimed that nothing wrong had happened; he was only counselling and comforting her. But decades later, another foster child, who was a couple of months older than Gail, said John had convinced Gail that they were meant to be together. Perhaps this is what Gail told Susan at the time. But, according to Constance, Susan blamed Gail. Denial was easier than holding John responsible. "She likely buried the truth of it as she'd buried everything else," Constance said of her mother.

Susan helped Gail move out of the house and into her own place, after which Susan could not look at a picture of Gail for a long time. In due course, however, Gail would return to the fold and once again attend family events at John and Susan's home. Given the history, most people in John's position would, I think, find Gail's presence mortifying, but not John, apparently.

While Susan buried and hid important realities from herself, she was at the same time also asserting a degree of autonomy, sometimes in defiance of John: supporting Ann's marriage preparations and attending her wedding, making her first visits back to the old country, and bringing Phil back to the family. But, noteworthy as these acts of independence are, they did not presage a break or even a fundamental shift in Susan's relationship with John. She was dedicated to staying with him. Despite sex being a frequent point of friction between them, she was happy to otherwise go along, apparently even permitting him occasional dalliances.

She had a childlike way of believing what she wanted to believe. This was part of her lack of agency in some areas of her life. One time she surprised me when she remarked with a certain resignation, "I never thought John would fall for anyone but me. The sex was not that good, but otherwise things were okay. You get used to everything."

John may have been threatened by Susan's expressions of self-determination. Constance said they were hard on him and that he increasingly used the "psychic stuff" that so impressed Susan to influence her. What is not clear is where conscious manipulation left off and genuine belief began in John's mind. No doubt the boundary between them ebbed and flowed with his emotional state. By 1973 and 1974, his beliefs about reincarnation and several of his alleged past lives and what they supposedly indicated he should be doing in his present incarnation had assumed a much more dominant place in his thinking.

Prior to leaving Susan during the spring of 1974, he wrote two essays, "Meditation," which is undated, and "About Meditation," which is dated March 4, 1974. "Meditation" is addressed to "Woman" and includes this:

> We consider living as a positive action—doing, thinking, the everlasting bustle, conflict, fear, sorrow, guilt, ambition, competition, the bustling after pleasure with its pain, the desire to be successful. All this is what we call living. This is our life, with its occasional joy, with its moments of compassion without any motive, and generosity without any strings attached to it. These are rare moments of ecstasy, of bliss that have no past or future. But going to the office, anger, hatred, contempt, enmity, are what we call everyday living. And we consider it extraordinarily positive.
>
> The negation of the positive is the only true positive. To negate this so-called living, which is ugly, lonely, fearful, brutal and violent, without knowledge of the other, is the most positive action. Are we communicating with each other?
>
> You know, to deny conventional morality completely is to be highly moral, because what we call social morality, the morality of respectability, is utterly immoral; we are competitive, greedy, envious, seeking our own way—you know how we behave. We call this social morality.... But when you deny it because you understand it, there is the highest form of morality. In the same way to negate social morality, to negate the way we are living—our pretty little lives, our shallow thinking and existence, the satisfaction at a superficial level with our accumulated things, to deny all that, not as a reaction but seeing the utter stupidity and the destructive nature of this way of living, to negate all that is to live. To see the false as the false—this seeing is the truth.... What we call love is torture, despair, a feeling of guilt.
>
> ... Probably [sex] is the only escape man has now, the only freedom; everywhere else he is pushed around, bullied,

violated intellectually, emotionally, in every way he is a slave to society, he is broken, and the only time when he can be free is in sexual experience. In that freedom he comes upon a <u>certain</u> joy and he wants the repetition of that joy. Looking at all this, where is love? Only a mind and heart that are full of love can see the <u>whole</u> movement of life. <u>Then</u> whatever he does, a man who <u>possesses such love is moral</u>, whatever and regardless of what society says, he is good and what he does is beautiful.

David Spangler, the American mystic, has written, "It is on the personality level that we must ground ourselves. I have seen too many people pull in energies and then be unable to handle them, for their personalities are not properly integrated. The result is usually one of emotional imbalance, but it can disperse a person mentally and physically as well…. it is quite effective as a way of stimulating conflict. It also cuts off incoming communication, isolating a person or a group within its own illusions, encouraging an increasing removal from reality."[530] John's words quoted above, are, in my view, an example of a person isolated "within [his] own illusions" and functioning at "an increasing removal from reality."

Susan told me it was not in her nature to see "the bad part" of John, but she was forced to face up to it after he left the marriage and "counselled" her about their divorce settlement. Manipulation rather than counselling would be a more apt term for what he did. His purpose, according to Susan in 2003, was "so that he wouldn't have to pay too much money"; he "implied it was what Jesus wanted." Her conclusion: "I was weak." But five years later, when we spoke about the divorce again, her conclusion had changed to, "I was stupid." She admitted she had overridden her lawyer, who had tried to talk her out of the settlement. But in 2008, she didn't say John had influenced her.

---

[530] David Spangler, "An Open Letter to the Findhorn Community," *Reflections on the Christ* (Findhorn, Scotland: Findhorn Publications, Third edition, 1981), 107–108.

I reminded her of her earlier comments, but she didn't respond. Six months earlier, however, she had told me his intentions were bad sometimes.

John's departure from the marriage was the biggest sadness in Susan's life, Constance told me. In 1975, when Susan went to the Netherlands for six months, the magnitude of what had befallen her became clear. "I almost died," she told me, referring to a broken heart. Constance described her mother as "soul sick" during this period and credited John's siblings, Miek, Wim, and Constant, with nursing her back to health. Miek said John wrote letters to Constant and Wim but not to her. She figured John thought she would not accept his explanation, but Constant and Wim might.

According to Constance, Susan was still in a desolate state of mind when she returned to Canada. Despite this and what she had been through, she never got mad at John, Constance said. In fact, Susan told me on at least two occasions that she held out hope he might return to her. She was dismissive of his subsequent common-law marriages. She referred to the first, which lasted almost eight years, as "a fling," while the latter, which occupied his last five and a half years, was "very superficial" in her estimation.

"When I die, I know he will be there. He promised. We agreed to it," Susan said in 2003.

She died in July 2009, at the age of ninety-one. Following her memorial service, Al Wagstaff spoke to Kitt on two or three occasions. Based on those conversations, he told me some of the girls in the Petersen house had led "horrifically terrible lives." He was referring to Kitt and Constance, although, as indicated, they were not the only young women John exploited and abused.

While Susan certainly contributed to the dysfunctional aspects of their marriage, there is little doubt the key factor in bringing it to an end and fissuring their family was John's erratic mental health and behaviour. Of the almost twenty-three years their marriage survived in Canada, from 1952 to 1974, Al Wagstaff was part of the family for only two, 1959 and 1960. But he had the advantage of the sensitive and observant outsider. He became aware "something didn't feel right" in the Petersen home. He said on another occasion that there was "a general stress over the whole household." These malign influences had a deleterious and cumulative effect on him, to the point he felt compelled to leave in mid-December 1960, before he'd finished high school. Prior to or upon returning home to Alberni, he suffered something akin to a nervous breakdown. He described it as a bout of severe anxiety.

"It took a couple of months to get rid of it," he said.

30

THE OTHER BOOK

"I believed everything," Susan told me in 2008.

"Everything" was pretty much anything John told her. This included his claim that he had access to the Akashic records, which was the source of his reputed knowledge of past lives. Science writer John Horgan describes the Akashic records when he refers to "the theosophical concept of 'thought forms,' which holds that every thought that has passed through a human mind is stored in a kind of eternal psychic ether, which can be tapped into with proper training."[531]

When John was sitting quietly in the living room, he was presumably engaged in what Constance referred to as his "deep thinking." In 2003, I asked Colleen to describe what she recalled about John's demeanour and mannerisms when we would ask him something about reincarnation or "the philosophy," which was a compendium of his spiritual beliefs that the word *the* implied was a fount of special knowledge.

"I can see him sitting back, reflecting," she said. "He moved into a place [where he was] very comfortable, very intense." It was as though he was "tuning in." She said he had an authority in that place,

---

[531] John Horgan, *Rational Mysticism: Dispatches from the Border Between Science and Spirituality* (Boston and New York: Houghton Mifflin, 2003), 109.

and when he spoke, he would often hold his hands prayer-like in front of him, and he frequently had a cigarette between his fingers.

John sometimes referred to being put on a pedestal because of his gifts. Constance said, "he looked like he had all the answers."

He said the pedestal was a lonely place he didn't want to occupy, implying he didn't deserve it because his gifts came from God. Constance agreed her father didn't deserve to be on a pedestal, but she added pointedly that he required it. "What was missing was reality."

"What he believed may not have been objectively true," Onno told me, "but it was true to him. He needed it to be true." John's granddaughter Helen (Harald's daughter) came to a similar conclusion: "He absolutely believed [what he was saying]; he had to."

It's not hard to see how a belief that he was special, that he had answers, that he could help people, could come to justify his wholly inappropriate intrusions into other people's lives, intrusions that too often had much more to do with gratifying himself and his delusions than serving and assisting others.[532]

"Dad had an incessant need to be the best, to be the boss, to be the guy everybody looked up to," Harald said. "He had a need to be adored.... He had a need to be his own god."

According to Constance, "Dad presented himself as beyond human."

"We were fascinated with him," Susan told me in 2002. She was referring to how she and the kids, some more than others, responded to John and his perceived gifts and his occult explorations. But what they and John didn't appreciate sufficiently when they were living together is how easy it is to go astray in these areas.

Horgan paraphrases and quotes Ken Wilber, the philosopher and writer on transpersonal psychology: "Mystical maturity does not necessarily lead to psychological maturity. In fact, powerful mystical

---

[532] In *Citadels of Pride: Sexual Assault, Accountability, and Reconciliation* (New York: W. W. Norton & Company, 2021), philosopher Martha Nussbaum writes that pride is "the vice that consists of thinking that you are above others and that other people are not fully real."

experiences can retard psychological development by giving you delusions of grandeur ... [W]hen gurus proclaim themselves to be perfect masters no longer bound by ordinary human ethics 'things start to get very, very ugly. It happens all the time. *All* the time.'"[533]

Discussing the abuse of psychic abilities, Spangler says: "Invasion of privacy, the domination of one mind by another, and a completely false assumption of authority or superiority based on having psychic contact with invisible worlds are among the misuses of psychic gifts that I have seen, not to mention the distortion, the delusions, and the mental and emotional imbalance that can come when a personality is unable to integrate psychic experiences in a healthy and grounded way or becomes obsessed by their glamour."[534]

I see John in Wilber's and Spangler's words.

I also see him in these words from psychiatrist M. Scott Peck: "Psychiatrists refer to [a variety of schizophrenia] as 'grandiosity.' Such people feel as if they are—or at least should be—great and powerful when, in reality, they are utterly lacking the personal, spiritual, or intellectual assets that make for greatness. Perhaps because they are unable to bear the disparity between the reality and the feeling, they bridge the gap by plummeting into a realm of pure fantasy where they believe they have already achieved greatness."[535]

There was an alarming episode around Christmas 1968. Constance called it the "three-day coma." Susan told me John had taken to his bed for several days because a number of family members were challenging him. No one remembers the reason John was being challenged, but they do remember the fallout, some more clearly than others. Constance maintained John was "punishing" Susan with his coma-like behaviour, during which Susan phoned Constance in a panic.

---

[533] Horgan, 61-62.
[534] David Spangler, *Emergence: The Rebirth of the Sacred* (New York: Dell Publishing Co., 1984), 146. In *The Perennial Philosophy*, Aldous Huxley writes (19-20): "Psychic preoccupations may be and often are a major obstacle in the way of genuine spirituality."
[535] M. Scott Peck, M.D., *A World Waiting to Be Born: Civility Rediscovered* (New York, Toronto, London, Sydney, Auckland: Bantam, 1993), 68.

"What do I do?" Constance recalled her mother saying. "It's all my fault!"

Constance, in turn, called Hans and Harald, and the three of them plus Susan gathered later that day at Constance's house. During the meeting they talked about having John committed. But they were interrupted. Suddenly recovered, John showed up at Constance's. She said they saw him through the sheers that covered the sliding glass door and that his unexpected appearance terrified them. "He had a look in his eyes that would hold us all terrified," she added. She "thought it was magic" that he had found them, but he probably knew where to look having overheard Susan on the phone. They never told him what they'd been discussing.

Not too many years later, John's belief in reincarnation expanded to include the conviction that he had been both John the Baptist and John the beloved disciple—the soul of the former, upon his beheading, moving into the latter. This conviction was part of his rationale for leaving Susan, which, along with the turmoil that preceded his departure, maimed the family. It was during this time that he wrote his December 1974 essay in which he referred to "time which up to now has covered up something which I did many years ago." About 1983, he told Harald that he had been crazy during that period.

How far did John take his psychic and occult explorations? I don't know the answer to this question, but I feel uncomfortably bound to address it. I am uncomfortable and somewhat conflicted because, by including the provocative material I'm about to introduce, I'm dwelling on and, in some ways, reinforcing a possibility that is only that—a possibility.

In 1978, Colleen and I purchased our first home in Colwood, to the west of Victoria. We were befriended by our next-door neighbours who, about that time, bought into the owner-operator group of the new Thrifty Foods grocery store located in the Fairfield Plaza across the street from Victoria's Ross Bay Cemetery. Sometime later, a strange book was found in one of the store's dumpsters. My neighbours thought that with my background in history, I might be able to identify the book. But it was equally mysterious to me. So, I took it to John. He knew what it was: a satanic bible.

Speaking about Satanism and his father, Onno told me, "I think he had a great knowledge of that practice." Onno saw it as a natural extension of John's interests, although it is a subject about which he and his father never had a specific conversation. Onno did, however, mention two disturbing but inconclusive exchanges he had with Susan. They both concerned John and Susan's youngest child, Helen Odelia, who was born in September 1957 but died three days later due to what John said was a defective pancreas.

John told me Susan hadn't wanted this child, but Constance said that Susan, while pregnant, had a sense the baby was not well and would not survive. Moreover, unlike her pregnancy with Onno, she made no nursery preparations for the pending new arrival. After Helen Odelia died, twelve-year-old Constance spent a lot of time with her mother. It "was like she was in a trance, like she was made of stone," Constance recalled. Susan rarely spoke of Helen Odelia again.

Like Constance, Onno maintained Susan "could hide things from herself." Once, Susan mentioned to him something about lying on a table surrounded by people, which later caused him to wonder if it was a satanic ritual. Another time when he asked Susan about Satanism in connection to Helen Odelia, "she appeared to slam the door on these memories," my notes read; "he saw a refusal [on Susan's part] to go there."

A curious and perhaps contradictory fact is that the 1953–58 period is the only time in John's life when he attended a single church over an extended period: All Saints' Anglican Church in Alberni. John and the children were probably introduced to the church by their friends, Jim and Jane Lett; Susan didn't attend.[536] The vicar was the Reverend Alan Peter Horsfield, who John clearly admired based on stories he told me about him. Five years younger than John, Horsfield served in the Merchant Marine during the war and became

---

[536] Although Harald said, "Susan isn't a believer," John was able to influence her by invoking Jesus's name.

a minister about 1949. John was baptized on October 31, 1954, and confirmed on January 22, 1955. He served on the church committee in 1956 and 1957, although he missed most of the monthly meetings in 1957, according to the minutes.[537] After Al Wagstaff completed his lengthy stay at Vancouver General Hospital's tuberculosis unit, Horsfield was probably the person who arranged for Al to board with the Petersen family so he could complete high school.

Harald, who was confirmed in June 1954, has suggested something may have been amiss during the first half of the year. His reasons: John didn't attend his confirmation, and Harald recalls that John was not involved at the church for a time. Harald speculated that there may have been a falling out between his father and Horsfield, but I have found nothing to support this. Constance, who turned nine that February, recalled John taking classes from Horsfield, which were undoubtedly related to his baptism and confirmation. She added that John also researched other religions during this period, which may have been the same time when, according to Hans, John read Bible stories to the family after dinner for several months.

Although John didn't attend Harald's confirmation, he did present Harald with a remarkable painting to commemorate the occasion. It's not one of John's better paintings; the composition is secondary to the directness and force of the message. In the background three crosses stand atop snow-covered Mount Arrowsmith. The large central cross casts a shadow to the foreground, where a boy stands, outlined in light, at the intersection of the shadow cross. Given John's troubled relationship with Harald, among other factors, perhaps the figure in the painting is less representative of Harald than it is of John.

---

[537] The minutes are held at the Anglican Archives for the Diocese of British Columbia, located in Victoria.

Figure 33. Titled "Confirmation" on John's list of paintings, the painting bears the date "Jan. 1954," the month Harald turned twelve, although it apparently was not presented until the ceremony took place in June.

Was Susan's paradoxical summation of John—a man of great inner strength and no inner strength—true because he compromised himself in an important way through involvement with Satanism, or was it true for some other reason, such as his fear of being alone and his dependency on women?

He warned me away from the occult, telling me, "If you need to know something, you will know it." I am grateful for his warning. I wonder what prompted it. Was it the result of his deep interest in and involvement with the occult, which, in turn, resulted in a regretted slide into Satanism?

When Onno and I spoke about John and Satanism, he told me John believed in Satan and evil as seen in Christian thinking. "It was almost [as if he were saying], I know what I'm speaking of."

***

During the final stages of preparing this book for publication, a few features of John's life took on an emergent quality in my mind as though they contained veins of valuable ore that hadn't been revealed. I, of course, went looking for those veins, not with a pickaxe, but with the radar of reflection and intuition.

Two of these veins, representing different aspects of John's experience, seem to intersect and may have run together for years or even decades. One aspect was something John said to me more than once: We are not to have expectations of the other side, of the subtle or invisible worlds that interlace our physical world. The other aspect was the role of the mysterious minister who turned up at the hospital just before an upset John was released in December 1946.

A key problem with having expectations of the other side is that expectations can be based on a sense of entitlement.[538] I now hear

---

[538] Such expectations based on a sense of entitlement stand in marked contrast to the idea of partnering with our spiritual allies and guides, meaning that two or more beings possessing their own sovereignty and agency come together with a shared purpose and for mutual benefit and learning. Opportunities for partnering are easy to miss as they can catch people unaware. To not miss them requires openness and receptivity, while engaging with them requires discernment, respect, and gratitude. In my experience, such partnering provides a wonderful sense of support and companionship. To make what I'm saying more real, consider the notion that a writer may have a muse, which has been a commonplace idea for centuries. I certainly feel and believe I have mine.

what John said about this almost as a warning, perhaps one based on his own experience. It would not surprise me if many of John's difficulties during the 1950s, '60s, and '70s were rooted not only in downswings in his mental health but also in expectations and a feeling of entitlement based on what he felt he had suffered in his life. Likely wrapped up in this were his sense of special ability, greatness, and possibly even godliness. Perhaps when they didn't manifest sufficiently for him, he turned to Satanism in and around 1957 to try to achieve what he wanted. He was certainly astray in 1959 when Kitt, as Ann, was sent to his bed and when he tried "to fix" Constance. Moreover, it was soon after these events that he had a notable conversation with Harald, in about 1960. According to this conversation, as Harald related it to me, God had told John that he would not be happy except for the last six years of his life, because he'd abused his gifts.

As for the mysterious minister, did he fan the flames of John's sense of entitlement born of his feelings of victimization? We have no proof of this minister's existence. Perhaps he's another fictitious creation of John's, like his artistic mentor Wiertz and the German army commander with whom John claimed a close association during the last years of the war. But even if the minister did not exist, the picture of him presented by John gives us insight into John's thinking.

"You're pretty bitter, aren't you?" the minister observed after entering John's room. (This is according to my notes based on what John told me.) "If you're angry at God, then why don't you tell him you think he's a bastard?"

John said he followed the minister's advice. He told God, "It is very unfair that I'm being sent back to camp" when he presumed his internment would stretch on for an indeterminant period. He did not know he would be freed that afternoon.

When necessary, it wakes me in the middle of the night with a gentle sense of urgency tied to an offering: a solution to a problem or a new perspective on something. These welcome encounters always galvanize me and see me set to work despite the hour.

We are now faced with at least a couple of possibilities, one ordinary, another extraordinary. On one hand, it can be good to vent anger rather than deny or suppress it, although how the venting occurs matters if it is not to create additional problems. On the other hand, what if John continued from time to time to view God as a bastard and intertwined this sentiment with a sense of entitlement born of suffering and victimization? Might such feelings and views have prompted his possible involvement with Satanism? Sussing out what is real and true in all this is beyond me, but I do know that John actively pursued his deep thinking and his interest in the other side during the years after he came to Canada. If nothing else, the confluence of events in the 1957–60 period is certainly provocative.

***

After John identified the satanic bible, I thoughtlessly left it in my old bedroom at my parents' home. This upset Tad, a family member,[539] when he found out about it. In fact, it so troubled him that he resolved to get rid of the book. His first plan was to burn it in the incinerator in the backyard, but fear prevented him from following through. His anxiety was such that he felt burning on his arm, particularly around his wristwatch. It bothered him so much that he threw the watch away. Even after he had disposed of the book in a waste receptacle in the shopping village down the road, he continued to be troubled by the experience. He discussed the matter with a minister. Sometime later, he told me of his upset, and I told John. John's response was noteworthy.

"Tell Tad he's protected."

I did. And this simplest of notions proved helpful. I didn't realize how much until decades later, when Tad reminded me of how John had helped him. During the intervening years, while I remembered the discovery and identification of the book and how it had upset Tad,

---

[539] Tad is a pseudonym.

I had completely forgotten about John's message to him. Once I had delivered it, I apparently put it out of my mind. But Tad didn't forget. Quite the contrary; for him it was one of those experiences that indelibly etch themselves into memory. Twenty-plus years later, he continued to be grateful for John's four brief but crucial words of support.

"What strikes me," I wrote in earlier versions of this account, "is what John said. How many people would presume or dare to say such a thing? Was it ego and grandiosity speaking? Was it foolishness? Or was it something else: some knowledge or some intervention? Or was it, as others have suggested, simply a wise and kind response that effectively met Tad's fear and upset on their own level?"

I do not ask these questions any longer.

John's words were certainly effective, as Tad has testified. I suspect they also reflect John's faith. The idea that we are providentially held throughout our lives is a belief I have also acquired in recent years.

31

A MYSTIC CEREMONY

Toward the end of John's life, a few years after he told Harald he'd been crazy during and prior to the time he left Susan, he spoke of himself as mentally unstable. According to Onno, he felt there was something wrong with his mind. Onno detected a "new level of truth" in his father at this juncture, that John was "being more authentic." This is especially noteworthy because, of all the children, Onno had been the most consistently critical of and challenging toward John. He had never put his father on a pedestal. While most people who viewed John as something of a guru suspected he knew more than he let on, Onno was adamant John knew less than he claimed. Onno, who died in 2016 at sixty-one, told me in 2010 that since the age of nine he had viewed his father as "fake."

Hans and Constance also detected changes in John. But, unlike Onno, they were not happy with them. They blamed John's new wife, Shirley. Constance said Shirley was "simple." John had to "live on the surface with her." When John and Shirley visited Constance and her second husband at their small farm in Oliver, British Columbia, John told Constance that he had put his "deep thinking in his pocket." Both Hans and Constance told me, separately, that John had "sold out."

I don't dispute that John told Constance he had put his deep thinking in his pocket, but I don't believe it was a permanent change on his part. I know his psychic and spiritual interests continued and that he shared them with Shirley. I suspect, however, that Shirley represented a change in his life in another way. My sense is he didn't use the "psychic stuff" and purported past lives to influence her as he had done with Susan and Mary. Among the reasons Mary left him were his "manipulations and lies" and his controlling. It appears such manipulation originated with his relationship with Susan, for there is no clear indication it was a factor in his relationship with Frie.[540] If John made such a change, it would be an important aspect of the "new level of truth" Onno saw in him.

There is another instance of a more truthful John. Although he had told Harald, Constance, and probably others that he would not have to reincarnate again, he subsequently advised Harald that he would "have to come back ... because [he had] not worked out [his] karma."

Like their mother and older brothers, Onno and Constance could speak as positively about John as they did critically of him. "I wouldn't have wished for a different father," Onno told me. "I like the person I am, and he was a major, major influence of that." Onno expressed gratitude for his father and summarized his influence as follows: "to live outside the box, to question beliefs, to instill a desire for personal growth and the exploration of spiritual traditions." Constance told me, "A lot of my basic philosophy comes from him." His teachings were "a gift. They allowed my spirit to grow." She said she remembers him mostly by "positive conversations," and noted that "usually, conversations with him ended on a wonderful high." In 2010, in the epilogue of an earlier version of this book, I wrote: "Despite [his] weakness and the damage that he did, there is also what he helped inspire in a number of others: a ... receptivity to a surpassing loving connectedness." I still believe this.

---

[540] Was John the primary architect of the scheme he and Frie pursued in furtherance of their divorce, that he'd admit adultery in return for her not contesting custody of Hans? If so, did he manipulate Frie to obtain her agreement to participate? It was Frie who backed out of their plan when she signed a document that disclosed their intention to deceive the court.

The mystical experience John and I shared also occurred during the "new level of truth" period. It happened one evening in his living room. I think John and I were alone, but it's possible Shirley was there too. The experience engulfed my attention. It was virtually all-consuming, but as I recall it now, I have a vague sense of Shirley on the periphery of my memory standing to one side of the experience.[541] John was sitting in his chair and I was standing facing him about eight feet away. I was about to take my leave when I became aware that something was happening. Something immaterial yet definite was behind and above me, cloaking me, and reaching out toward John at the same time. It was sublime and wondrous, a tangible yet transcendental manifestation of love. Almost simultaneous with my awareness of it, I said to John, "I feel very close to you right now."

"That's because Jesus is here," he replied.

I had no sense of a particular soul or identity. I was entirely caught up in the surpassing marvel of those moments. The sense of being cloaked, of a sublime presence and lovely warmth enfolding me while also reaching out to John, was the essence of it. It is notable that when John first described Jesus coming to him in the dark cell in 1945, he said it "felt warm ... like someone putting a cloak around him." I had forgotten this when I first described my experience with him. *Showings* is an account by Dame Julian of Norwich (1342–circa 1423) of sixteen visions or revelations she experienced. In it she writes of "our Lord" that "He is our clothing, for he is that love which wraps and enfolds us."[542]

But was what I experienced truly a mystical event? Or was it another of John's manipulations? Close to twenty years later, when I first talked at length with Constance, one of the subjects she raised was her father's interest in hypnosis. It fascinated him, she said.

---

[541] I suspect Shirley was in the kitchen rather than in the living room or in the adjoining dining room. A pitched cathedral ceiling covered all these areas. While walls separated the living room and dining room from the kitchen and adjoining eating area, these walls were about eight feet tall, meaning that all these areas flowed together above that height.

[542] "Showings" (Short text), Chapter iv, *Julian of Norwich: SHOWINGS* (New York, Ramsey, New Jersey, Toronto: Paulist Press, 1978), 130.

"Do you remember this?" she asked me as we sat in her living room. She was twiddling her thumbs in a slow, deliberate manner, rotating them forward for a short time, then backward, then forward again, and so on.

And I did remember. It was something John sometimes did while he talked. I hadn't thought of it in ages, perhaps not since I'd seen him do it. Constance also reminded me he would rub his thigh in a slow and repetitive manner. He employed these techniques to mesmerize people and make them vulnerable to suggestion, she claimed. Onno said the thumb-twiddling was "a form of entrainment" to bring about similar thinking. He said John used programming techniques and had an instinctive understanding of making people believe. As to John's explanation—"That's because Jesus is here"—Onno contended that John had "incorporated his belief system into his interpretation of the experience."

I was never voluntarily hypnotized by John. Nor do I have any sense of having been involuntarily hypnotized by him. As far as I can remember, the only time the subject of hypnosis came up was when he told me the story about the guard being hypnotized at the Muiden camp when he was interned there. But after Constance prompted my recall of John twiddling his thumbs in that distinctive way and rubbing his thigh, I could not help but wonder if there was a connection between one of these entrainment techniques and the marvellous experience of being cloaked that I had in his presence. Had the thumb-twiddling occurred earlier that evening? Had John used it to hypnotize me? Was my experience the product of implanted suggestion? While my memory of it continued to be strong and deeply positive, it now resided under a shadow of some doubt.

In 2010, I investigated my doubt and questions by consulting two psychologists, Dennis Payne and Mark Jackman, who sometimes used hypnosis in their practices.[543] I also consulted a transformational coach and energy healer who does not use hypnosis, but who, as a twelve-

---

[543] Dennis Payne died in July 2011.

year-old, received hypnosis to successfully treat a speech impairment. I read to each of them an earlier version of the above information starting with "The mystical experience John and I shared" and ending with "it now resided under a shadow of some doubt."

The two psychologists offered similar assessments.

"I don't think he hypnotized you," was Dennis Payne's conclusion.

Mark Jackman was definitive. It was "not hypnosis," he said.

At the same time, they both agreed that the thumb-twiddling could be used to introduce an altered state of consciousness. Payne said the thumb-twiddling "would be a way to get a person's attention" preliminary to "trance induction" or "attentional absorption." Jackman agreed. He used the term "hypnotic induction," which "takes a person out of the normal range of expected social behavior." He said, "You can set up conditions for something like that." The coach/healer also felt that John may have opened the door or prepared the way for the experience I had, but she stressed it was my experience. She judged the experience genuine because it was so positive and loved-based (as opposed to fear-based).

"I think you had a special, special experience," Payne remarked. "I trust you had a genuine experience."

The event "was real," Jackman told me. "You certainly experienced it. Your description is exactly how mystical experiences occur."

The coach/healer recommended that I expand the either/or, mysticism/manipulation dichotomy I had posited because there is a whole range of possibilities between those poles. She said she had the experience of being cloaked many times, always in conjunction with finishing a project or course (e.g., a developmental stage in the healing arts). Her description prompted me to liken each of her cloaking experiences to "a ceremony of completion." Then it occurred to me that this phrase might also apply to the mystical experience John and I shared, that it was a special acknowledgement of his central role in my life and, in a sense, that I was taking my leave of him.

In February 2021, when I followed up with Mark Jackman for permission to refer to him by name, he advised that the feeling of "divine love" is characteristic of mystical experiences, whereas a sense of deep relaxation and well-being is typical of hypnosis. This distinction between the two states had immediate resonance for me based on an experience of hypnosis I'd had with Dennis Payne, circa 1993 or 1994. Learning this difference also had the effect of removing any lingering doubt I had about the mystical experience I shared with John.

Remember my alternate title for this book, *Captain Aye Aye and the Power of Belief*? Where Captain Aye Aye typifies the laughable downside of that power, my mystical experience with John represents its mysterious, inspiring, and inspiriting upside.

EPILOGUE

There can be no genuine hope of recovery and renewal for either an individual or an institution without an honest facing up to the past.... truth demands my allegiance over everything—truth acted upon in love.

—Tom Harpur, *The Pagan Christ: Recovering the Lost Light*

For a human being, the truth is and must remain entirely subjective.

—Randall Sullivan, *The Miracle Detective*

The soul of all things follows the one-pointedness of a true human being as thread follows needle.

—Rumi, *The Soul of Rumi*

THE EVOLUTION OF A BOOK TITLE

Back in the day, when John told me his story, we spent some time considering a couple of options for the title of the book I would eventually write. I proposed *A Kind of Glory*, taken from John

Steinbeck's *East of Eden*, but John didn't like it. My next proposal, *Of Love and Power*, was a winner. It came from Alan Paton's *Cry, the Beloved Country*: "When a man loves, he seeks no power, and therefore he has power"—a statement that seared itself into my consciousness when I first read it in my Grade 12 English class. For years after our decision, the acronym OLAP was my private code for the book to be.

When the rose-coloured glasses I had been wearing concerning John finally came off, I realized the title of the book had to change. As Colleen adroitly observed, John's behaviour often used power and control as substitutes for love and did so most egregiously on those occasions when he showed little, if any, consideration for the young women he manipulated and abused.

Although I don't remember precisely when *A Snake on the Heart* became the new title, since that time, it has always seemed the obvious choice, given the evocative image John said he carried with him during the war because of the "double game" he played. It was only much later that I realized the snake, with its multiple meanings, could also be applied to me and my story, the developmental stages of which often occurred in tandem with progress I made on John's story.

THE PAGES OF JOHN'S BOOK

John told me numerous times that, as he went through the first half of his life, his constant plea was "Please, God, don't let the pages of my book be blank." He gave his plea a heroic tenor, for he also repeatedly said that, despite the many hardships he had suffered, he would not change anything that had happened to him. At some point during the long process of sorting out his story, the meaning of this supplication shifted in my mind. What I heard instead of stoic heroism was fear and regret: fear of blank pages and regret for lost and squandered opportunities. This fear was intertwined with his victimhood, romanticism, and grandiosity, those qualities that had spawned a veritable cascade of tall tales over the decades.

During much of the 1980s, when Colleen ran a family daycare for preschoolers in our home, John would often come for lunch on Mondays and stay during nap time that followed. Colleen had the impression from the last of these visits prior to his death that he was disappointed, particularly in not having devoted more time to art and painting, but also by how things had turned out.

Despite John's blighted personal history—his role in the SD and the Holocaust and the sexual and psychological abuse and suffering he imposed on others—there is no doubt that he also helped some people during the war and later as a social worker. While some of his social-work colleagues were critical of him and his lack of formal education, my eulogy quoted a description of him as more than a social worker, as the granddad to a lot of kids, a family patriarch you could always turn to, for many of the troubled kids he helped kept coming back to see him when they were older. But, in 2021, the person who provided this description in January 1988 would no longer endorse it (and has requested not to be identified in this book). Having heard disturbing opinions during the interim, this individual now harbours deep uncertainty and grave doubts about John.

Although essentially repudiated, the granddad-to-a-lot-of-kids assessment did exist for a time and is probably the best possible interpretation that could be given to John's life as a social worker from 1963 to 1980. Colleen was certainly one of John's grateful and admiring clients. She said he had "real wisdom" and was "hugely influential" in her life when she was fifteen. But when she learned how his self-serving distortions and lies broke trust and selfishly and gravely damaged the lives of others, she was furious with him. Given the repeal of the once laudatory granddad assessment, it appears that aspects of the ugly, hidden parts of John's life that have been revealed in these pages had been bubbling to the surface for years in the form of rumours and conjecture.

Along with Colleen and my parents, John was one of the most important and influential people in my life. He both honoured and manipulated me when he made me the custodian of his story. When

I started to see him more clearly in the mid-1990s, my sense of being honoured and privileged was largely replaced, especially by 2002, by a near compulsion to learn the truth and to bring multiple perspectives to bear on his story. While the broad strokes of what he told me were true, his telling was polluted with numerous falsehoods and omissions, which I had to identify for myself. In summary, John's journey shifted in my mind from a remarkable story to a cautionary tale, one that is bizarre and compelling and ultimately stark and mysterious.

"He didn't practise what he preached," Susan told me in 1995.

According to Constance, he agreed with this assessment, at least some of the time. She paraphrased him in the following way: "Do as I say, but not as I do—because I can't live up to it. But what I say is important."

Although Susan told me numerous times, "I still love him," she also said he was a "very complicated and disturbed man [who] created a lot of disharmony and trouble [and] caused so much grief and misery in his own family"; he was a "very strange man, very pacifist, a real con man. He could talk white black."

"How can a man—who so often spoke of 'love and truth'—live the life he did?" Miek asked me in a letter in 2004. "Didn't he ever get in conflict with the moral side of his doings?" She added that when he went to Canada "he had the opportunity to start this 'new life.' But gradually he went overboard and brought misery to a lot of people."

In addition to claiming academic credits he had not earned and achievements that were not his, some of John's fictitious stories were his way of adding drama and flair to the pages of his book, as though what he had actually done and experienced was not enough. He was apparently able to influence the person who prepared the prosecution document of November 14, 1946, for it makes no mention of John's disastrous sea career, which is reinvented as a success story and includes an untrue statement about John holding a "Certificate Chief

Mate in deep sea navigation."[544] Hans's suggestion that some of his father's dubious assertions about his time at sea may have been borrowed from Constant's more successful nautical career may be true. This possibility is consistent with my conclusion that John pirated a portion of his friend Koos's work history to add flesh to the bones of his lie that his work for the SS was to instruct new recruits. While the latter case was a deliberate cover-up, most of his tall tales were exercises in compensatory behaviour: They reflected his insecurity and his need for validation and recognition. Behind his charm and grandiosity, he was a needy individual who wanted to belong.

"He was a very lonely man," according to Susan. "He said he always felt like he was an island."

The idea that John borrowed details from Constant's life to embellish his own intertwines with another idea: John may have felt he suffered in comparison to his younger brother. When he told me he felt torn during the war by his conflicting loyalties to the Netherlands and to Germany, he said, "It was like having to kill your brother to save your father." This extraordinary analogy has mythic dimensions, especially in the light of his brother's name: Constant. Presumably, the father to be saved was their biological father who died when John was barely three, the father he idealized and about whom he told heroic and highly romanticized stories.

Somewhere along the way, in response to the different traumas he experienced during the 1920s and '30s, the fantasy he relied on for

---

[544] Per the prosecution document of November 14, 1946, John not only blamed his initial sea career problems on his nationality, he also extended the length of that career from a few months to more than three and a half years: "Dutch companies did not want to hire him, being German. He then tried German companies; because of his Dutch certificate they did not want him either. After that he [did] a variety of work [with] Hudig & Veder [until] May 1940." Had the person who prepared the prosecution document done a more thorough review of what he termed "the case," he would have noted that John admitted in his collaborator statement of October 29, 1946, that he only made "one trip as [an] apprentice deck officer" and had been told he "would never [be] hired as a regular deck officer," statements that contradict assertions reported as facts in the prosecution document.

succour apparently became habitual. Although he was a genuine victim in some ways, this habit established a pattern of deluding and re-victimizing himself, and sometimes damaging others in the process. Speaking of his father's neediness, Onno told me it was the basis for a lot of John's "inner contradictions and motivations and his manipulations."

From time to time in these pages, I have asked if some of John's tall tales may have been the result of alternate realities he created for himself. One example is his claim that he jumped ship in Canada in 1933. Another is his elaborate story of his fear-induced flight from his German army unit in The Hague in the winter of 1945, his hiding with another German army unit during the last months of the war, and his arrest, trial, death sentence, and timely liberation by Canadian soldiers.

These and other apparent alternate realities were prompted and fed by various emotional storms that beset him: his fraught relationships with his mother and stepfather; the loneliness and isolation he felt at times growing up; his troubled experiences at sea; his mother's stinging criticism that he was in danger of becoming "a good-for-nothing" following the demise of his sea career; the sense he may have been unflatteringly compared to Constant who lived a steadier, more conventional life; the apparent breakdown he suffered following the end of his marriage to Frie, much of which became "a blank," he claimed; how, when he and Susan became a couple, he seemingly projected onto her the emotional turmoil he had experienced after his marriage—that she had supposedly been on "the brink of losing all interest in life" following a nonexistent love affair he claimed she had while working as an au pair in France; the fear he felt prior to and following his interrogations by the German army and the SS during the last year or so of the war; the paranoia he said he suffered during 1947 and 1948, following his release from internment; and the possibility he experienced more memory gaps in the late 1940s and early 1950s prior to leaving the Netherlands, in particular regarding his adored mentor, Timperley, who, I suspect, may have challenged him in ways he didn't appreciate.

THE TRIUMPH OF FANTASY: KEEPING THE TRUTH AT BAY

John once told me that, to be an artist, to have a chance at succeeding as an artist, you need to be prepared to dedicate your life completely to that pursuit. Constance believed that her father's false narrative of being a student at the National Art Academy for a year and being offered a Prix de Rome bursary to finish his studies in Italy represented the life he would have preferred to have lived. But while John tried to live an artist's life prior to and likely, at times, during his marriage to Frie, he was not successful. He was tripped up by circumstances and his responses to them. Those circumstances included the global depression, his lack of a practical means to sustain himself financially, and emotional factors tied to his childhood and youth.

In May 1976, when he began to tell me about his life, he concluded our third session by noting that, since he'd been a child, he'd had a special woman in his mind. She always loved and cared for him and he trusted her and "wanted to serve" her. In November 1984, he added that "life was like a love, a beautiful woman, but [he always] got rejected." Nonetheless, "he never got bitter, he always stayed in love." This attitude empowered the fable of his success at the National Art Academy, where he not only said he found his niche but also sacrificed the illusory bursary on a point of principle: his defence of his right to fall in love. This was a re-creation and favourable distortion of what he said occurred when he married Frie, namely that he overrode the advice of people who cared for him, ploughed quickly and blindly ahead, and crashed headlong into disaster. The fable insulated him from "a failed marriage [and a] child born too soon," a breakdown, and the fear he would not amount to anything.

Such alternate worlds were havens of solace and succour for him. They were like his "dreams of a perfect woman," which, he told me, were "safe from life's harsh realities and wouldn't get shot through with holes." But these alternate worlds prevented him from seeing vital truths about himself and denied him the opportunity to embrace those truths as necessary abrasives in the service of self-discovery.

The truth is critical to John's story. To know ourselves, to see clearly, we must nurture and protect the truth within ourselves, especially when it comes to our limitations and failings, for, without that clear seeing, distortion and self-deception will keep us from the bedrock of self-knowledge and fundamentally inhibit our ability to discover and adhere to our best selves.

John believed each of us has a soul, but he didn't give adequate attention to his. To find and embrace our soul, to travel with our soul in fidelity, we must also find and acknowledge the truth of who we are and adhere, with a warrior's devotion, to that hard-won and precious truth.

INNER KNOWING AND THE NEED TO REFRAIN FROM DISTORTING REALITY

In *Quiet Heroes: True Stories of the Rescue of Jews by Christians in Nazi-Occupied Holland*, André Stein writes, "The rescuers insisted time and time again that what they did had nothing to do with heroism. Instead, it all had to do with who they were and what, being who they were, was required of them in order to remain unchanged." They did what they did because of inner knowing and a requirement that they act in alignment and fidelity with that knowing. One of the rescuers profiled by Stein says, "I am involved in helping Jews because a voice inside me told me that I had to do it…. that's all there is to it. If I disobeyed that voice, I would no longer be me."[545]

In his June 1951 letter, John intimates he possessed some of the same spiritual bedrock. "Many times I was able to do something for the Dutch people, that I loved, although it had exterminated me," he wrote. "I don't want to make the impression that I was a sort of hero, but I have always done that, which I held for my duty. I could not do otherwise!" But in the same paragraph, immediately before these sentences, is this, which I have quoted before: "Whatever I did in the

---

[545] Stein, 306, 20.

war, it was always a result of a position, into which I was forced, and that I have always tried to choose the least worse of the two!" Thus, while he claims he always did his duty and couldn't have done otherwise, he also states he was "forced" into situations where all he could do was try "to choose the least worse" option.

If we accept John's claim that during the war he was trapped and compromised by his circumstances, presumably related to the roundup of the Jews, no such excuse is available to him for the sexual and psychological abuse he inflicted on several young women, including his daughters. The gaping void on this subject, the lack of comment on it in his subsequent writing, reminds me of what Spangler says about "a completely false assumption of authority or superiority based on having psychic contact with invisible worlds," and that, as Wilber notes, such contact "can retard psychological development."

I remember a time visiting at John's, about 1980, when he quietly talked about Constance, who I had not met at that point. Constance was his troubled and unhappy daughter who had mental health problems, I recall him saying, as if he were removed from the situation, as if he were saying with cool dispassion that wasn't really sadness that it's too bad things have to be this way. The memory is one of those things that has been bearing down on me, seemingly trying to make something known or at least clearer. What strikes me now is the charade he performed about his troubled and unhappy daughter, a charade that said it was an unfortunate situation that had nothing whatsoever to do with him or with the cascading and compounding events of his relationship with Constance over the last twenty years. It is a memory of his free choice to deny the truth. But that free choice was also circumscribed because he was a trapped man, trapped because he was not prepared to face and admit what he'd done. He was caught in a trap of his own making. Such traps are deepening pits of malevolence because that is what is served by the long-term and repeated expression of the false.

Yet despite being trapped by an unknown number of issues in his life, John's spiritual focus persisted and centred him when the trapping, threatening issues lay dormant. On March 7, 1972, his fifty-seventh birthday, he wrote an aspirational poem:

> *Let my words reflect your wisdom, o God,*
> *so they can penetrate*
> *the wall of misunderstanding,*
> *that separates me*
> *from another human being.*
> *Let my silences be deep and watchfull [sic],*
> *so I can comprehend*
> *with my mind, heart and soul,*
> *the whispered needs and confessions.*
> *Let me never condemn,*
> *judge or interfere,*
> *with another life's unfolding,*
> *for I do not even know*
> *the purpose of my own destiny.*
> *Let there always be*
> *enough warmth and space in my Self,*
> *to welcome and shelter*
> *the homeless longing of the lost ones,*
> *and*
> *let me never feel lonely,*
> *when the wayfarer*
> *leaves on his journey again,*
> *but may I release him with love*
> *in his search*
> *for fullfilment [sic].*

On October 10, 1974, thirty-one months later and several months after he left Susan, he wrote:

How to be free.

Come to involve yourself with activities and people you don't really enjoy. You know what they are. Your deeper self tells you of the things you do from a false sense of duty, from false loyalty, from public pressure, from trying to please unpleasant people so that they will be pleased with you.

Learn to live as you like by no longer living a life you dislike.

But you must rebel against your own mental chains and nothing else.

No offensive individual and no social illness can keep you down.

We are responsible for our own chains and we are capable of our own liberation.

One is often enslaved by false ideas of what it means to live your own life—ideas, incidentally, imposed upon you by a confused society.

When you really live as <u>you</u> like, you are free and genuinely happy.

Man seeks his inward unity, but his real progress depends on his capacity to refrain from distorting reality in accordance with his desires.

How conscious or aware was John of the wisdom contained in this short piece, especially its last sentence? If he was conscious of it at all, I don't think that consciousness lasted long, given the tumult of that period, particularly the turmoil in his relationship with Susan and how it affected other members of his family. I suspect he channelled this information and recorded it through automatic writing. In it, especially the last sentence, I suspect we are hearing the voice of his soul.

When he died, about 11:00 p.m. on January 8, 1988, John and Shirley were making love.[546] Why should he have had such a nice, quick death? Constance wondered. She didn't think it was fair. There is another question: Why were John and I privileged with our joint mystical experience? Although I agree with John that he had not worked out his karma, I believe he will have to address it. I suspect my use of the future tense here is not entirely accurate. I suspect John has been addressing and will continue to have to address his karma. (See Appendix 3–John Petersen and the post-mortem realms.) I also suspect that commonplace judgments of this world are not necessarily those of the next. I cannot explain the experience of that wondrous cloaking aura we shared beyond what I have already written, except to add that I view it as a dispensation of grace and love from a surpassing power.

FROM EULOGY TO A NEW COMPLETION

When I wrote John's eulogy, I was alone in my office in an empty building during the dark of night, relying exclusively on what he'd told me. Now, after much consultation and research, over many years, I have presented him in a fuller and more rounded form, achieving what I believe is a reasonable approximation of the truth.[547] I've also described how wrestling with him and his story has contributed to my life. The snake that oppressed him with the truth

---

[546] John's official date of death is January 9, 1988. In the aftermath of John's death, Shirley told Colleen that she and John had been making love when he died; Colleen told me. Shirley—who died at sixty-one, thirteen months later when, according to a newspaper account, "an unoccupied truck rolled over her ... in a freak accident"—probably told others as well. John and I had the same family doctor. At an appointment with the doctor in January 2006, I mentioned the book I was writing and who it was about. "He died having sex," the doctor said, recalling this distinctive detail. "He was a charmer," the doctor added, "probably a real lady's man."

[547] During the final months of completing this book, I encountered new information on a couple of occasions that contradicted or undercut more of John's stories and claims, which perhaps indicates that the phrase "reasonable approximation" should be downgraded to "rough approximation of the truth."

of his falseness became for me a symbol of healing and growth. Where John was obviously the protagonist in his own life, he and his story became antagonists in mine. At the same time, surrounding all this is the mystery of the mystical dimension and our shared experience. That dimension and our connection to it is the true source of the love and power that he wanted to be the title of the book by which he would be remembered.[548]

Despite his grievous failings, I am grateful to John, the companion of my long novitiate, for what he added to my life. The snake that mesmerized and trapped him helped me to find my way.

---

[548] As incarnate souls, it is my understanding that human beings also have the capacity to act with love and power and that this capacity is inherent to their sovereignty and agency, which they must discover and develop in conjunction with their souls.

AUTHOR'S NOTE

As mentioned in the prologue, I made 118 pages of notes during my sessions with John in 1976. These were supplemented with additional notes based on subsequent sessions, mostly in 1984 and 1985. My notes occasionally include direct quotations. More commonly, they consist of my paraphrasing what John told me. In finalizing the book for publication, I've generally sought to use John's original point of view, although in a few cases, whether in relation to John or another interlocutor, I do reference "my notes" directly.

My additional human sources consisted of twelve other members of the Petersen family, as well as another fourteen individuals, nonfamily members, who knew John. I had more than 250 in-person and telephone sessions with these people. My sessions with five of them, principally John's son Harald, were supplemented with numerous email exchanges.

With documentary sources, such as John's 1951 letter and the collaborator statements he and his brothers, Constant and Wim, gave to Dutch officials during internment after the war, I have preserved the original quotations, so spelling and style may be inconsistent in the book. In rare instances where I have not done this, as with the translation of John's April 1944 Dutch SS Intelligence Service report on Pieter Heerema, I have identified the exception and explained why I made it (see footnotes 238 and 571).

Preparing the book for publication, my editors and I found and corrected numerous errors. Mistakes have a disconcerting way of turning up on what, until discovery, had appeared to be unblemished pages. I am responsible for any errors not found.

A Snake on the Heart is a biography with a lot of uncertainty attached to it, which is why I viewed the researching and writing of it as a pursuit of truth and one reason why the word *mystery* is in the first subtitle. Perhaps I could have achieved greater certainty with more research, but I am mindful of historian Barbara W. Tuchman's wise observation, "One must stop before one has finished; otherwise, one will never stop and never finish."[549] I'm hopeful that the book's publication will prompt more disclosures about John; in particular, his attitudes and actions during the Second World War, and information and insight from people who knew him in Canada, for better or worse, including his possible involvement with Satanism. If new revelations contradict some of my conclusions, so be it. The pursuit of truth—or, less grandly, of a better understanding—goes on.

---

[549] Douglas E. Abrams, "Historian Barbara W. Tuchman on the 'Art of Writing' (Part II)," *Precedent,* Winter 2015, accessed October 18, 2021, 18, https://scholarship.law.missouri.edu/cgi/viewcontent.cgi?article=1873&context=facpubs.

APPENDICES

APPENDIX 1

PIETER SCHELTE HEEREMA

(Further to Chapter 12)

Pieter Schelte Heerema (1908–81) was a Dutch member of the Waffen SS who claimed to have "switched sides and joined the resistance in 1943." His relationship with the resistance and the handling of his collaboration case by the Dutch courts in 1946 are both subjects of controversy. In 1947, he returned to Venezuela to continue his career as a marine engineer. In 1963, he went home to the Netherlands where he pioneered the development and expansion of its offshore oil industry.[550]

He became a figure of controversy once again in the twenty-first century when his son, Edward Heerema, owner of the Swiss-based Allseas Group, sought to honour his father's marine-engineering legacy by naming the world's largest construction vessel the *Pieter Schelte*. Given Pieter Heerema's Nazi past, this provoked public outcries in 2008 and again in early 2015 when the vessel was being completed, at which time Allseas relented and

---

[550] Toby Sterling, Associated Press Writer, "Dutch outcry over naming giant ship after Nazi," *San Francisco Chronicle*, November 7, 2008 (switched sides). "The troubled life of offshore lifting pioneer Pieter Schelte Heerema," *Energy Global News* website, June 2, 2019 — http://www.energyglobalnews.com/the-troubled-life-of-offshore-lifting-pioneer-pieter-schelte-heerema/ — accessed May 12, 2020 (Venezuela; 1947; marine engineer; pioneer). Ed Vulliamy, "Jewish outrage as ship named after SS war criminal arrives in Europe," *The Guardian*, January 24, 2015 (returned).

renamed the ship *Pioneering Spirit*, keeping the initials of Pieter Schelte.[551]

While working for Henk Feldmeijer's Dutch SS Intelligence Service during the Second World War, John Petersen compiled information and wrote a short report on Heerema, dated April 26, 1944, after Heerema had allegedly switched sides, disappeared, and been arrested in Switzerland the month before. According to the report, Heerema "was a member of the N.S.N.A.P., but joined the Dutch SS after it was founded" in May 1940. The report indicates that he and John knew each other. It states that Feldmeijer, who was also leader of the Dutch SS, sent Heerema to Munich at the end of 1940 "to appraise S.S. trainees [possibly including John] slated to become officers." When Heerema returned to the Netherlands, he "became 'Standaardleider' of the 'Standaard 4' [in which John served]." During this period, "he occupied himself with gathering information about [NSB party leader A. A.] Mussert," an activity that may also have involved John.[552]

At the start of the war, Pieter was "very pro-German" and "very anti-communist."[553] "The German race is the model," a report on a speech he gave in 1941 quotes him as saying. "The Jewish race, by comparison, is parasitic ... therefore the Jewish question must be

---

[551] *Energy Global News* article (world's largest; renamed). Sterling ("new ship [is] to be used for laying oil pipes and decommissioning North Sea oil rigs"). Vulliamy (Swiss-based; "a pipelayer for the oil and gas industry"). Mark Odell, "Shell to use ship named after Nazi war criminal," *Financial Times*, February 5, 2015. "Dutch owners change name of vessel called after Nazi," *The Times of Israel*, February 6, 2015.
[552] The report is in Dutch National Archives CABR file 91103.
[553] Email of June 11, 2009, from Sierk Plantinga, Dutch National Archives, to the author. According to Ian Gallagher, "Nazi millions and the Royals' favourite British fizz: His bubbly has beaten Bollinger to be named the world's best, but the man behind Nyetimber is son of an SS war criminal," *Daily Mail*, February 12, 2017, "Pieter expressed fervent support of Nazism." Vulliamy quotes historian David Barnouw saying Heerema was "a member of a small fascist party before the war, but was in Venezuela when the Germans invaded. [Heerema] saw it as a reason to return." Ton Biesemaat says Heerema belonged to the virulently anti-Semitic Dutch National Socialist Workers Party (NNSAP)—see Ton Biesemaat, "Your tax money and the Fourth Reich," accessed May 18, 2009, www.tonbiesemaat.nl.

resolved in every Aryan country."⁵⁵⁴ Different sources make contradictory statements about his time with the SS. According to the Dutch National Archives, he trained at Sennheim in 1941 from August 29 until October, and then at Klagenfurt until March 1942, when he "was [sent] to occupied Russia."⁵⁵⁵ Although he said he "never [saw] action in Russia," a 2015 *Financial Times* article maintains he "saw active service with the elite 5th Panzer Division Wiking in 1941 and 1942 in the former Yugoslavia and on the eastern front near Rostov and the Caucasus."⁵⁵⁶

Heerema's rank in the SS is another subject of conflicting information. A 2017 *Daily Mail* article says that "he rose rapidly to become an Untersturmführer—the equivalent of a second lieutenant."⁵⁵⁷ Although the article doesn't give dates, this statement may align with the contention in Petersen's report that Heerema was the SS Standaardleider of Standaard 4 in 1941. Moreover, Heerema presumably was an SS officer when Feldmeijer sent him on his review mission to Munich in late 1940. Petersen's report also indicates that Heerema "was an 'S.S.-Onderstormleider in the Dutch S.S.'" prior to his dishonourable discharge. But, according to the Dutch National Archives, Heerema, while at Sennheim, "entered the Waffen SS on 26-10-1941" and about the same time "accepted a one-year appointment as SS-Mann." The Dutch National Archives also states that "Heerema was never a commissioned Officer in the SS; he held the rank of Pionier, an equivalent to an ordinary soldier (private)."⁵⁵⁸

In addition, the Dutch National Archives advised me that Heerema was "suddenly dismissed" from the SS on June 26, 1942. He

---

⁵⁵⁴ For Heerema quotation, see Sterling or Odell or Gallagher. Sterling and Odell say the speech was given in 1941. Biesemaat says the speech was given at "the Hague Odeon" in June 1941.
⁵⁵⁵ Email from Plantinga.
⁵⁵⁶ Email from Plantinga (never saw action). Odell, *Financial Times*. Plantinga's email says Heerema "was placed in the SS-Pionier Ersatz Battillon, 1st Engineering Cy."
⁵⁵⁷ Gallagher, *Daily Mail*.
⁵⁵⁸ Email from Plantinga.

was sent back to the Netherlands where, on behalf of the SS, he worked for the Nederlandsche Oost Compagnie (Netherlands East Company) from November 1942 to June 1943 as "a technical director" responsible "for arresting Dutch men who were forced to work in the Baltic areas of Eastern Europe occupied by the Nazis; many hundreds died." Historian David Barnouw states that Heerema "commandeered 4,000 for forced labour."[559]

When Heerema married Erna Kühnen in December 1942, Hanns Albin Rauter, the head of the SS in the Netherlands, was the guest of honour.[560] *Storm*, the Dutch SS magazine, ran "a cover story of the marriage."[561] Six months later, however, after Stalingrad and the turning of the war's tide, Heerema joined "the resistance-espionage group 'Vogel-Reinaert',"[562] although he continued working for the Nazis until he had "a falling out with his German superiors in August 1943" when he "disappeared."[563] Sought by the Gestapo, he fled in March 1944 via Paris to Switzerland where he was arrested and interned that same month.[564]

According to the Dutch National Archives, "The Special Criminal Court in The Hague (Bijzonder Gerechtshof Den Haag) sentenced [Heerema] on 25 July 1946 to two years in prison, with reduction in sentence for time already served (since 29 August 1945). The court took in account his SS-past, but also his turn to the resistance in 1943 and the internment in Switzerland since March 1944. The Court of Appeal (Bijzondere Raad van Cassatie) agreed with the reasoning of

---

[559] Email from Plantinga. Gallagher (technical director). Vulliamy (November 1942 to June 1943; Barnouw quote). "Pieter Schelte Heerema," Wikipedia, accessed May 18, 2020, https://nl.wikipedia.org/wiki/Pieter_Schelte_Heerema (many hundreds died in Baltic areas).
[560] Gallagher. *Energy Global News* article.
[561] "Pieter Schelte Heerema," Wikipedia.
[562] Email from Plantinga (resistance-espionage group).
[563] Email from Plantinga. Sterling (falling out; disappeared). Vulliamy quotes an Allseas's document that says "Heerema lost his sympathy for the Nazi regime and defected in June 1943."
[564] Email from Plantinga (March 1944; Gestapo; fled; interned). Sterling (March 1944; arrested).

the Special Criminal Court but in its sentence of 4 November 1946 reduced the years in prison from two years into one year and two months, with the effect that Heerema then was released."[565]

A 2008 Associated Press story in the *San Francisco Chronicle* says the courts "recognized his unspecified but 'very important' services to the resistance between August 1943 and March 1944."[566] The 2017 *Daily Mail* article also states that "several resistance fighters testified in his favour" and that "information he collected was used by the Allies."[567] But the 2015 *Financial Times* article maintains Heerema's renunciation of the Nazis and his work for the resistance have been "discredited."[568] Barnouw has called Heerema's trial a "farce" and, as reported in the *Daily Mail* article, "said the resistance group [Heerema] assisted comprised 'about two people' and served as a cover for collaborating Dutchmen who had a sudden 'change of heart'." On the other hand, Professor E. J. H. Schrage, another historian, contends "the resistance unit was 'legitimate' and says [Heerema's] sentence was justified."[569]

John spoke to his Intelligence Service supervisor, Gerardus Andreas Scholte, about various people, including Pieter and Tine Heerema. Sometime later, according to John's statement of April 22, 1947, "SCHOLTE came to me with someone from the S.D. The S.D. man asked me to go with him to Binnenhof 7 in 's-Gravenhage [The Hague] to gather more information about Piet HEEREMA. This I did and compiled a transcript of the conversations."[570] Here is John's report on Heerema, quoted in full:

> There has been a lot of talk in the S.S. lately about a certain Heerema, who until recently was an "S.S.-Onderstormleider in the Dutch S.S."

---

[565] Email from Plantinga.
[566] Sterling.
[567] Gallagher.
[568] Odell.
[569] Gallagher.
[570] Dr. M. Blauw's attachment, p. 3, to her email of December 9, 2009, to the author. John's statement of April 22, 1947 (DNA, CABR 91103).

Generally speaking, it is said that H. went into hiding after he was summoned for the "S.S. Kriegsgericht" [military justice] by Rauter. At this moment it is said he is the leader of an organisation helping people to go into hiding in the Achterhoek [an area in the province of Gelderland near the German border]. Heerema was suspected of espionage and of undisciplined behaviour concerning the marriage of S.S.-Obersturmführer Gerhards.

An acquaintance of H. told me that H. had said that he was imprisoned shortly before May 1940 in South America, suspected of espionage for Germany. By bribing some eminent persons, he managed to flee to Europe by clipper. He arrived in the Netherlands via the Balkans.

At first, he was a member of the N.S.N.A.P., but joined the Dutch S.S. after it was founded. At the end of 1940, as he told, he was sent by the leader to München to appraise S.S. trainees slated to become officers. After his short stay there he returned to the Netherlands and became "Standaardleider" of "Standaard 4". During this same period, he occupied himself with gathering information on Mussert, about whom he possessed a complete file.

He avoided serving at the front for a long time, but he finally went when ordered to do so by Feldmeyer [Feldmeijer]. When he left the front, he told a comrade at the train station not to worry about him because he would make arrangements to avoid any further front service.

After he returned to the Netherlands from the Waffen-S.S., it appeared that H., who formerly was a strong supporter of the S.S., had completely changed his mind about this. He became convincingly anti-German and roused feelings against the S.S. and against everything that was German. He told comrades about all kinds of S.S. abuses and advised them not to join the Waffen-S.S. He told them.: "The Dutch were good enough to serve as cannon fodder, but would never receive any rights." That was clear to him now.

Due to the "case Gerhards" [the marriage], Heerema was dishonorably discharged from the Dutch S.S., after which we went into hiding.

This case caused a lot of stirring in S.S. circles, mainly in The Hague, where it was a well-known case. It was also a hot topic in the N.S.B. 1698/nr. 13. Rijswijk 26.4.1944. [571]

---

[571] The report was translated for the author by both Léon van der Hoeven and Elisa Goudriaan. The author melded and modified their translations for clarity. As presented here, the report is not a literal translation but is consistent with the meaning and spirit of the original Dutch text.

APPENDIX 2

THE REST OF JOHN HEYMANS'S WARTIME STORY

(Continued from Chapter 13)

In "The Final Story about Hugo Heijmans," John Heymans writes that the first survivors of the death marches from the east started to arrive at Theresienstadt in March 1945. "Frozen noses, hands and feet [were] very common." Most of them had not "eaten any food for days, some had eaten grass." John writes that his father, David, a family physician who worked as an anesthetist in Theresienstadt, told the family that he "could not give prescriptions for urgent needed medication because there was no medication at all. The only thing he could give his patients [who were often terminally ill] was his full attention." He sat at their bedsides "night after night" listening to their stories, which he also "wrote [down]." While doing this, he "made efforts to get information … from Dutch survivors concerning his elder brother Hugo." In due course, he received confirmation that Hugo had been on one of the death marches and, when "he was not able to walk anymore," was presumably executed by one of the German guards.[572]

---

[572] John Heymans, "The final story about Hugo Heijmans," accessed March 7, 2019, https://www.joodsmonument.nl/en/page/550398/the-final-story-about-

In February 1947, Dr. Heymans, his wife, Sara, and their twin children, Johnny and Wilhelmina, celebrated their survival and the twins' tenth birthday by travelling in the family's "old secondhand car" to all the addresses where they had been hidden in 1942 and 1943. At the Van Leeuwen's place at Loosdrechtseweg 23 in Hilversum, Johnny's "dear friend Peter" gave him a rapturous welcome. The dinner party for all those who had helped hide them "was a great success." A decade later, in 1957, John immigrated to Israel.[573]

After Dr. Heymans's death at the age of eighty, in Haarlem, in 1986, John, Willy, and their younger brother, Hugo, who was born January 1, 1947, and named after their uncle, "found the testimony evidence" of the death march survivors their father had recorded in 1945. In February 1996, they donated it to Yad Vashem, Israel's official memorial to the victims of the Holocaust, in Jerusalem. Yad Vashem engaged Dr. Alexander Dasberg to translate the documents into Hebrew. Dasberg's father, Rabbi Nathan Dasberg of Hilversum, knew Barend van Leeuwen.[574]

---

hugo-heijmans. Zuzana Justman, in "My Terezin Diary," *The New Yorker*, September 16, 2019, says (45) "given the lack of medicines and of nutritious food, there was little [the doctors] could do to combat the diseases that ravaged the place."

[573] Attachments to John Heymans's emails of March 14 and 18 and April 10, 2019, to the author. "The final story about Hugo Heijmans" (Sara's given name; her maiden name is also noted).

[574] "The final story about Hugo Heijmans" (died 1986; age eighty; brother Hugo). Attachment to John Heymans's email of March 21, 2019, to the author (found the testimony evidence; donated February 1996; Dr. Dasberg). Barend van Leeuwen's statement of October 17, 1946 (mentions "Rabbi Dasberg of Hilversum").

APPENDIX 3

JOHN PETERSEN AND THE POST-MORTEM REALMS

Testimony of Light: An Extraordinary Message of Life after Death by Helen Greaves is based on communications she received from her long-time friend Frances Banks after Frances died in November 1965. Greaves, who was said to have possessed "a gift that [enabled] her to penetrate to the next dimension of consciousness," described the book as a "work of telepathy and communication 'between the worlds.'" Banks, "a seeker all her days," had been an Anglican nun known as Sister Frances Mary for twenty-five years until her vows were annulled and she was able to pursue and explore spirituality with greater freedom.[575]

Describing her "location" in the post-mortem realms (PMR), Frances says, "this plane is only a few rungs or so higher than the earth plane." There is no compulsion, Frances explains, "to review one's past life on earth as soon as one arrives and the new life here begins. Some take a long while to tackle the problem. They dread to see the effects of mistakes and failures." She adds, "Yours is the judgment. You stand at your own bar of judgment. You make your own

---

[575] Helen Greaves, *Testimony of Light: An Extraordinary Message of Life after Death* (New York, Jeremy P. Tarcher/Penguin, 2009), xiii (gift), xix (telepathy), xxi (25 years), xxii (seeker), 155 (annulled).

decisions. You take your own blame.... You are the accused, the judge and the jury." [576]

Noting that "quite a few souls in this Rest Home have become immobilized," Frances is soon one of those trying "to help them along, but only when they have made the 'inner desire' to right their wrongs. Until that decision I do not know what happens to them, but I should think that they are 'prisoners of the self.'" One who had made such a decision and was known to her "had been a Nazi leader [who] had committed suicide" (not Hitler) and who "had been 'lodged in the shadows' [and] 'wandering in the lower places.'" Frances says, "for twenty earth years, he had been imprisoned by his own evil."[577]

Elsewhere, Frances comments, "Some of the souls who come to our side and who have perpetrated much evil, take a great deal of advising and helping on this point. Remorse overwhelms them and often they choose to live in the gloom of regret." They shut "themselves away from the very Light which could illumine their minds, dissolve their guilts and bring a constructive ray to bear on their problems ..." She refers to the "Land of Shadows" and to the "lower regions," calling the latter "terrible" and places "of semi-gloom, of unwholesome 'sticky' emotions, of utter distortion of all that is beautiful. One's feelings are wrung by the pitiful sights; compassion flows out for those poor half-alive creatures in their self-darkness."[578]

During the last few years when I was completing this book, I often thought of John and wondered if he was stuck in the lower regions of the PMR. If so, he would have been there for thirty or more Earth years, which I sensed was entirely possible. When I revisited and finalized what I wrote about him and Satanism, I, at one point, had the sense of being visited by a malign presence. I was in bed. The

---

[576] Greaves, 22 (earth plane), 19 (life review), 20 (judgment).
[577] Greaves, 20 (inner desire), 40 (Nazi; lodged in shadows; imprisoned by his own evil).
[578] Greaves, 78–79 (remorse overwhelms; illuminating Light; lower regions; terrible, semi-gloom), 85 (land of shadows).

presence was in what I took to be the middle distance of the dark, far enough away that I didn't feel threatened. The sense of distance and lack of threat undercut my initial perception of malevolence. More recently, as I suggested several times in latter parts of the book, I've been helped by unknown or hidden aspects of John's life that I felt bearing down on me and that ultimately broke into my comprehension. It would not surprise me if these prompts and intuitions were inspired by John, likely in the company of helpers who were aiding the process, all of whom were partnering with me to add some important final details to *A Snake on the Heart*.

ACKNOWLEDGEMENTS

In completing *A Snake on the Heart*, I have required considerable assistance over many years. Underlining this fact is the number of people who have helped and have since retired or died. The late Martin van der Weerd, the father of a colleague with the British Columbia Public Service, is a poignant example. Marty did some translating for me. After examining the first documents I sent for his review, he replied in an email of November 15, 2002: "This is a story that doesn't sit well, as I lost quite a lot of family during the war and my own Father was picked up by persons like John—we called them Dutch SS—and my father was gone for 3 years in a concentration camp and his brother was shot to death as an underground fighter." Despite his family's losses and suffering and the feelings they still engendered, Marty kindly agreed to help.

In addition to Marty, the late Harry Eerkes, Haydee Oord, Léon van der Hoeven, Elisa Goudriaan, and Will Collishaw (and his mother) also assisted with translations.

My understanding of the life and work of John's father, Hans, in the Far East, particularly in British North Borneo and the Dutch East Indies, was greatly aided by three researchers. R. W. (Bob) O'Hara searched the National Archives of the United Kingdom. His findings were subsequently augmented by those of Henk van der Velde of

Oosterbeek, Netherlands, and Uwe Aranas of Cologne, Germany, which they graciously shared with me.

Dr. Maili Blauw undertook several research projects for me at the Dutch National Archives and elsewhere. Nico van Horn was the first to review files on my behalf at the Dutch National Archives. I was also assisted by numerous staff at the Dutch National Archives, and I particularly want to thank Sandra Sacher, Liesbeth Strasser, Tontje Jolles, and Sierk Plantinga. Dr. Hans de Vries of the Netherlands Institute for War Documentation and Zwanet Plomp of the Netherlands Central Bureau for Genealogy also provided stalwart support over many years.

I gratefully acknowledge the assistance of authors Bob Moore, Gerhard Hirschfeld, Frank van Riet, and Jacques van Gerwen, amongst other historians referenced in the book. Important help was also provided by Erika Bartsch, archivist at the Statarchiv in Flensburg; Reiner and Dirkje Bobbe; Professor Manfred Brusten, University of Wuppertal; G. J. de Raad, Municipal Archives of Blaricum, Hilversum, Laren, and Wijdemeren; Dr. N. C. H. M. Heitman; Tinie Kerseboom, Head of Collections, Rijksakademie; Marjolein Kranse, Library, Leiden University; Dr. Janjapp Luijt; Herman Meijer, chief editor of VARA Documentaries in Hilversum; Edwin Meinsma, creator of the website Nederlanders in de Waffen-SS; Dr. Ulrike Schrader, Begegnungsstätte Alte Synagoge Wuppertal; Saskia Spiekman, librarian, Museum voor Communicatie; Ralph Tiller, Krishnamurti Education Centre of Canada; Marloes van der Beek, Museum Hilversum; Eric van der Ploeg; Miguel Sehested Zambras of 7seasvessels.com; The Hague City Archives; Dr. Kriszti Vákár, F. van der Most, and Dr. Hans Wijgergangs, all of the Netherlands Institute for Art History; Margaret Horsfield for information about her father, the Reverend Peter Horsfield; psychologists Mark Jackman and the late Dr. Dennis Payne; and, Anthony Beks of Capital Stenographic Services, Victoria, B.C.

I must also acknowledge the vital role played by Iguana Books, especially by Greg Ioannou and my successive editors, Paula

Chiarcos, Amanda Feeney, and Cheryl Hawley, whose recommendations and prompts resulted in numerous improvements.

A research highlight occurred late in the day when I made the acquaintance of John Heymans, via the internet, in March 2019. It was a delight to learn his remarkable survival story and that of his parents and sister.

I was delighted as well by vital support and assistance from family, particularly my brothers, Michael and Peter, my good friend and former wife, Colleen, and at least half a dozen other friends, most notably Thelma Fayle, Barbara Greeniaus, Dave Young, and Kirk Longpre, who read the manuscript on one or more occasions. Kirk convinced me to give greater scope to my personal journey in writing the book, which was critical in determining its final shape and bearing.

I must thank Bert Elliott for his support when I was pondering taking early retirement from the B.C. Public Service to devote myself more fully to this project, and David Spangler for being an invaluable resource.

Finally, I am indebted to the members of the Petersen family for their incredible cooperation over the decades.

SELECTED BIBLIOGRAPHY

This bibliography is not a complete record of all the works and sources used during the writing of this book. It itemizes those sources and works that I found most important in providing context and rounding out the information I obtained from the Petersen family and others, namely family documents, photos, and verbal and written recollections.

ABBREVIATIONS USED BELOW AND IN FOOTNOTES

DCBG (Dutch Central Bureau for Genealogy)

DNA (Dutch National Archives)
- BG *Bijzonder Gerechtshoven* (Special Courts)
- CABR *Centraal Archief Bijzonder Rechtspleging* (Central Archive Special Courts)
- MJ *Ministerie van Justitie* (Ministry of Justice re: applications for Dutch naturalization)
- NBI *Nederlands Beheersinstituut* (Department responsible for supervising the property of enemies and betrayers)
- PRA *Politieke Recherche Afdelingen* (Political Investigation Department)

NAUK (National Archives of the United Kingdom)
- CO Colonial Office
- FO Foreign Office

SELECTED PRIMARY DOCUMENTATION

Jacobus Jan (Koos) Doornbos
- DNA, CABR 109056
- DNA, NBI 58652

Jacobus Hermanus (Ko) Elhorst
- DNA, CABR 64049
- DNA, NBI 3309 and 75853

Johanus Grootveld—see entry for Jan Jürgen Petersen
Pieter Schelte Heerema—see entry for Jan Jürgen Petersen
- DNA, email of June 11, 2009, from Sierk Plantinga to the author

Tine Setske Heerema—see entry for Jan Jürgen Petersen
Willem (Wim) Kempen
- DNA, CABR 107966
    - Various documents including Kempen's collaborator statements of August 3 and October 23, 1946
    - Barend van Leeuwen's statement of October 17, 1946
- DNA, CABR 94285/PRA Hilversum, dossier 3619A
- DNA, NBI 99047

Adriaan Korteland—see entry for Jan Jürgen Petersen
Constant Wilhelm Petersen
- DNA, CABR 70629
    - Various documents including two letters to his wife and his collaborator statements of September 14, 1945; January 7, 1946; October 24, 1946; November 26, 1946; and February 14, 1947
- DNA, CABR 96529/PRA Rotterdam, dossier 11323
- DNA, MJ—1934: 02.09.22 inv. #10252 and #20252
    - Records related to applications for naturalization
- DNA, NBI 146852

Jan Jürgen Petersen
- DNA, CABR 109786
  - J. J. Petersen's collaborator statements of October 8, 1945, and October 29, 1946
  - J. J. Petersen's *Stamkaart Nederlandsche SS* card
  - Witness statements from
    - Antonius Johanus Grootveld, dated October 28, 1946
    - Susan Petersen, dated October 22, 1946
    - Dr. H. Schouten, dated October 29, 1946
    - Adrianus Cornelis Smit, dated October 30, 1946
    - Theodorus van Schouwen, dated October 28, 1946
  - Testimonial letters from
    - J. G. Siewers, dated October 26, 1946
    - Barend van Leeuwen, dated October 28, 1946
    - Johan Veltmeijer, dated October 26, 1946
  - Two-page handwritten document date-stamped November 14, 1946, that provides case information and advice to Special Prosecutor F. Hollander
  - A note of December 16, 1946, from Special Prosecutor F. Hollander ordering J. J. Petersen's release
- DNA, CABR 91103/PRA The Hague, dossier 21717. G. A. Scholte is the primary focus of this file. There are subfiles on eight other suspects, including John whose file includes
  - J. J. Petersen's collaborator statement of April 22, 1947
  - A card on J. J. Petersen's internment history
  - The SD Intelligence Service Report of April 5, 1944, on Tine Heerema signed by J. J. Petersen
  - The SD Intelligence Service Report of April 26, 1944, on Pieter Heerema

- Witness statements from
  - Tine Setske Heerema, dated January 25, 1947
  - Adriaan Korteland, dated April 14, 1947
  - Gerardus Andreas Scholte, dated April 8, 1947
- DNA, MJ—1934: 02.09.22 inv. #10252 and #20252; and 1937–39: inv. #11681 and #11668
  - Records related to applications for naturalization
- DNA, NBI 146868

Gerardus Andreas Scholte—see entry for Jan Jürgen Petersen
Jan Gerrit Siewers—see entry for Jan Jürgen Petersen
Adrianus Cornelis Smit—see entry for Jan Jürgen Petersen
Barend van Leeuwen—see entry for Willem (Wim) Petersen
Theodorus van Schouwen—see entry for Jan Jürgen Petersen
Johan Veltmeijer—see entry for Jan Jürgen Petersen

PRINCIPAL SECONDARY SOURCES

Anderson, Anthony. "A Forgotten Chapter: Holland under the Third Reich." Transcript of a lecture presented at the University of Southern California, October 17, 1995. Accessed online February 7, 2002.

Anderson, Anthony. "Anne Frank Was Not Alone: Holland and the Holocaust." Transcript of a lecture presented at the University of Southern California, October 24, 1995. Accessed online February 7, 2002.

Berben, Paul. *Dachau, 1933–1945: The Official History*. London: Norfolk Press, 1975.

Cornwell, John. *Hitler's Pope: The Secret History of Pius XII*. New York: Viking Penguin, 1999.

Craig, Gordon A. *Europe since 1815*, 2nd ed. New York, Chicago, San Francisco, Toronto, London: Holt, Rinehart and Winston, 1966.

de Jong, Louis. "The Dutch Government in Exile." *Holland at War Against Hitler: Anglo-Dutch Relations, 1940–1945*. Edited by M. R. D. Foot. London: Frank Cass, 1990.

de Jong, Louis. *The Netherlands and Nazi Germany*. Cambridge, Massachusetts, and London, England: Harvard University Press, 1990.

de Jong, Louis, and J. W. F. Stoppelman. *The Lion Rampant: The Story of Holland's Resistance to the Nazis*. New York: Querido, 1943.

Frank, Anne. *The Diary of a Young Girl: The Definitive Edition*. Edited by Otto H. Frank and Mirjam Pressler. Translated by Susan Massotty. London: Penguin Books, 2001.

Gisevius, Hans Bernd. *To The Bitter End*. Boston: Houghton Mifflin, 1947.

Goodwin, Doris Kearns. *No Ordinary Time: Franklin and Eleanor Roosevelt: The Home Front in World War II*. New York: Simon & Schuster, 1994.

Graber, G. S. *History of the SS*. New York: David McKay Company, 1978.

Hackett, John. "Operation Market Garden." *Holland at War Against Hitler: Anglo-Dutch Relations, 1940–1945*. Edited by M. R. D. Foot. London: Frank Cass, 1990.

Hanson, S. E. *Underground Out of Holland*. London: Ian Allan Ltd., 1977.

Hillesum, Etty. *An Interrupted Life: The Diaries, 1941–1943 and Letters from Westerbork*. Translated by Arnold J. Pomerans. New York: Henry Holt and Company, 1996.

Hirschfeld, Gerhard. *Nazi Rule and Dutch Collaboration: The Netherlands under German Occupation, 1940–1945*. Translated by Louise Willmot. Oxford, New York, Hamburg: Berg Publishers Ltd., 1988.

Hockenos, Matthew. *Then They Came for Me: Martin Niemöller, the Pastor Who Defied the Nazis*. New York: Basic Books, 2018.

Horn, Michiel. *A Liberation Album: Canadians in the Netherlands, 1944–45*. Edited by David Kaufman. Toronto, Montreal, New York: McGraw-Hill Ryerson, Ltd., 1980.

in 't Veld, N. K. C. A. *De SS en Nederland: documenten uit SS-archieven, 1933–1945*. 2 vols. The Hague: Martinus Nijhoff, 1976.

John, David W. and James C. Jackson. "The Tobacco Industry of North Borneo: A Distinctive Form of Plantation Agriculture." *Journal of Southeast Asian Studies*. Vol. 4, Issue 1, March 1973.

Kamphuis, Piet. "Caught Between Hope and Fear: Operation Market Garden and its Effects on the Civilian Population in the Netherlands." *Holland at War Against Hitler: Anglo-Dutch Relations, 1940–1945*. Edited by M. R. D. Foot. London: Frank Cass, 1990.

Kershaw, Ian. *Hitler, 1889–1936: Hubris*. London: Penguin, 1998.

Kershaw, Ian. *Hitler, 1936–1945: Nemesis*. London: Penguin, 2000.

Kersten, Felix. *The Kersten Memoirs: 1940–1945*. London: Hutchinson, 1956.

Maass, Walter B. *The Netherlands at War: 1940–1945*. London, New York, Toronto: Abelard-Schuman Ltd., 1970.

MacMillan, Margaret. *Paris 1919: Six Months that Changed the World*. New York: Random House, 2003.

Mason, Henry L. *The Purge of Dutch Quislings: Emergency Justice in the Netherlands*. The Hague: Martinus Nijhoff, 1952.

Moore, Bob. *Victims and Survivors: The Nazi Persecution of the Jews in the Netherlands, 1940–1945*. London: Arnold, 1997.

Paape, Harry. "How Dutch Resistance Was Organized." *Holland at War Against Hitler: Anglo-Dutch Relations, 1940–1945*. Edited by M. R. D. Foot. London: Frank Cass, 1990.

Padfield, Peter. *Himmler: Reichsführer-SS*. London: MacMillan, 1990.

Rutter, Owen. *British North Borneo: An Account of its History, Resources and Native Tribes*. London, Bombay, Sydney: Constable & Company Ltd., 1922.

Shirer, William L. *The Nightmare Years, 1930–1940*. Boston, Toronto: Little Brown and Company, 1984.

Smith, Marcus J. *The Harrowing of Hell: Dachau.* Albuerque: University of New Mexico Press, 1972.

The SS. The Third Reich series. Alexandria, Virginia: Time-Life Books, 1988.

Stein, André. *Quiet Heroes: The True Stories of the Rescue of Jews by Christians in Nazi-Occupied Holland.* Toronto: Lester & Orpen Dennys, Ltd., 1988.

Tregonning, K. G. *A History of Modern Sabah, 1881-1963.* Kuala Lumpur: University of Malaya Press, 1965.

van der Zee, Henri A. *The Hunger Winter: Occupied Holland 1944-5.* London: Jill Norman and Hobhouse, 1982.

van Riet, F. A. M. "Enforcement under the new order: The political history of the Rotterdam police during the Second World War." PhD diss., Amsterdam Institute for Humanities Research. https://dare.uva.nl/search?identifier=78ea43ea-1b64-4567-a646-528c92b313c0. Accessed June 5, 2021.

Velghe, Brita. "Antoine Wiertz (1806-1865)," Brussels: Royal Museums of Fine Arts of Belgium, 2000.

von Below, Nicolaus. *At Hitler's Side: The Memoirs of Hitler's Luftwaffe Adjutant 1937-1945.* Translated by Geoffrey Brooks. London: Greenhill Books, and Mechanicsburg, PA: Stackpole Books, 2004.

INDEX

A

Akashic records, 407
Alcoholics Anonymous, 375, 388
Ann (foster/later adopted child), 286, 366, 386–92, 398, 400–1, 415, xi, xiii, xxv, xvii
  picture of, xi
Atlantic Wall, 242, 336
Auschwitz concentration camp, 146, 191, 211
Avegoor (SS training facility), 169, 177, 182

B

Barbarossa. *See* military operation
Battle of the Bulge. *See* military operation
Blitzkrieg, 124
British North Borneo, 5, 7, 11–16, xv

C

Captain Aye Aye, 62–64, 73, 423
Central Office for Jewish Emigration (Zentralstelle für jüdische Auswenderung), 190–93
Chowhound. *See* military operation
Churchill, Winston, 35–36, 125, 291, 295
Colijn, Dr. Hendrik, 136
Collaboration, 46, 75, 135–37, 141, 170–71, 193, 196, 254, 260, 310, xxiii–xxiv
  . See also Hatchet Day
Crailoo (prison camp), 345, 360

D

Dachau
  concentration camp at, 133, 143, 145–46
  SS school at, 133, 143

D-Day, 253
Den Hartog, Barend, 218–19, 261–63, 303–4
de Ridder, Constance Wilhelmina. *See* Petersen, Constance Wilhelmina (Stanni)
Dolle Dinsdag (Mad Tuesday), 247, 254–55, 258
Doornbos, Door, 115, 268, 275, 375–76
Doornbos, Jacobus Jan (Koos), 114–15, 169–70, 268, 305, 368–69, 372, 375–77, 429
Duindorp (prison camp), 305–7, 336–45, 347, 349

E

Eastern front, 174, 249, 270
Eichmann, Adolf, 190
Eisenhower, General Dwight D., 255, 290–92, 295
Elhorst family, 74, 94
Elhorst, Frie, 430
   first marriage of, 90–92, 94–96, 98
   relationship with John Petersen of, 76–77, 86, 88–89, 101, 370–71, 419
   second marriage of, 101
Elhorst, Jacobus Hermanus (Ko or Joe), 214
   deception and fraud (actual and alleged) of, 74–75, 97–98, 104–5
   friendship with John Petersen, 31, 68, 74–75, 88–89
   imprisoned, 75, 105
   picture of, 82, 88
   work with John Petersen, 75–77, 81–82, 97–99, 102–4

F

Feldmeijer, Johannes Hendrik, 171–76, 178–180, 238, 444–45, 448
Five-Day War, 123–27, 133, 228, 255, 292
Frank, Anne, 173, 210–11, 228, 243

G

Gail (foster child), 401–2
Gerbrandy, Pieter, 258, 264–65, 275, 290–91
German Order Police (Ordnungspolizei). *See* Order Police
Germanic SS in the Netherlands, 137, 177
. *See also* SS Standarte "Westland"
Germany
   1919–1940, 35–37
   armed forces of, 153–54
   capitulation of, 294–95
   "gentle hand" policy of, 134–35, 140, 150, 163
   hostages held as death candidates, 172, 204, 242, 288

invasion of Netherlands of, 123–27, 152
Nazi ideology in, 75, 157–58
occupation of Western Europe by, 134, 154, 188
reprisal policy of, 156–57, 172, 236, 242, 256, 258–59, 296–97
total war policy of, 225, 228
. *See also* Hitler, Adolf; Holocaust and Nazi ideology
Gisevius, Hans Bernd, 37, 155, 205, 207
Goebbels, Joseph, 150, 188, 278
Göring, Hermann, 139, 194
Great Depression, 36, 59–60, 63, 74, 431
Green Police. *See* Order Police
Grootveld, Antonius Johannes, 240, 361–62

H
Hanson, S. E. (Stan), 210, 236, 299
Hatchet Day, 254–55, 295–96
. *See also* Collaboration
Heerema, Pieter Schelte, 175–76, 179–80, 183–84, 439, 443–49
rank of, 445
resistance and, 446–47
Heerema, Tine, 175, 183–86, 198, 363, 447
Heymans, John, 212, 214, 219–22, 262, 450–51, 457

Hillesum, Etty, 121, 210–11
Himmler, Heinrich, 134–35, 146–47, 155–56, 157, 161, 166, 172–73, 180–82, 188, 193, 204, 294, 296–97
Hitler, Adolf, 1, 35–37, 39–40, 132–34, 140, 152–53, 157, 170, 188, 203, 223, 228, 253–54, 270, 294, 312
. *See also* Germany; Holocaust and Nazi ideology
Holland. *See* Netherlands
Hollander, Dr. F., 230, 362, 363
Holocaust and Nazi ideology, 39–40, 157–58, 163–64, 188–93, 197, 224
Horgan, John, 407–8
Hunger Winter. *See* Netherlands (Hunger Winter)

J
Jackman, Mark, 421–23
Jewish Council, 166, 190, 210, 212–13

K
Kempen, J. W., 18–19, 22–25, xxiii
picture of, 19
Kempen, Miek, 18–19, 68, 69, 72–73, 94, 96, 97–98, 105, 111, 133, 171, 174, 264, 271, 297, 306, 309–10, 366, 374–77, 380, 383, 405, 428, xxiii, xxvii
"big secret," 310

birth of, 18
marriage of, 365
picture of, 91, 117, 365
. *See also* Kempen, J.W.
Kempen, Wim, 375, 405, 439
    arrest and imprisonment of, 261–63, 302, 303–4, 346, 348, 351, xxiii
    birth, 18, 22
    hiding, went into, 207, 263, 307
    Jews and, 208–9, 214, 262
    life during the Second World War of, 141, 187, 208–9, 218–19, 233, 241, 271
    marriage (first), 241, 364
    marriage (second), 364, 365
    picture of, 92, 365
    personality of, 208
    relationship with brother (John), 208–9, 233, 241, 351
    release of, 364
    resistance and, 141, 187, 261–62, xxiii
    SS and, 174, 241, xxiii
    works for Germans, 207, 233, 241, 261, 263
    . *See also* Kempen, J. W.; Muiden (prison camp)
Kempen-de Ridder, Constance. *See* Petersen, Constance (Stanni)
Kitt. *See* Ann (foster/later adopted child)

Korteland, Adriaan, 183, 238, 246–49, 253, 305–6, 363
Krishnamurti, Jiddu, 198–99, 373–74

L

Landstorm, 242
Landwacht, 226, 242, 269
Leopold III, King of Belgium, 124–25, 134

M

Malang, 16–19, 26–28
Manna. *See* military operation
Market Garden. *See* military operation
Mauthausen concentration camp, 146, 166, 190
military operation
    Barbarossa, 153, 174, 187, 253
    Battle of the Bulge, 269–70, 272
    Chowhound, 292, 293
    Manna, 292–93
    Market Garden, 255–56, 257, 291
Muiden (prison camp), 345, 346–50, 354, 360, 421
Mussert, Anton Adriaan, 40, 139, 171–73, 176, 203–4, 242, 444
    arrest and execution of, 296
    SS and, 40, 172–73, 181, 182–83
    . *See also* Nationaal-Socialistische Beweging (NSB)

N

Nationaal-Socialistische Beweging (NSB), 40, 136, 139, 165–66, 172–73, 176, 178–79, 182, 192, 203, 204–5, 212, 226, 242, 255, 312, 313
    Weerafdeling (W.A.) or Defence Section, 165
    . *See also* Mussert, Anton Adriaan

National Socialist Dutch Workers Party (NSNAP), 40, 165, 175, 444, 448
    Sturmabteilung (S.A.), paramilitary section, 165

Nazi ideology. *See* Holocaust and Nazi ideology

Netherlands
    black market in, 224–25, 267, 301–2
    bombing of The Hague in, 275–76, 278
    bombing of Rotterdam in, 125–26, 130
    Canadian troops in, 295–97, 301–2, 308–9, 314, 332–35
    collaborator camps in, 311–14, 318
    economy/economic policy of, 59–60, 64, 77, 224, 242, 377
    food shortages of, 264, 266, 271, 290, 292
    German occupation of, 74, 134–35, 223, 228, 257, 261
    Germany's invasion of, 123–27
    Hunger Winter (1944–45), 226, 242, 258, 271, 287, 291, 301
    Jewish refugees in, 59–60
    Jews of, 165–66, 188–93, 210–11, 224, 255, 312
    last months of the war and, 257–59, 263–65
    liberation of, 290–93, 301–2
    martial law in, 228
    neutrality of, 39, 127
    onderduikers (people in hiding), 204, 229, 243, 255–56, 263
    razzias (forced labour manhunts), 263
    recovery after the war of, 301–2
    resistance movement in, 5, 41, 126, 137, 156, 167, 187, 202–6, 210, 234, 236, 242, 246–47, 256, 258, 260, 270, 303, 314, 315, 316
    royal family of, 102, 124–25, 139–41, 223, 265, 297, 299, 303, 306, 307
    "September Warriors" of, 260
    strafing in, 276–77
    strikes in, 163, 166–68, 228–29, 256–57
    treatment of Jews in, 59–60, 163–66
    tribunals in, 311–12
    underground press in, 140–41, 167, 189, 205

women in, 307–9
work service in Germany, 228–29, 312
. *See also* Hatchet Day; Holocaust and Nazi ideology; Hunger Winter (1944–45); military operation; Mussert, Anton Adriaan; Nationaal-Socialistische Beweging (NSB); Order Police; Schalkhaar Police Academy; SS Standarte "Westland"
Netherlands East Company, 172, 233, 241, 261, 446
Niemöller, Martin, 37, 56, vii

O

Order Police (Ordnungspolizei) a.k.a. Green Police (Grüne Polizei), 163, 168, 175, 189, 194, 202

P

Packford, Bernice Levitz, xiv
Payne, Dr. Dennis, 421–22
Peck, Dr. M. Scott, 409
Petersen, Constance, 108, 114, 170, 275, 302, 306, 365, 366, 369, 373, 375, 377, 385–89, 392, 395–401, 405, 407–12, 419–21, 428, 431, 433, xi, xxv, xxvii
  birth of, 273, 275, 287
  brother Hans and, 286
  marriages, 399
  personality of, 107–8, 394–95, 398–401
  pictures of, 365, 373, xi
  relationship with father, 396–98, 400, 415, 419, 436
  relationship with mother, 386, 391, 399–400
Petersen, Constance Wilhelmina (Stanni), 3, 6, 10, 16, 18, 22–23, 33, 57, 87, 91, 94, 95–96, 99, 108, 174, 181, 187, 241, 248, 252, 264, 275, 280, 307–9, 349, 365, 375
  death of, 110
  picture of, 6, 19, 91, 365
  . *See also* individual members of Kempen and Petersen families
Petersen, Constant, 187, 310, 405, 429, 430, 439
  arrest of, 307
  birth and death of, 16, 73
  at the front, 194, 207
  Germany's invasion of Netherlands and, 120, 133, xxii–xxiii
  imprisoned, 145–48, 364, xxiii
  marriage, wife, and sons, 71–72, 120, 133, 255, 261, 307–8
  nationality and, 8, 57, 77, 120, 377–79
  NSB and, 182
  personality of, 69–70, 71–72, 73, 148, 429

picture of, 19, 92, 117, 365
rank of, 182, 194, 207
relationship with brother
   (John), 23, 60, 69–73, 120,
   138, 206–7, 209, 233, 248–
   49, 252–53, 429
relationship with stepfather, 18
release of, 364, 377
roundups of Jews and, 193–95,
   212, 378, xxiii
sea career of, 60, 120
SS and, 138, 160–61, 182, 193,
   378
SS training of, 143–48, 158
war wound and recovery, 207,
   233
work for Dutch SS of, 160–61,
   193–95, 206–7
. *See also* Avegoor (SS training
   facility); Holocaust and
   Nazi ideology
Petersen, Hans (1936–2022),
   130, 162, 181, 187, 207, 248,
   274–77, 297, 302, 364, 365,
   369, 380, 399–400, 410, 412,
   418, 429, xxvii
appendix of, 95
beatings and whipping of, 303,
   370–71
birth and death of, 94, 289
food drops, 293–94
food shortages and, 243, 264–
   66, 271, 274

personal testimony of in 1991,
   265, 280, 282–84, 287–88,
   370–71
picture of, 117, 365, 373, xi
psychic experiences of, 280–81
relationship with and views on
   father of, 111, 170, 265,
   279–84, 286, 302–3, 315,
   367, 370
relationship with mother of,
   98, 370
relationship with stepmother
   of, 95, 108, 286–87, 370–71
schooling, 282, 297, xiii
strafing and, 284–85
truth and, 286–87
wartime experiences of, 209–
   10, 279, 282–86, 288–89
Petersen, Hans Nis Jürgen
   (1868–1918), 3–12, 14–17, 20–
   22, 37–39, 281
death of, 16
picture of, 6, 17
Petersen, Harald, 111, 207, 248,
   264, 265, 271, 274–77, 285,
   302, 336, 365, 385, 399–400,
   408, 410, 418, 419, 439, xxvii
birth of, 181–82
confirmation of, 412–13
food shortages, 266
picture of, 365, 373, xi, xii
relationship with father, 25,
   130, 198, 200–1, 206, 371–
   73, 412, 415

relationship with mother, 206, 370–71
Petersen, John (Jan Jürgen)
animals and, 26–27
anti-Semitism of, 59, 197, 394
. See also Petersen, John (Jews and)
aphorisms of, 260, 426
arrest of, 128, 297, 302, 305, 315
artistic pursuits of, 34, 77–79, 81, 87, 100, 110, 339, 412–13, 427, 431
. See also Petersen, John (paintings by)
aspirations, spiritual and other of, 31, 33, 34, 81, 110, 373–75
baptism and confirmation of, 412
"best lie" rule, 97, xx–xxi
birth and death of, 5, 43, 436
clergyman and, 359, 381, 414–15
collaboration case of, 361–63
"deep thinking" of, 407, 416, 418
"double game" and "reckless game" of, 121, 205–6, 209, 241, 426, xix–xx
entitlement and, 414–16
eulogy for, 436, xi, xxv–xxvi
faith of, 29–30, 411–14, 417, 432–33
finances of, 225

food shortages and, 243–45, 266–69
German army commander and, 232–34, 237, 252, 267–68, 272, 415
Germany, views on, 35–37, 39, 58, 127, 151, 156, 170, 209, 240, 279, 281
Germany's invasion of Netherlands and, 39, 128, 132–33, xxii–xxiii
girlfriend of, 30–31, 50, 67
at the hospital, 354–59
imprisoned, 128–29, 145–48, 275, 305–7, 315–60, xxiii
Indigenous people and, 26–28, 394
injuries of, 198, 350–53, 366, xiii
investigations on, 248–52, 272, 274, 430
Jews and, 209–10, 214–18, 221
. See also Petersen, John (anti-Semitism of)
Jews, roundup of, 193, 197–202, 212, 427, 433, xxiii
love affairs of, 88–9, 368–70, 379, 386–87, 401–2
marriage to Susan, 111, 115, 181, 198, 368–69, 376, 383, 385–88, 391–93, 402, 405, 409, 419, xxvii
mental health and PTSD of, 79, 81, 84, 85–86, 109, 115,

205–6, 237, 272, 274–75, 366–67, 373, 380, 397, 401–2, 405, 409, 415, 418, 430–31, xix–xxi, xxiv
minister and. *See* Petersen, John (clergyman)
mystical experiences of, 327–30, 420–23, xxiv
National Art Academy and, 84–86, 431
nationality of, 8, 10–11, 33–34, 38, 42–43, 57–59, 61, 77, 96–97, 99, 101, 111, 127, 133, 147, 177–78, 209, 240, 260, 377, 430, xxi–xxii, xxiv
. *See* Petersen, John (sense of belonging of)
at nautical school, 43–56
NSB and, 40, 101, 138
pacifism, politics, and independent action of, 41, 73, 127, 170, 193, 209, 217, 223, 241, 294
paintings by, 79, 412–13
personality of, 3. 21–25, 28–31, 34, 43, 46–47, 50, 65–66, 68–69, 73, 87–88, 96, 98, 100, 101, 107, 109, 113–114, 150, 170, 174, 185, 206, 208, 239, 315, 322, 353, 355, 362, 369, 372, 373, 376, 379, 386, 388–90, 394–96, 398–404, 407–8, 413, 415–16, 419, 426–31, xiii, xviii, xix–xxii, xxiv, xxvi
photographic memory of, 70, 235
picture of, 6, 17, 19, 29, 48, 88, 90, 103, 112, 117, 119, 352, 365, 367, 381, xvi
poems of, 321, 330, 340–41, 368–69, 372, 434
post-injury recovery of, 364, 366–67
post-mortem realms (PMR) and, 436, 452–54
as predator, 69
psychic abilities/experiences of, 26–28, 53–54, 280–81, 397, 408
race and homosexuality, views of, 108, 197, 393–95, 399
"reckless game." *See* Petersen, John ("double game")
rank of, 175, 217, xviii–xix
reincarnation and, 21, 112, 375, 402, 407, 410, 419, xviii
relationship with brother Constant, 23, 60, 69–73, 187, 206, 209, 233, 248–49, 252
relationship with brother Wim, 23, 187, 208–9, 233, 241
relationship with father of, 7, 8, 11, 20, 25, 429

relationship with mother of, 23–25, 33, 50, 60, 67–68, 98, 430, xviii
relationship with stepfather of, 18, 22–23, 430
resistance and, 202–3, 212, 223, 225, 235–36, 260, 283, xxiii
Satanism and, 410–11, 413–16, 440, 453
schooling (prior to nautical school) of, 28–29, 33, 34, 79
as Schutzgruppe member, 121, 195–96, 201, 205, 216–17, 223, 225–27, 230, 233, 235, 237, 240, 247, 249, 251, 259, 262, 268, 274, 275, xix
sea career of, 57, 60, 61–67
sense of belonging of, 47–48, 101–2, 132–33, 151, 153, 170–71, 377–79
. *See* Petersen, John (nationality of)
spiritualism (séances, Ouija board) and, 21, 109, 110, 375–77, 402–4
SS and, 138, 142, 177–78, 182, 196, 201–2, 209–10, 217, 223, 240, 362, 379
SS training of, 108, 133, 144–45, 148–59, 243–44, 287, 342
status and, 11, 33–34, 92–94, 95
story of, 3, 81, 249, 260, 425–28, 436–37, xv–xvi, xviii–xxvii
strafing and, 276–77
"the philosophy," 407, xviii
truth and, 31, 76, 94, 146, 369, 418–20, 431–33, 436, xxiv
work
  as social worker, 33, 61, 71, 109, 397–98, 400, 427, xiv–xv
  at Amersfoort of, 227–28, 230–32
  at ANAK insurance company, 238–41, 259–60, 362
  business ventures, 75–76, 81–82, 102–4, 116
  for Canadian army, 332–35
  at De Centrale insurance company, 176–80, 183, 216, 238–39, xix
  for Dutch SS, 137–38, 160–62, 176–77, 182, 216–17, 239, 379, 427, xix
  for Dutch SS Intelligence Service, 161, 175, 178–79, 183, 186, 238–39, 246–48, 259, 305–6, 361, 363, 444–45, 447–49
  for German army, 232–36, 244–45, 252, 259, 260–61
  at grocery business of, 96–98
  at Holland Life Insurance Company, 87, 116, xiii
  while interned after the Second World War, 320–21, 322–24

odd jobs, 75, 77–78, 89, 96, 106
for Siewers Photography Shop, 116, 119, 128, 132
writing/essays of, 198–9, 389, 402–4, 410, 433, 435, 439
youth of, 28–30
. *See also* Avegoor (SS training facility); Duindorp (prison camp); Elhorst, Frie; Elhorst, Jacobus Hermanus (Ko or Joe); Muiden (prison camp); Petersen family; Scheveningen (prison); individual members of Petersen and Kempen families

Petersen, Onno, 112, 114, 115, 366, 370, 373, 385–87, 393, 396, 408, 411, 414, 418–19, 421, xi, xxv–xxvii
birth and death of, 110, 418, xiii
picture of, 392, xi
relationship with father, 418–19

Petersen, Susan, 138, 276–77, 280, 281, 285, 286–87, 294, 302, 305–06, 315, 348, 349, 361, 364, 365, 379, 429
birth and death, 106, 405
children and, 95, 113, 274–75, 298, 370, 385–86, 399–402, 411
daughter Constance and, 142, 273, 275, 386, 391, 396
faulty memory of, 287
food shortages, 243, 264, 268, 271
John's eulogy and story and, xxv–xxvi
marriage to John, 181, 368–69, 419, xxvii
personality of, 108, 111–14, 370–71, 376, 386, 391–92, 398–99, 401–2, 404–5, 407, 411, xiii
picture of, 112, 365, 392, 403, xi
relationship with John Petersen of, 85, 109–16, 162–3, 181–82, 206, 209, 298, 376, 383, 385–88, 391–93, 401–2, 405, 407, 409–10
relationship with mother-in-law (Stanni), 23, 110, 308
relationship with stepson Hans, 95, 108, 286–87, 297, 370–71
separation and divorce from John Petersen of, 403–5, 410
strafing and, 276–77
. *See also* Petersen family; Posthumus family

Petersen family
after the Second World War, 364–66
Christmas and, 24–25
Danish roots, 4–5, 9

foster care and boarders with, 385–86, 392, 396, 401–2, 405–6, xiii–xiv

life in Canada of, 385–86, 405–6, xii–xiii

photo of, 6, 17, 19, 365, 392, xi

spiritualism and, 386

. *See also* Ann (foster/later adopted child); Gail (foster child); Phil (foster/later adopted child); Wagstaff, Al (boarder); individual members of Kempen and Petersen families

Phil (foster/later adopted child), 366, 385, 392–93, 394, xi, xiii, xxvii

Posthumus family, 106–9, 113, 115, 365–66

Pouwels, Pieter, 32, 40, 80, 86, 379–80

Prince Bernhard of Lippe-Biesterfeld. *See* Netherlands (royal family of)

R

Radio Orange, 125, 263, 278, 291

Rauter, Hanns Albin, 193, 204, 242, 446, 448

arrest of, 296–97

conflict with Seyss-Inquart and, 164–65, 204, 267

conflict with NSB and, 179, 204

Dutch SS and, 172, 181, 228

. *See also* Schalkhaar Police Academy

Roelants family, 379, xii

Roelants, Hans (also referred to as Henry), 195, 199–200, 366, 379, xix, xxi

Roodenburg, John, 392, 394, xi

picture of, xi

Roodenburg, Sandra, 392.

Rost van Tonningen, Meinod Marinus, 171, 172, 180

Rothschild, Arnold, 117–18, 212–18, 221, 303

S

Schalkhaar Police Academy, 169, 193

Scheveningen (prison), 305–6, 314–31, 336–38, 345, 348, 349

Scholte, G.A., 178–79, 238–39, 247, 305–6, 363, 447

Schouten, Dr. 353–54

Schutzgruppe, 195, 227, xix

Seyss-Inquart, Dr. Arthur, 134–35, 150, 152, 164–65, 167, 172, 180, 189, 203, 258, 292, 294, 296, 312

Shirley (John Petersen's third wife), 418–20, 436, xxvii

Siewers, Jan Gerrit, 116, 119, 196, 230–32, 361, xix

Smit, Adrianus Cornelis, 216n, 362

Spangler, David, 404, 409, 433, 457
SS, 154–57, 228
SS Intelligence Service, 179, 246
SS-Schule Avegoor, 169, 177, 182
SS Standarte "Westland", 137, 138, 158
SS supporting members (BL), 173–74, xxiii
Stalin, Joseph, 253
Stalingrad, 194, 204, 225, 446
Sturmabteilung (S.A.). *See* National Socialist Dutch Workers Party (NSNAP)

T

tall tales
  about family in British North Borneo and Java, 8, 9, 11, 14, 16, 18
  about father's death, 20–22
  about nautical school, 43–44, 45, 47, 49–50, 53n, 56
  about sea career, 59, 60, 61, 64, 67–68, 73, 428–29
  about various events in life, 33, 89–90, 379–81
  about wartime experiences, 127–31, 152, 252, 260, 272–74
  about work at SS, 159, 168–70, 177–78, 235–36, 237
  of John Petersen, 274–75, 428–32, xx–xxi
Theresienstadt, 220, 450

Timperley, William (mentor), 31, 32–33, 34, 44, 63, 100, 380–81, 397, 430
Treaty of Versailles, 35–36, 153

U

Underground newspapers. *See* Netherlands (underground press in)

V

V-1, 253–54
V-2, 267, 269, 275–77, 285, 288, 348
Van den Elsakker, 218–19, 261–63, 303–4
Van Leeuwen, Barend, 116–18, 131, 141, 187, 196, 202–3, 207–8, 218–19, 261–63, 303–5, 361–62, xix
  Jews and, 141, 212–15, 217–19, 303, 451
  picture of, 117
  relationship with John Petersen, 116–18, 131, 202–03, 212, 218–19, 230–31, 241, 361–62, xix
  resistance and, 131, 141, 187, 202–03, 261–63, 303, 451, xix
  . *See also* Heymans, John; Kempen, Wim; Rothschild, Arnold
Van Leeuwen, Dina, 208, 218–19, 233

arrest of, 261–62, 303–4
divorce of, 364
marriage of, 141, 187, 208, 241
. *See also* Kempen, Wim
Van Schouwen, Jacobus Theodorus, 240, 259, 361–62
VE Day, 294–95, 302, 307
Veltmeijer, Johan, 40–41, 74, 97, 140–41, 196, 322, 361, xix

W

Wagstaff, Al (boarder), 200–1, 386, 390, 396, 405–6, 412
Weerafdeling (W.A.). *See* NationaSocialistische Beweging (NSB)
Westerbork concentration camp, 190–92, 201, 210–11, 220, 224, 364
Western Europe. *See* Germany (occupation of Western Europe by)
"Westland". *See* SS Standarte "Westland"
Wilber, Ken, 408–9, 433
Wiertz (mentor), 31–32, 60–61, 78–81, 84, 93, 99, 100, 214, 233, 379–80, 415
Wiertz, Antoine Joseph, 34, 80, 81–83
Wiertz, Henri Louis (Joub), 80
Wilhelmina, Queen. *See* Netherlands (royal family of)
Winkelman, General Henri G., 124, 126, 140

Z

Zentralstelle für jüdische Auswenderung. *See* Central Office for Jewish Emigration

Printed in the USA
CPSIA information can be obtained
at www.ICGtesting.com
JSHW020046141023
50080JS00004B/13

9 781771 806183